Spring 1865

Great Campaigns of the Civil War

SERIES EDITORS

Anne J. Bailey
Georgia College & State University

Brooks D. Simpson
Arizona State University

Perry D. Jamieson

SPRING 1865

The Closing Campaigns of the Civil War

UNIVERSITY OF NEBRASKA PRESS
LINCOLN & LONDON

Maps by Erin Greb

Manufactured in the United States of America

Library of Congress Cataloging-in-Publication Data
Jamieson, Perry D.
Spring 1865: the closing campaigns of the Civil War / Perry D. Jamieson.
pages cm.—(Great campaigns of the Civil War)
Includes bibliographical references and index.
ISBN 978-0-8032-2581-7 (hardcover: alk. paper)
ISBN 978-0-8032-7470-9 (epub)
ISBN 978-0-8032-7471-6 (mobi)
ISBN 978-0-8032-7472-3 (pdf)
1. United States—History—Civil War, 1861–1865—Campaigns.
2. United States—History—Civil War, 1861–1865—Peace. I. Title.
E470.J36 2015 973.7'31—dc23 2014034907

Set in Swift by Renni Johnson.

For Stephanie Deats Jamieson

CONTENTS

ILLUSTRATIONS

MAPS

PREFACE

Unlike other books in this series, this one covers campaigns that took place in both of the major theaters of the American Civil War, the eastern and the western, and it touches on a few events that occurred beyond them. It would have been impossible to synthesize such wide-ranging operations without the help of some excellent secondary sources. This volume benefited from a number of valuable works on the last campaigns of the Civil War. Their titles appear in the bibliographical essay, and some of the most helpful ones are mentioned in the text.

To treat fairly the campaigns that took place during the final months of the war in the length of a volume in this series, it was necessary to focus on planning and operations at the strategic and operational levels of warfare. Some readers may want more details about tactics or more human-interest stories. They will find them in the campaign and battle studies mentioned in the bibliographical essay.

Although this work concentrates on the senior leaders of each side, their subordinates are not forgotten. The junior officers and soldiers in the ranks suffered the brunt of the operations described in this book, and they did much to decide the outcome of the battles and campaigns. Some superb archival collections made it possible to give their perspectives, and those of some civilians, on events that took place during a few extraordinary months in America's past.

Ultimately, however, most attention necessarily went to the senior military and political leaders of the North and South. In Virginia revered commander Gen. Robert E. Lee skillfully led his devoted men until field operations were no longer a reasonable course of action. He was confronted by Lt. Gen. Ulysses S. Grant, another of the most determined leaders in American history, who relentlessly used his soldiers and other resources until victory was secured. Behind General Grant and the other Union field commanders stood President Abraham Lincoln, who maintained an unwavering focus on restoring the Union.

In the Carolinas, Maj. Gen. William T. Sherman became the ally of his friend Grant in the difficult task of gaining victory in a long and costly war. Opposing General Sherman was a Confederate commander in chief, President Jefferson Davis, who persisted in resisting against hopeless odds. President Davis's field leader in the Carolinas, Gen. Joseph E. Johnston, held a more realistic view of the South's military prospects. Probably by February 1865, and certainly by April of that year, General Johnston had concluded that the essential question was no longer how to win a military victory for the Confederacy but rather how to gain the best possible peace terms for the South.

Twenty-first-century Americans should know about the experiences of these senior leaders and those of the soldiers and civilians around them. These people witnessed some of the most harrowing months in our country's history. Their stories help today's citizens understand how an unimaginably painful, and extremely crucial, American war came to an end.

ACKNOWLEDGMENTS

When the hard work of writing a book is done, it is a great pleasure to thank the people who helped the effort. In this case, there were so many that I am almost certain to forget some of them. I apologize in advance for my omissions.

My first thanks go to the staff of the University of Nebraska Press. They remained patient with me during the long time I worked on this project. I greatly appreciate the professionalism of Bridget Barry, Sabrina Ehmke Sergeant, Kathryn Owens, Kyle Simonsen, Ann Baker, Tish Fobben, and others at the press.

Several archivists and librarians made this book possible. During the first years I worked on it, I received valuable support, as I often have, from Richard J. Sommers, David Keough, Pamela Cheney, and Louise Arnold-Friend at the United States Army Heritage and Education Center. Later in my research, I enjoyed seeing Master Sgt. Rich Baker, USAF (Ret.), who brought to his job equal measures of professionalism and humor. I am especially grateful that I was helped by Arthur W. Bergeron, Jr., himself a highly accomplished historian whose works appear in the bibliographical essay of this book. He left us, too soon, in February 2010.

It was thanks to the suggestions of Frances Pollard, the chief librarian of the Virginia Historical Society, that I was able to make the most of my time at her institution. I also benefited from the assistance of Matthew Turi, the manuscripts reference librarian at the Wilson Library at the University of North Carolina–Chapel Hill. Like the staff of the Virginia Historical Society, the professionals at the Wilson Library do a praiseworthy job of managing a superb collection.

Two institutions with regional holdings proved helpful to this project. Lisa Kobrin directed me to useful sources in the local history collection of the May Memorial Library in Burlington, North Carolina. And I owe particular thanks to Rebecca Owens of the Johnston County Heritage Center in Smithfield, North Carolina. One rainy Monday in August 2010, she helped me learn about the history of the Bentonville area. More important, she kept me in communication throughout that day with my wife, Stephanie, who had left me at the heritage center that morning and then, through no fault of hers, became involved in a car accident. Fortunately no one was hurt, but the episode made for some stressful hours.

Thanks go to Anne J. Bailey and Brooks D. Simpson for inviting me to contribute to the Great Campaigns of the Civil War series. Vicki Chamlee diligently copyedited my manuscript and greatly improved it. Erin Greb converted my rough ideas into a superb set of maps. Frank Surdu, a longtime friend whose computer skills far outrun mine, helped me find and prepare the illustrations. Frank and I appreciate the information we received from Amanda Brantley of the Bentonville Battleground State Historic Site and the images we obtained from John W. Guss of the Bennett Place State Historic Site in Durham, North Carolina, and from Christopher M. Calkins of the Sailor's Creek Battlefield Historical State Park in Rice, Virginia.

A few friendly critics looked at my manuscript and offered ideas that improved it. I am particularly grateful to Judkin Browning of Appalachian State University. His insightful suggestions, and those of others, strengthened this book. Any errors that remain are mine.

Some relatives and friends helped in wide-ranging ways. They variously informed me about Civil War politics in Johnston County, North Carolina, and about the trees in that state; they ran down elusive citations; and they bolstered my morale.

Thanks go to Thomas G. Clemens, Ted Daniel, Fred Deats, James Michael Denham, Judith Schafer, and Frank (Mickey) Schubert. I send a special thank-you to my sister-in-law Phyllis Deats, who toured Fort Fisher with me on a particularly hot August day. My last and largest thanks go to my wife, Stephanie. She remained patient while I was writing this book instead of painting and otherwise improving our early twentieth-century western Maryland farmhouse. In recent years Stephanie and I have enjoyed trips to Alaska, France, and spring training and World Series games. We also have experienced terrible diseases and other adversities in our family. In good times and bad, Stephanie keeps making things better. As the dedication page says, this one is for her.

SERIES EDITORS' INTRODUCTION

Americans remain fascinated by the Civil War. Movies, television, and video—even computer software—have augmented the ever-expanding list of books on the war. Although it stands to reason that a large portion of recent work concentrates on military aspects of the conflict, historians have expanded our scope of inquiry to include civilians, especially women; the destruction of slavery and the evolving understanding of what freedom meant to millions of former slaves; and an even greater emphasis on the experiences of the common soldier on both sides. Other studies have demonstrated the interrelationships of war, politics, and policy and how civilians' concerns back home influenced both soldiers and politicians. Although one cannot fully comprehend this central event in American history without understanding that military operations were fundamental in determining the course and outcome of the war, it is time for students of battles and campaigns to incorporate nonmilitary themes in their accounts. The most pressing challenge facing Civil War scholarship today is the integration of various perspectives and emphases into a new narrative that explains not only what happened, why, and how but also why it mattered.

The series Great Campaigns of the Civil War offers readers concise syntheses of the major campaigns of the war, reflecting the findings of recent scholarship. The series points to new ways of viewing military campaigns by looking beyond the battlefield and the headquarters tent to the wider political and social context within which these campaigns unfolded; it also shows how campaigns and battles left their imprint on many Americans, from presidents and generals down to privates and civilians. The ends and means of waging war reflect larger political objectives and priorities as well as social values. Historians may continue to debate among themselves as to which of these campaigns constituted true turning points, but each of the campaigns treated in this series contributed to shaping the course of the conflict, to opening opportunities, and to eliminating alternatives.

Perry Jamieson's volume details the closing campaigns of the war. In hindsight, of course, we see that the Confederacy's days were numbered, but that was not necessarily the case at the time to the presidents, generals, soldiers, and people. In the first few months of 1865, Union forces made their way through the Carolinas, and by March they were hovering south of Virginia. Coastal operations securing the fall of Fort Fisher and Wilmington, North Carolina, in January were overshadowed in popular memory by William T. Sherman's fiery march through South Carolina in February. Meanwhile, both Ulysses S. Grant and Robert E. Lee awaited the advent of spring and dry roads to resume operations around Richmond and Petersburg. The Confederate commander planned to escape the capital in hopes of uniting with Joe Johnston's army in North Carolina before turning on either Grant or Sherman. Eager to prevent such an event, Grant also hoped to make sure that even if Lee evacuated Richmond and Petersburg, he would not get far. As it turned out, his pursuit of Lee's retreating legions during the first nine days of April 1865 proved masterful, resulting in Lee's surrender at Appomattox Court House on Palm Sunday. Once the Army of Northern Virginia was no more, other Confederate commanders eventually followed suit, with both Johnston and Sherman exceeding the directives of their superiors at Durham's Station, North Carolina. In the end Sherman heeded his superiors, especially Grant, while Johnston ignored Jefferson Davis. Nevertheless, the road to Confederate submission was at times a rough one, and the Confederacy did not quite go quietly. Jamieson's account reminds us of the choices men made and the alternatives they left on the table.

Spring 1865

CHAPTER ONE

Terrible Times of Shipwreck

Col. Joseph Frederick Waring, the commander of Mississippi's Jefferson Davis Legion, was a well-read and observant Confederate cavalry officer. He concluded one Saturday in the dead of the winter of 1864–65 that the season of the year affected the morale of Southern civilians. "The people give way every winter to despondency," Colonel Waring wrote in his diary on January 14, 1865. "I have seen it now for four winters." It was an observation that rang truer than ever during the gloomy weeks of late 1864 and early 1865.[1]

Less than four years earlier, the Confederacy had gone to war in a springtime of optimism. Then season followed season, the casualty rolls lengthened, the Federal armies advanced again and again, and Southern spirits dropped. Now the fourth winter of the war settled across a beleaguered Confederacy. From Virginia to Texas, Southerners despaired of victory.

In their mansions, houses, and log cabins, women prayed for the return of their loved ones. Only a few still believed that these men would come home to an independent Confederacy. In mid-January 1865 Mary Boykin Chesnut, a well-connected South Carolinian, learned there would be peace negotiations between the North and South, but the news brought her no cheer. She wrote tersely in her diary: "No hope—no good. Who dares hope?" That same winter Lydia Johnston, the wife of Gen. Joseph E. "Old

Joe" Johnston, wrote from Lincolnton, North Carolina, to her friend Charlotte Wigfall in Richmond: "Oh these terrible times of shipwreck—everything looks hopeless to me now, and then if we are to go down—we are so far apart that we can see nothing of each other, but the glimpse of a distant pale face as it sinks out of sight!"[2]

While Southern civilians despaired of victory, their soldiers suffered stern hardships. The men of the Army of Northern Virginia, tied down in the siege at Petersburg, Virginia, had little to eat. Many days the troops received either meat or a starch—cornmeal or flour—but not both. After four or five meatless days, their commissary officers tried with varying success to supply them with some sorghum or sugar. "To these deficiencies of food," wrote division commander Maj. Gen. Joseph B. Kershaw, "I attribute the number of desertions daily occurring and a general feeling of depression existing."[3]

The Army of Northern Virginia lacked food and firewood. The Confederates had been well settled around Petersburg since the previous June and had used many of the trees around them to construct fortifications and winter quarters. "We suffered for firewood," a South Carolina veteran reported. "The growth about the camp, never heavy, was soon consumed by the troops; and for the last two months of our stay here we were obliged to carry logs on our shoulders for the distance of a mile or more, in order to have any fire at all." Historian Earl Hess, citing a late twentieth-century study, states that during the more than nine months the soldiers spent in the area, they cut down more than half of its timber.[4]

Lt. Gen. James "Old Pete" Longstreet, the Army of Northern Virginia's senior corps commander, imposed a rational policy on timbering north of the James River. His soldiers were to cut first the trees in front of their lines and save those to the rear for later use. Wood rationing became a standard practice. In the Forty-ninth North Carolina, for example, each company drew ten sticks of green pinewood and a bushel of coal a day.[5]

Partly because the Southerners lacked firewood, warm clothing, and food, many of them began leaving the Petersburg trenches.

On February 25, 1865, Gen. Robert E. Lee was forced to report a brutal truth to the Confederate adjutant general: "Hundreds of men are deserting nightly and I cannot keep the army together unless examples are made of [convicted deserters]."[6] During ten days of that month, more than a thousand men left the ranks. At the end of that dismal February, General Lee told the secretary of war that desertion "proceeds from the discouraging sentiment out of the Army, which, unless it can be checked, will bring us calamity." The arrival of a new month did not improve the situation. Reports covering the period from February 15 through March 18 showed that more than three thousand men deserted the Army of Northern Virginia.[7]

That winter Lee's men wrote letters and diary entries that reveal they accepted desertion as a routine fact of life. An Alabamian informed his wife in early March that "the spirit of the army is very low[,] desertion is getting to be a daily thing." "Fourteen left our Brigade last night," another soldier wrote his spouse on March 15, "& went over to the yankees. . . . Numbers go over to the yankees every night." He added: "And what speaks worse for the spirit of the army, is that the men on the picket line fire off their guns into the air & will not try to shoot down those who are in the act of deserting to the enemy." A third veteran wrote to his aunt: "[W]hen I got Back the Boys Said to me what did you com back for all the other Boys has Runaway."[8]

Confederate senior officers recognized that alarming numbers of soldiers were leaving the ranks, and they often offered what historian Tracy Power has called "an administrative interpretation of desertion." In their efforts to explain why so many veterans were abandoning the army, some commanders emphasized physical hardships—shortages of food and other essentials—and they pointed to the government's failure to meet its commitments for pay and authorized leaves. These explanations offered at least some hope, because they held out the possibility that stronger logistics could address the desertion problem.[9]

The letters written by the troops, however, suggest that the causes were more fundamental, and more difficult to resolve, than their officers wanted to acknowledge. The correspondence from the men of the Army of Northern Virginia suggests that, as Power has framed it, "many soldiers deserted because they believed that the war was already lost or that their families needed them more than the Confederacy did."[10]

By the winter of 1864–65, letters from loved ones to Lee's men, appealing to them to come home, had become sadly common. Pvt. Robert Stiles referred to correspondence that "could not be read without tears—letters in which a wife and mother, crazed by her starving children's cries for bread, required a husband and father to choose between his God-imposed obligations to her and to them and his allegiance to his country, his duty as a soldier." Col. Walter Taylor of Lee's staff stated that he knew of "hundreds of letters" in which mothers, wives, and sisters lamented their hardships and asked their loved one to return home.[11]

Married men were receptive to these appeals; fathers were particularly so. A scholarly statistical study by historian Joseph Glatthaar shows that over the course of the war married men in the Army of Northern Virginia "were nearly a third more likely to desert. Even more powerful was the motivation to look after one's children. Fathers were 80% more likely to flee the army than childless soldiers."[12]

Appeals from the home front encouraged so much desertion that in early March a Virginia officer acknowledged: "It is useless to conceal the truth any longer. Many of our people at home have become so demoralized that they write to their husbands, sons and brothers that desertion *now* is not *dishonorable*." "Friends write, imprudently they communicate their despondent feelings to friends in the army," a Georgian wrote to his sister on March 21, 1865, "and you see the legitimate result—desertion. People at home have done more harm by discouraging the army than they have any idea." Lee himself sadly concluded that civilians contributed significantly to desertion rates. "It seems that the men are influenced by the representations of their friends at home," he reported to the Confederate secretary of war, "who appear to have become very despondent as to our success. They think the cause desperate and write to the soldiers, advising them to take care of themselves, assuring them that if they will return home the bands of deserters so far outnumber the home guards that they will be in no danger of arrest."[13]

The Confederates suffered the same problems of high desertion and low morale in the region west of Lee's army, the critically important area defended by the Army of Tennessee. The field force in the western theater had tried for years to protect a front that ran for several hundred miles and was more than two and a half times longer than the one assigned to the more prestigious Army of Northern Virginia.[14] The Army of Tennessee became the hard-luck outfit of the South, racked by feuding among its leaders, neglected by Richmond, and defeated in battle time and again.[15]

By the winter of 1864–65, the western Confederates had suffered so many reverses that they despaired of victory. After Gen. John Bell Hood's disastrous Tennessee campaign, one veteran wrote to his wife: "Our army was badly whipped and it seems that they are not going to get over it Soon, especially if Gen. Hood remains in Command." On January 17 another observer informed Brig. Gen. Basil Duke: "Genl Hood's army is . . . the worst whipped army you ever saw." Describing morale on the North Carolina front, an infantryman referred to the same fundamental problem that afflicted the Army of Northern Virginia. "The men are all very much disheartened," he related, "and the people at home are even more so and they write that strain to the soldiers and that makes them more dispirited . . . there would be very few deserters if the soldiers letters [from home] were of a cheerful tone."[16]

Still farther west, in the Trans-Mississippi Confederacy, four years of Civil War had brought unrelenting grief. After a two-week foray through parts of Louisiana and Arkansas in January 1865, a Federal officer painted a stark landscape. "No squad of men, much less an army," he reported, "can live anywhere we have been. The people have neither seed, corn, nor bread, or the mills to grind the corn in if they had it." Some Trans-Mississippi farmers continued to produce decent harvests, but they found it nearly impossible to ship them. Wagons had worn out, draft animals suffered exhaustion, steamboats had fallen into disrepair, and rail lines lay in shambles.[17] Shortly after the war ended, a journalist lamented: "There is nothing in the State of Texas so sadly out of joint, out of repair, out of time, out of efficient officers, and as we are led to believe, out of money, as our Railroads. . . . A discreet person never thinks of taking passage on a Texas Rail-road without first getting his life insured, saying his prayers, and then writing to some friendly freighter, to meet him half-way along the track, and transport him to the depot."[18]

Confederate morale in the Trans-Mississippi had collapsed. In February 1865 a furloughed Southern soldier made his way back to Texas only to find that nearly every resident of his region "appeared dispirited and whipped." By then many of the troops were putting themselves on leave—permanently. Whole regiments seemed to melt from the ranks. Early that January, newspapers in Galveston and San Antonio ran a column and a half of names of men who were listed officially as deserters. A fugitive from the garrison at Alexandria, Louisiana, reported that the soldiers of that state "are discouraged and are deserting daily, some going to Mexico, some to the Federal lines. They have not been paid for more than a year."[19]

In the Trans-Mississippi and elsewhere that winter, desertion and sickness crippled the Confederacy. In December 1864 fewer than half the men on the rolls were in fact with their regiments. As officially reported, only 196,016 out of 400,787 Southern soldiers, or 49 percent, were present for duty. By April 1865 these numbers would decline to 160,198 out of 358,692, or 45 percent. While many men had fallen too ill to continue to fight, others had abandoned the cause. They agreed with one of Lee's veterans, who in January 1865 confessed: "There are a good many of us who believe this shooting match has gone on long enough. A government that has run out of rations can't expect to do much more fighting, and to keep on in a reckless and wanton expenditure of human life."[20]

While Southern morale was low on every front, one Confederate remained as determined as ever—President Jefferson Davis. Lee met with the chief executive in March 1865 and came away impressed both with his superior's faith about the outcome of the ongoing struggle and with his strong will power. Historian Steven Woodworth, a careful student of both President Davis and General Lee, believes that the greatest difference in their views during the last months of the war lay in the president's "increasingly unrealistic faith in the continued possibility of Confederate victory." Davis's biographer William C. Davis observes that, as late as February 1865, "Jefferson Davis simply would not countenance that his desperate cause did not still have a chance."[21]

Many Southerners hoped that Lee would be able to reverse the fortunes of their cause. The most successful of their field generals, he had saved Richmond in the early summer of 1862 and then had given the Confederacy other dramatic victories. "The greatest single factor engendering Confederate hope after the midpoint of the war," writes historian Gary Gallagher, "was trust in Robert E. Lee and the Army of Northern Viriginia."[22]

Since the day Lee had taken command of the Army of Northern Virginia, his authority had been limited to that organization. If he were given control of all of the Confederacy's armies, many believed, greater results would follow. "It is to be hoped," Waring of the Jeff Davis Legion wrote on January 14, 1865, "that Gen. Lee will be made Generalissimo. If he is made so, it will give great confidence to the people."[23] Three days after Waring expressed this opinion, the Virginia legislature recommended in a secret bill that Lee be appointed commander of all Confederate field forces.

This proposal would help centralize and strengthen the South's strategic planning, to some extent at the expense of the military authority of the civilian commander in chief. President Davis nonetheless replied to the Virginia lawmakers that he supported the idea. In the past, he told them, Lee had been reluctant to assume this larger role while still directly commanding the Army of Northern Virginia. This position stated by the general himself and nothing else, Davis asserted, prevented Lee's taking greater authority. The president then wrote to his most successful army commander and reopened the subject. Lee promptly answered that he was pleased with Davis's confidence in him, but he questioned what he could accomplish if his responsibilities were expanded.

The matter did not end there, because the Confederate Congress forced the issue. On January 15, two days before the Virginia legislature voted in secret, the Confederate Senate had passed overwhelmingly a resolution calling for Davis to make Lee general in chief. On January 19, the Confederate House concurred with the Senate on this appointment.

Davis and Lee accepted the congressional mandate. The president endorsed the elevation of Lee, given his record in the field. Davis did see to it that the final version of the bill gave the general in chief "command of all the military forces of the Confederate states," wording that the chief executive believed protected his own authority as commander in chief. On February 1 Davis gave the new position to Lee, who set aside his earlier reservations and on the ninth assumed the broader responsibilities.[24] During the weeks following the general's promotion, it became evident that his increased role did not change either his personal or his professional relationship with the president.[25]

The Federal counterparts to the Davis-Lee command team were capable leaders, committed to waging war until a Union victory was won. When the conflict began, President Abraham Lincoln lacked any significant experience with military affairs, but as the fighting continued, he grew into his role as commander in chief. President Lincoln had many qualities that helped save the Union: an ability to identify and use the strengths of others, an appreciation of sound ideas, a skill at developing political support for the war effort from diverse quarters, and a determination to stay the course through years of appalling bloodshed.[26] As commander in chief, he maintained an unwavering focus on restoring the Union. "With razor-like acuteness," writes historian Joseph Glatthaar, "Lincoln sliced away all the extraneous concerns until only a single, core issue remained: the reunion of the states. Nothing else mattered."[27]

Lincoln benefited not only from having appointed a general in chief nearly a year before the Confederacy did so but also from the qualities of the soldier who held this position. Lt. Gen. Ulysses S. Grant was a straightforward man who presented an ordinary appearance. Officers found him at his headquarters wearing a slouch hat and a short coat, with no display of the three-star rank that he uniquely held. In his modest dress and other traits, General Grant modeled himself on Maj. Gen. Zachary Taylor, who, with brevet Lt. Gen. Winfield Scott, had shared billing as the two preeminent heroes of the Old Army. As a young officer, Grant had served under General Taylor, nicknamed "Old Rough and Ready," in the northern theater of the Mexican-American War. Late in his life, as the retired president, Grant would write of Taylor what many others said of Grant himself: "No soldier could face either danger or responsibility more calmly than he. These are qualities more rarely found than genius or physical courage."[28]

Grant's strong suit was his fixed determination to campaign relentlessly against Lee until a victory was secured. When Grant arrived in the eastern theater, Confederate general Longstreet, who had known him since their West Point days, grimly predicted: "We must make up our minds to get into line of battle and to stay there; for that man will fight us every day and every hour till the end of this war."[29]

Grant's persistence in the face of ghastly battlefield losses was so strong that some considered him a cold-blooded butcher, but those who knew him well thought otherwise. "Stolid as Grant appeared to be," one officer wrote, "I have no doubt that he felt as deeply about the horrors of war as those who were more demonstrative." Adam Badeau, the general's military secretary, believed that Grant had an extraordinary ability to keep his feelings in check. "I sometimes wondered whether he was conscious of his own emotions," Badeau reflected, "they were so completely under control; but they were all there, all alive, all active, only enveloped in a cloak of obstinate reserve and majestic silence which only at the rarest intervals was torn aside by misfortune or lifted for a moment to a friend."[30]

Grant's friend Maj. Gen. William T. Sherman became his equally determined ally in the hard business yet to be finished. General Sherman had made a record of devoting himself to whatever task was at hand and reliably getting it done. In January 1865 his men had just completed a devastating march through Georgia, and during the months ahead, they would wreak even greater damage in South Carolina. After the war, many white Southerners would depict Sherman as a destructive monster. He was in truth a dedicated professional soldier, driven by an unwavering sense of duty and an uncompromising integrity.[31]

Grant assigned Sherman a major role in the operations that would begin that winter and, he hoped, would end the war. The two generals would execute a grand strategy that relentlessly would exploit their advantage in numbers. The North, like the South, had suffered high casualties during three and a half years of combat, but its larger population had allowed it to replace its manpower losses far better than the Confederacy had.

In December 1864 Lee's Army of Northern Virginia had a scant 66,500 effectives and was stretched thin to hold its trenches around Petersburg. Grant could bring to bear three leviathans against this small, ill-supplied Southern command. At his elbow was Maj. Gen. George G. Meade's Army of the Potomac, numbering more than 80,000 soldiers and pinning down the threadbare Confederate forces that held the Petersburg lines. Grant also had at hand Maj. Gen. Benjamin F. Butler's Army of the James, which totaled about 40,700 men and cooperated with General Meade in the siege of Lee. The third force stood nearly five hundred miles south of Petersburg, at Savannah, Georgia, where Sherman's roughly 60,000 soldiers were resting at the end of December. If these men joined those with Generals Butler and Meade, their combined strength would doom Lee's ragged and beleaguered command.[32]

At first Grant had intended to move Sherman's soldiers by water, but his trustworthy subordinate convinced him that he could reach Virginia by marching through the Carolinas. On December 27 the senior general told Sherman: "Your confidence in being able to march up and join this Army [of the Potomac] pleases me and I believe it can be done. . . . Without waiting further directions then you may make preparation to start on your Northern expedition without delay. Break up the rail-roads in South & North Carolina and join the Armies operating against Richmond as soon as you can."[33] With those words, Grant endorsed his friend's strategic proposal for the western theater: Sherman would drive overland through the Carolinas.

In carrying out their operations, Grant and Sherman would benefit from strong logistics. Sherman's force was served by the talented chief quartermaster Brig. Gen. Langdon C. Easton. During the March to the Sea of November and December 1864, the Federals had moved about 65,000 soldiers, 19,500 mules, 14,500 horses, 5,500 cattle, and 2,500 wagons from Atlanta to Savannah. By mid-January 1865 Sherman's command had been resupplied and stood ready for its advance into the Carolinas. His powerful combat units would outnumber considerably any Confederates they might encounter. Yet at the same time Union logistics were, as officers of a later era would put it, "lean and mean." Sherman had reduced his cavalry and artillery, thus cutting by 4,000 the number of animals he would have to support. He would begin the Carolinas campaign with about 2,700 wagons, and his ratio of these vehicles to soldiers would be slightly higher when he started north than it had been during the March to the Sea.[34]

General Easton was so confident that Sherman would reach Goldsboro, North Carolina, that he prepared a huge supply base and built from scratch a depot and wharves at Morehead City, some ninety miles to the southeast and on the Atlantic coast. Maj. Gen. John M. Schofield, victor of the Battle of Franklin, provided fifteen hundred men from his XXIII Corps to the working parties and guard details needed for this impressive project. To get a sawmill running, Easton bought up the lumber in the area and then brought in timber from Savannah. Civilian carpenters, mechanics, and laborers came from Washington DC and New York.[35]

Sherman also marshaled a high-achieving corps of engineers and shattered their enemy's assumption that South Carolina's tidewater swamps would stop the Federal hordes. "My engineers," General Johnston stated, "reported that it was absolutely impossible for an army to march across the lower portions of the State in winter." Sherman's pioneer battalions of soldiers and freedmen refuted this claim. Brig. Gen. Orlando M. Poe, Sherman's able chief engineer, reported that his engineers and mechanics corduroyed four hundred miles of road during the Carolinas campaign; the entire Federal force reworked almost eight hundred miles.[36]

Sherman's talented engineers and strong logistics were matched by Grant's. Nowhere were Federal riches in supplies and transportation more evident than at Grant's massive base at City Point, Virginia. During 1864 Union military might had converted this quiet hamlet into one of the world's thriving seaports. At City Point, the wealth and efficiency of the industrial North contrasted with the shortages and incapacity of the failing Confederacy. On a typical day during the Petersburg campaign, forty steamboats, seventy-five sailing vessels, and a hundred barges tied up or anchored at the wharves and docks that ran far along the James River and up the Appomattox River. A twenty-one-mile railroad tied Grant's huge command at Petersburg to City Point's vast complex of warehouses, bakeries, blacksmith shops, wagon-repair barns, and barracks.[37]

While Grant and Sherman prepared to use their enormous resources to finish the war by military operations, a remote prospect beckoned that it could be ended by peace negotiations. This small hope began to twinkle on December 15, 1864, when Horace Greeley, the influential editor of the *New York Tribune*, suggested to Francis P. Blair, an equally prominent Maryland editor, that a war-weary North Carolina, with its share of Unionists, might be persuaded to abandon the conflict. Blair optimistically expanded this idea to encompass the entire Confederacy and asked its president for permission to visit Richmond. The former Jacksonian Democrat, now in his seventies, had known Davis before the war. Blair told his old acquaintance he had arrived at a plan that might lead to peace and wanted to discuss it with him. Davis agreed to a meeting.

The two men held a long session on January 12, 1865. Blair contended that the issue of slavery was dead and that the two sections should end their war and join forces in support of the Monroe Doctrine. Specifically he proposed a wild scheme in which the North and South would form an alliance to defeat Napoleon III's puppet government in Mexico. Davis at once saw the obvious obstacles to Blair's extravagant idea, and while he continued to believe that Southern arms would win the Confederacy's independence, he nonetheless expressed a willingness to negotiate. In the immediate circumstance, Davis saw an opportunity to warn Lincoln, through the Maryland editor, how costly it would be to occupy the South—assuming, and Davis himself emphatically did not, that the Confederacy could be defeated. For the longer term, the Confederate president may have seen a political opportunity. He sent Blair back to Washington with an offer to send commissioners to a "conference with a view to secure peace to the two countries."[38]

On January 22 the self-appointed emissary met with Lincoln. The president said that if he personally entered normal peace negotiations with the Confederates, his already considerable domestic political problems would grow worse. He told Blair that he was willing to entertain the idea of a preliminary meeting between Grant and Lee to establish a cease-fire, which then might lead to further discussions between civilian leaders. Lincoln had no interest in a Mexican adventure, but he was receptive to peace talks. He gave Blair a letter to show Davis that said that the Southerners might informally send agents to Lincoln "with the view of securing peace to the people of our one common country."[39]

Lincoln's letter underlined the crucial point in any bargaining between North and South: Davis spoke of negotiating a peace between "the two countries" while Lincoln referred to "our one common country." The two phrases could not be reconciled. The national union was either permanent, as Lincoln believed, or not, as Davis contended.

Davis was amenable to a Lee-Grant meeting, but by the time Blair returned to Washington, Lincoln apparently had come to recognize that he could not entrust peace negotiations to military officers. The two chief executives turned instead to a conference of civilian commissioners. Lincoln had stated he would give an audience to Southern agents, and in late January the Confederates put together a delegation.[40]

The selection process was hindered by a deep rift that divided Davis from his vice president, Alexander H. Stephens, who had once compared the president to "my poor old blind and deaf dog." Their feud ran through the war, becoming so bitter that the president more than once told his friend Confederate congressman James Lyons of Virginia that he would resign—if Stephens would also.[41]

Stephens, an old friend of Lincoln's, had championed the idea of talks with the North albeit with Confederate independence as a precondition for a peace settlement.[42] The Confederate vice president had set out on a mission to Washington during the Pennsylvania campaign, which was abruptly ended by the Union victory at Gettysburg.[43] In January 1865 while the Confederate cabinet was discussing the names of possible negotiators, the Senate was preparing to pass a series of resolutions, backed by Stephens, calling for an all-states convention that would formulate a peace agreement.[44]

When it came time to pick the commissioners, the president's first thought was to keep Stephens off the delegation. Secretary of State Judah P. Benjamin agreed with Davis, out of loyalty to him. Senator Benjamin Hill of Georgia, Secretary of the Navy Stephen R. Mallory, and others persuaded the chief executive to include Stephens if only to get him out of Richmond and derail his peace resolutions.

Davis changed his mind, put his vice president on the delegation, and created a favorable political situation for himself. While insisting that the mission was a genuine peace initiative, the president bound his commissioners with instructions that doomed in advance the negotiations with the Union leaders. Davis may have expected that the Federals would demand humiliating conditions, the conference would fail, and after the terms were published, Confederate morale would climb. The Southern peace movement would be discredited and the war effort reinvigorated. Events did not play out quite so well as Davis hoped, but he did score a rare double victory in public relations and in personality politics. As it turned out, many Southerners would blame Northern leaders for the collapse of the peace talks and would link the failed conference to Alexander Stephens.[45]

Stephens, accompanied by Assistant Secretary of War John A. Campbell and Senator R. M. T. Hunter of Virginia, arrived at Grant's City Point headquarters on the evening of January 31. They almost went no farther. Truculent secretary of war Edwin

M. Stanton wanted nothing to do with the Rebel emissaries and might well have had them sent back to Richmond if Grant had not intervened.[46]

Grant handled the situation properly. He put the three agents onto a steamer in the James River, notified Lincoln of their arrival, and asked his civilian superior for instructions. The tough Federal general, of course, had his own opinion of the matter. Grant had seen a great deal of bloodshed on many battlefields, and doubtless he wanted it to end. He also had made a military calculation: if an armistice were declared, desertion would unravel Lee's army.

Grant talked to Stephens and Hunter and concluded they were sincere about their mission. He urged the commissioners to put their intentions in writing, making the text vague enough that Lincoln would conclude he could meet with them without granting any legal recognition to the Confederacy. The Southern agents took Grant's advice, and Lincoln telegraphed that he would confer with them at Hampton Roads.[47]

On February 3, 1865, Lincoln and Secretary of State William H. Seward met with the three Confederate commissioners on the steamer *River Queen*. A few days earlier the president had prepared written instructions for Secretary Seward, and he held fast to them himself during the long meeting at Hampton Roads. Lincoln insisted on three points, which he had told his secretary of state were "indispensable": "1 The restoration of the National authority throughout all the states. 2 No receding by the Executive of the United States, on the slavery question. . . . 3 No cessation of hostilities short of an end of the war, and the disbanding of all forces hostile to the government."[48]

These three points left Stephens and his colleagues with no room to negotiate. As one Confederate officer tersely put it: "Lincoln told our Commissioners that we must submit." In any event, the Southern delegation was bound by Davis's instructions, which were as inflexible as Lincoln's to Seward. Stephens raised the proposal that had initiated the conference—Blair's Mexican scheme. Hunter suggested an armistice, followed by a convention of the states. Lincoln dismissed both ideas. Dejected, the three Southerners returned to Richmond.[49]

The futility of the Hampton Roads peace conference had been announced in advance, as noted previously, in the correspondence between the two presidents during the Blair mission. Davis had written about a peace between "the two countries" while for Lincoln there could be only "our one common country." Another harbinger of failure was a reminder of the irreconcilable differences between the sections. When the three Confederates had arrived in front of Grant's lines at Petersburg, one Federal officer saw "that the *bone of contention* between the two armies . . . came with them in the shape of a black man carrying a valise."[50]

The failure at Hampton Roads no doubt pleased many Federal soldiers. By the winter of 1864–65, they had seen large numbers of comrades killed and maimed and others carted off to hellish prison camps. Many veterans believed these casualties should be the price of a military victory, not a negotiated settlement. An infantryman serving on the Cape Fear River front in North Carolina voiced a common sentiment when he told a Philadelphia reporter that he wanted "a soldier's peace, not a politician's peace." When the journalist pursued the question, the Union warrior explained what he meant by a "soldier's peace": "To fight till one side is completely whipped, whipped till they own up, that sir, is a soldier's peace."[51]

The Hampton Roads meeting had come to nothing. The winter would give way to spring, the weather would improve for active campaigning, and the North would renew its offensives. The Federals would pursue the war until a soldier's peace was won. On the last day of 1864, Sherman informed his wife, Ellen, from Savannah: "It will not be long before I sally forth on another dangerous & important Quixotic venture." Shortly before Sherman communicated with his spouse, one of his artillery officers offered a prediction. "It appears to me now," he wrote to his brother, "that next spring will finish this war, but there will be some very heavy fighting to be done yet."[52]

CHAPTER TWO

Fort Fisher and Wilmington

Lt. Gen. Ulysses S. Grant's grand strategy for 1865 called for Maj. Gen. William T. Sherman to sweep north through the Carolinas toward Petersburg, Virginia, where Gen. Robert E. Lee stood pinned in his trenches. Wilmington, North Carolina, loomed large in General Sherman's operations. The city was vital to the Confederates as their only remaining open port, and its location—roughly halfway between Savannah, Georgia, and Richmond, Virginia—also made it potentially valuable to the Union. Federal occupation of Wilmington would ease Sherman's supply arrangements and speed his advance toward Virginia. He could draw men and provisions from the Cape Fear River and from the railroads that entered this port city from three compass points.[1]

South from Wilmington ran Federal Point, a sandy peninsula with the Atlantic Ocean on the east and the Cape Fear River on the west. On the lower end of Federal Point stood Fort Fisher, a massive fortification named after Charles Fisher, the colonel of the Sixth North Carolina who had been killed on Henry House Hill during the First Battle of Manassas.[2] Fort Fisher defended the favorite approach of the blockade runners who, during the winter of 1864–65, were still slipping into Wilmington.[3] Col. William Lamb, who redesigned and commanded the great post, summed up its significance in a single sentence: "General Lee sent me word that Fort Fisher must be held, or he could not subsist his army."[4]

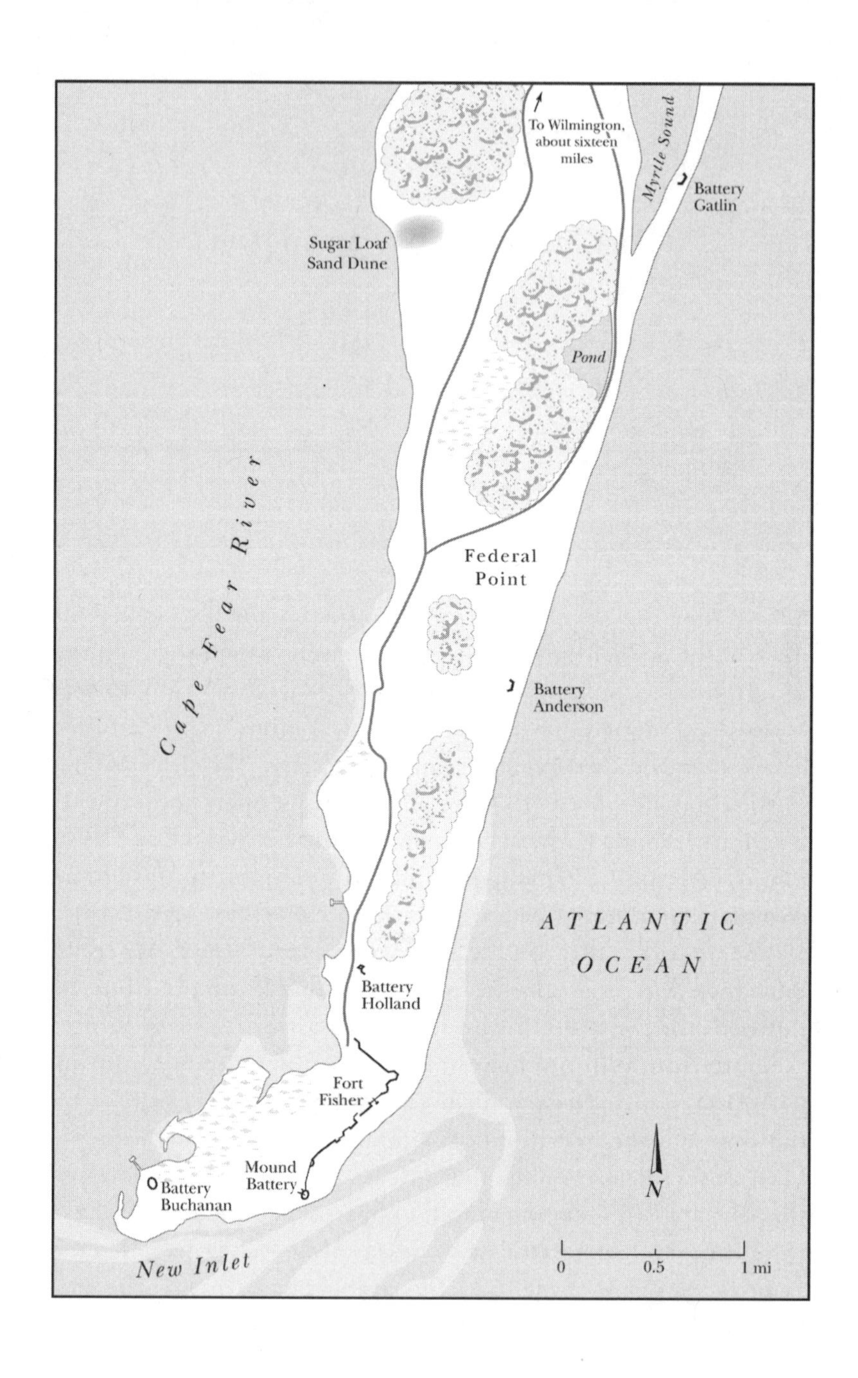

MAP 1. Federal Point Peninsula and Fort Fisher

The Federal high command fully understood Fort Fisher's importance and made an effort against it near the end of December 1864. General Grant dispatched from the Petersburg front about sixty-five hundred men from the Army of the James: one full white division, two brigades of an African American division, an artillery battery, and a small support force. Fort Fisher fell within the jurisdiction of the Department of Virginia and North Carolina, so its commander, Maj. Gen. Benjamin F. Butler, directed the expedition although few Northerners had much confidence in his generalship.[5] General Butler took his forces down to North Carolina on transport ships, intending to link up with sixty-four vessels under Rear Adm. David Dixon Porter.[6]

General Lee countered the Federals by reluctantly dispatching from his own army Maj. Gen. Robert F. Hoke's command. Best known for his brilliant capture of Plymouth, North Carolina, in April 1864, General Hoke led a division of more than sixty-four hundred soldiers.[7] Lee sent these veterans to help Colonel Lamb's fewer than fourteen hundred men and boys hold the enormous Fort Fisher and its defenses.[8]

Historian Chris Fonvielle, Jr., superbly details the Union operations against Fort Fisher and Wilmington in his clearly written work *The Wilmington Campaign: Last Rays of Departing Hope*. As Fonvielle relates, the initial Federal expedition against Fort Fisher made a fitful start. Butler's transports arrived off Masonboro Inlet after sunset on December 15. Admiral Porter's fleet did not show up until three days later, and bad weather further delayed the operation until December 23.[9]

In this initial attack on Fort Fisher, the Federals used a novel weapon—a powder ship. The attackers intended to detonate the USS *Louisiana*, a 143-foot screw steamer carrying 215 tons of gunpowder, and blast away the sand walls of the fortification. They tried the stratagem during the early morning hours of Christmas Eve day but failed to get the vessel close enough to Fort Fisher. Many of the Confederates inside the works hardly noticed the explosion. Capt. Thomas O. Selfridge, Jr., of the U.S. Navy described it honestly as "an ignominious failure." Writing in more colorful terms, the Federal chief of staff Maj. Gen. Henry W. Halleck distanced himself from the fiasco in a dispatch, which when published in the *Official Records* was rendered: "Thank God I had nothing to do with it, except to express the opinion that Butler's torpedo ship would have about as much effect on the forts as if he should — at them."[10]

After the powder ship debacle, the Northerners abandoned novelty and tried a conventional operation, one of extraordinary weight. On December 24 and 25 Porter's fleet delivered an unprecedented bombardment of Fort Fisher. His ships fired more than twenty thousand projectiles against the bastion—that is, one shell every two seconds, or fifteen for each defender. The holiday shelling was monumental but failed to reduce the post.[11]

On Christmas Day launch boats began bringing Union infantrymen ashore, landing up the beach well north of the Confederate stronghold. By that evening only about a third of Butler's force had debarked while the waters grew rough. Confederate prisoners told their captors that Hoke's Division was approaching. Butler knew that this unit would outnumber greatly the bluecoats he had been able to get ashore. He decided they could neither be left on the beach nor be reinforced quickly enough to stave off Hoke's command. Butler abruptly broke off the action, ordered a re-embarkation, and departed the day after Christmas for Hampton Roads, Virginia. Captain Selfridge complained, "Words cannot express the bitter feeling and chagrin of the navy. We all felt the fruit was ripe for plucking and with little exertion would have fallen into the hands of the army."[12]

Grant agreed that with a more determined effort and with a general other than Butler in command, Fort Fisher could have been taken. The operation commanded greater urgency now than it had in mid-December. The stakes increased after Sherman had captured Savannah on December 22 and began preparing for his advance into the Carolinas. Seizing Fort Fisher represented one step toward a larger goal of capturing Wilmington and making that river-and-railroad center available to Sherman.[13]

Grant had not wanted Butler to command the first expedition against Fort Fisher and made certain he did not lead the second. The general in chief's choice for this next attempt was brevet Maj. Gen. Alfred H. Terry, a non–West Pointer who was well regarded for his performances at Port Royal, South Carolina; at Fort Pulaski, Georgia; and with the Army of the James. Capt. Solon A. Carter, an observant Union staff officer, reflected the views of many Federals when he said he feared Butler would lead the second expedition and was glad to learn that instead "a good soldier" would be in command.[14]

The force for the second Fort Fisher expedition, General Terry's Provisional Corps, consisted of essentially the same troops that Butler had taken on the first attack. The addition of a heavy artillery siege train and some other units bolstered its numbers to about ninety-six hundred men. A sizable Federal infantry force also was en route to the Carolinas. On January 7, 1865, Brig. Gen. Cuvier Grover's division of the XIX Corps, no longer needed in the Shenandoah, left the great valley. Taking the rails to Baltimore and steamers to Savannah, it made the trip in less than two weeks.[15]

While this army division was changing stations, the navy also was preparing for the second effort against Fort Fisher. After the first expedition, Porter repaired and refitted his armada at Beaufort, North Carolina. The Union fleet, with army and naval vessels combined, had grown larger since the failure in mid-December. The second attack on Fort Fisher would be the largest land-sea operation of the Civil War.[16]

The Confederates did not wait idly for this next blow to fall. They beefed up their garrison, and Lamb set his soldiers to work restoring the damage inflicted by the Christmastime naval bombardment.[17] He remained convinced that the Federals would return. So did Maj. Gen. William H. C. Whiting, who in June 1862 had been instrumental in winning the Confederate victory at Gaines's Mill and now served as second in command of the District of the Cape Fear. Hoke's Division stood available, and General Whiting urged that it be held near enough to Fort Fisher to give the garrison a secondary force.[18]

Gen. Braxton Bragg, Whiting's immediate superior, disagreed with this proposed deployment.[19] In the autumn of 1864, General Bragg had become commander first of the District of the Cape Fear and later also of its larger entity, the Department of North Carolina. As a gesture to Whiting, Bragg kept him as second in command in the district. Bragg was burdened with a reputation for failure, the worst of any Southern field commander. Years later Lt. Gen. James Longstreet insisted that a newspaper had greeted his appointment with the announcement: "We understand that Gen. Bragg is ordered to Wilmington! Good-bye Wilmington!"[20]

Bragg had lost more than his share of campaigns, but unlike Whiting, he seemed confident about holding Fort Fisher. He drew a generalization from the repulse of the first Federal expedition and became more optimistic than the facts warranted. Bragg concluded that Butler's defeat proved "the superiority of land batteries over ships of war," thanks to "the genius of the engineer." During the three weeks after the first expedition against Fort Fisher, Bragg initiated no improvements in its defenses and instead wallowed in carping and complaining.[21]

Convinced that the Federals had given up their designs against the massive fort, Bragg sent off some of Lamb's garrison to Goldsboro, North Carolina. He also withdrew two brigades of Hoke's Division from Sugar Loaf, an enormous sand dune that offered an important defensive position on the Cape Fear River north of Fort Fisher.[22] These two units joined the rest of their division at Camp Whiting, just east of Wilmington.[23] Thanks to Bragg's misjudgment, Hoke's Division was deployed miles too far north to support Fort Fisher in the role Whiting had envisioned.[24]

The Federals did not give the Confederates time to recover from Bragg's error. On the night of January 4, 1865, and into the morning of the fifth, Terry boarded his troops at Bermuda Hundred, Virginia, and sailed to join Porter's squadron off Beaufort. Storms delayed the expedition, but it reached the waters of Fort Fisher on the night of the twelfth. "We did not arrive off Federal Point until nearly night-fall," Terry reported, and Porter decided not to begin disembarking the troops until the next morning.[25]

After midnight, word reached Bragg that the Northerners had returned, and now he tried to correct his faulty deployment of Hoke's Division. The Southern infantrymen would need about seven hours to march from Camp Whiting back to Sugar Loaf.

They could make better time going by water, but the Confederates lacked the steamers to accommodate them. During the early morning hours of January 13, Brig. Gen. William W. Kirkland's Brigade marched to the Wilmington docks to board the available ships, and three other brigades struck out overland for Sugar Loaf.[26]

At 7:20 a.m. on the thirteenth, Porter opened fire against Federal Point with more than a hundred guns on thirteen ships, and about forty minutes later Terry's infantrymen began debarking at Battery Gatlin, just more than a mile east of Sugar Loaf and roughly five miles north of Fort Fisher. When the Federals began coming ashore, Hoke had only General Kirkland's Brigade at hand to meet them, and he was reluctant to fight at the beachhead. He threw out a line of skirmishers and waited while his other three brigades arrived at Sugar Loaf. When they did reach the great sand dune, Hoke had them take up a defensive position. He decided that the fire of the Federal gunboats offshore was so strong that he could not contest the landing. By 3:00 p.m. Terry's force of ninety-six hundred men had arrived safely ashore.[27]

Just as Grant had hoped, Terry pushed the operation with a vigor Butler had not. About two hours after completing its landing, the Provisional Corps started down Federal Point toward Fort Fisher. Terry left a brigade to cover his beachhead, and Hoke sat watching from Sugar Loaf while the main Union force, Brig. Gen. Charles J. Paine's African American division and Brig. Gen. Adelbert Ames's white one, marched south. General Paine came from a prominent Boston family; he was a Harvard graduate and the direct descendant of a signer of the Declaration of Independence.[28] General Ames had graduated fifth in his 1861 West Point class, soon went into the field, and had been severely wounded during the First Battle of Bull Run.[29]

The infantrymen of Ames's and Paine's divisions halted about two miles north of Fort Fisher. During the earliest hours of January 14, they began entrenching a line east–west across Federal Point. By 8:00 a.m. Terry had a chain of breastworks that would hinder Hoke or others who might arrive from the north and try to interfere with Terry's operations. He now could move with confidence against the great Rebel post to the south.

That same morning Bragg and Hoke rode out to learn what they could about the Union deployments. Just as Bragg expected, he found the Federals in large numbers within their beachhead. But that was not the end of it. Bragg was taken aback to learn that the enemy also had moved in strength well down Federal Point. He issued a discretionary order to Hoke to attack the invaders. The division commander studied the fortified Northern line and decided he could not carry it. Bragg readily agreed but made certain in his official report to Richmond that the burden was put on his subordinate. It was *Hoke*, he emphasized, who considered it "too hazardous to assault with such an inferior force." Hoke's Division retreated to Sugar Loaf and covered itself with fieldworks.[30]

While Bragg and Hoke hesitated, their opponents continued to act with determination. After 10:30 a.m. on the fourteenth, Porter renewed the naval bombardment, a fearsome cannonade that pounded into the next day and eventually expended about twenty thousand rounds of ammunition.[31] Around 4:00 p.m. brevet Brig. Gen. N. Martin Curtis's brigade of Ames's division cleared Battery Holland.[32] This fortification stood on Howard's Hill, about 900 yards north of Fort Fisher, and from there Terry carefully studied the Confederate main defenses. After nightfall General Curtis made further progress, digging a series of rifle pits that eventually reached within 175 yards of the fort.[33]

During January 15 Porter's shells continued to rain down on the defenders, and a volunteer landing party of about twenty-two hundred sailors and marines led by Fleet Capt. K. Randolph Breese came ashore. Terry marshaled his troops for a concerted effort against Fort Fisher. Paine's division and Col. Joseph C. Abbott's brigade were to hold the line that ran east–west across the rear of the Union corps and to keep the Southerners from intervening from that quarter. Curtis's New York brigade would lead the rest of Ames's division in an assault against the western, or Cape Fear, end of the great fort, and Captain Breese was to storm the northeast bastion on the Atlantic end.[34] A misunderstanding between Porter and Terry led the navy captain to believe the attack was scheduled sooner than actually intended.

Breese prematurely advanced his men to within a half mile of Fort Fisher, and they fell into disorder.[35]

At 3:20 p.m. on January 15, Ames sent word to Terry at Battery Holland that his division was ready to attack. Porter's fleet broke off its shattering cannonade, and at 3:25 p.m. the Union ships announced the assault by sounding their whistles. Colonel Lamb described the noise as "a soul-stirring signal both to besiegers and besieged."[36] Alerted by the penetrating sound, the Confederate colonel passed on his final orders for the defense of Fort Fisher.[37]

Breese's sailors and marines had been misdeployed and had waited anxiously on the beach for the attack order. After the whistles sounded the assault, they stormed toward the northeast bastion—and into a blizzard of fire. The attackers got within five hundred yards of the fort and lay down under a storm of artillery rounds. Some made another effort and rushed another two hundred yards before falling prone again. Still fewer—perhaps 150, perhaps 200 men—gained the palisade east of the bastion.

The outcome was decided quickly. The Confederates, including Lamb and Whiting, poured lead down on the unfortunate attackers. A handful of sailors reached the base of the fort's ramparts. "We were now so close that we could hear the voices of the rebels," Ens. Robley D. Evans recalled, and then added primly, "and what they said need not be written here." The heroic Ensign Evans suffered multiple wounds but survived the battle. Breese's storming party fell back, having lost about 300 sailors and marines, who were killed and wounded. Selfridge believed it had been a fundamental mistake to expect sailors "collected heavily from different ships, unknown to each other, armed with swords and pistols, to stand against veteran soldiers armed with rifles and bayonets."[38]

Selfridge and other naval officers sought solace in claiming that this assault had created a diversion for the army's attack to the west.[39] In this sector, Curtis led his brigade forward as soon as he heard the 3:25 p.m. signal. The defenders at once blasted his men with artillery rounds and showered them with rifle fire. In addition to this resistance, Curtis and his New Yorkers encountered a stretch of low ground in front of their center and right. A wagon bridge had been built across this morass, but the Confederates had largely dismantled it.

The Rebel artillery pounded the attackers, but the Federals pressed on and reached the palisade. Axmen hacked through log obstacles, clearing the way for the infantry, and the Northerners began to scale the walls of the fort. At the eastern end of the post, Whiting, Lamb, and their men had fired down on the attackers from the ramparts; here at the western end, the defenders tried to fight from the gun compartments. This position gave the Federals the respite of a dead space at the base of the walls.

Many of the attackers regained their wind and their courage in the sheltered area, then clambered toward the top of the fort. Curtis himself was among the first to reach the summit. A vicious fight began for Shepherd's Battery, the stronghold at the western end of Fort Fisher.

The assault might have stalled out, but Terry ordered the brigade behind Curtis's—under the direction of twenty-year-old Col. Galusha Pennypacker—to press the action. Ames and his staff officers advanced with this supporting unit and sent it against the fort. Colonel Pennypacker's brigade—three Pennsylvania regiments and two New York ones—attacked with the same determination shown by Curtis and his command. Their young leader carried the flag of the Ninety-seventh Pennsylvania, his former regiment, onto a traverse and fell severely wounded.[40] Below this desperate fight for the ramparts, the Federals seized control of the "Bloody Gate," where the Wilmington Road entered the great fort.[41]

The last of Ames's brigades to join the fight was Col. Louis Bell's, and it capitalized on the efforts of the two ahead of it. Colonel Bell's men poured through the western gate and into the interior of Fort Fisher. Bell was shot through his chest but insisted on staying at the front. Propped up and smiling, he watched as the battle flag of his old unit, the Fourth New Hampshire, was taken to the top of the massive defenses. Bell died the next morning. "He was an able and efficient officer," Ames lamented, "and not easily replaced."[42]

With Fort Fisher's defenses crumbling, Whiting decided that the best hope was an attack from the north and into the Union rear. He tried to rouse Bragg at Sugar Loaf: "The enemy are assaulting us by land and sea. Can't you help us?" He followed this appeal with another one: "We still hold the fort, but are sorely pressed. Can't you assist us from the outside?"[43] After receiving these petitions, Bragg made an optimistic prediction about Fort Fisher. "If defended, as I believe it will be, by your veterans and the former garrison," he told Lee at Petersburg, "it cannot be taken. It is not invested and cannot be unless the fleet passes."[44]

While Bragg remained blasé and at his post, Whiting threw himself into the fight. He struggled with a Federal color bearer over a flag, and rifle fire brought him down. Whiting's soldiers took him out of the swirling combat and moved him to the safety of a hospital on the eastern side of the fort.

Lamb also put himself into the thick of the action. He pulled together some of the defenders for a counterattack but was wounded before he could get the movement under way. The command eventually fell to Maj. James Reilly.

At around 5:30 p.m. the battle reached its crisis. Curtis, who already had multiple injuries, suffered a ghastly face wound and was carried out of the fight. The darkness of January 15 settled over Fort Fisher. Terry seemed to recognize that a turning point was at hand. Since Bragg made no move from the north, the Union commander could draw troops from the defensive line across Federal Point. Terry took Colonel Abbott's brigade from this front and called on it to break the resistance inside the fort.[45]

Abbott's men stormed the works in a night action, an unusual operation in Civil War combat. Around 9:00 p.m., with the Third New Hampshire leading the way, the brigade carried the northeast bastion of Fort Fisher. The defense collapsed, and the Federals began a prisoner roundup. Escaping through a hail of spent bullets, Confederate stretcher bearers carried Whiting and Lamb to Battery Buchanan, nearly two miles to the southwest down Federal Point.[46]

Having lost the main works of Fort Fisher, Major Reilly reached for his last straw. The defenders would rally under the cover of

Battery Buchanan's seacoast guns and gain the support of its naval contingent. It was Reilly's final hope as this fortification stood perilously close to the end of Federal Point, and from there the Confederates could retreat no farther. Perhaps five hundred Southerners reached Battery Buchanan only to learn that the naval force had boarded its boats and fled into the night. Lamb later minced no words: "Captain R.F. Chapman, of our navy, . . . following the example of General Bragg, had abandoned us to our fate."[47]

Abbott's brigade, reinforced by one of Paine's regiments, pursued the Confederates through the darkness. The Federals moved guardedly, securing the batteries along the east face of the fort as they moved slowly south. At about 10:00 p.m. the pursuers surrounded Battery Buchanan and rendered helpless the surviving defenders.

Whiting and Lamb lay suffering on their litters in the sand. The general asked for the Federal commander, and Terry introduced himself. Whiting offered to surrender, asking only for the good treatment of his men. Terry promised as much, gathered the prisoners, and marched back north to Fort Fisher.[48]

Pennypacker had been wounded so badly that his surgeons had ordered a coffin for him. He endured a long hospital recovery at Fort Monroe, Virginia, and eventually received the Medal of Honor.[49] Curtis, like Pennypacker, was wounded so horribly his men believed he could not live, but he too survived and was awarded the Medal of Honor.[50]

The highest estimates of Union casualties exceeded fourteen hundred in killed, wounded, and missing.[51] Fort Fisher's main powder magazine exploded early on the morning of January 16 and killed another two hundred or so Northern and Southern soldiers. The U.S. Navy officially reported that nearly four hundred sailors and marines had been killed and wounded in either the battle or the explosion.[52]

The most accurate accountings of the Confederate casualties were no more than estimates. Probably five hundred of the defenders were killed or wounded and about fourteen hundred captured. The severely wounded Lamb, as well as the other officers, went off to a prison camp for the rest of the war. He survived his injuries and lived until 1909.[53] Whiting proved less fortunate. The Federals shipped him to Fort Columbus in New York Harbor, where, weakened by his wounds, he died of dysentery on March 10.[54]

During the few weeks of life left to Whiting, he denounced Bragg's failure to advance from Sugar Loaf and relieve Fort Fisher's beleaguered defenders. The angry Mississippian pressed his case from his hospital bed. Two days after the loss of the fort, Whiting prepared a pointed account of the disaster for Lee. He insisted that the post could have been held "if the commanding General had done his duty" and asked for an investigation of Bragg's conduct. The captured Whiting was reluctant to send his report through the Federal lines and did not dispatch it until February 19, and nothing came of his request for an inquiry.[55] The embittered general fired a last volley from his deathbed: "That I am here, and that Wilmington and Fisher are gone, is due wholly and solely to the incompetency, the imbecility and the pusillanimity of Braxton Bragg."[56]

President Jefferson Davis, in distant Richmond, did not share Whiting's angry despair. In a fit of wild optimism, he asked Bragg: "Can you retake the fort?" Bragg quickly disabused the commander in chief of this pipe dream. The Northern naval forces, if not their infantry and artillery, would crush any Southern march against Fort Fisher. His best hope, Bragg told President Davis, was to hang on to Sugar Loaf.[57]

With Fort Fisher lost, many Confederates feared for Wilmington. Judith Brockenbrough McGuire, a Richmond woman, took a view common among Southerners. "Fort Fisher has fallen," she wrote on January 16, "Wilmington will of course follow. This was our last port into which blockade-runners were successful in entering, and which furnished us with [an] immense amount of stores."[58]

The capture of Wilmington might prove as inevitable as Mrs. McGuire expected, but the Federals would have to expend some effort to make it so. Terry's men restored Fort Fisher for their own purposes, and then the Northerners made their way up Federal Point. A reconnaissance showed them that Hoke still held a stout defensive line at Sugar Loaf. The two contestants squared off again, each suffering under the winter's cold rains and winds. Captain Carter, the staff officer who had praised Terry at Butler's expense, described a "tremendous rain storm" that blew in from the northeast one night in early February. The winds ripped off his shelter-tent roof, and the torrents left his clothes "pretty well soaked" and his boots half full of water.[59]

While the Federals hunkered against the weather, Grant came down to North Carolina at the end of January and met with Terry and Porter. He brought with him Gustavus V. Fox, the dynamic assistant secretary of the navy, and Maj. Gen. John M. Schofield, commander of the XXIII Corps. These senior officers gathered on the USS *Malvern*, Admiral Porter's flagship, and considered their next move. Sherman, they knew, soon would be leaving Savannah and moving north toward Goldsboro. With Fort Fisher secured, the group focused its attention on Wilmington. This port would prove valuable as a supply depot and a staging point for a Federal force to advance on Goldsboro in concert with Sherman's approach. The assembled strategists believed that the operation against Wilmington should be pressed to a successful conclusion. Grant, whose opinion counted most, agreed.[60]

Porter believed that capturing the city would take more soldiers than were available then on the Wilmington front. Grant already had determined to bring the XXIII Corps to the Carolinas; thus he had the unit's commander accompany him to the *Malvern* conference. The commanding general had considered using General Schofield and his corps either to support Sherman or to take Wilmington, and he now decided on the latter course. Grant put Schofield in charge of the operation as the commander of a revived Department of North Carolina, which would include the units of his own corps as they reached the scene and Terry's force already in place.[61]

Grant's selection of Schofield was a sound but double-edged choice. The leader of the XXIII Corps had proven he could handle assignments such as taking Wilmington. At the same time, Grant's decision put Schofield in command over Terry, the officer who had just won Fort Fisher.[62]

While the Federals had been operating against that crucial post, Sherman's troops were preparing to leave Savannah and begin their drive north. They represented a powerful force, full of veterans and well supplied. Sherman's command was separated into two large wings, with each in turn divided into two corps.

The Left Wing, or the Army of Georgia, consisted of the XIV and XX Corps. Its commander was Maj. Gen. Henry W. Slocum, a New Yorker who had seen extensive service in the eastern theater through Gettysburg and had then moved to the west. General Slocum had never delivered a lightning stroke on any battlefield, but neither had he ever committed a blunder. The darkest smudge on his record was entered on July 1, 1863, when he had been slow to get his XII Corps into the developing battle at Gettysburg.[63]

Sherman's Right Wing, or the Army of the Tennessee, included the XV and XVII Corps and was commanded by Maj. Gen. Oliver O. Howard. A brave officer, General Howard had lost his right arm during the Battle of Fair Oaks or Seven Pines. Despite Howard's personal courage, his commands had not fared well in battle. His Philadelphia Brigade had been outflanked at Antietam and his XI Corps routed at Chancellorsville and again, almost exactly two months later, at Gettysburg.[64]

On January 3 Howard's Right Wing had begun moving by ships from Savannah into the Broad River and past Hilton Head, which one day would become a popular resort, and Parris Island, which would become a famous U.S. Marine Corps training facility. The infantrymen debarked inland, and by the seventeenth most of the wing had deployed in the area around Pocataligo, South Carolina.[65]

Sherman intended that while Howard's units moved by water, Slocum's wing would march overland from Savannah—a movement that demanded thorough preparation. Slocum's men repaired and corduroyed the causeway that the Federals had built through the rice fields outside the city, and they threw a sturdy pontoon bridge across the Savannah River. Their work was undone by bad weather. Before the campaign started, heavy rains flooded the river, broke the pontoon bridge, and put the causeway four feet under water. Slocum took his men some thirty-five miles upstream to Sister's Ferry, but even here the inundated stream and its bordering bottomlands presented a barrier almost three miles wide. It was the first week of February before all of Slocum's command moved into South Carolina.[66]

While the weather delayed Sherman, he received at least one bit of good news: General Grover's division arrived in Savannah from the Shenandoah Valley. On January 19 Grover began relieving Maj. Gen. John W. Geary's division of the XX Corps of the task of holding the Georgia port. Grover's arrival meant that Sherman could send his entire command on the drive north.[67]

Slocum's soldiers put the weather delays behind them and began pouring into the Palmetto State. Every regiment, the wing commander claimed, gave three cheers as it entered South Carolina. "The men seemed to realize that at last they had set foot on the State which had done more than all others to bring upon the country the horrors of civil war." Howard's units that had traveled by ship were waiting for them in the interior. The two large wings of Sherman's command now stood poised to march through South Carolina.[68]

The Federals also were marshaling troops for a renewed effort on the Wilmington front. Bragg still held the Sugar Loaf line with Hoke's Division, but Schofield assembled powerful numbers against him. Four brigades of the XXIII Corps would contribute decisively to the next Union operation. Three of them formed a division commanded by Maj. Gen. Jacob D. Cox, who had helped organize the Republican Party in Ohio and then served in both the eastern and western theaters of the Civil War.[69]

In a letter to his wife, Emily, Solon Carter, the observant staff officer, noted the arrival of General Cox's men and others. He also sadly reported that the ocean voyage proved hard on a number of the animals shipped to Federal Point. "So many of the horses that have been brought here," Carter told his wife, "have been more or less injured. One of our brigades has lost every horse they had = 30 odd =[.] The sea was rough and the stalls broke and they were obliged to throw them overboard."[70]

While the Federals massed men, horses, and equipment on the Wilmington front, the Southerners made a change near the top of their command structure. On February 1 Lee had become the general in chief of all Confederate field forces. When Bragg had reported to North Carolina in 1864, he had retained his position as military adviser to Davis. A group of his staff officers had remained in Richmond, and through them the general had continued to counsel the president from Wilmington. After Lee assumed his expanded responsibility, Bragg's military secretary in the capital believed he should return there and help smooth the transition to the new command arrangement.[71]

Communications passed back and forth between Richmond and Wilmington, with Bragg's staff officers in Virginia urging him to join them there while the general insisted that his presence was required in North Carolina. Bragg clearly saw that the situation in Wilmington was deteriorating and told Davis he did not "feel authorized to leave here in the present condition of affairs." On February 9 he received what he wanted—a direct order to report to Richmond, giving him authority to be away from the front while the impending Southern disaster in North Carolina took place. Bragg left for the capital the next day and spent a week there.[72]

Bragg's stratagem served his purpose, but it did nothing for Wilmington or the rest of the Confederacy. The defenses of the port city became vulnerable when Schofield opened operations west of the Cape Fear River, a strategy that Terry and Porter had suggested at the *Malvern* conference. The sole obstacle to the Federals in this sector was Brig. Gen. Johnson Hagood's Brigade at Fort Anderson, which stood opposite Sugar Loaf on the Cape Fear. Unless the Confederates could hold this crucial post, Wilmington was lost.

Schofield sent Cox's division to outflank Fort Anderson while Porter's ships bombarded it. General Hagood concluded that his position was untenable, and early on the morning of February 18 he withdrew from the vital fortification. Schofield's foot soldiers promptly occupied it and found that the greatest difficulty of the operation was to get their own navy to stop its shelling. Staff officer Carter recounted the action for the benefit of his wife: "On the 19th we learned at daylight that a body of our troops which had crossed the [Cape Fear] river the day before were in possession of Fort Anderson and a few minutes later it was reported that the rebels had evacuated their line of works immediately in our front. We were all stirring in a twinkling and started out after the Johnnies without waiting for our breakfast."[73]

On the morning of the nineteenth, Hagood halted and took up a line on the north bank of Town Creek, the last piece of promising terrain for a stand west of the Cape Fear. Over on the east bank, Hoke now gave up Sugar Loaf. This position had proven valuable to the Confederates during much of the campaign, but after the loss of Fort Anderson, the Southern division commander probably feared the Federals would land behind his lines and interpose between them and Wilmington. Hoke aligned his retreat on Hagood's and fell back to the outskirts of the city.[74]

Schofield pressed the pursuit, with Cox following Hagood on the west bank of the Cape Fear River, Terry shadowing Hoke on the east bank, and Porter steaming unopposed up the river between them.[75] On February 20 Cox crossed Town Creek below Hagood's left and turned his defensive line, outflanking him just as he had at Fort Anderson. The Union commander explained his success: "In the attack upon the enemy's position at Town Creek the wooded nature of the field gave our troops good cover in advancing and made the fire of the enemy so uncertain that it produced little damage, our loss in that charge being but thirty in killed and wounded. The positions of the enemy were captured by rendering them untenable, and the labor and courage of the troops were expended rather in overcoming the great physical obstacles in the nature of the country than in hard fighting." With this victory of maneuver at Town Creek, Cox opened the western approach to Wilmington, and the Confederates kept him out of the city only by some desperate bridge burning.[76]

During the morning of that same twentieth of February, Terry dogged Hoke northward. The Confederates continually waged small actions to delay their pursuers. At Forks Road, about three miles south of Wilmington, they made a stand behind a line of well-constructed earthworks and waited for the mid-afternoon approach of the Federals.[77] Here Hoke blunted Terry's first effort to continue his advance on Wilmington.

For a time Hoke kept the Northerners at bay, but when he learned of Hagood's defeat at Town Creek, he knew the game was up. He recognized that Cox surely would take Wilmington from the west and that he could do no more than stall Terry. Hoke removed as many stores and prisoners from the port as he could and infested the Cape Fear River with mines.[78]

Bragg's self-serving trip to Richmond ended on February 21, when he returned to the Department of North Carolina. He resumed his command just in time to declare that the situation had become hopeless during his absence. The Confederates spent the day of Bragg's return preparing to evacuate Wilmington, and they retreated north from the city after midnight.[79]

On February 22 Cox's and Terry's converging forces streamed into Wilmington. Bragg emphasized in bold relief that the defeat had been sealed in his absence. "I find on arrival," he told Lee on the twenty-first, "that our forces are driven from the west bank of the Cape Fear." Bragg used the phrase "on my arrival" in a communication to Gen. Pierre Gustave Toutant Beauregard, commander of the Military Division of the West. And he took pains to explain to Brig. Gen. L. S. Baker, the commander of the Second Military District, at Goldsboro: "Enemy had driven our forces across the river when I arrived."[80]

Bragg's posturing for the record was no compensation for the fall of Wilmington. Schofield, Cox, Terry, and Porter had closed the South's last port and shut off the Confederacy from the rest of the world.[81] Wilmington's valuable facilities were lost to the Confederates and instead became available to Sherman.

By the time of this victory, the Federals also were doing well elsewhere in the Carolinas. Writing again to his wife, Emily, from the Wilmington front, Solon Carter emphasized that Sherman was "playing hob with them down in South Carolina. . . . Matters look very favorable for our cause at present."[82]

CHAPTER THREE

In the Carolinas

With Wilmington secured, Maj. Gen. John M. Schofield, the commander of the Department of North Carolina, turned his attention about ninety-five miles northeast to New Bern, a city that had been in Federal hands since 1862. The Union's logistical arrangements already were strong, and General Schofield saw that this port could improve them further. He had no rolling stock and few wagons at Wilmington; New Bern could supply them. This city on the Neuse River also might become a valuable railhead once work crews put in shape the Atlantic and North Carolina Railroad line, which ran west from the port toward Kinston.[1]

On February 26, 1865, four days after capturing Wilmington, Schofield dispatched Maj. Gen. Jacob D. Cox to New Bern. The Ohioan pulled together troops who had been garrisoning the region for almost two years, added a division of the XXIII Corps that Schofield sent him, and formed a provisional corps. General Cox promptly began repairing the railroad and preparing to move on Goldsboro, North Carolina.[2] There he could link up with Maj. Gen. William T. Sherman, whose February 28 muster rolls showed more than fifty-seven thousand soldiers.[3]

Challenged by these numbers and Union activity, many Southerners looked to Gen. Pierre Gustave Toutant Beauregard to save their cause. A hero early in the war at Fort Sumter and the First

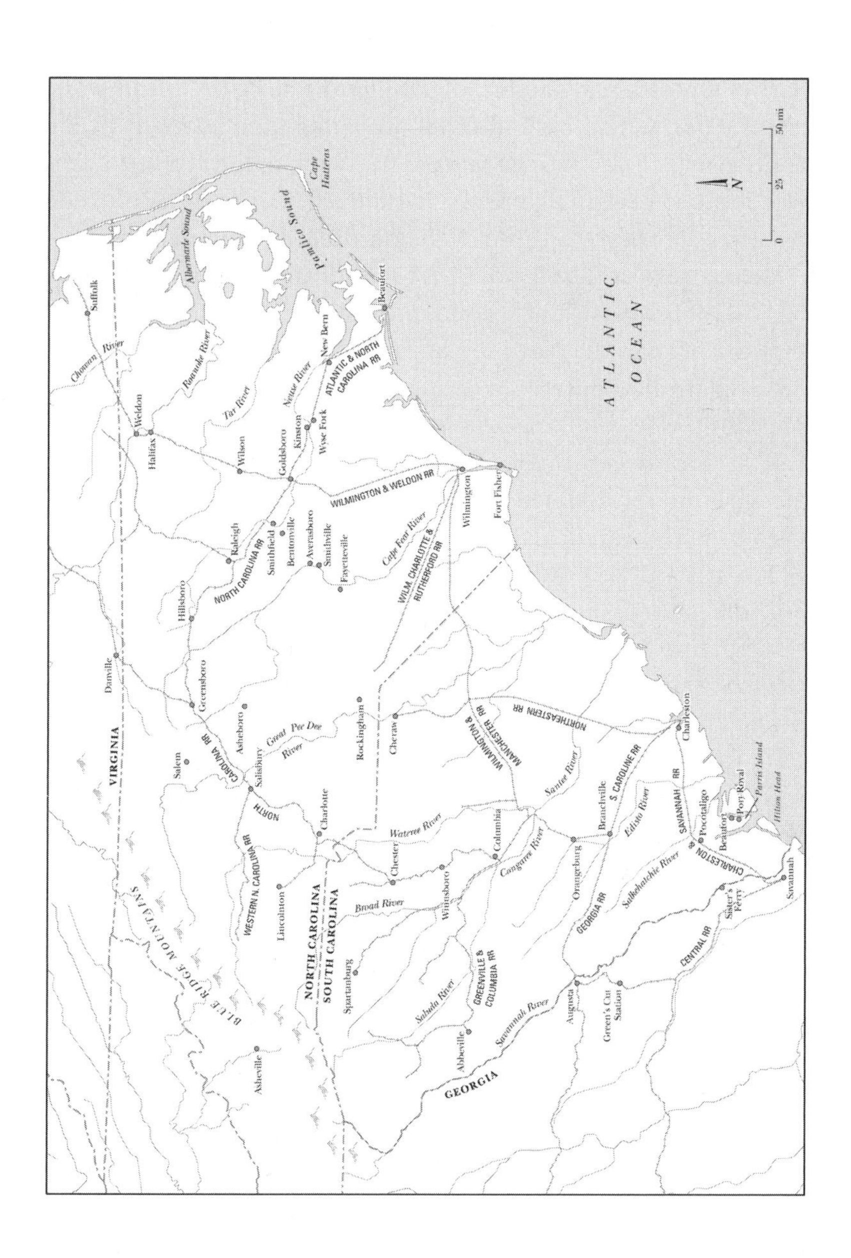

MAP 2. The Carolinas

Battle of Manassas, General Beauregard had gone to the western theater, where he had fared no better than so many other Southern generals had. He fancied himself a grand strategist and was fond of positing campaigns that required men and other resources far beyond those of the hardscrabble Confederacy.[4]

Beauregard suffered two other handicaps: poor health and a bad relationship with his commander in chief, dating to the early months of the war.[5] Not long after the First Battle of Manassas, Beauregard had entered a series of disputes with Confederate president Jefferson Davis and his advisers over supplies, military law, and army command. President Davis had tried to cooperate with his opinionated general but found he could not remain patient with him. Davis eventually lost trust in Beauregard.[6]

Beauregard also was hindered by practical limitations to his authority. He desperately needed to pull together the scattered Confederate forces in his theater so they could contend against General Sherman. Beauregard commanded the Military Division of the West and in theory could have ordered a concentration of forces, but in reality, his authority over the generals around him was vague. Throughout most of February 1865, neither Beauregard nor any other Confederate general exercised centralized control over the western theater. On the twentieth of that month, Col. Joseph Frederick Waring, commander of the Jeff Davis Legion, made a worried entry in his diary: "Sherman has it all his own way. When will we concentrate troops against him [?]"[7]

Even if Beauregard could make the concentration that Colonel Waring and others saw was needed, the Confederates still would be sorely outnumbered. By Beauregard's own favorable estimate in early February, he could gather only a little more than half of Sherman's strength. Moreover, this figure represented his "best-case" number, which assumed the largest possible gathering of the troops in the region. In stark fact, Beauregard faced the Federals with a little more than a quarter of their numbers.[8]

On February 2 while the Northerners readied for their final operation against Wilmington and while Sherman advanced into South Carolina, Beauregard huddled with three other general officers at Green's Cut Station, Georgia, on the Augusta and

Savannah Railroad south of Augusta.[9] Lt. Gen. William J. Hardee, commander of the Department of South Carolina, Georgia, and Florida, had earned the nickname "Old Reliable" on the battlefields with the Army of Tennessee and was one of the Confederacy's most able corps commanders.[10] Maj. Gen. Daniel Harvey D. H. Hill, responsible for the District of Georgia, had left the Army of Northern Virginia to serve in the western theater and became one of Gen. Braxton Bragg's many critics.[11] Maj. Gen. Gustavus W. Smith, commander of the Georgia state militia, briefly had directed the Army of Northern Virginia after Gen. Joseph E. Johnston had been wounded during the Battle of Fair Oaks or Seven Pines. This level of responsibility had paralyzed General Smith, and Davis had dispatched Gen. Robert E. Lee from Richmond to replace him. Smith's later career was marked by protests when officers junior to him were advanced ahead of him.[12]

General Hill had received a cavalry report that Sherman's objective was Branchville, South Carolina, which stood about halfway between Augusta and Charleston. The town posed a likely target because it was due north of the bulk of Sherman's two wings and included an important rail point. The South Carolina Railroad ran down from Columbia through Orangeburg to Branchville. Here it turned west for Augusta while sending another line east to Charleston.[13] Beauregard's subordinates thought this strategic junction might be the place to intercept Sherman and bring him to battle, and they suggested concentrating their forces there.[14]

Beauregard swept aside this plan. He believed that Sherman's force, larger than the scattered Confederates', could reach Branchville before they could gather there. Davis insisted that Charleston be defended, and Beauregard remained undecided whether his opponent would march against that city or Augusta. He believed he should try to hold both places at least until the result of the then ongoing Hampton Roads peace conference was known.[15]

The peace talks (which soon were to end in futility), Beauregard's vague authority, and his confusion about Sherman's objective—all these factors worked together to keep the Confederate units dispersed across the region. For his own part, Beauregard assembled a hodgepodge force to cover Augusta: Georgia militia, remnants of the Army of Tennessee, and workers turned out from the factories of Macon and Augusta itself. General Hardee was to hold Charleston with a garrison command and young Maj. Gen. Joseph Wheeler's cavalry corps. Between Hardee and Beauregard, a third ragtag force—some local South Carolina troops and a corps of the Army of Tennessee—gathered below Columbia.[16]

With the Confederate forces scattered and their leaders uncertain whether their opponent would advance on Augusta, Charleston, or another point, Sherman pressed his two wings north through the Palmetto State and headed for Columbia. Weather and terrain posed larger obstacles to him than Southern soldiers did. On January 22 the Union commander wrote to his brother Senator John Sherman: "We have had such storms & rains that the whole country is under water." Maj. Gen. Henry W. Slocum, commander of the Left Wing, recalled: "The march through South Carolina [was] greatly delayed by the almost incessant rains and the swampy nature of the country. More than half the way we were compelled to corduroy the roads before our trains could be moved."[17]

In early February Maj. Gen. Oliver O. Howard's Right Wing began making its way out of Pocataligo, and the XVII Corps executed an impressive crossing of the formidable Salkehatchie. Although nominally a river, in the area where the Federals pushed through it, it was in fact a mile-and-a-half-wide swamp. Hardee, from his vantage point in Charleston, later acknowledged that when he "learned that Sherman's army was marching through the Salkehatchie swamp, making its own corduroy roads at the rate of a dozen miles a day or more, and bringing its artillery and wagons with it, I made up my mind that there had been no such army in existence since the days of Julius Caesar."[18]

The Union soldiers in the Carolinas were strangers in a strange land. They marveled at sights beyond their previous experiences. An Illinois veteran was impressed by the Salkehatchie: "A dog could scarcely make his way through the swamp, much less a horse. . . . So immense are the trees, and so thickly set, that the eye cannot reach half pistol range; and they are so abundantly covered with foliage that the light of day is shut out." An officer from the same state related an episode that took place in early February: "Some of our boys shot an alligator about 7 feet long and dragged it to our camp. It caused quite an excitement. Men came from all directions to see it." Six weeks into the campaign, another Illinois soldier found it remarkable that "there has not been a flake of snow here this winter. The gardens are full of flowers."[19]

While the Northerners looked in wonder at their environment, they wreaked destruction on it. When Sherman's men reached the Charleston–Augusta rail line, they took up the hard work of demolishing the railroad. On February 10 a Union company officer recorded in his diary: "Our Regt [the Sixty-third Illinois] tore up about 1400 yards of R.R. today. There is bout 30 miles torn up in this country. We commenced tearing up at the 50 mile post from Augusta and tore up toward Charleston."[20]

After the war General Slocum offered a tutorial on the destruction of railroads. He emphasized that the men should be assigned, and the work organized, on the night before the day's efforts and that the laborers should be given a hearty breakfast. After Slocum described in detail how to tear up and heat the rails, he patiently explained how to destroy them. The final step, he insisted, "should be in command of an efficient officer who will see that the work is not slighted. Unless closely watched, soldiers will content themselves with simply bending the [heated] rails around trees." Such half-hearted destruction would not do. "A rail which is simply bent," the Federal general warned, "can easily be restored to its original shape. No rail should be regarded as properly treated till it has assumed the shape of a doughnut; it must not only be bent but twisted."[21]

While the Northerners went about this destruction and while Confederate despair mounted in South Carolina, some Southerners looked to a native son for help. On February 15 Wade Hampton took a promotion to lieutenant general and accepted command of all the cavalry in the state. A wealthy antebellum planter, he was a veteran of many mounted operations in the eastern theater.[22] Generals Hampton and Beauregard reported to Columbia, but they brought with them no magic that would save the capital. The few Southern units that could reach the scene were a motley mix: some of General Wheeler's cavalry, part of a corps of the Army of Tennessee, and a division of horsemen, totaling only about three thousand infantry and cavalry.[23]

On February 16 General Howard's wing closed directly on Columbia while Slocum's paralleled it to the west and reached the Saluda River upstream from the capital. The next day, with the city all but lost, Davis relented on his earlier guidance to Hardee. Old Reliable could abandon Charleston, the commander in chief now said, and join Beauregard in defending Columbia.[24]

Davis had taken far too long to reverse himself. On the day he did, the seventeenth, Beauregard and Hampton conceded Columbia to Sherman's masses. The Confederate cavalry chief initiated a retreat and then directed Mayor Thomas Jefferson Goodwyn to surrender the city. Goodwyn collected three aldermen, a white flag, and a carriage. Sometime between 8:00 a.m. and 9:00 a.m. these four civilians rode out of Columbia, intercepted the approaching Federals, and made the capitulation.[25]

On the night of February 17–18, fire devastated the city, and the cause of this disaster became a matter of dispute for decades. At the direction of Maj. Allen J. Green, the Columbia post commander, Southerners had rolled hundreds of bales of cotton into Richardson Street and other avenues of the commercial district and elsewhere across the municipality on February 15 and 16. Fires broke out the night of the sixteenth and seventeenth, possibly ignited by explosive shells thrown by the Union artillery. Columbia held large stores of liquor, and very likely, drunken Northern soldiers set more fires during the morning and afternoon of the seventeenth. These flames were put out by mid-afternoon, but that night the city suffered a conflagration that could not be controlled.[26] A strong wind blowing from the northwest and gusting in all directions defeated efforts to fight the fire. The city's business community was virtually destroyed. On Richardson Street alone, the flames claimed 101 stores; throughout Columbia, 193 businesses and public buildings were lost. Four hundred and fifty-eight structures—about a third of the city—burned.[27]

One Federal soldier recorded the tragic scene in his diary. "At Columbia," he wrote, "a horrible show took place. At night the entire sky was lit from the fires, and plundering was at a high point and many perished when the houses collapsed. Twenty Union men who were robbing homes died when the houses collapsed." Plunderers and drunks appeared in many accounts. One Northern officer acknowledged: "I seen as I marched through the city men with boxes of tobacco & most everything else a soldier could make use of & a good deal that they could not carrying to camp and lying about the streets but a great many were too drunk to move at all."[28]

The same officer toured Columbia on the morning of February 18 and described the aftermath of the fires. "I got a pass this morning," he wrote, "and went down to the city with Capt Wm F. Davis, Lieut Dill, Jefferies and Hunter and never in my life did I see such destruction of property, so many desolate looking people. some of them had managed to get some of their goods out of their house before it was burned and were sitting in the streets and square guarding them & hardly a place to go for safety."[29]

Two days after the destruction of Columbia, General Lee, who had become general in chief on the first of the month, voiced a vote of no confidence in Beauregard. "Genl Beauregard makes no mention of what he proposes or what he can do," Lee wrote to Davis, "or where his troops are. He does not appear from his despatches to be able to do much." On February 21 Davis received one of Beauregard's wildly unrealistic schemes: The Confederates should concentrate thirty-five thousand infantrymen and artillerymen against Sherman, crush him, and then confront Lt. Gen. Ulysses S. Grant's enormous force in Virginia. After defeating it, they should capture Washington and dictate a peace. When the president forwarded this flight of fancy to his general in chief, Lee punctured it with a few sharp words: "The idea is good, but the means are lacking."[30]

With Beauregard unable to come to terms with the realities of the situation, the best choice to command the western theater might well be General Johnston, an able defensive fighter who had the support of the Confederate Congress. A joint resolution of January 19 had called on Davis not only to appoint Lee as general in chief but also to reinstate Johnston as commander of the

Army of Tennessee. Lee recognized that the western commands must be united and believed that Johnston was the sole leader who held the confidence of the western army and its home front.[31]

Lee also knew it would be difficult to convince Davis to reappoint Johnston. The president had, if anything, even less regard for Johnston than he had for Beauregard. A bitter, long-running feud between the president and his senior officer had begun with a dispute over Johnston's standing: Davis had ranked him fourth among the Confederacy's full generals; Johnston believed he should have been first. Bad blood flowed between the two men throughout the war. In an October 1863 diary entry Mary Chesnut wrote that "the president detests Joe Johnston for all the trouble he has given him. And General Johnston returns the compliment with interest."[32] Their feud had culminated in Davis's firing of Johnston as Sherman approached Atlanta.

Lee understood that Davis would be reluctant at best to reinstate this commander, but faced with catastrophe in the Carolinas, he might. On February 19 Lee gingerly raised the idea with John C. Breckinridge, the new secretary of war. He mentioned the reports of Beauregard's poor health and then suggested that if it became necessary to replace him, Johnston was "the only officer" for this command. Two days later Lee directly asked Secretary Breckinridge to have Johnston report so that he could assign him to Beauregard's position.[33]

Lee carried his point with Davis. On February 22, the day the Federals streamed into Wilmington, Breckinridge put Johnston under the orders of the general in chief, who promptly put him in command of the Army of Tennessee. Lee also told the reinstated commander, who then was at Lincolnton, North Carolina, to succeed Hardee at the head of the Department of South Carolina, Georgia, and Florida.[34] Several days later Davis explained to a friend that he had complied with Lee's wish "in the hope that Genl. Johnston's soldierly qualities may be made serviceable to his country when acting under General Lee's orders, and that in his new position those defects which I found manifested by him when serving as an independent command[er] will be remedied by the control of the General in Chief."[35]

Johnston traveled southeast from Lincolnton to Charlotte, North Carolina, and took up his assignment. The new commander held few illusions of winning a victory in the field. Johnston began his duties, he later wrote, "with a full consciousness on my part, however, that we could have no other object, in continuing the war, than to obtain fair terms of peace; for the Southern cause must have appeared hopeless then, to all intelligent and dispassionate Southern men. I therefore resumed the duties of my military grade with no hope beyond that of contributing to obtain peace on such conditions as, under the circumstances, ought to satisfy the Southern people and their Government."[36]

Before assuming command, Johnston met with Beauregard. Writing a decade later, Johnston said that Beauregard evidenced no resentment at being replaced, particularly in view of his poor health. Beauregard endorsed the new leader's strategy of concentrating the Army of Tennessee in the area of Charlotte and informally agreed to serve as his second in command. The two Confederate generals faced enemies of daunting strength: Sherman and his more than fifty-seven thousand men, who were preparing to leave Columbia, and Schofield and his more than thirty thousand men, who had just captured Wilmington.[37]

Johnston would have to contend against these masses with meager forces. The pathetically small Army of Tennessee began to gather around Chester, South Carolina, south of Charlotte. This field command had faded to a pale ghost of the force that had waged the Shiloh, Chickamauga, Atlanta, and other campaigns. It remained an army in name only; its rolls in mid-March gave its effective strength as about four thousand troops.[38]

In addition to the Army of Tennessee, Johnston had been given Hardee's Department of South Carolina, Georgia, and Florida. It too was pitifully small, numbering fewer than eight thousand men. Unable to contribute to the defense of Columbia, Hardee had headed north for Cheraw, South Carolina, just below the North Carolina border.[39]

Johnston also held authority over the Department of North Carolina, or the forces led by General Bragg, although they added fewer than another six thousand men.[40] On February 23

Lee advised the reinstated commander that if his operations brought him near Bragg's troops, "of course you will direct their movements." Having lost Wilmington, the unpopular Bragg had retreated about 80 miles north along the Wilmington and Weldon Railroad to Goldsboro.[41]

This movement left the Confederates dispersed, with Bragg more than 110 miles northeast of Hardee at Cheraw and nearly 200 miles on roughly the same line from the Army of Tennessee's assembly area around Chester. The rail distances were even greater than the road ones. Trains carrying Confederates from Chester to Charlotte would travel about 45 miles on the Charlotte and South Carolina Railroad, and from there the cars would run along the North Carolina Railroad on a 220-mile arc through Salisbury, Greensboro, and Raleigh before they reached Bragg's position at Goldsboro.[42]

It would take considerable time to pull together these scattered commands. The two months spent drifting under Beauregard's murky standing could never be regained. Johnston now had the authority to carry out a concentration, but it could not be done quickly. The new commander had no more than grasped the reins when he fired off a disclaimer to Lee: "It is too late to expect me to concentrate troops capable of driving back Sherman. The remnant of the Army of Tennessee is much divided. So are other troops."[43]

Sherman did not intend to give his enemies time to use the rail lines to concentrate, and if they did try, he believed they could accomplish little. The decisive point of the campaign already had passed or at least so it seemed to the Union commander in the afterglow of victory. "From the moment my army passed Columbia S.C.," Sherman claimed in 1868, "the war was ended. All after that were the necessary consequences of foregone conclusions, the manner of the conclusion being left only for Johnston." On February 20 Sherman left the ashes of Columbia behind him and marched on Winnsboro, some twenty-five miles north.[44]

Foragers—and vandals—moved in front of the army and looted the village and surrounding area. Perhaps as many as thirty of Winnsboro's buildings were destroyed.[45] Among them was Christ Episcopal Church in the northwest corner of town. In a macabre act of vandalism, Union soldiers dug up a coffin in the churchyard cemetery, opened it, and propped it up so that the corpse could "watch" the burning of the sanctuary.[46]

The acts of vandalism that occurred in Winnsboro took place elsewhere in South Carolina. Sherman had anticipated that the campaign would prove destructive. In mid-December 1864 he had speculated to General Grant, in the harsh language he often indulged in: "We can punish South Carolina as she deserves. . . . I do sincerely believe that the whole United States, North and South, would rejoice to have this army turned loose on South Carolina to devastate that state, in the manner we have done in Georgia, and it would have a direct and immediate bearing on your campaign in Virginia." Later on the eve of the Carolinas campaign, Sherman declared: "The truth is the whole army is burning with an insatiable desire to wreak vengeance upon South Carolina. I almost tremble at her fate, but feel that she deserves all that seems in store for her."[47]

Doubtless many Union soldiers agreed with their commander: South Carolina had begun the war and deserved to suffer the consequences. One of Sherman's Ohioans flatly declared that "this state was largely responsible for the rebellion." Another Buckeye echoed the point: "Our men had the idea that South Carolina was the cause of all our troubles." An Illinois soldier wrote darkly: "It seemed to be decreed that South Carolina, having sown the wind, should reap the whirlwind."[48]

Much of this destruction was the handiwork of Sherman's "bummers," a term generally applied to the regular foragers of his command who were detailed daily to collect supplies. The invaders considered this task routine. A company commander in an Illinois regiment gave a matter-of-fact accounting of some foraging done in early February and acknowledged his superior's role in it. "We got plenty of all kinds of forage today," Capt. George F. Glossbrenner recorded in his diary. "Robinson gave me 3 nice hams, A[.] Holman 3 chickens. the Col. gave three to our mess and Walker 2 muscova ducks."[49]

Some members of the XX Corps—men who had fought in the eastern theater and had been moved to the west—used a different definition of the term "bummer." They drew a distinction between foragers, or soldiers who were sent by their officers to gather supplies, and bummers, or wanderers who set out on their own to loot and destroy. Capt. Daniel Oakey of the Second Massachusetts, XX Corps, for example, believed that the army had "regular" foragers who were restrained and bummers who were not. After the Northerners had entered North Carolina, Captain Oakey watched magnificent pine trees go up in flames and commented: "It was sad to see this wanton destruction of property, which, like the firing of the resin pits, was the work of 'bummers,' who were marauding through the country committing every sort of outrage. There was no restraint except with the column or the regular foraging parties."[50]

Unlike Oakey, white Carolinians who suffered property losses saw no distinction between bands of marauding bummers and parties of organized foragers. Most of Sherman's own men agreed with them, regarding any soldier a bummer if he foraged routinely with or without authorization. And while Oakey separated foragers from bummers, he also boasted about their prowess: "We were proud of our foragers. They constituted a picked force from each regiment, under an officer selected for the command, and were remarkable for intelligence, spirit, and daring." Oakey bragged about their skill at requisitioning: "Many a forager had nothing better than a bit of carpet and a rope halter; yet this simplicity of equipment did not abate his power of carrying off hams and sweet-potatoes in the face of the enemy."[51]

In addition to looting and burning, white Southerners suffered another form of property loss when their African American slaves left their plantations and farms and fell in behind Sherman's advancing columns. Through Georgia and the Carolinas, Slocum recalled, the "refugee-train following in rear of the army was one of the most singular features of the march. . . . It was natural that these poor creatures, seeking a place of safety, should flee to the army, and endeavor to keep in sight of it." Writing to Maj. Gen. Alfred H. Terry, the commander of the Provisional Corps at Wilmington, Sherman estimated that by the time he reached Fayetteville, North Carolina, "20,000 to 30,000 useless mouths" had attached themselves to his command. He complained that these "refugees, white and black, . . . have clung to our skirts, impeded our movements, and consumed our food." In another communication he characterized them as "a dead weight."[52]

Racial prejudice against African Americans ran strong in Sherman's command, but the experiences of many Northern soldiers during the Carolinas campaign led them to change their views. The white veterans were inspired by the sight of thousands of blacks leaving their plantations and seeking freedom. They also were grateful to those African Americans who helped Union prisoners of war escape captivity, who assisted foraging parties, or who otherwise aided the Federals. "What they have done for the army entitles them to their freedom," an officer argued, "or whatever they may desire." A chaplain wrote: "The more we become acquainted with the negro character, both as men and Christians, the more we are compelled to respect them."[53]

In late February neither black nor white Carolinians knew where the Federals were headed. Sherman's advance from Columbia to Winnsboro had put him on a course straight for Charlotte. After pillaging Winnsboro and its region, however, the Northerners changed direction. The Union leviathan now turned east toward Hardee's little force at Cheraw on the Great Pee Dee River. By February 23 all of Sherman's command had closed on the Wateree River, and some divisions had crossed it.[54]

On March 2 Confederate cavalry skirmished with units of the Left Wing's XX Corps at Chesterfield; the Federals were only ten miles west of Cheraw. On the same day, the Confederate horsemen learned that the XVII Corps of Howard's Right Wing was nearing the same city from the southwest. Hardee evacuated Cheraw that night, retreating north toward Rockingham.[55]

"We marched into Cheraw," the company officer Oakey fondly recalled, "with music and with colors flying. Stacking arms in the main street, we proceeded to supper, while the engineers laid the pontoons across the Peedee River." Another officer reported: "This town Cheraw is a very nice town numbering about 3,000 inhabitants. Large churches and public building[s]. There was a great amount of cotton here, also all kinds of munitions of war." Slocum remembered the town for another reason—a fine libation. "On the 3d of March we arrived at Cheraw," the general recounted, "where we found a large supply of stores sent from Charleston for safe-keeping. Among the stores was a large quantity of very old wine of the best quality, which had been kept in the cellars of Charleston many years, with no thought on the part of the owners that in its old age it would be drunk from tin cups by Yankee soldiers."[56]

With the Federals poised on the North Carolina border, the Confederates still had not concentrated their small and scattered forces. Hardee had retreated from Cheraw with his fewer than eight thousand men while Bragg remained at Goldsboro with less than six thousand men. Fayetteville stood about halfway between them, and Johnston concluded that this city on the Cape Fear River was the place to gather his forces and confront Sherman. On March 4, the day of President Abraham Lincoln's second inauguration and the day after the Northerners entered Cheraw, Johnston moved his headquarters to Fayetteville from Charlotte. That same day he ordered the Army of Tennessee to take the train from Chester—moving through Charlotte, Greensboro, and Raleigh—to Smithfield, North Carolina. Here this small but veteran command would stand within forty-five miles of Fayetteville and would be well situated between Hardee and Bragg.[57]

Hard rains and swampy rivers had delayed Sherman in South Carolina as much as any Confederate general had slowed him, but the Federals seemed concerned that pattern would change with Johnston's return to command. Sherman learned of the reinstatement on March 6, and after the war he wrote: "I knew then that my special antagonist, General Jos. Johnston was back, with part of his old army, that he would not be misled by feints and false reports, and would somehow compel me to exercise more caution than I had hitherto done." A Union artillery officer offered his opinion: "I do not imagine for a moment that this change of Rebel commanders will influence General Sherman in his purpose, yet it will alter the modus operandi, for Johnston cannot be treated with the contempt Sherman shows for Beauregard." After the war Howard praised Johnston as an "astute Confederate commander."[58]

Johnston may have been astute, but his strategy of concentrating at Fayetteville died young. The "slow working of the railroad," he complained, delayed transporting the units of the Army of Tennessee. Despite "its enormous amount of rolling stock," Johnston reported on another occasion, the line brought "only about 500 men a day" to Smithfield. On March 6 he told Hardee that it was "too late to turn to Fayetteville. Take the best route to Raleigh." That city, sixty miles north of Fayetteville, now became the focus of the commander's thinking. On the seventh he warned Bragg at Goldsboro that Sherman was advancing from Cheraw on Fayetteville, and there was "nothing to impede his march." The Southern forces would have to make their juncture in the Raleigh-Smithfield area, farther north than Johnston initially had hoped.[59]

On March 7, the same day that Johnston sent his warning to Bragg, the Federals pushed into the Tar Heel State. "As we advanced into the wild pine regions of North Carolina," Captain Oakley remembered, "the natives seemed wonderfully impressed at seeing every road filled with marching troops, artillery, and wagon trains. They looked destitute enough as they stood in blank amazement gazing upon the 'Yanks' marching by." At night, some of Sherman's bummers set fires in the sap cavities of the great turpentine trees, lighting the way for the marching Union columns.[60]

For the most part, though, in North Carolina the invaders indulged in less of the capricious destruction that they had inflicted in South Carolina. Drawing a distinction between the two states, Sherman ordered brevet Maj. Gen. Judson "Kill Cavalry" Kilpatrick: "Deal as moderately and fairly by the North Carolinians as possible, and fan the flame of discord already subsisting between them and their proud cousins of South Carolina. There never was much love between them." In addition to this theory held by their commander, the Union soldiers themselves seemed to have spent their bitterness in South Carolina, the state many of them blamed for causing the war. North Carolina, in contrast, was not a Deep South state, had many Unionists, and had been the next-to-the-last state to secede. As the historians who edited Sherman's letters point out, "In such a case the olive branch might prove more effective than the sword in drawing these people back to the Union."[61] When Sherman eventually reached Fayetteville, it was significant that his men destroyed only its arsenal and other buildings of military value. "Since entering North Carolina," one Federal officer claimed, "the wanton destruction has stopped." After nearly a month of campaigning in North Carolina, an Illinois soldier drew a contrast: "Every man in Sherman's army wanted to see South Carolina suffer, have it feel the full weight of the war. . . . I have not seen half a dozen houses fired in [North Carolina]."[62]

As the campaign moved from South to North Carolina, Johnston knew that Schofield's forces inevitably would weigh in against him. By the first of March, Cox had finished organizing his Provincial Corps, and construction crews had started reopening the Atlantic and North Carolina rail line.[63] The new command, which mustered more than eleven thousand men, promptly headed from New Bern toward Kinston while covering the work being done on the railroad behind it.[64]

When Cox started his advance, Bragg still held Goldsboro, where the Wilmington and Weldon Railroad intersected the Atlantic and North Carolina line. The Confederate general was outnumbered but nonetheless determined to defend Kinston against the oncoming provincial corps. On March 6 Bragg asked Johnston for the two thousand or so soldiers of the Army of Tennessee who had been able to detrain at Smithfield. The commander agreed, with a proviso: after these veterans, under Hill's command, fought in any battle, they were to return to Smithfield. "Keep your [railroad] cars," Johnston instructed Hill, "and return the moment it is over." Pointedly referring to the bad blood between Hill and Bragg, the army commander added: "I beg you to forget the past for this emergency."[65]

In addition to Hill's two thousand men, Bragg had perhaps another six thousand or more troops. The Confederates held a strong position at the Wyse Fork crossroads, four miles east of Kinston. Cox's approaching Provisional Corps far outnumbered the Southerners, but Bragg nonetheless was determined to strike a blow. On March 7 he promised Johnston: "No delay will occur in making an issue." Bragg's blood was up, and he laid out an ambitious plan. Hill would contain the Union advance in front of Wyse Fork while other Confederates would hit the enemy's left flank. When the Federals gave way, Hill was to take the offensive and complete the victory.[66]

On Wednesday, March 8, Bragg began the Battle of Wyse Fork. (Some called it the Battle of Kinston, and others used the Second Battle of Kinston since a small fight had taken place in the area in December 1862.) Shortly before the fighting began near Wyse Fork, in an area back toward New Bern an Illinois soldier dashed off a letter to his family. He soon would be off to join his regiment, he told them, "for now while I am writing I hear heavy cannonading in the direction of Kingston. last week there passed through here about ten thousand soldiers all going in the direction of Kingston. . . . as I write I can hear the booming of the cannon more plainly and more rapid."[67]

The anxious soldier had overheard an artillery prelude to the Battle of Wyse Fork. Although local African Americans had alerted the Federals that the Confederates were on the move, the Southerners were able to cut off a Union brigade that had deployed about a mile from its main body. Its commander acknowledged 884 men and officers were missing; nearly all of them must have been among the "several hundred prisoners" claimed by Bragg.[68] In addition to encircling an entire brigade, the Southerners captured a field piece from Battery I, Third New York Light Artillery.[69]

The Confederates overestimated the importance of their initial success. Bragg ordered a pursuit, but his men found that they could accomplish little more on March 8.[70] The Federals reformed their lines, threw out skirmishers, and consolidated their position.[71]

The next day Bragg probed for an opportunity to renew the initiative, but he had lost control of the battle. Cox's men had spent much of the night entrenching, and their skirmish lines fended off the Confederates. "The 9th was employed in extending and strengthening our works," a Union senior officer reported. "The enemy at one time drove our skirmishers from their advance rifle-pits, but they were soon afterward retaken." Bragg hounded his subordinates to make a "vigorous and determined" attack, but the day ended in frustration for the Southerners.[72]

The Battle of Wyse Fork sputtered to an end on March 10. At 9:30 a.m. Johnston reminded Bragg of the proviso that had accompanied the loan of Hill's force. Sherman was moving on Fayetteville, and "all troops must be concentrated in his front, south of [the] Raleigh and Goldsborough Railroad." By the tenth the Federals were strongly entrenched, and Hill reported: "My officers had stated to me the unwillingness of the men to attack earth-works, their experience in the late campaign not being favorable to such an undertaking." That afternoon Bragg gave up hope of achieving anything further against Cox. He left it to Hoke to conduct a rearguard action against the Northerners and retired to Goldsboro.[73]

Bragg's offensive east of Kinston had netted some prisoners, but it had done little to delay Cox's advance. Worse yet for Johnston, the Confederates were unable to arrest Sherman's march on Fayetteville. On March 10, the same day Bragg broke off his action against Cox, the Southerners tried a cavalry foray. Hampton launched a surprise attack against two brigades of Federal troopers under General Kilpatrick at Monroe's Crossroads on the Morgantown Road about twenty miles west of Fayetteville. The reckless Kill Cavalry was caught unawares, but he recovered and gave a fair account of himself. After a vicious fight that produced scores of casualties on each side, the Confederates withdrew. While both contestants claimed a victory, the Union advance through North Carolina continued.[74]

On the eleventh Sherman took Fayetteville, the first sizable city he occupied in North Carolina, and opened communications with General Terry and his corps at Wilmington. "The effect was electric," as Sherman remembered it in the glow of the postwar years, "and no one can realize the feeling unless, like us, he had been for months cut off from all communications with friends." On the twelfth Capt. Solon A. Carter, a staff officer on the Wilmington front, wrote to his wife: "We have had such a succession of brilliant victories lately, & every one of Sherman's seems greater than the last."[75]

In Slocum's perhaps narrow view, there was more than one reason for enthusiasm. "The opening of communication with Wilmington not only brought us our mails and a supply of clothing," he believed, "but enabled us to send to a place of safety thousands of refugees and contrabands who were following the army and seriously embarrassing it. We were dependent upon the country for our supplies of food and forage, and every one not connected with the army was a source of weakness to us." Pvt. Edwin Williams informed his family on March 22: "The darkies have been planting potatoes for the last two or three weeks. there are here in and under the protection of Newberne no less than 4000 negroes old and young."[76]

While Sherman camped around Fayetteville, sending off his African American refugees and destroying the city's arsenal buildings, machine shops, and foundries, Johnston considered his own dispositions. Most of two corps of the Army of Tennessee—including the troops Hill had taken to Kinston—now were at Smithfield. A good part of another corps was stalled at Salisbury, the victim of an enormous railroad backup.[77] Hardee had retreated from Fayetteville and halted at Smithville, a large plantation about five miles south of Averasboro. Bragg, his command reduced by Hill's departure, remained at Goldsboro until Johnston ordered him to Smithfield on the thirteenth.[78]

On March 11, the day Sherman entered Fayetteville, Johnston assessed the strategic situation in North Carolina for Lee. What did the enemy intend to do next? Johnston saw two possible moves for Sherman, both of which were dire for the Confederacy—a drive against Raleigh or one on Goldsboro.

If the Federals took Raleigh, they would cut one of the rail lines to the Army of Northern Virginia at Petersburg. Johnston anxiously asked Lee about the consequence of this action and advised him that it would not be easy for Johnston to detect, let alone arrest, a Union move on Raleigh if the Northerners took their best line of advance.[79] "Should the Federal army move upon Raleigh from Fayetteville," Johnston told Lee, "the course of the Cape Fear might conceal his movements to within thirty miles of the place, and prevent my meeting it near the river, where its columns are most likely to be separated."[80]

The second Federal option, a drive toward Goldsboro, probably posed an even greater threat. This maneuver would link Sherman with Cox's Provisional Corps and eventually Terry's force. Should Sherman combine even with Cox alone, Johnston warned Lee, "their march into Virginia cannot be prevented by me."[81] Prudent commanders always assume that their foes will pursue their best available strategy, and Johnston was inclined to believe that Sherman would head for the Goldsboro-Kinston area and join Cox. "It seems to me probable," he thought, "that General Sherman intends to unite the troops near Kinston with his own army."[82]

Anticipating Johnston's question about Raleigh's importance, Lee had written to him on the same March 11. If the city and its railroad were taken, Lee believed the Army of Northern Virginia could not be supplied. If Johnston retreated north from Raleigh, both Southern armies would starve.[83]

A few days later Lee answered Johnston's communication of the eleventh, offering what counsel he could from the distance of Petersburg. The general in chief thought it more likely that Sherman would order Schofield to Raleigh and would march to join him there rather than in the Goldsboro-Kinston region. In either case, the enormous Federal force would have to leave Fayetteville on more than one road. Lee advised Johnston to remain alert for any opportunity to destroy one of Sherman's columns on the march.[84]

The Union leviathan left Fayetteville on March 15. It used three lines of march because it was so large and because its multiple routes would keep Johnston uncertain whether the Federals' destination was Raleigh or Goldsboro. Slocum's Left Wing struck north on the Raleigh Plank Road.[85] One corps of Howard's Right Wing moved on Slocum's right and headed directly for Goldsboro.[86] Howard's other corps pushed out on Sherman's far right and also steered for Goldsboro.[87]

Sherman was keenly aware that his marching columns would offer the Confederates an opportunity to inflict a defeat in detail, and he intended to guard against that possibility. Before he left Fayetteville he told Terry, in a message that showed better strategic foresight than proper grammar: "I can whip Joe Johnston provided he don't catch one of my corps in flank, and I will see that my army marches hence to Goldsborough in compact form." Sherman also saw that his enemy was running out of viable choices. Just before departing Fayetteville, he remarked to Howard: "I do think it is Johnston's only chance to meet this army before an easy junction with Schofield can be effected."[88]

Torrents of water and quagmires of mud hindered the Federal advance. A Union officer described the conditions: "We built corduroy roads and took ropes and fastened [them] to the wagon tongue and pulled at them. the wagons went down to the hubs in the mud & the mules would fall down and have to be unhitched before they could get up." Higher in the chain of command, Sherman himself explained the dilemma to Terry: "It is now raining hard and the bottom has fallen out, and we will have to corduroy every foot of the way."[89]

On the second day out of Fayetteville, March 16, Slocum's wing pushed through the mud on the Raleigh Plank Road and closed in on Averasboro. South of the town and south of the plank road's junction with the Goldsboro road, Hardee stood ready to meet the Federals with two divisions.[90]

Sherman, riding with Slocum's van, had arrived at the correct estimate of his enemy's intention very early that morning. "Hardee is ahead of me," he informed Terry, "and shows fight."[91]

Sherman's estimate of the Confederate blocking force, ten thousand men, proved to be reasonably correct if a bit high. The key point was that the Federal commander knew the strength of Slocum's wing. Its total numbers, infantry and cavalry combined, were double Hardee's presumed ten thousand troops. Sherman felt confident that once Slocum deployed his full force, he could open the road to Averasboro.[92]

The rain eased during the night of March 15–16, and in the morning the Federals prepared to push Hardee out of their way. Kilpatrick's cavalry opened the action around 6:00 a.m., and the Union horsemen spent the next three hours in a spirited effort to learn more about the Confederate position. Slocum brought up his infantry, and as an officer of the Twenty-sixth Wisconsin related, a "very hot skirmish" took place.[93]

The Battle of Averasboro developed into a good-size engagement. Around 9:00 a.m. two divisions of the XX Corps, Slocum's lead unit, began deploying for battle. This corps was commanded by brevet Maj. Gen. Alpheus S. Williams, once the postmaster of Detroit and now a veteran of hard fighting in both the eastern and western theaters.[94] Well aided by their corps's artillery, General Williams's infantrymen approached the entrenched Confederate front line and engaged it in hard combat.[95]

Sherman himself was at the front and became annoyed as the Confederate resistance continued through the morning. About 10:30 a.m. he ordered Slocum to send a brigade off to the left and turn the right flank of the defenders. Four regiments moved through the woods and over a ravine and carried out this mission. At the same time, their comrades renewed the frontal assault up the Raleigh Plank Road. A sergeant of the Twenty-second Wisconsin, which made this rush at the double-quick, wrote about it on the same day. The men in the frontal assault, he said, were "fully expecting to meet a charge of . . . canister, but nothing came but a volley of musketry . . . and fortunately for us . . . the bullets nearly all went over us."[96]

The Confederate front line had made a stout fight all morning, but now, struck in front and flank, it broke and gave way. Men from the Union brigade that had made the turning movement became the first to enter the Southern works, and soon those who had made the frontal attack joined them. The Federals captured three field pieces, and the noncommissioned officer from Wisconsin learned why at least one of the cannon had not been fired. He counted six white horses, "dead and horribly mangled," that apparently had been hitched to a limber chest that had exploded. The "gunners and drivers were laying about," he recorded, "what was left of them, mangled . . . past recognition; it was no wonder that gun was silenced."[97]

The Federals gathered their prisoners, and about 1:00 p.m., Williams's infantrymen and Kilpatrick's cavalrymen pressed on against the second Confederate line of defense. The Union officers persisted in their advance, threatened the flanks of the defenders, and wore down their resistance. The second Southern position deteriorated, but Hardee reorganized his defense, integrating his two divisions. The infantrymen were joined by Wheeler's cavalry corps of two divisions. While Wheeler said he arrived in the morning, Hardee made it the late afternoon; whenever, his aid was welcomed.[98] The two divisions of troopers deployed on Hardee's right, extending it to the bluffs on the east bank of the Cape Fear River.[99]

The Union numbers were building as well. As Sherman had foreseen, Slocum's wing eventually would greatly outnumber the blocking force in its front. Early in the afternoon units of the Slocum's other corps, the XIV Corps, entered the battle. This corps was led by a brevet major general with the most ironic name in the Northern army—Jefferson C. Davis. General Davis's reputation had been scarred by two events: in September 1862 he had shot and killed his former commander, Maj. Gen. William "Bull" Nelson, and in December 1864 he had abandoned hundreds of African American refugees in the face of Confederate cavalry at Ebenezeer Creek, Georgia.[100] Beyond these negative marks, Davis made a creditable record from Fort Sumter to the close of the war. Sherman admired him, and as Davis's biographers point out, he was "entrusted repeatedly with independent expeditions, with the advance, with the dangerous flank."[101]

Davis's lead division first was ordered into camp, but with the Battle of Averasboro heating up, it was sent to the left of Slocum's line. This fresh unit moved west of the Raleigh Plank Road, hoping to turn the right flank of what now was Hardee's third position.[102]

Given the Federal advantage in strength, the Union plan seemed well founded, and yet it could not be carried out. The targeted flank was not in the air but stoutly anchored by Wheeler's cavalrymen on the bluffs of the Cape Fear. The flanking Federal division crossed some ravines west of the Raleigh Plank Road only to meet resistance and frustration. Its discouraged commander reported that "it would have been worse than folly to have attempted a further advance. I was much disappointed in the results, being confident that the movement would outflank the enemy's position."[103]

When Slocum's turning attack became stymied, he put another fresh division into the action. It fared no better than its predecessor in large part because the rains had made the roads difficult and slowed the Union advance. Daylight began to fail, and Sherman decided to break off the action.[104]

The total Southern casualties in the Battle of Averasboro came to around 500; the Northern losses were higher, about 680. With the advantage of numbers and with the momentum gained by persistence, the Federals had driven their enemy from two successive positions. But Hardee had waged a successful delaying action at Averasboro. From early January 1865 until March 16, Sherman's progress through the Carolinas had been, as Wade Hampton pointed out, "entirely unobstructed"; but at Averasboro, Hampton said, Hardee made "a spirited fight." Old Reliable himself carried the point a step further, telling his men that they had given "the enemy the first serious check he has received since leaving Atlanta."[105]

CHAPTER FOUR

Bentonville

While Lt. Gen. William J. Hardee's soldiers fought at Averasboro, Gen. Joseph E. Johnston gathered the rest of his units around Smithfield. General Johnston finally achieved the concentration of forces that the Confederates had so long needed in the western theater. Once at Smithfield, Johnston formally combined his commands into the Army of the South: the remnants of the Army of Tennessee, now led by Lt. Gen. Alexander P. Stewart, who was nicknamed "Old Straight" by his men; the Department of North Carolina troops commanded by Gen. Braxton Bragg; the Department of South Carolina, Georgia, and Florida soldiers in a corps under General Hardee; and the cavalry under Lt. Gen. Wade Hampton.[1] A general order of March 16 confirmed officially that Gen. Pierre Gustave Toutant Beauregard would serve as Johnston's second in command, a role the Creole already had accepted.[2]

The Army of the South, except Hardee's Corps, stood near Smithfield. Having fought at Averasboro, Hardee moved his command from that battlefield to Elevation, located along the main road between Averasboro and Smithfield.[3]

The Federals were on the move as well. On March 17 Maj. Gen. Henry W. Slocum's Left Wing left the Averasboro battlefield and headed for Goldsboro, moving to within twenty miles of Bentonville. To the south, Maj. Gen. Oliver O. Howard's Right

Wing moved more slowly. Its commander later reported, somewhat tersely: "March 17, being yet uncertain as to the result of the engagement of the day before [at Averasboro], I moved forward toward Bentonville but six miles."[4]

Maj. Gen. John M. Schofield was at Kinston, with Maj. Gen. Jacob D. Cox's Provisional Corps. Since the battle against General Bragg on March 10, the Federals had been exerting themselves. "Immediately upon the occupation of Kinston," General Schofield said, "I put a large force of troops to work upon the railroad, in aid of the construction corps under Colonel [William W.] Wright, rebuilt the wagon bridge over the Neuse, and brought forward supplies preparatory to a farther advance." Schofield's other Provisional Corps, under Maj. Gen. Alfred H. Terry, had left Wilmington on the fifteenth and was headed north toward its comrades.[5]

With Schofield moving to join Generals Slocum and Howard, Johnston's window of opportunity to undertake an initiative was closing rapidly. Even after concentrating the Army of the South around Smithfield and after making use of Hardee's Corps at Elevation, Johnston could bring only about sixteen thousand soldiers into a battle.[6] Maj. Gen. William T. Sherman's March 1 muster rolls put his effective strength at more than fifty-seven thousand men. Johnston was ignorant of that number, but he certainly knew that he was heavily outnumbered. Despite this disparity in personnel and despite Johnston's usual caution in the field, on March 17 he was determined to seize the operational and tactical offensive. At 7:00 p.m. he wrote to Hardee: "Something must be done to-morrow morning, and yet I have no satisfactory information as to the enemy's movements."[7]

Why did the usually defensive-minded Johnston decide to attack a force much larger than his own? Historian Mark Grimsley has suggested some likely reasons. First an operational initiative would comply with general in chief Gen. Robert E. Lee's guidance to look for an opportunity to destroy one of General Sherman's columns while on the march.[8] Grimsley also argues that Johnston believed a hard blow against Sherman would strengthen the Confederate government's position in any peace negotiations. Johnston stated in his memoir that when he returned to command, he did not believe victory could be won in the field; thus his objective was "to obtain fair terms of peace." A powerful attack on Sherman would show that the Southern army remained a viable force and would bolster the hand of Confederate negotiators.[9]

Grimsley offers a third reason that is particularly compelling: Johnston decided to attack because he believed that taking the initiative would raise the morale of his men. Grimsley concludes that "the morale effect was critical." Johnston claimed in his memoir that one "important object was gained" by attacking Sherman: "restoring the confidence of our troops, who had either lost it in the defeat at Wilmington, or in those of Tennessee. All were greatly elated by the event." Less than a week after the Battle of Bentonville, Johnston made the same assessment in a report to General Lee.[10]

For these reasons, Johnston had concluded the evening of March 17 that the troops had to act the next morning, but he had to acknowledge that he lacked information about the Federals' movements.[11] He needed firm intelligence before he could plan an attack on Sherman.

To gain that intelligence, at 10:00 p.m. Johnston sent General Hampton, his senior cavalry commander, a dispatch that asked several questions. How many Federal columns were on the march? Where were they? How far apart were they? What was their distance from Goldsboro? In addition to answers to these questions, Johnston wanted Hampton's opinion of a concept of operations that he had in mind: would it be "practicable" to strike south from Smithfield and attack the Federals below the Neuse River before they reached Goldsboro?[12]

Hampton's cavalrymen had been active, and he soon gave Johnston the location, but probably not the identity, of the Union forces.[13] After the war Johnston recalled, "About daybreak, on the 18th, information came to me from General Hampton, that the Federal army was marching toward Goldsboro."[14]

In answer to Johnston's questions, Hampton knew the Federals were moving in two columns. The northernmost was marching

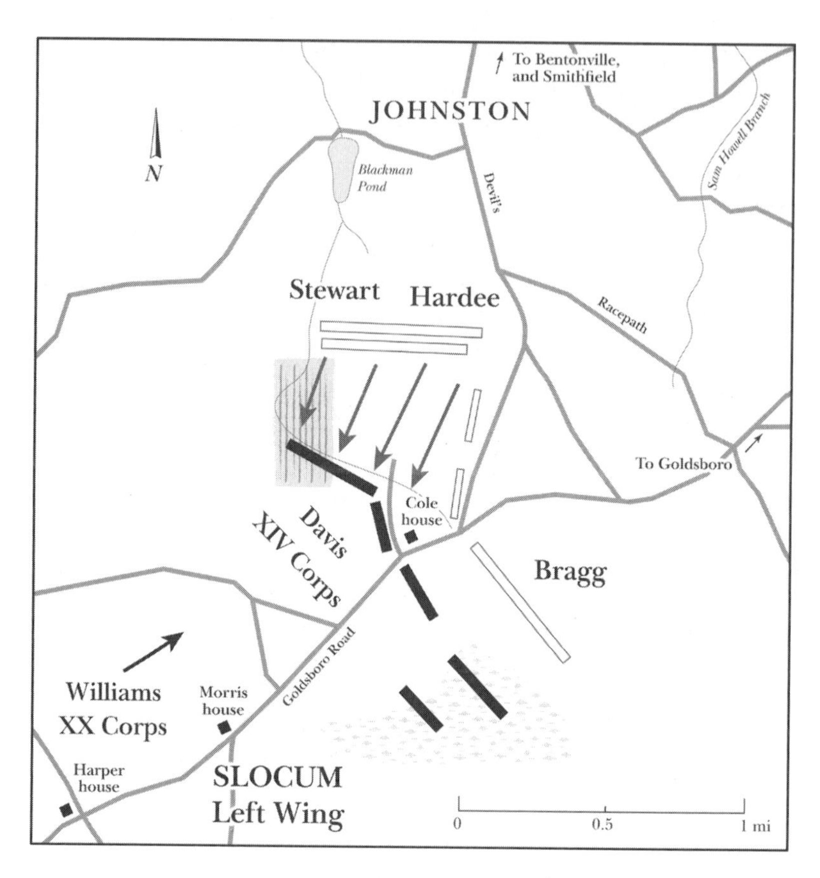

MAP 3. Battle of Bentonville, First Day, March 19, 1865

eastward on a main road to Goldsboro. (Although it is virtually certain that Hampton did not know it at the time, this column was Slocum's Left Wing, with the XIV and XX Corps.) The other column was moving in the same direction but on a parallel road to the south. (Although it is again almost certain that Hampton did not know it, this column was Howard's Right Wing, the XV and XVII Corps.) How far apart were these two columns? Hampton may not have answered this question precisely for Johnston at the time. Even in an account written after many years had passed, he put it vaguely: they were "some miles" apart.[15] Johnston stated after the war that his cavalry reports told him that one Federal wing was about half a day's march in advance of the other. How far was each column from Goldsboro? If Hampton offered Johnston any estimates, no record of them survived.[16]

Johnston also had asked for Hampton's opinion of his operational concept of striking south from Smithfield and attacking the Federals while they were on the march to Goldsboro. The cavalryman endorsed the idea and made recommendations about it. From Hampton's suggestions, a plan emerged for attacking Sherman.[17]

The plan's starting point took into account that two Union columns were marching toward Goldsboro on parallel roads. Johnston used what he called "the map of North Carolina" or "the State map," which probably was the official state map at the time. The Confederate commander began with the intelligence report from his cavalry that one Federal column was a half day's march ahead of the other. He factored in the distance between the parallel roads as given on his map and concluded "that there was probably an interval of a day's march between the heads of the two columns."[18]

The enemy force closest to Johnston at Smithfield was the northernmost Union column, Slocum's wing, which was heading east on the Goldsboro Road. It would become the objective of the Confederates. Johnston intended to defeat Sherman's two columns in detail by smashing Slocum's wing before Howard's could come to its aid.[19]

A Confederate blocking force would stop Slocum's movement on the Goldsboro Road. Early in the morning of March 18, Johnston directed Bragg first to advance his command, about fifty-five hundred soldiers, from Smithfield to Bentonville.[20] Then Bragg would move south from Bentonville and form a line across the Goldsboro Road—one of the deployments Hampton had suggested. Bragg would serve as a blocking force, preventing Slocum's column from going any farther east on the Goldsboro Road.[21]

While Bragg held the Federals on the Goldsboro Road, Johnston's other two major commands—Hardee's Corps and General Stewart's Army of Tennessee—would strike them from the north. Hardee would bring roughly fifty-four hundred infantrymen into the fight. The Army of Tennessee was an army in name only as Stewart led about four thousand soldiers.[22]

The Confederates would be outnumbered in the battle that would develop south of Bentonville. Slocum was able to bring about twenty thousand soldiers to the battlefield. On the eve of the engagement, Johnston's total strength was probably about sixteen thousand men.[23]

When Hampton recommended a position for Bragg's blocking force, he chose a heavily wooded area with "dense thickets of blackjack." The Confederate cavalryman saw a potential tactical advantage in the close stands of these oak trees, which are also known as jack oak or blackjack oak. The dense thickets of these trees would provide cover for Bragg's infantrymen.[24]

Marching on a stretch of the Goldsboro Road that ran northeast, Slocum's column would reach the two-story whitewashed house of Willis Cole at a point less than two miles south of Bentonville.[25] (Cole's property was ill-fated: during the Battle of Bentonville, Confederate skirmishers would burn down the house and surrounding outbuildings.[26]) Hampton described the Cole farm as surrounded on the north, east, and south by thickets of blackjack oak trees. The woods, standing a half mile north of the Goldsboro Road, would screen Hardee and Stewart while they moved into position to strike southward. Only Bragg's blocking force would be in view to the approaching Federals. South of the Goldsboro Road, across from the Cole house, were more thickets and marshes and swamps.[27] It was an area where the Federals would have difficulty moving from marching column to fighting line and where their advantage in numbers would count for less. Doubtless Hampton and Johnston hoped that these terrain features would help balance the numerical odds.

From his Smithfield headquarters, Johnston directed Hardee, Stewart, and Bragg into their positions to carry out the plan.[28] In a dispatch dated 7:40 a.m., March 18, Johnston told Hampton: "The scheme mentioned in my note, which you pronounce practicable, will be attempted."[29]

Sherman recognized that while his forces marched in two columns on parallel roads they would be vulnerable to precisely what Johnston had in mind—an attack on one column before the other could come to its assistance. Before he left Fayetteville, Sherman had told General Terry that he intended to make a compact march to Goldsboro to guard against Johnston's hitting one of his corps in the flank. Sherman also saw that his opponent was running out of viable strategic choices. Just before departing Fayetteville, he remarked to Howard that Johnston's only remaining chance was to attack Sherman's forces before they joined with Schofield's.[30]

Given the available road net, Sherman was quite successful at keeping his two wings near each other. Historian Mark Bradley's remarkably detailed *Last Stand in the Carolinas: The Battle of Bentonville* provides a fine account of the final engagement between Johnston and Sherman. Bradley points out that on the afternoon of March 18, just before the battle began, Sherman's front extended twelve miles, the most compact it had ever been while on the march.[31]

On the evening of March 18, the head of Slocum's column encountered Hampton's cavalry, deployed both north and south of the Goldsboro Road and west of the Cole house. The South Carolina planter heard one of his own troopers remark: "Old Hampton is playing a bluff game, and if he don't mind[,] Sherman will call him." The Federal infantry did in fact "call" Hampton, who continued to resist the Federals' advance into the next morning, when he handed off the fight to Bragg's blocking force.[32]

The early daylight hours of Sunday, March 19, 1865, the first day of the Battle of Bentonville, featured a clear blue sky. "A more beautiful morning I never saw," declared an Ohio private. The day proved warm and cloudless.[33]

The morning sun beamed down on Bentonville, a quiet North Carolina hamlet that would have been ignored by history had not the last large battle in the Civil War's western theater been waged just south of it. In March 1865 it featured a carriage shop operated by John C. Hood, who was then in his mid-thirties. Five years earlier, along with other inhabitants, the national census takers had listed Hood, his wife Martha, and three young children. In addition to Hood's carriage shop, Bentonville boasted a general store, a blacksmith shop, a Methodist church, and a few other buildings.[34] East of this little community stood John Benton's log house, and his farm became Johnston's headquarters.[35]

The land around Bentonville supported farms and featured the majestic pines common to North Carolina. Local workers exploited these trees to produce what since colonial days had been called "naval stores"—that is, turpentine or pitch used to caulk wooden ships. Just north of Bentonville ran Mill Creek, an area landmark that carried more immediate military significance than the region's noble pines. This impassable stream might prove a dangerous obstacle to the Southerners if their battle plan for Bentonville miscarried since only one bridge across it was readily available to them.[36]

The Federals entered the area south of Bentonville much as Hampton and Johnston had expected. Slocum's van had dealt with Hampton's cavalry and then encountered Bragg's blocking force. To the south, Howard moved his brother command along a road roughly parallel to Slocum's. The head of Howard's column was six miles south of Slocum's, but the tail was only about two miles from it.[37]

By 9:00 a.m. Slocum's lead units had forced Hampton's troopers to retire. When the Federals approached the Cole house, they encountered the stiffer resistance of infantrymen rather than that of cavalrymen. Bragg's force of fifty-five hundred did what the Hampton-Johnston plan asked it to do and conducted a determined holding action. To the north, Stewart formed the Army of Tennessee and prepared to drive south into the Federals.[38] The opening phase of the battle developed much as Hampton and Johnston had planned.

But the disadvantages of low numbers and a desperate strategic position left the Confederates with very little tolerance for any setbacks. If the Southerners were to win at Bentonville, every important tactical outcome had to turn their way. And when the battle began developing on the morning of March 19, so did the Confederates' problems.

The first difficulty was that the Bentonville operation was flawed before the Southerners began to carry it out, because the map that Johnston had used to make his plans contained errors. It understated the distance that Hardee would have to march to reach the jump-off point to attack the Federals' flank on the Goldsboro Road. Johnston's map showed that Hardee's Corps at Elevation was twelve miles from its assembly area on the Bentonville battlefield; in reality, the unit had farther to travel. Compounding matters, Johnston's map exaggerated the distance between Slocum's and Howard's wings. It put the two Federal columns more than twelve miles apart; in reality, they were much closer. Misled by his cartography, Johnston assumed that Hardee would be able to attack Slocum sooner than in fact he could and that Howard would take more time to reinforce Slocum than in fact he would.[39]

Unfortunately for the Confederates, Hardee's map was no better than Johnston's. It also understated his distance from Bentonville.[40] Hardee had other problems as well. His soldiers had fought at Averasboro on the sixteenth and made a hard march through rain and mud to Elevation the next day. It is not surprising that Hardee's exhausted men made a late start on March 18. The corps did not leave its bivouacs at Elevation until midday. Hindered by poor maps and confusion as to the best route, Hardee's command marched fifteen miles on the eighteenth and halted about six miles northwest of Bentonville.[41]

Hardee and his staff officers rode another mile and took lodging for the night in a private residence. It was the home of a Unionist named Snead, probably George Poindexter Snead.[42] Mr. Snead's political views were not uncommon in Johnston County, nor did they prevent him from offering his Confederate guests "unbounded hospitality."[43]

The next morning, March 19, as historian Nathaniel Cheairs Hughes, Jr., puts it in his scholarly, insightful book on this battle, "Hardee and his men wandered cross-country to Bentonville." Their march from Snead's house to the battlefield was yet another difficult one, and they did not reach their destination until 9:00 a.m., or well after the battle had begun.[44] This delay was the first setback in the Confederate plan for a Hardee-Stewart attack that would crush the Federals on the Goldsboro Road.

When the senior Confederate leaders on the battlefield realized that Hardee would be late maneuvering his corps to its intended position at right angles to Bragg's line, they adjusted their tactical plan. Hampton proposed, and Johnston agreed, that the cavalryman should deploy his two horse batteries where they could cover Bragg's front and link up with Stewart's Army of Tennessee when it came on line.[45]

Hampton's suggestion bought time for the Confederates, and Stewart's men began arriving from the north. The Army of Tennessee maneuvered into position, hinging its left at a right angle to the right of Bragg's line. While these veterans were getting into place, one of Stewart's brigade commanders, Ohio native Brig. Gen. Daniel H. Reynolds, suffered a shell wound. A projectile, perhaps intended for Hampton's nearby horse batteries, grievously injured the general and killed his mount, Old Bob, and another horse.[46]

After the wounding of General Reynolds, Stewart moved his units on line and poised to attack. Before he could do so, the Federals moved deliberately forward through the marshy, tangled ground south of the Goldsboro Road. The Confederates contained this advance, but the Union effort had been determined enough to make Bragg anxious about holding his position.[47]

While Bragg worried and the morning of March 19 came to an end, Hardee deployed his two divisions, which were led by two bushy-bearded commanders—Maj. Gen. Lafayette McLaws of Georgia and Brig. Gen. William B. Taliaferro of Virginia. Hardee reached the battlefield just as Bragg's concerns about the Union attacks below the Goldsboro Road were peaking. The North Carolinian appealed to Johnston to reinforce his position, and the senior commander acquiesced. General Taliaferro's Division deployed on Stewart's right, as originally planned, but Hardee's lead unit, General McLaws's Division, was sent to Bragg's assistance. Historian Hughes asserts: "This was a critical moment at Bentonville, perhaps *the* critical moment for the Confederates. Johnston conceded to Bragg's alarm and diverted Hardee's largest division—McLaws's—to aid [Maj. Gen. Robert F. Hoke's Division of Bragg's command]."[48]

By midday that Sunday, the fundamental element of Johnston's plan—Stewart's and Hardee's drive south to crush Slocum's wing on the Goldsboro Road—had suffered two setbacks. First Hardee's late appearance had prevented him from attacking in concert with the Army of Tennessee. Then when Hardee reached the field, his effort with Stewart was diluted because Bragg's anxiety caused a sizable part of Hardee's command to be diverted.

The mistake of diverting McLaws's Division was compounded when, as the afternoon wore on, Bragg made no use of it. Hardee accordingly asked to have the unit returned to him, and Johnston granted this request. The result was that McLaws spent the day marching and countermarching rather than fighting. Four of his brigades finally made an attack as the sun was setting, but they accomplished nothing.[49]

Johnston came to regret sending McLaws away from the Army of Tennessee. Six years later, he wrote to one of Bragg's subordinates: "I believe that Genl Bragg's nervousness when you were first attacked at Bentonville, was very injurious—by producing urgent applications for help—which not only made delay, but put a large division out of position." And in his 1874 memoir, Johnston again acknowledged that the diversion of McLaws had been "most injudicious."[50]

While McLaws's command was deploying and redeploying, Sherman and Slocum corresponded during the early afternoon of March 19. Sherman had been riding with Slocum's Left Wing for several days, but on the morning of the nineteenth, he decided to reduce his courier distance from the corps of Generals Cox and Terry by accompanying Howard rather than Slocum.[51] At 1:30 p.m. Slocum wrote to Sherman, alerting him that he was fighting against Confederate infantry, which was "in strong force in my front," and recommending that the Right Wing come to his assistance. Sherman answered Slocum at 2:00 p.m., assuring him that four divisions of Howard's wing were coming to his aid. Far down in the chain of command from these senior generals, a XV Corps soldier noted in his diary that the Right Wing was not far from Slocum's battlefield: "We heard very heavy firing to the left and to the rear of us all afternoon. Very heavy cannonading."[52]

Johnston was ignorant of the details of Howard's approach, but the Confederate commander knew he must overpower Slocum's wing soon before its brother command came to its aid. Johnston continued to press his attacks, but Slocum put up a creditable defense. He brought up fresh units, massed his formations, and moved some of his men behind improvised fieldworks. "A line of defense was at once selected," Slocum later related, "and as the troops came up they were placed in position and ordered to collect fence-rails and everything else available for barricades. The men used their tin cups and hands as shovels, and needed no urging to induce them to work."[53]

Through the afternoon of that March Sunday and into the darkness, the Confederates renewed their efforts against Slocum's wing. Lt. Col. Allen L. Fahnestock, commander of the Eighty-sixth Illinois, related that at one point the "bullets flew like hail among the Pine trees." Capt. Will Robinson of the Thirty-fourth Illinois reported to his father: "All agree it was the hottest place we were ever in." Another officer of the same regiment elaborated on the point. Noting that the Thirty-fourth had fought at Shiloh, Stones River, Kennesaw Mountain, Jonesboro, and elsewhere, he contended that "for a desperate resistance and a determination to whip them on the part of our own men, we saw nothing in four years of army life to compare with that 19th of March at Bentonville."[54]

Striking hard, the Confederates crushed Brig. Gen. William P. Carlin's division. (General Carlin, writes scholar Hughes, "fought bravely but impetuously.") The Southerners also roughly handled another division, which was commanded by the dependable and popular Brig. Gen. James D. Morgan. The official returns showed that General Morgan's division lost 410 total casualties; Carlin's division, 453.[55]

The Confederates won these and other tactical successes, but hindered by the delayed arrival of Hardee's Corps and the misuse of McLaws's Division, they failed to achieve their operational objective of destroying Slocum's wing. The Federals weathered the storm on March 19 and inflicted more damage than they received. During the first day's fighting at Bentonville, Johnston lost about two thousand of his sixteen thousand soldiers engaged. His losses were almost double Slocum's as the Federal losses were roughly eleven hundred of their twenty thousand men on the field.[56]

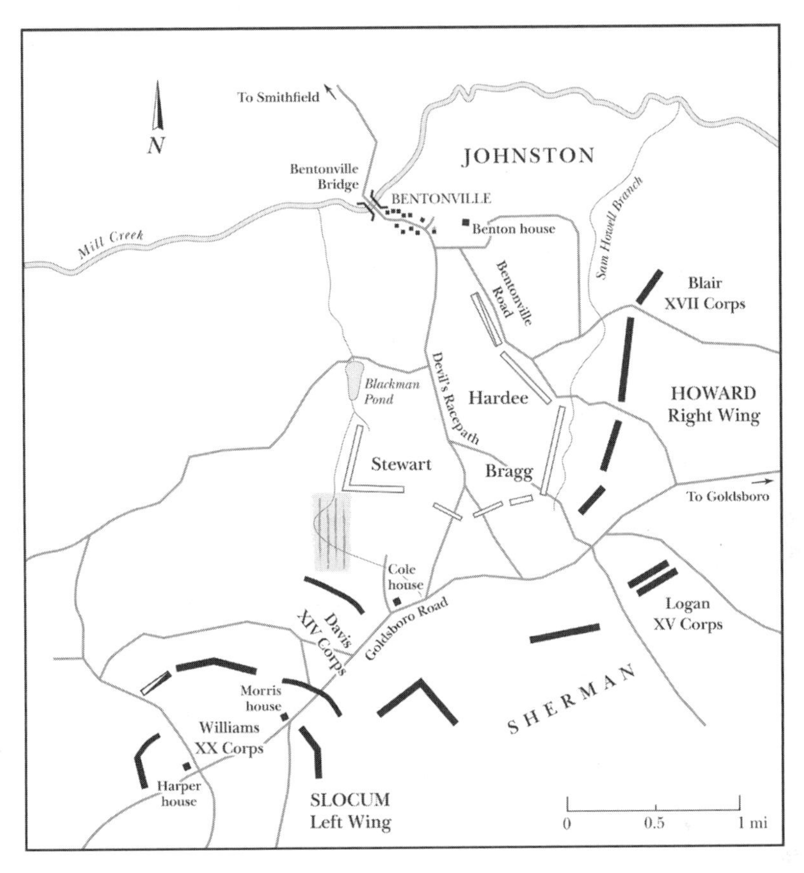

MAP 4. Battle of Bentonville, Second Day, March 20, 1865

The first day at Bentonville, Sunday, March 19, 1865, in some ways resembled the second day at Gettysburg, Thursday, July 2, 1863. In each case the Confederates attacked, fought hard, and were successful up to a point but fell short of decisive victory. The Federals on March 19, as on July 2, always seemed able to commit fresh units just in time to meet each successive crisis. The Northerners at Bentonville, as at Gettysburg, frustrated the sustained efforts of their opponents. The first day at Bentonville ended in a draw. And a draw meant a Southern defeat, for Johnston's hopes rested entirely on crushing the Left Wing while it fought alone. Once Howard began reinforcing Slocum, the Confederates had no reasonable chance of winning an operational victory.

The second day of the Battle of Bentonville, Monday, March 20, fell on what one Federal called a "very warm" day. Johnston acknowledged that his operational plan had failed, and he went on the defensive. He withdrew a short distance north from the March 19 battlefield and into a narrow horseshoe-shape line that extended from east to west. In his rear stood Bentonville and, just beyond it, Mill Creek. This stream, which ran generally southwest to northeast, could be crossed only at the Bentonville Bridge.[57]

Johnston remained in Sherman's front in this dangerous position even though he had virtually no chance of winning a victory. Why did he do so? In his official report on Bentonville, Johnston gave two reasons why he offered battle on March 20. Reflecting his understanding of the advantages of the tactical defensive, he said he hoped Sherman's "greatly superior numbers might encourage him to attack." Johnston's second intention was "to cover the removal of our wounded." (Because of a shortage of ambulances, compounded by what the Confederate commander characterized as "very bad roads," it took two days to get his stricken soldiers off the battlefield.) In his 1874 memoir Johnston said nothing about hoping that Sherman would attack but emphasized the time needed to remove the injured. "There was now no object in remaining in presence of the enemy," he acknowledged, "but that of covering the bearing off of our wounded."[58]

Historians have suggested other reasons beyond these two. Johnston's able biographer Craig L. Symonds writes: "Perhaps, too, [Johnston] was loath to withdraw lest his critics be provided with yet another example of his willingness to surrender territory." Historian Grimsley, who argues that Johnston attacked at Bentonville in part to raise the morale of his men, also contends that he remained on the battlefield for the same reason. "The successful initial attack on Sherman's Left Wing," Grimsley observes, gave the Southern soldiers "a valuable tonic; Johnston risked the possibility of total disaster so that his troops might carry it from the battlefield. . . . A stout defense and a departure in its own good time made the battle seem a success."[59]

The total disaster Grimsley mentions was indeed a possibility, because before the end of March 20 Johnston faced Sherman's united command. During the mid-afternoon of that Monday, the first of Howard's infantrymen began arriving on the battlefield, and by 4:30 p.m. Howard had his entire force in place, with four divisions on line and three in reserve.[60] Arriving with Howard's wing, Sherman made his headquarters on a farm in the rear of the northern part of the Union front.[61] Probably more than fifty-five thousand Federals, with Slocum's wing deployed on the left and Howard's on the right, firmly held a line along the Goldsboro Road. They confronted Johnston's horseshoe-shaped line, which, even after receiving some cavalry reinforcements, was defended by only about eighteen thousand men.[62]

Probing Johnston's new line, the Federals challenged the Confederates as they withdrew northward, but for the most part Monday, March 20, passed quietly. The losses on each side that day did not remotely compare with those suffered during the first day's battle. One Confederate return suggests that the Army of Tennessee lost just nine men; General Hoke's Division, sixty-two.[63] The Fourteenth Michigan and Sixteenth Illinois did some sharp fighting and together probably suffered about a hundred total casualties.[64]

Late in the afternoon of the twentieth, Johnston told his subordinates that he planned to retreat from Bentonville, but then he changed his mind. On Tuesday, March 21, the Confederates remained in place, continuing to hold their bridgehead south of Mill Creek. Why did Johnston continue to stand at Bentonville, when he was so heavily outnumbered and had only one line of retreat? He did not answer this question in his official report, implying that the reasons he gave for staying in place on March 20 still obtained the next day. When Johnston addressed the point in his memoir, he explained that because of his shortage of ambulances and the bad condition of the roads, removing his wounded men took two days. Grimsley's suggestion, that Johnston defied Sherman and left Bentonville at his "own good time" in order to strengthen the morale of his soldiers, applies as well—or better—to Johnston's conduct on the twenty-first as on the twentieth.[65]

Tuesday, March 21, brought a gloomy morning that turned to rain. On the third day at Bentonville, the XVII Corps of Howard's

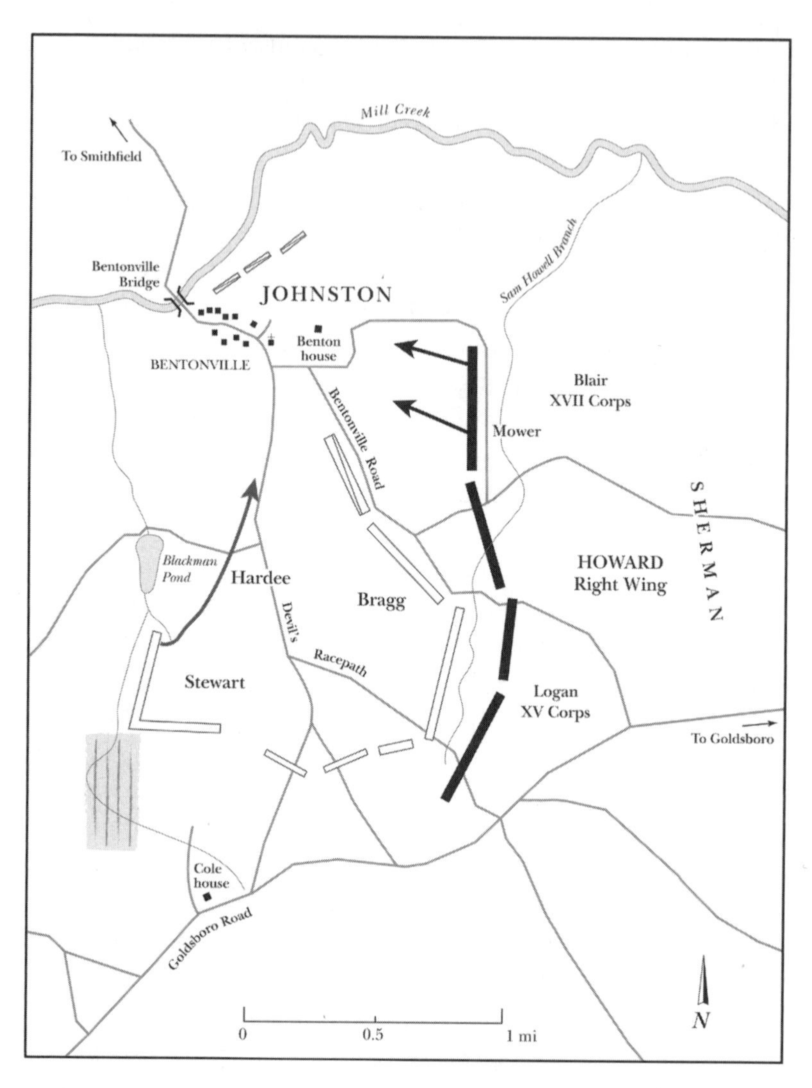

MAP 5. Battle of Bentonville, Third Day, March 21, 1865

wing held the Union right.[66] One of its divisions was commanded by Maj. Gen. Joseph A. "Fighting Joe" Mower, a New Englander whom Sherman called "brave to a fault" and "ever rash."[67] General Mower secured his corps commander's permission to make a "little reconnaissance," which he escalated into a two-brigade attack. The division commander recognized that he lacked the strength to cut off Johnston's sole line of retreat across the Bentonville Bridge. But Mower no doubt anticipated that if he drove deeply enough into the Confederate left, Sherman would send reinforcements to support his initiative.[68]

In fighting that took place in a rainstorm, Johnston used his reserves to frustrate Mower's improvised attack. During this action, the Eighth Texas Cavalry staged a dramatic mounted charge. General Hardee's only son, sixteen-year-old Pvt. William "Willie" Hardee, rode in this attack and was fatally wounded in the chest.[69]

In Mower's unsuccessful offensive, the day's only major action, the Federals lost just 166 officers and men. A Confederate return for March 21 reported 154 total casualties, but this accounting excludes those of Hardee's Corps and the cavalry.[70]

Nor did the casualties suffered during the entire three days at Bentonville brook any comparison with the wholesale slaughters at Shiloh, Murfreesboro, Chickamauga, or elsewhere in the western theater. They nonetheless were terrible enough in their own right. The Federals reported their total losses as 1,527; the Confederates, 2,606. Doubtless historian Bradley is correct in characterizing both of these numbers as "probably low."[71]

With Mower's attack checked, Sherman ordered him back and was content to let the Battle of Bentonville come to an end. In his memoirs, the Federal commander acknowledged that this decision may have been an error. "I think I made a mistake there," Sherman wrote, "and should have rapidly followed Mower's lead with the whole of the right wing, which would have brought on a general battle, and it could not have resulted otherwise than successfully to us, by reason of our vastly superior numbers."[72]

On March 21, 1865, Sherman focused more on his strategic than his tactical and operational opportunities. He was more interested in continuing his march to Goldsboro than in attacking Johnston. Sherman confidently assumed that once he joined forces with Schofield, his numerical strength would be strategically decisive.[73]

Across the battlefield, Johnston recognized that he could remain no longer at Bentonville. He could hope that the heavy blows given Slocum on the nineteenth and the defiance offered during the next two days would bolster the spirits of the Army of the South. Late in the night of the twenty-first and into the early morning hours of the twenty-second, the Confederates gave up their lines south of Bentonville. They pulled back across Mill Creek and withdrew through a relentless rain toward Smithfield.[74]

Lacking enough ambulances, Johnston was forced to leave behind many of his most severely wounded men. At John and Amy Harper's fine residence on the north side of the Goldsboro Road and in other buildings throughout the area, local citizens tried to help the Southern unfortunates and the Federal casualties as well. The Harper house became the field hospital of the XIV Corps, and here some of the abandoned Confederate wounded, along with hundreds of Union soldiers, received care. Six of the nine Harper children were at home at the time of the battle; their parents kept them upstairs while they aided the stricken soldiers in the four rooms downstairs.[75] A Confederate cavalry scout who returned to Bentonville a week after the battle took note of the wounded Southerners he found in the Harpers' impressive two-story, double-chimney home. "They are in a suffering condition," he wrote, "for the want of proper supplies, and there is no surgeon to attend them. Mr. Harper and family are doing all their limited means will allow for the sufferers."[76]

Johnston's departure allowed Sherman to continue his march to Goldsboro. Terry had left Wilmington on March 15, and on the day after the Battle of Bentonville, the twenty-second, Sherman linked up with his corps west of Goldsboro.[77] On March 23 Sherman and Terry joined Schofield, with Cox's corps, at the same city.[78] This concentration gave Sherman a force of about eighty-one thousand soldiers.[79]

The numerical odds against Johnston now had grown so great that he was strategically bankrupt. Two days after Bentonville, Johnston telegraphed Lee: "Sherman's course cannot be hindered by the small force I have. I can do no more than annoy him. I respectfully suggest that it is no longer a question whether you leave [your] present position; you have only to decide where to meet Sherman. I will be near him."[80] By the time Johnston sent this communication, Lee was dealing with grave problems of his own.

CHAPTER FIVE

Late Winter at Petersburg

As 1864 drew to an end, Gen. Robert E. Lee's Army of Northern Virginia held its extensive trenches around Richmond and Petersburg with a threadbare force of about 66,500 effectives. The Confederates had stretched their lines to cover their capital and the crucial railroad center south of it. The winter weather, supply shortages, and depressing letters from home reduced the spirits of the defenders. On the day after Christmas, General Lee sent Secretary of War James A. Seddon a somber message, warning that the front along his army's far left flank "had to be in a measure abandoned and the rest very thinly manned." The enemy was concentrating his forces and apparently preparing to attack. "If so," Lee despaired, "I do not see where I am to get troops to meet him, as ours seem rather to diminish than to increase."[1]

The Confederate commander had excellent reasons for his concerns. The Federals besieging Lee held a great advantage in logistics, well illustrated by the enormous supply base they had built at City Point, Virginia. The Northerners also enjoyed superior numbers. Lt. Gen. Ulysses S. Grant had two field forces at hand—the Army of the Potomac, which in January 1865 mustered more than 80,000 soldiers, and the Army of the James, another 40,700.[2]

Maj. Gen. George G. Meade, best known for his victory over Lee at Gettysburg, commanded the Army of the Potomac. After that signal success, General Meade's star declined. He conducted an able pursuit of Lee from Gettysburg, but President Abraham Lincoln was disappointed that the Confederates returned to Virginia. Meade then led the Army of the Potomac through the inconclusive Bristoe and Mine Run campaigns. When General Grant became the Union general in chief, he considered replacing Meade with Maj. Gen. William F. "Baldy" Smith, who held Grant's high confidence. Grant decided instead to leave Meade in place, remain at his elbow, and shield him and the other Army of the Potomac generals from political pressures.[3]

The other field force, the Army of the James, had come under the leadership of Maj. Gen. Edward O. C. Ord after Maj. Gen. Benjamin F. Butler's failure with the first expedition against Fort Fisher. General Ord had the liability of being a conservative Democrat, but he had learned to keep his political views to himself and had been a favorite of Grant's since they served together in 1862. Ord had been severely wounded at Fort Harrison in September 1864.[4] Recovering and returning to duty, he replaced General Butler, who had greater political than military value to the administration and had become expendable after the election of 1864.[5]

Overseeing the operations of the armies of Ord and Meade, Grant had held Lee at bay at Petersburg since June 1864. When the New Year 1865 arrived, the outcome of the campaign still hung in the balance. The prize at stake was a vitally important logistics and communications center that stood about twenty miles directly south of Richmond. Railroads connected Petersburg with cities and military depots throughout the South, and they in turn were tied into the capital by a north–south rail line. Grant concluded that if the Federals won this beleaguered city, they almost certainly would gain Richmond as well.

In addition to being a communications center, Petersburg boasted a considerable population. In 1860 its more than eighteen thousand residents made it the second-largest city in Virginia and the eleventh in the South. African Americans comprised nearly half its population. Among Southern cities Petersburg had the greatest number of free blacks, or more than three thousand freedmen who were working as barbers, blacksmiths, boatmen, and stable keepers and in other occupations.[6]

Soldiers and, later, historians often referred to the struggle for this population and railroad center as the "siege of Petersburg." The phrase was accurate as far as it went, but two points should be kept in mind. First Grant's powerful forces lay siege not only to Petersburg but also to Richmond. The Confederate trench lines ran well north of the James River to protect the capital against a Federal advance from the east.

Second the term "siege" might suggest a static state of affairs, with the two opponents deeply entrenched and neither side—particularly the defenders—enjoying much mobility. Although both contestants constructed sophisticated fieldworks that were much more extensive than those of earlier campaigns, neither force was immobilized. Historian Earl Hess observes that "Petersburg was less of a siege than it was a traditional field campaign with some limited aspects of siege warfare."[7]

Mobility was in fact an important element in Grant's strategy for capturing Petersburg. He recognized that his advantage in numbers allowed him to conduct active operations. Grant also realized that the strong fieldworks that his men had built during the second half of 1864 not only kept them well protected but also meant that his long lines could be held securely by fewer soldiers, freeing others for tactical and operational offensives.

Rather than conducting a static siege, Grant took initiatives that extended his lines farther and farther to the south and west of Petersburg. This operational plan followed from the achievements of Maj. Gen. Gouverneur K. Warren and his V Corps at Globe Tavern, a few miles south of Petersburg on the Halifax Road, during August 18–21, 1864.[8] Before the Petersburg campaign, General Warren had made a mixed record. He had been a hero at Gettysburg and Mine Run but had faltered in the Wilderness and at Spotsylvania.[9] At Globe Tavern, Warren made a fundamental contribution to the North's ultimate success at Petersburg. He seized a stretch of the Weldon Railroad, an important Confederate supply artery; built strong fieldworks that ensured the Federals would continue to control this valuable rail line;

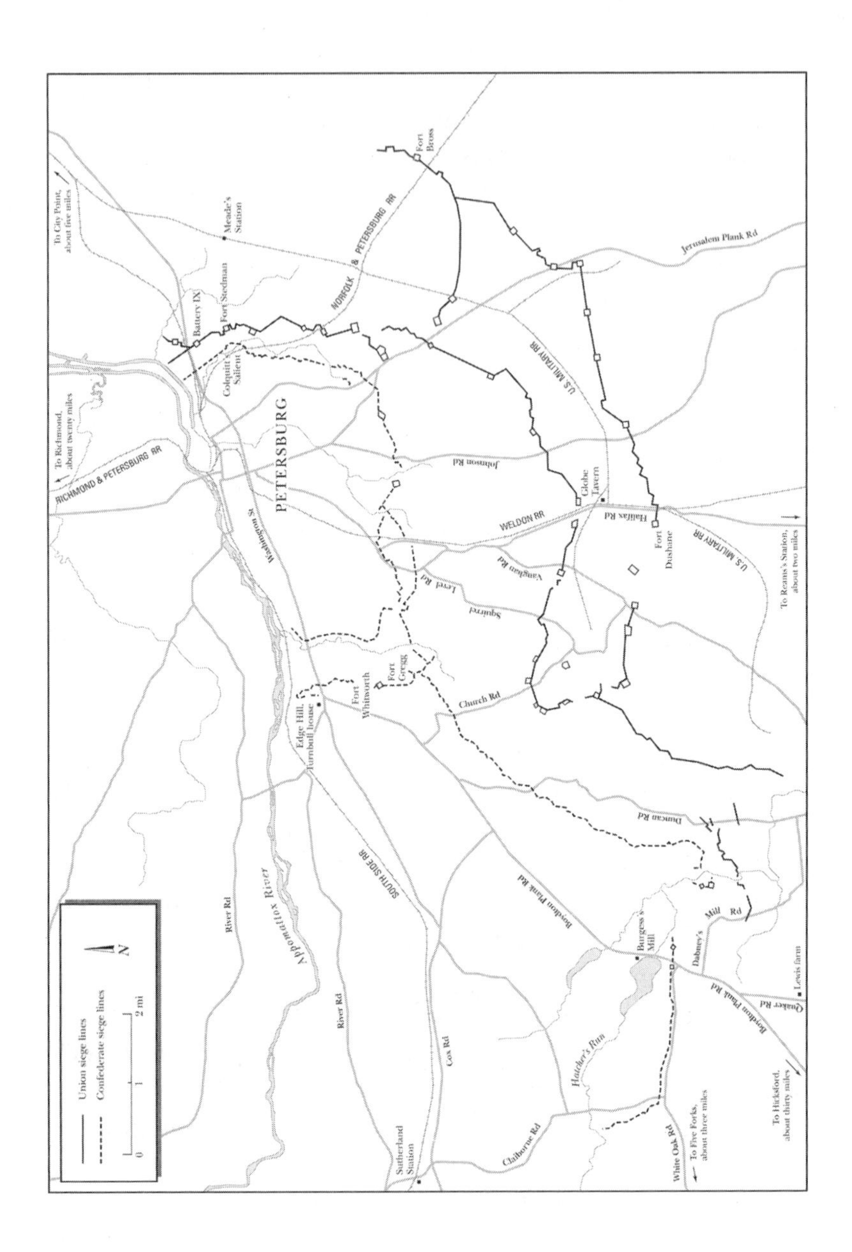

Map 6. Petersburg, Winter 1864–65

and extended the Union siege lines westward. Warren's accomplishment, as historian Hess notes, "pointed the way for future operations: make short movements to the left to extend the line in stages, something the Army of the Potomac was fully capable of doing."[10]

While it was Warren who hit upon the concept of moving westward and then entrenching his extended lines, his superior was ultimately responsible for conducting the campaign. Grant deserves credit for recognizing the value of the Globe Tavern motif and making it the fundamental Union operational plan at Petersburg. The Federal commander originally intended that Warren destroy some of the Weldon Railroad and draw the Southern infantrymen out of their fortifications. After Grant considered the larger consequences of what his subordinate had accomplished at Globe Tavern, he made it a model for his operations for the remainder of the Petersburg campaign.[11]

Grant's operational plan that followed from Warren's accomplishments at Globe Tavern carried several benefits to the Federals. Each time the Union commander stretched his lines westward, he forced Lee to do the same. The Confederates, with fewer infantrymen and artillery pieces than their enemy had, were forced to defend the same length of front. By early 1865 the opposing lines ran about thirty-seven miles from the Mechanicsville Turnpike northeast of Richmond to Hatcher's Run southwest of Petersburg.[12]

The Union's active operations also wore down the Army of Northern Virginia although on a reduced scale from the previous spring's battles of attrition in the Wilderness and around Spotsylvania. Through the autumn of 1864 and into the winter, Grant hit at Lee time and again north and south of the James. Striking on both sides of the river became a "familiar ploy" of Grant's, as historian Brooks Simpson points out, and served to keep his opponent off balance.[13] This motif also produced a number of small but costly battles. The attrition from these combats, and from desertion, continually depleted the Southern units.

By pushing their lines to the south and west, the Federals gained in still another way. Their movements threatened the highways and railroads that ran into Petersburg, carrying the economic lifeblood of what remained of the Confederacy. If the Northerners severed all of these lines into the city, its residents and Lee's soldiers would be rendered helpless.

In February 1865 a few key routes to the west and south still remained open: the River Road, the Cox Road, and, most important, the South Side Railroad. To shield these arteries, the Confederates had dug a line of works about seven miles long, reaching from the main defenses of Petersburg southwest to Hatcher's Run. To the west, another line of field fortifications covered the Boydton Plank Road in the area of Burgess's Mill. The main Federal works paralleled the Confederate defenses, and their western extensions reached toward the Boydton Plank Road at a point about ten miles southwest of Petersburg.[14]

During the first week of February 1865, while Maj. Gen. William T. Sherman was taking his first strides into South Carolina, Grant turned his attention to the Boydton Plank Road, which remained an important Southern supply route. In December 1864 the Federals had destroyed that line as far south as Hicksford, about forty miles below Petersburg. Grant had received intelligence that the Southerners were bringing supplies by train to that point and transferring them to wagons. These vehicles then carried the matériel upstream along the Meherrin River, west to the Boydton Plank Road, and took the highway through Dinwiddie Court House to Petersburg. Grant directed an operation against this Confederate line of supply that historian Earl Hess identifies as the "Seventh Union Offensive" at Petersburg.[15]

This offensive began when a Union cavalry division forayed out to seize the Boydton Plank Road at Dinwiddie Court House and to capture or destroy whatever wagons it could surprise. The Union troopers left their camps at 3:00 a.m. on February 5, moved through Reams's Station on the Weldon Railroad, and went on to Dinwiddie Court House. They rode through icy weather, the worst conditions of what already had been a hard winter at Petersburg.[16]

Warren's V Corps supported these cavalrymen, and the II Corps also participated in the operation. It was led by Maj. Gen. Andrew A. Humphreys, who had been the Army of the Potomac's chief of

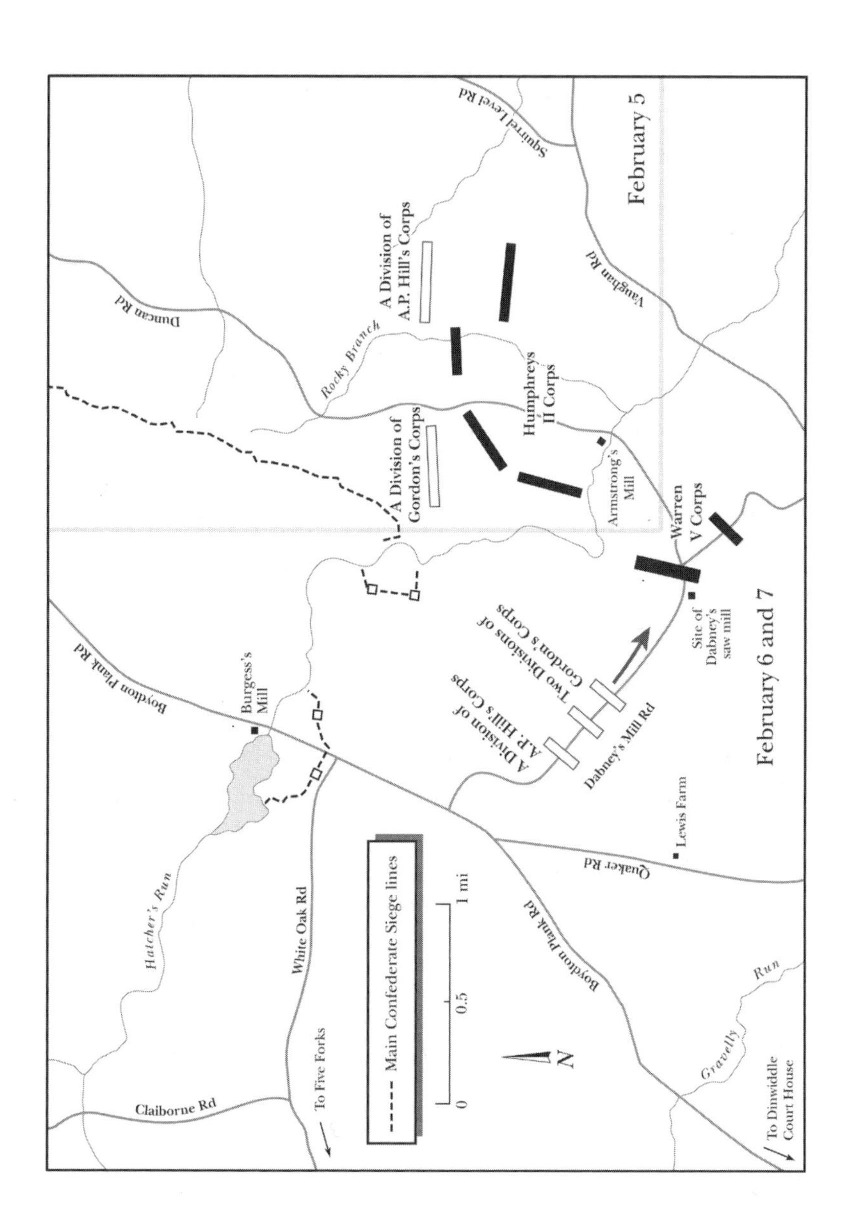

MAP 7. Battle of Hatcher's Run, February 5–7, 1865

staff and then succeeded the popular Maj. Gen. Winfield Scott Hancock as corps commander. General "Hancock's departure created an opening for which [General Humphreys] was eminently qualified," writes historian A. Wilson Greene. "His appointment was met with wide approval throughout the army."[17]

Between Humphreys and Warren, the former drew the more dangerous mission as his men would move against the main line of the Confederate defenses, whose fieldworks the Southerners had improved during the winter. Humphreys commanded three divisions. Leaving one in its own siege line entrenchments, he deployed the other two at the Armstrong's Mill and the Vaughn Road crossings of Hatcher's Run, a tributary of Rowanty Creek. Warren put all three of his divisions on the march, dealt with some Confederate pickets he encountered, and bridged Rowanty Creek. On the afternoon of February 5, the V Corps took up a position south of the II Corps.[18]

That Sunday, the fifth, passed rather quietly for the Federal cavalrymen. The Union riders gained their objective—the Boydton Plank Road at Dinwiddie Court House. From there they scouted the highway, both north and south, and their senior officer reported that they captured "some wagons and prisoners." Having determined that the Confederates were not making much use of the Boydton Plank Road, the Federal horsemen pulled back to Rowanty Creek.[19]

To the east, the II Corps took up a good position but found itself stymied by Confederate forces in its path. One division pushed across Hatcher's Run at Armstrong's Mill and deployed to cover this crossing point, resting its right flank on a little swamp. Its men found a line of sophisticated Confederate fieldworks a thousand yards in their front that had been prepared during recent weeks. The Union advance was halted.[20]

Back in Petersburg, Lee, who had recently become the general in chief of all Confederate armies, was attending church when he was told about the Federals' movement to the Boydton Plank Road and Hatcher's Run. At first he seemed unconcerned by the news, but when it came time to take communion, the general did not, as always, wait his turn. He instead went to the chancel with the first group of worshippers, received the elements, gathered his hat and gloves, and left the sanctuary.[21]

Before Lee reached the front, he was well served by his alert subordinates, who did not intend to let the Federals advance to the Boydton Plank Road and Hatcher's Run without a challenge. Lt. Gen. Ambrose P. Hill's Corps held the western end of the Petersburg lines. General Hill had led the Light Division and then, beginning with the Pennsylvania campaign, a corps. To his left was Maj. Gen. John B. Gordon's Corps. General Gordon had been severely wounded in Sharpsburg's Bloody Lane, had been promoted to major general in May 1864, and became a corps commander during the Petersburg campaign.[22]

Two divisions, one each from Gordon's and Hill's Corps, were the units that had blocked the Federals at Armstrong's Mill. During the late afternoon of February 5, the Confederate artillery opened fire, and then their infantry attacked. The Federals fended off this advance, but the Southerners made a determined showing and kept up their cannon fire after they fell back.[23]

This Confederate riposte drew the attention of the commander of the Army of the Potomac. During the night of the fifth, Meade ordered Warren to advance to support Humphreys. The army commander also directed the V Corps's leader to recall the Union cavalry from its disappointing raid on the Boydton Plank Road and use it to cover his march toward the II Corps. The Federal troopers reported to Warren before daylight on February 6.[24]

On the afternoon of Monday, the sixth, the V Corps moved up behind the II Corps. The Union horsemen scouted toward Gravelly Run, another tributary of Rowanty Creek, while Warren's infantrymen advanced toward Dabney's Mill, where a large pile of sawdust marked the site of an antebellum steam-powered sawmill.[25] Warren ordered the cavalrymen to cover the left of the infantry. The Federal troopers and soldiers pressed ahead into uninviting terrain, which a Pennsylvania colonel described as "rolling and principally covered with a heavy growth of wood, part of it with thick underbrush, a swamp, and several old fields."[26]

The Federals encountered another of Gordon's divisions, commanded by Brig. Gen. John A. Pegram, who was a veteran of the western theater, the Wilderness, and the 1864 Valley campaign and recently a groom.[27] The Union troopers and soldiers had the advantage of numbers, and they began gaining ground. General Pegram was pulling back his men slowly when the division to his left shifted away from the Armstrong's Mill front and came to his aid. The Confederates waged a stout fight, and a third division joined them.[28]

Warren saw that the advantage of numbers had swung to the Southerners. Writing about the battle later, he concluded that the deciding factor had been that "the enemy got up re-enforcements faster than I could." A staff officer agreed with Warren: "I do not wonder at our men breaking, since the enemy had three divisions against us, or about three men to our one, and one of those divisions was quite fresh while our men had been on foot for fifty hours and were nearly played out."[29]

The Confederates then launched a determined assault that proved too much for the V Corps's soldiers. Warren acknowledged in his official report: "Our line, despite all the exertions of the prominent officers and much good conduct among those in the ranks, gave way and fell back rapidly, but with little loss after the movement began." The general's remarks off the record were more candid: "We are getting to have an array of such poor soldiers that we have to lead them everywhere, and even then they run away from us." A veteran of the Twentieth Maine, a regiment famous for its fighting at Gettysburg's Little Round Top and Spotsylvania's Laurel Hill, despaired that his unit "got frightened and 'skedaddled' back through the woods like a flock of sheep." A noncommissioned officer of the 143rd Pennsylvania was fortunate to remain in his regiment's camp during the battle and serve as sergeant of the guard. Many years later, he recalled the "stragglers and shirks . . . coming into camp with tales of terrible slaughter. Along came a force of Provosts and gathered them up, and took them back to the front."[30]

The Confederate attack that put the Federals into flight proved to be the last main action of the day. The Southern success was marred when a sharpshooter killed Pegram just south of the Dabney's Mill Road. Col. Henry Kyd Douglas later recalled: "General Pegram was shot through the body near the heart. I jumped from my horse and caught him as he fell and with assistance took him from his horse. He died in my arms, almost as soon as he touched the ground." Pegram's funeral was held in Saint Paul's Episcopal Church in Richmond, where, three weeks before, he had been married.[31]

The Confederates had lost a division commander but had turned back Warren, Humphreys, and a cavalry division. After the fighting on February 6, the two sides suffered a cold and icy night. A young Confederate artilleryman recalled that "the weather was of a freezing kind—raining and freezing. Then, too, the soldiers were so poorly clad."[32]

A Pennsylvania cavalryman gave a bleak description of the next day's weather: "February 7, 1865, extremely disagreeable; raining and sleeting." The fighting on that Tuesday was "not so hard" as on the previous day, one V Corps veteran jotted in his journal. Warren reformed his units, tested the Confederate picket lines a bit, took into account "the severe storm which prevailed all day," and decided to break off the action.[33] The Battle of Hatcher's Run sputtered to a desultory end.

"Our loss," Lee said of the engagement, "is reported to be small." No official account of Confederate casualties at Hatcher's Run survived the war; historians commonly estimated them as totaling about 1,000.[34] Warren reported that the total losses in the V Corps came to more than 1,100.[35] Humphreys stated that his command lost 138 killed and wounded in the encounter at Armstrong's Mill.[36]

Hatcher's Run represented one of several small but hard-fought engagements of the Petersburg campaign. In its aftermath, the Southerners believed they had won an operational victory. They thought they had thwarted a Federal effort to gain permanent control of the Boydton Plank Road. (The Confederates did not know that the Northerners, having determined that their opponents were not making much use of that highway, became less interested in holding it and more interested in extending the siege lines westward.) The fight at Hatcher's Run and the return to active operations bolstered Southern spirits. By mid-March the desertion rate in Hill's Corps had dropped.[37]

For the Northerners, the chief benefit of their seventh offensive of the campaign, as with a number of other Union operations around Petersburg, was that it allowed them to stretch their field fortifications farther west. After the Battle of Hatcher's Run, Grant made the last continuous extension of his line westward. "Our entrenchments were now extended," Humphreys pointed out, "to Hatcher's Run at the Vaughn road crossing."[38] Along the segment of the front from the Appomattox River downstream from Petersburg to Hatcher's Run, the Federals now held fifteen miles of connected infantry and artillery fieldworks.[39]

Grant's last extension of his lines westward forced Lee to defend a front that was too long for his available manpower. Well before the Battle of Hatcher's Run, the Confederate commander understood the implications of his opponent's operations, but he had no remedy at hand. Lee lacked the soldiers and field guns to defend adequately a line that stretched roughly thirty-seven miles. As Gordon remembered the situation long after the war, by March 1865 his own corps was so attenuated that his "men stood like a row of vedettes, fifteen feet apart, in the trenches."[40]

The Battle of Hatcher's Run was followed by another peace initiative. On February 21, two weeks after the Confederate commissioners returned to Richmond from the failed Hampton Roads conference, Ord sent a flag of truce across the lines to Lt. Gen. James Longstreet, a prewar acquaintance who now was Lee's senior corps commander. The commander of the Army of the James suggested a meeting to discuss a routine matter, and General Longstreet surmised that the Federal general had something weightier in mind. Longstreet answered quickly, naming a date and place where he would see Ord.[41]

When the two generals met, Ord's real business became apparent. He told Longstreet that the Northern politicians were afraid of the peace question and that only the military leaders of the two sides could approach the subject. He proposed a cease-fire, then a meeting between Grant and Lee, followed by an exchange of social visits by Northern and Southern senior officers and their wives. He hoped the meetings would lead ultimately to "terms honorable to both sides."[42]

Longstreet reported his conversation with Ord, and President Jefferson Davis considered the Union general's proposal with Secretary of War John C. Breckinridge, Lee, and Longstreet. The group agreed to pursue this peace initiative, beginning with another Longstreet-Ord meeting.[43]

The two generals conferred again, and Ord asked that Lee write to Grant and propose a meeting. On March 2 Lee sent two letters to Grant. The first, dealing with political prisoners, was a blind cover for the second, which asked for an interview to discuss "the possibility of arriving at a satisfactory adjustment of the present unhappy difficulties by means of a military convention."[44]

On the same day Lee wrote to Grant, March 2, the final act of a Confederate disaster played out in the Shenandoah Valley. Maj. Gen. Philip H. Sheridan, the hard-driving Federal commander known as "Little Phil," smashed up what remained of Lt. Gen. Jubal A. Early's command in the Battle of Waynesboro. Lee predicted that the Union force that had conquered the Shenandoah Valley—almost twenty thousand men, he believed—now would join the masses Grant already had around Petersburg.[45]

While the Federals celebrated their triumph in the Valley, President Lincoln advised Grant on how to answer Lee's correspondence. On March 3 the chief executive wrote to his senior general through Secretary of War Edwin Stanton and forcefully made known his views. Grant was to meet with Lee only to receive his surrender or to discuss "some minor and purely military matter."[46]

While Lee awaited Grant's reply, he could only hope that something would come of this political initiative, for the Confederacy's military outlook was bleak on every horizon. The Shenandoah Valley had been lost. General Sherman was moving through South Carolina, and Gen. Joseph E. Johnston was trying to pull together enough units in North Carolina to resist him.

Lee's own immediate situation in early March offered more cause for despair. Spring would return to Virginia, and the Federals would resume active campaigning. Grant inevitably would force Lee yet again to extend his already tenuous siege lines. The Confederates lacked the resources to answer indefinitely every

Union threat north and south of the James. Eventually Lee's thin line would become untenable.

Lee considered what he could do to alter this chain of events. After the calamitous news had arrived from the Valley, the Confederate commander struggled with his strategic problems during the night of March 3–4.[47] During those hours Lee also waited for Grant's answer to his request for a military convention though he held little hope for that initiative. On March 2 he had confided to President Davis: "I have proposed to Genl Grant an interview, in the hope that some good may result, but I must confess that I am not sanguine."[48]

During the dead of night on March 3–4, as Gordon told the story many years later, Lee summoned him rather than his more experienced commanders because the young officer was closer at hand than either Longstreet or Lt. Gen. Richard S. Ewell, and Hill was not available. Gordon reported to Lee's headquarters in the William Turnbull residence known as Edge Hill, on the Cox Road west of Petersburg, during the early morning hours of March 4.[49]

Given the late date of Gordon's account, it is difficult to say what passed between the two generals that night. According to Gordon, Lee presented him with the gloomy news from every front and asked for his views.[50] Lee did not tell his young subordinate about the Ord-Longstreet peace initiative; the Confederate president alone was privy to Lee's correspondence with Grant. According to Gordon, Lee told him that he was going to Richmond, and after his return he would send for the young corps commander again.[51]

On the morning of March 4, the day that Lincoln would deliver his second inaugural address, Lee traveled to Richmond, conferred with Davis, and learned that Grant's reply to his request for a military convention had arrived. With Lincoln's guidance at hand, the Federal commander had thrown cold water on the proposed meeting. "I have no authority," Grant stated, "to accede to your proposition for a conference on the subject proposed. Such authority is vested in the President of the United States alone."[52]

With the peace conference dead, Lee and Davis turned to the strategic possibility of joining the forces in Virginia with those in North Carolina. Lee proposed abandoning Petersburg and Richmond, linking with General Johnston, and striking Sherman and then Grant. Davis seemed resigned to the loss of the capital and questioned only why his general did not set out immediately. Lee explained that the horses of the Army of Northern Virginia were too weak to pull the wagons through the winter mud. The movement must wait for the early spring weather to dry the roads, for the animals to be strengthened, and for stores to be positioned along the South Side and Danville Railroads.

Returning to the Petersburg front, Lee conferred again with Gordon. He told his subordinate that the Petersburg defenders must fight Grant. The remaining question was one of timing. On the one hand, Lee knew it would take weeks to address the logistical issues that he had discussed with Davis. On the other hand, General Sheridan soon would bring his command from the Valley to join Grant. Little Phil's arrival would give the Federals overwhelming strength, and they would use it to close out the Petersburg siege.[53]

On March 11 Sherman captured Fayetteville and opened communication with Maj. Gen. Alfred H. Terry's Provisional Corps at Wilmington. Johnston wrote to warn Lee that if the Union commands in North Carolina united, he could not stop them from moving into Virginia. At the end of this dark dispatch, Old Joe suggested a new strategic plan: perhaps Lee should not take all of his forces out of Petersburg and Richmond; instead, he possibly could hold the inner defenses of the capital with part of his command and "meet Sherman with the other, returning to Richmond after the fighting."[54]

Johnston's suggestion—Longstreet had proposed something along the same lines—appealed to Lee because it would avoid, at least for a time, abandoning Richmond to the enemy. The first step in executing this plan would be to deliver a hard blow against Grant. Lee directed Gordon to study the Union siege lines and determine if they could be broken. This directive took the first step toward what later would be called the "Third Confederate Offensive" at Petersburg.[55]

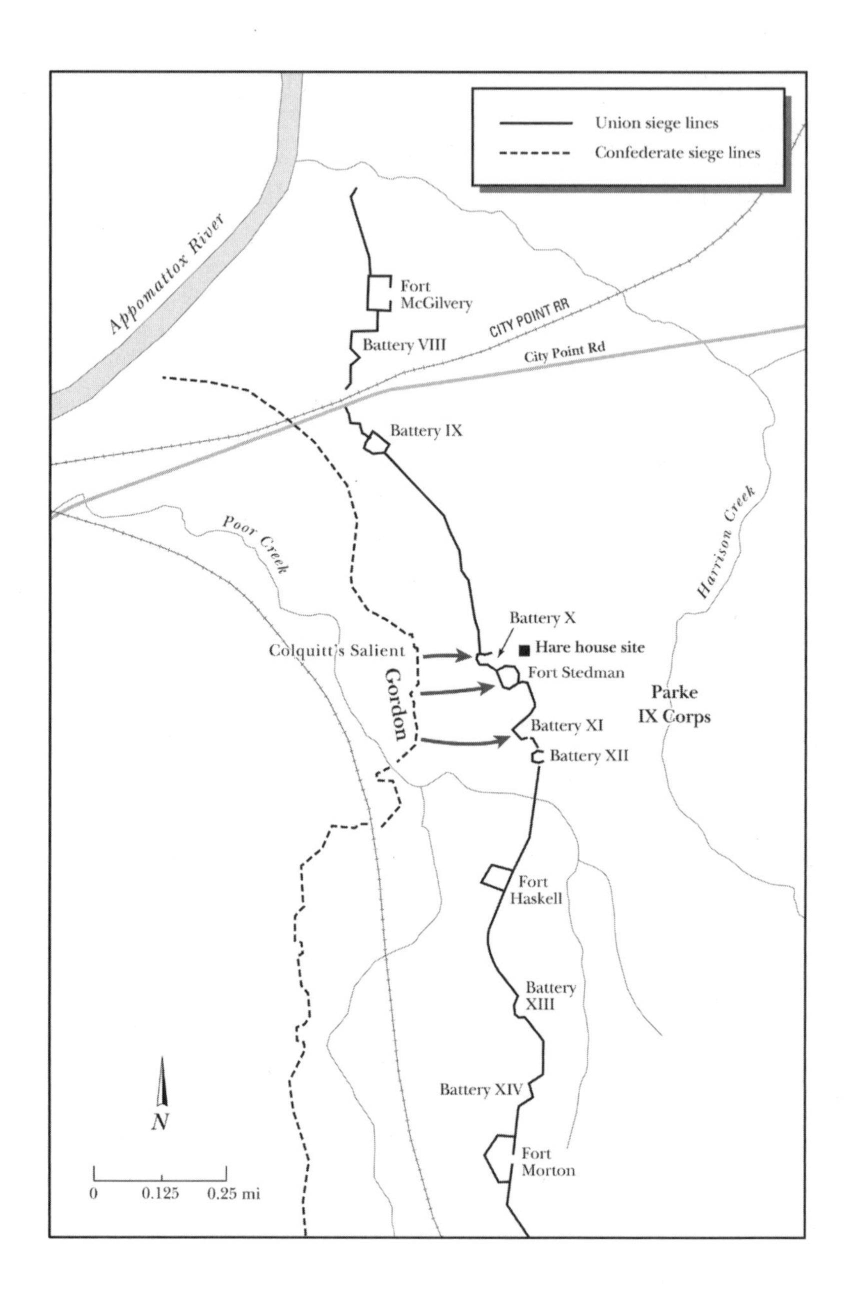

MAP 8. Battle of Fort Stedman, March 25, 1865

Gordon and his officers collected valuable information from Union prisoners and deserters and from close scrutiny of the enemy's works. After a thorough study, the corps commander reported to Lee that he could take Fort Stedman, a fortification that stood less than a mile northeast of the already famous Crater. The term "fort" might call to mind the wooden stockades associated with frontier posts, but the forts of the Petersburg siege were the heavily fortified strongpoints that stood along each contender's main trench line. There was no firm standard as to precisely how formidable a redoubt had to be to rate the designation "fort"; the Federals used the term far more freely than the Confederates did.[56]

The Northerners had constructed Fort Stedman at the eastern end of a small plateau called "Hare's Hill." This terrain was named after Otway P. Hare's house, which stood on it until June 18, 1864, when it was destroyed during the initial assaults on Petersburg. From here, the Federals commanded an open field of fire toward the Confederate trench lines.[57] They named the fort for brevet Brig. Gen. Griffin A. Stedman, Jr., of Connecticut, who had been fatally wounded on August 5, 1864, while reconnoitering this part of the Petersburg front with Brig. Gen. Adelbert Ames.[58]

Stedman was an oddity among the Petersburg forts in that several trees remained standing inside it; the men had left them to offer shade to the garrison. By March 1865, very little natural growth or farm fencing remained anywhere else in the area. The soldiers had used most of the region's trees, scrubs, and fences to construct defenses, to supply firewood, or to build huts.[59]

Fort Stedman stood only about 260 yards from Colquitt's Salient, a strongpoint on the main Confederate siege line.[60] The Southerners had named this fortification for Brig. Gen. Alfred H. Colquitt, a brigade commander in Lee's army and a veteran of the Battle of Olustee, Florida.[61] General Colquitt's men had been the first to occupy this stronghold.[62]

Gordon's scouts could see the vulnerabilities of Fort Stedman. So could the Southern pickets, who were deployed only about fifty yards from their counterparts covering the fortification. It was small, relative to other Petersburg works of its kind, taking up only about three-fourths of an acre. Fort Stedman's parapet had deteriorated as it had not been properly compacted and frost had loosened its dirt.[63] An almost entirely fallow cornfield lay between Fort Stedman and Colquitt's Salient. This open ground and the short distance between the two fortifications had prevented the Federals from making any repairs to Stedman.[64]

Gordon appreciated the advantages the Confederates enjoyed along this sector of the siege lines. The low ground behind Colquitt's Salient would allow the Southerners to form for an assault unseen by their opponents. A dash across the old cornfield would put the attackers into the Union works. And a worthy target beckoned not far behind Stedman. About a mile and a half east of the fort stood Meade's Station on the United States Military Railroad, the line that supplied the besieging Federals from their enormous base at City Point. Destruction of this rail depot, at least for a time, would disrupt Union operations against Petersburg.[65]

The odds against an attack succeeding were long but not impossible. While Grant had forced Lee to stretch his lines, he likewise had had to extend his own. For example, the IX Corps, which had about eighteen thousand men on its returns on March 20, had to cover a front of seven miles.[66] Taking into account soldiers who were ill, under arrest, or for whatever reasons not on duty and allowing for reserves, the unit's manning of its front line was limited.

Reflecting this larger situation, Fort Stedman's garrison, provided by the IX Corps, was modest in size. Four twelve-pounder Napoleons of the Nineteenth Battery, New York Light Artillery, commanded by Capt. Edward W. Rogers, stood within the fortification.[67] These guns were supported by eight companies of Maj. George M. Randall's Fourteenth New York Heavy Artillery. The soldiers assigned to the heavy artillery regiments had been trained to man the large guns of Washington DC's defenses. They also knew how to handle a shoulder arm, and when Federal losses began mounting during the spring of 1864, Grant transferred some of these soldiers from the forts around the national capital to the front lines in Virginia.[68]

The Fourteenth New York "heavies" supported the four smoothbores of the Nineteenth New York Battery, but that was not their only responsibility. They also had to cover Battery X, the next Federal emplacement along the siege line to the right and just northwest of Stedman. And the heavies held another hundred yards of the main Federal trenches beyond Battery X.[69]

Fort Stedman stood between Federal Batteries X and XI, which were stout earthworks that protected some of the most important Union artillery positions. Their numerals began with I, which was given to a gun emplacement at Rushmore's, the colonial plantation of Thomas Rushmore lying between the Appomattox River and the River Road. The battery numbers increased as the Union line ran south to Battery XXXI near Fort Dushane on the Weldon Railroad. From there, a major line of trenches covered the Federal rear area by running east and ending near Battery XLII, which was north of Fort Bross.[70]

Defending the Fort Stedman sector of the front was the responsibility of the IX Corps, an organization whose leadership had improved during the Petersburg campaign. The corps had labored under Maj. Gen. Ambrose E. Burnside until shortly after the Battle of the Crater on July 30, 1864. About two weeks after that debacle, the able Maj. Gen. John G. Parke replaced General Burnside in command of the IX Corps.[71]

Lee concluded that a well-planned attack on the IX Corps's sector might break the Federals' hold on Fort Stedman and its neighboring defenses. Even if Gordon's attack fell short of gaining Meade's Station, it still might disrupt the Union front and force Grant to tighten his lines. Then Lee would be able to hold Petersburg with fewer defenders and to dispatch a sizable command to join Johnston and operate against Sherman.[72]

Failing these efforts, if the Federals turned back Gordon's attack, the strategic situation would be no darker for the Confederates than before his attempt. Beyond whatever losses the attackers incurred, the Southerners would be no worse off. Lee and Davis already had resigned themselves to abandoning Petersburg and Richmond and taking the entire Army of Northern Virginia toward a junction with Johnston. If Gordon's attempt failed, that option remained open.[73]

During March 19–21 Johnston fought Sherman at Bentonville. The engagement raised Southern morale, but it fell short of winning a strategic or even an operational victory. On March 23 Johnston informed Lee that he could do no more than "annoy" Sherman. In Johnston's view, only one strategic option remained to the Confederates: Lee would have to elude Grant and join Johnston in contending with Sherman.[74]

By the twenty-third Lee concluded that Sheridan had joined the Federals at Petersburg, adding a heavy weight to the scales that tipped against the Confederate defenders. Soon Grant would be operating again to the west of Petersburg, either cutting the last Southern supply lines or stretching their defenses beyond endurance. Lee would wait no longer. That night he approved the attack on Fort Stedman.[75]

The assault's main force was composed of nearly all of Gordon's three divisions. Those few of his soldiers who did not make the attack were left to hold the siege line for their entire corps. Gordon's main body included two other brigades, which came from the one division that remained assigned to the corps of Lt. Gen. Richard H. "Fighting Dick" Anderson. These two brigades and Gordon's Corps totaled about 11,500 effectives.[76]

Other Confederate units were given roles in the breakout effort. Two brigades from Hill's Corps, or another seventeen hundred men, stood in support of the main attack force. Gordon also expected one of Longstreet's divisions to shift from the north side of the James River to the Fort Stedman sector. This unit could contribute another sixty-five hundred soldiers to the effort, but Lee doubted it could reach the scene in time to help. Finally a cavalry division was positioned to exploit any success the infantrymen won. In all, nearly half the Confederate army would either make or support Gordon's assault.[77]

Gordon meticulously planned the attack on Fort Stedman. In the predawn darkness of Saturday, March 25, advance parties would clear away the obstacles that protected their own front and would open up lanes for the assault troops to follow. (Removing these defenses any sooner would alert the Federals to the attack.) Handpicked soldiers then would advance quietly and carry out the dangerous work of silencing the Union pickets and clearing routes through the enemy's abatis, or a defensive obstacle of felled trees whose branches could ensnare attackers. Fraises—pointed stakes—also bristled in front of Stedman and its neighboring batteries. Fifty Southerners carrying axes would chop through these obstructions. Following on their heels, three storming parties of a hundred men each would execute the essential mission: they would overpower the garrisons of Stedman and of Batteries X, XI, and XII.[78]

Gordon's study of the Union position led him to believe that several strongholds were in the rear of Stedman.[79] Once the fort and its nearby batteries had been captured, local guides, selected by Lee himself, would lead three groups farther east. These parties, again consisting of a hundred men each, would raid deeper into the Federal position and would locate and secure the strongpoints behind Stedman.[80] Once these fieldworks were in Confederate hands, Gordon's three divisions would widen the gap opened in the Union siege line. The two follow-on brigades then would attack, and the cavalry division would ride through the breach and raid into the enemy's rear.[81]

The attack against the Fort Stedman sector began in the early morning gloom of March 25. Confederate advance parties cleared away their own obstructions in front of Colquitt's Salient. As Gordon related the story decades later, a private fired a signal shot that launched the attack but only after gallantly calling out a warning to the Union pickets.[82]

This signal shot rang out shortly after 4:00 a.m., or about half an hour before daybreak. A division commander recalled the advance of his soldiers: "The cool, frosty morning made every sound distinct and clear, and the only sound heard was the tramp! tramp! of the men as they kept step as regularly as if on drill." A private related that his storming party "with unloaded muskets and a profound silence, leaped over our breastworks, [and] dashed across the open space in front."[83]

When the Confederates rushed forward, at least one Federal on the picket line escaped to raise a frightened alarm. Two cannons, three-inch ordnance rifles, barked out from Battery X, but Gordon's men quickly stormed over the fortification and captured it. The commotion from this action to the northwest alerted Captain Rogers inside Fort Stedman. "The guard of my pieces [the Napoleons of the Nineteenth New York Light Artillery]," he related, "immediately discharged the guns, which were kept loaded with canister." Unhappily for the Federals, these tubes were trained on the main Confederate works, not on Battery X, and did nothing to relieve their immediate tactical problem. Gordon's men swarmed over Fort Stedman. "The Confederates climbed over the parapets and in at the embrasures," one Northerner remembered, "and it was so dark that the garrison could not distinguish their own men from the enemy."[84]

Gordon's carefully planned formations and storm tactics won initial successes along the Union front. The Confederates quickly secured Fort Stedman. A Union brigade commander rode into the fortification only to find it full of Southerners and himself a prisoner.[85] To the south of Stedman, Gordon's men overran Battery XI before it could fire a shot, and farther down the main Federal line, they captured Battery XII. "Up to this point," Gordon wrote long afterward, "the success had exceeded my most sanguine expectations."[86]

The three raiding parties fanned out in search of the forts that Gordon believed stood in the rear of Stedman and its neighboring batteries. The Confederate corps commander now suffered his first setback. He received a report from one of the raiding parties: it had lost its guide during the advance from Colquitt's Salient, had wandered around in a maze of supporting trenches east of Stedman, and had failed to find the objective forts. Equally discouraging reports soon arrived from the other parties.[87]

Many years later, Humphreys offered a simple explanation for the enemy's dilemma: Gordon had worked from faulty intelligence. In "point of fact," the commander of the II Corps explained, "there were no such forts." Union artilleryman brevet Brig. Gen. John C. Tidball, however, contradicted Humphreys and identified the three objectives as Fort Friend, Battery IV, and Fort Avery. Whatever the merits of this dispute, the Confederates certainly gained initial successes, but then they lost valuable time searching in the rear of Stedman for strongpoints—whether they were nonexistent or elusive.[88]

The rising sun brightened the area that the Confederates had seized, and the time came for the secondary units to help the first attackers. Cars of the Richmond and Petersburg Railroad were to bring a division from north of the James to the Stedman front, but as Lee had thought, the unit did not arrive soon enough to help. Gordon did have the two brigades from Hill's Corps already at hand, but for whatever reason, he made no use of them.[89]

When the Confederates failed to exploit their initial success, the defenders overcame the shock of Gordon's bolt out of the predawn darkness. Fortunately for the IX Corps, it had forces available to meet the crisis. Brig. Gen. John F. Hartranft, who had led the Fifty-first Pennsylvania across Burnside's Bridge during the Battle of Antietam, commanded its reserve division in the area.[90] The left flank of General Hartranft's division, composed of six regiments from the Keystone State, rested behind Fort Prescott, and the right was only about a mile northeast of Fort Stedman. Hartranft did not officially report the strength of his command, but long after the war he estimated that "nearly 4000 men" counterattacked the Confederates that morning.[91]

Hartranft learned about the Stedman attack around 4:30 a.m., or about half an hour into the action. He dispatched a staff officer to investigate the alarm and readied his two brigades for action. He rode toward the headquarters of another IX division and, along the way, encountered his own 200th and 209th Pennsylvania Regiments, which already were moving forward. "It was not yet light enough to see the enemy," Hartranft wrote, "nor could any sound be heard, owing to the direction of the wind, but the white puffs indicated musketry-firing, and, being in the rear of our lines, disclosed unmistakably an attack in force, and not a feint."[92]

The 200th and 209th Pennsylvania Regiments made preliminary, and unsuccessful, advances against the Confederates at Fort Stedman and the breach around it. Hartranft built up his strength in the area and began hemming in Gordon's soldiers. By 7:30 a.m. the Federals had regained Batteries XI and XII and had driven the Confederates back into Fort Stedman and Battery X.[93]

General Parke, the leader of the IX Corps, temporarily commanded the Army of the Potomac that morning in Meade's absence. At Grant's invitation, the commander in chief and his wife, Mary Todd Lincoln, had arrived at City Point on March 24 to visit the general and Julia Dent Grant. In addition to the social occasion, the men were to conduct military discussions, and as the commander of the Army of the Potomac, Meade would attend them. Ord already was at City Point, Meade spent the night of the twenty-fourth and twenty-fifth there, Sheridan would arrive on the twenty-sixth, and Sherman was expected on the following day. During the Stedman attack, the Confederates cut the telegraph line to the key Union supply base. With Meade out of communication, Parke, as the army's senior ranking army corps commander, became its acting head.[94]

Parke believed that the momentum had shifted to the Federals, and about 7:30 a.m. he ordered Hartranft to retake Fort Stedman and Battery X. The division commander formed his Pennsylvanians in a long semicircle that reached around the Confederate intruders. Hartranft described the action years later: "The long line of the 211th [Pennsylvania] lifted itself with cadenced step over the brow of the hill and swept down in magnificent style toward Fort Stedman. . . . The enemy, apparently taken by surprise and magnifying the mass pouring down the hill into the sweep of a whole brigade, began to waver, and the rest of the Third [Hartranft's] Division, responding to the signal, rose with loud cheers and sprang forward to the charge." The attack succeeded.[95]

Lee rode from his headquarters at the Turnbull house and watched the breakout attempt. At about the time Hartranft was preparing his counterblow, the Confederate commander arrived at the same assessment of the situation that Parke had. Lee gave Gordon permission to break off the action.[96]

By then, however, retreating to Colquitt's Salient had become a dangerous option for the Southerners. "The cross-fire of artillery and infantry on the space between the lines," Humphreys pointed out, "prevented the enemy who were in our works from escaping, and reinforcements from coming to them." The artillery fire was dangerously heavy. Ordnance Sgt. James W. Albright, an artilleryman in Anderson's Corps, entered in his diary: "Our battalion had 20 guns engaged for 35 minutes and showed by [a] report filed with me that 744 shells were fired. The explosion of shell looked as thick as lightning bugs over [a] meadow because where we fired one shot[,] the Yanks fired 10 to 20." Rather than run the gauntlet of this artillery and small arms fire, many of Gordon's men preferred to surrender; nearly two thousand of them did so.[97]

After the Confederate prisoners had been rounded up and the Union victory sealed, Lincoln and Grant traveled from City Point to visit Fort Stedman. Arriving just hours after the fighting ended, they saw the stark aftermath of recent combat. The president viewed the dead of both sides and the wounded who had not yet been removed from the field. At Meade's headquarters, the army commander greeted the commander in chief: "I have just now a dispatch from General Parke to show you." Lincoln pointed to a large collection of Southern prisoners who stood nearby. "Ah," the president said, "*there* is the best dispatch you can show me from General Parke!"[98]

Senior Union officers estimated that their opponents suffered total casualties of about 4,000 in the Fort Stedman attack. Parke reported that the IX Corps lost 1,044: 72 killed, 450 wounded, and 522 captured or missing.[99]

Gordon's effort against Fort Stedman represented the third—and last—Confederate offensive at Petersburg. It ended in total failure. Grant's hold on his siege lines remained firm. Lee knew that the Army of Northern Virginia could not stay in Petersburg much longer.

CHAPTER SIX

The Fall of Petersburg

On March 28, 1865, three days after the attack on Fort Stedman, President Abraham Lincoln, Lt. Gen. Ulysses S. Grant, Maj. Gen. William T. Sherman, and Rear Adm. David Dixon Porter met on the *River Queen* at a wharf in City Point, Virginia. General Grant described the strategy he would implement that spring. He intended to continue moving west until he cut off Gen. Robert E. Lee's right flank and ended any chance that his opponent could link with Gen. Joseph E. Johnston. Severing the last rail and road lines into Petersburg from the west, Grant would leave General Lee with the dismal choices of attacking at hopeless odds, starving in place, or retreating from the Cockade City and Richmond. Meanwhile, General Sherman would press his campaign against General Johnston.[1]

President Lincoln, who had just seen the gruesome aftermath of the attack at Fort Stedman, asked Grant and Sherman if the war could be ended without another large battle. Neither general offered Lincoln any hope on this count. Sherman later wrote: "Both General Grant and myself supposed that one or the other of us would have to fight one more bloody battle, and that it would be the *last*."[2]

Sherman asked the president what kind of peace he envisioned, thereby moving the subject of the meeting from strategy to policy. What was to be done with the defeated Southern armies?

How were the Confederate political leaders to be treated? Should they be permitted to escape?[3]

Lincoln cheerfully answered that he was ready for peace. He wanted the Confederates paroled and promptly sent to their farms and other workplaces. The president's worst fear was that the defeated enemy soldiers would not return to their homes and accept federal citizenship and that anarchy would prevail in the South. Lincoln did not say directly but strongly implied that it would be best if Confederate president Jefferson Davis fled the country.[4]

While Sherman took the opportunity of the *River Queen* conference to question Lincoln about the war's end state, Grant did not join this discussion of military policy. The general in chief seemed to understand already the president's ideas about closing out the conflict and restoring the country. Earlier that month, Grant had received the president's guidance that he was to meet with Lee only to receive the surrender of the Army of Northern Virginia or to discuss a specific military issue. National policy was reserved to the authority of the commander in chief. Grant also was familiar with Lincoln's guidance of "let 'em up easy." On the *River Queen*, the senior general was content to present his strategy for the springtime ahead.[5] If Grant had been more active in the discussion of military policy and the end of the war, he might have solicited information from Lincoln that would have benefited Sherman. But Grant had no reason to do so.

Without Grant's further probing of Lincoln's views, Sherman came away from the meeting impressed by the president's desire to end the conflict quickly. In his memoirs, the general recalled that Lincoln had said that "to avoid anarchy," he would grant de facto recognition to the existing Confederate state governments until Congress established other ones. "I know, when I left him," Sherman wrote, "that I was more than ever impressed by his kindly nature, his deep and earnest sympathy with the afflictions of the whole people, resulting from the war . . . and that his earnest desire seemed to be to end the war speedily, without more bloodshed or devastation, and to restore all the men of both sections to their homes."[6] In view of what would happen the next month at the Bennett Place in North Carolina, it appears that Sherman was misled by the discussion on the *River Queen*. He took from the meeting an overemphasis on the president's concern for ending the bloodshed quickly.

By the time of the *River Queen* conference, Grant had ample forces for his drive west, which he described to the president. Maj. Gen. Philip H. Sheridan had arrived from the Shenandoah Valley and was available for new tasks. His veteran and well-equipped mounted command would provide an ideal strike force against Lee's far western flank. And Grant had strong confidence that General Sheridan would pursue this important mission aggressively.[7]

The day before the attack on Fort Stedman, Grant had informed Maj. Gen. George G. Meade, Maj. Gen. Edward O. C. Ord, and Sheridan of his plan for the springtime operations. "On the 29th instant," he directed these subordinates, "the armies operating against Richmond will be moved by our left, for the double purpose of turning the enemy out of his present position around Petersburg and to insure the success of the cavalry under General Sheridan, which will start at the same time, in its efforts to reach and destroy the South Side and Danville railroads."[8]

To reach the first of these objectives, the South Side Railroad, Sheridan would sweep around the Confederate right flank. The South Side Railroad represented a valuable target. It was the Army of Northern Virginia's most important remaining communications line and the only set of tracks into Petersburg that the Confederates still controlled. The South Side Railroad was Lee's last connection to the regions west and south of the beleaguered city and to Johnston.[9]

Sheridan began his mission by assembling three cavalry divisions, or about nine thousand troopers, along the military railroad that brought Federal supplies to the Petersburg siege lines from City Point.[10] On March 29 Sheridan led these cavalrymen down to Reams's Station on the Weldon Railroad, across Rowanty Creek, and west toward Dinwiddie Court House. This movement began what later was called the "Eighth Union Offensive" against Petersburg.[11]

Two large infantry units, Maj. Gen. Andrew A. Humphreys's II Corps and Maj. Gen. Gouverneur K. Warren's V Corps, were assigned to support Sheridan's movement against the Confederate right. These same two commands had made Grant's last major shift west, which had ended in the Battle of Hatcher's Run. Lt. Gen. Richard H. Anderson, who had responsibility for this western stretch of the Rebel defenses, opposed them. General Anderson commanded what was nominally a corps. In reality, he had only one division, which was led by Ohio-born Maj. Gen. Bushrod R. Johnson.[12]

Sheridan's operation soon produced the small engagement of the Battle of the Lewis Farm or the Battle of the Quaker Road. One division of the V Corps encountered General Johnson's command on Joseph M. Lewis's 285-acre farm just east of the Quaker Road. The Federals lost about 380 total casualties; the Confederates, a bit fewer. The fight resulted in the Federals' gaining control of the junction of the Quaker and Boydton Plank Roads.[13]

While General Warren fought at the Lewis farm and General Humphreys covered his right, Sheridan's horsemen started for Dinwiddie Court House. On March 29 they met only a few Confederate mounted patrols, but muddy roads delayed them. Annoyed by this hindrance, the impetuous Sheridan determined to gain speed by dropping off his supply wagons. Leaving one division to guard them, he pushed two others to Dinwiddie Court House.[14]

Lee anticipated this threat to his far right flank and moved to counter it.[15] On the thirtieth, he ordered a force of about 10,600 infantrymen, cavalrymen, and artillerymen to a vitally important crossroads roughly fourteen miles southwest of Petersburg.[16] The Confederates needed to hold this crucial junction and keep their opponents from approaching the city's western defenses and the South Side Railroad, Lee's last link to Johnston and the rest of the Confederacy. Here the Dinwiddie, Scott's, and Ford's (or Church) Roads ran away from the White Oak Road, forming a star pattern that gave the crossroads its name—Five Forks.[17]

The officer responsible for the defense of Five Forks was Maj. Gen. George E. Pickett, whose name was forever connected to one of the most famous infantry assaults in American history, at Gettysburg. To defend the vital Five Forks crossroads, General Pickett had three of his own brigades and two from another division;

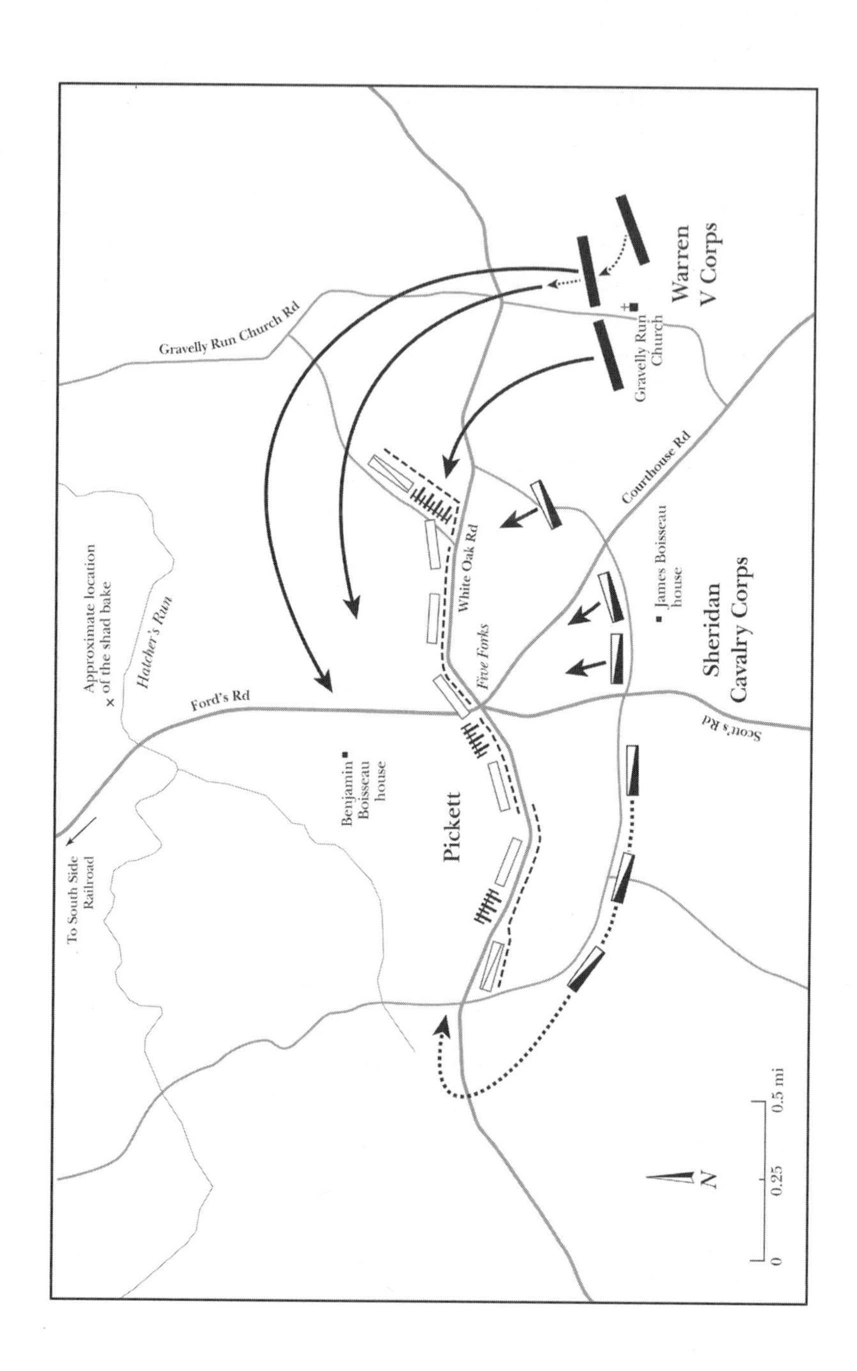

MAP 9. Battle of Five Forks, April 1, 1865

some units of the cavalry corps headed by Maj. Gen. Fitzhugh "Fitz" Lee, the army commander's nephew; and six field guns directed by Col. William J. "Willie" Pegram, a younger brother of Brig. Gen. John A. Pegram.[18]

While Pickett and his mixed command got under way, Sheridan and his two divisions spent March 30 around Dinwiddie Court House. Torrents of rain fell from the evening of the twenty-ninth until the morning of the thirty-first, creating road conditions that frustrated the Northern cavalry. The troopers passed a quiet day on March 30.[19]

The next day Sheridan's two divisions moved north from Dinwiddie Court House and began probing the roads toward the crucial Five Forks crossing. In what was later styled the Battle of Dinwiddie Court House, Pickett struck at the Union horsemen with both his cavalry and infantry. Late in the afternoon, Sheridan brought up most of his reserve division, and the engagement ended in a tactical draw. Sheridan lost roughly 350 total casualties; the Confederates, about 760.[20]

Three miles to the northeast, another battle took place on March 31. Here the Southerners attacked and began an action that was called the Battle of the White Oak Road or the Battle of Gravelly Run. Four brigades representing three Confederate divisions swept two V Corps divisions south across Gravelly Run. Warren was not able to stabilize his position until some men of II Corps came to his aid, but the Federals then successfully counterattacked. The total Union losses came to more than 1,800, the Confederates probably about 800. For their greater casualties, the Federals gained a significant tactical success. Warren tied his right flank to Humphreys's left, and the Southerners retired into the entrenchments at the western end of the main Petersburg defenses.[21]

To the southwest, at Dinwiddie Court House, Sheridan saw that the Confederate retreat after the Battle of the White Oak Road had left Pickett isolated. Moreover, Sheridan was gaining reinforcements. With the Battle of the White Oak Road won, Warren ordered one of his brigades to march to the Union cavalry. Early in the morning of Saturday, April 1, young Brig. Gen.

Ranald S. Mackenzie brought a small but strong cavalry division from the Army of the James to Sheridan's aid.[22]

Sheridan welcomed these units, but what he really wanted was the VI Corps. Maj. Gen. Horatio G. Wright, although not an inspiring or innovative leader, had reliably commanded this unit since the popular Maj. Gen. John Sedgwick's death at Spotsylvania. The men of the VI Corps had won Little Phil's good opinion during his brilliantly successful Shenandoah Valley campaign. Sheridan requested this unit, but Grant told him that it was deployed too far east to join him promptly. Further General Wright had declared that he could break Lee's main defenses in his front, demonstrating a self-assurance that was rare among corps commanders in the history of the Army of the Potomac. The soldiers of the VI Corps and their confident leader would be needed where they were when—and it might be soon—Grant ordered a general assault against Petersburg.[23]

So in place of the corps he wanted, Sheridan got the V Corps. The aggressive cavalryman was unenthusiastic about Warren's generalship, which he considered apathetic. Nor did Warren enjoy a high standing with Grant, who believed him both too quick to worry about how other corps would support his own and too prone to fight his own command piecemeal. "His difficulty," Grant concluded, "was constitutional and beyond his control."[24]

Grant's opinion of Warren boded ill for the New Yorker's future, and so did a dispatch that the senior commander sent from his Dabney's Mill field headquarters at 10:45 p.m. on March 31. This message told Sheridan that General Mackenzie's cavalry and Warren's infantry had been detailed to him and assured him that the V Corps would arrive "by 12 to-night." It is hard to understand how any officer at Grant's headquarters believed the unit could meet this arrival time. It required the corps, which had just fought a hard battle, to throw a bridge across Gravelly Run, march through the dead of night on muddy roads, and cover six miles in an hour and a quarter. When the V Corps failed to do the impossible, Sheridan regarded it as late and blamed Warren.[25]

North of Dinwiddie Court House that night, Pickett was concerned about the designs of the Federals. Three weeks later Gen.

Fitz Lee explained that sometime during the hours of darkness, the Confederates learned that "the Fifth Corps . . . was marching to the support of Sheridan . . . which would have brought them directly upon our left flank," and "at daylight on the 1st we commenced moving back to our former position at Five Forks."[26] By defending this crossroads, Pickett could cover the vital South Side Railroad.[27]

Pickett reported to Lee his decision to fall back. While his infantrymen and cavalrymen withdrew northward, the independent commander received a pointed directive from his chief. "Hold Five Forks at all hazards," Lee instructed Pickett. "Protect road to Ford's Depot and prevent Union forces from striking the Southside Railroad."[28]

Pickett deployed his command facing south along a stretch of the White Oak Road about a mile and three quarters long and roughly centered on Five Forks. His infantrymen entrenched and made a sharp angle in their line when they refused their left flank a short distance to the north. A cavalry division covered each end of their position. Colonel Pegram placed three of his guns at Five Forks and the other three farther west, where they supported the right of the infantry line.[29]

While the Confederates established their position at Five Forks, powerful Federal units gathered against them. Sheridan held one division near Dinwiddie to guard his wagon trains and sent two others north in pursuit of the Southerners.[30] South of Five Forks, these troopers deployed on a long line that confronted Pickett's along the White Oak Road, with one division forming west of Scott's Road and the other east of it.[31] During the morning of April 1, the V Corps linked with the cavalry. One division marched down the Boydton Plank Road, turned westward, and reached the Five Forks front at about daylight. Warren brought up his other two divisions between 7:00 and 8:00 a.m. while Mackenzie's cavalry took station on the Union forces' right flank.[32]

Warren probably brought about 12,000 soldiers to Five Forks. The Union troopers numbered roughly 9,000 and gave Sheridan a total of more than 21,000 effectives.[33] Pickett's mixed command originally had mustered about 10,600, and by the time it prepared to defend Five Forks, it probably had 9,000 to 10,000 men.[34] Sheridan enjoyed an advantage of about two to one.

The Northerners held the edge in numbers, but a spirit of distrust ran through their high command that first day of April. Months later Warren recalled conferring with Sheridan late that morning and commented: "When I met him at about 11:00 a.m. his manner was friendly and cordial." Perhaps so, but unknown to Warren, he would enter the Battle of Five Forks with a sword over his head. Less than an hour before his meeting with Sheridan, as Grant's aide-de-camp Lt. Col. Horace Porter later recounted it, an event took place that boded ill for the V Corps's commander. Lt. Col. Orville Babcock, another of Grant's staff officers, "came over from headquarters and said to Sheridan: 'General Grant directs me to say to you, that if in your judgment the Fifth Corps would do better under one of the division commanders, you are authorized to relieve General Warren, and order him to report to General Grant, at headquarters.'"[35]

About 1:00 p.m. Warren received an order from Sheridan to bring up his corps. Warren formed his command with two divisions on line in a position just east and a little south of Five Forks. One division deployed west of the Gravelly Run Methodist Episcopal Church, another went to the east of this simple white frame building, and a third division formed behind the right-front one. It took the infantrymen until about 4:00 p.m. to get into position. Sheridan complained that "General Warren did not exert himself to get up his corps as rapidly as he might have done, and his manner gave me the impression that he wished the sun to go down before dispositions for the attack could be completed."[36]

While Sheridan bridled at what he perceived as Warren's lack of energy, the Confederate leaders seemed to feel no sense of urgency on their side of the field, either. Two days earlier Maj. Gen. Thomas L. Rosser, who commanded a division of Virginia cavalry regiments, and Brig. Gen. James Dearing, his subordinate, had caught some shad. These fish, which belong to the herring family, are a favorite of Tidewater Virginians. During the early afternoon of the first, Pickett and Fitz Lee joined General Rosser for a shad bake at his camp north of Hatcher's Run and well back in the Confederate rear.[37]

While Pickett and his senior officers were enjoying their fish, the Federals began their advance, but the V Corps did not step off until after 4:00 p.m., which was inexcusably late in Sheridan's view.[38] Whether Warren could have moved sooner became a point of controversy, but it was certain that he acted on bad tactical intelligence. A poor map and inadequate scouting led the Federals to believe that the Confederate left flank was farther east than it was. Warren's two frontline divisions drove northwest from Gravelly Run Methodist Episcopal Church, crossed the White Oak Road, and delivered an attack that landed in the air. The Federals at first encountered only light musketry as Pickett's refused left flank lay several hundred yards away, farther west down the roadway.[39]

Sheridan and Warren, accompanied by Lieutenant Colonel Porter, had trotted into the action at the left front of the V Corps. Warren soon moved off, quite properly, to a position where he could better direct his whole corps. Sheridan remained with Warren's left-front division.[40]

To the right of the V Corps, Mackenzie had driven back Col. Thomas Munford's cavalrymen. He rode up to Sheridan and reported his success. The Federal commander ordered him to strike toward Hatcher's Run, turn west, and cut off the Confederate line of retreat along Ford's Road.[41]

Soon after Mackenzie received this directive from Sheridan, as Porter later recalled events, Warren's left-front division came under a nasty enfilade from Pickett's veterans. As Porter described it, the Federals "met with a heavy fire on their left flank and had to change direction by facing more to the west. As the troops entered the woods and moved forward over the boggy ground and struggled through the dense undergrowth, they were staggered by a heavy fire from the angle [in Pickett's line, at his refused left flank] and fell back in some confusion."[42]

The Union line swung to the west and struck the angle in Pickett's position. Sheridan energized the assault. Rienzi, the black horse that had carried the general on his famous ride from Winchester to Cedar Creek, now pranced among Warren's men at the point of the attack. "Where is my battle-flag?" Sheridan demanded. When a sergeant rode up with the red-and-white swallow-tailed guidon, the impetuous commander took it and galloped along the front, urging on his men.[43]

This swing to the west opened a potentially dangerous gap between Warren's two frontline divisions.[44] The two units lost contact, and Warren ordered the right division to close on the left. The corps commander also sent some of his staff officers to bring up his reserve division.[45] While Warren gave these orders, he remained where he could oversee his entire command. Doubtless this decision contributed to Sheridan's later complaint that Warren "did not exert himself to inspire" confidence in his men—particularly at a time when Sheridan himself was at the front doing precisely that.[46]

Warren could not quickly close the gap between his two frontline divisions, but fortunately for the Federals, the left division broke through the angle in Pickett's line before the Confederates could exploit this opening. In Porter's account of the high point of the battle, the Federals "with fixed bayonets and a rousing cheer dashed over the earth-works, sweeping everything before them, and killing or capturing every man in their immediate front whose legs had not saved him. Sheridan spurred 'Rienzi' up to the angle, and with a bound the horse carried his rider over the earth-works and landed in the midst of a line of prisoners who had thrown down their arms and were crouching close under their breastworks."[47]

Once some of the attackers got inside the angle, the Federal assault gained momentum. Acting on Warren's orders, the reserve division pressed into the gap between the other two. This fresh division attacked west across Robert Sydnor's open farm field and began rolling up the Southern line above the angle. To the north, the men on the right of the V Corps joined Mackenzie in driving back the dismounted cavalrymen in their front. The end of the advancing Union line had reached Ford's Road when Warren rode up and directed a wheel to the left, followed by a drive south into the Confederate rear at Five Forks.[48]

The senior Confederate generals, meanwhile, remained ignorant of the Union successes until it was too late to reverse them.

While the Federals pressed their advantages, Pickett, Fitz Lee, and Rosser were still in the rear, enjoying their shad bake. The heavily wooded terrain evidently kept much of the noise of the battle from reaching Rosser's campsite. Also, it had rained from the evening of March 29 until the morning of the thirty-first, dampening the dense stands of pine trees and making them a particularly effective sound buffer.[49]

Shortly after 4:00 p.m. Pickett asked Rosser to have a courier carry a dispatch to Five Forks. In the interest of ensuring delivery, the cavalryman sent off two riders at an interval. The lead courier was captured while Pickett looked on. Alarmed that the Federals were so far north, the general rode south until he saw the Union infantrymen pressing in from the east. "Do hold them back," Pickett told a cavalry officer, "till I pass to Five Forks." The concerned commander then continued south and found that his line along the White Oak Road was crumbling.[50]

Fitz Lee also intended to ride to the front, but by then the enemy had cut Ford's Road. He and Rosser were forced to remain north of Hatcher's Run. The shad bake forgotten, the Confederate generals formed Rosser's men on the far bank of that stream, facing south, in an effort to keep the Federal infantry from gaining the South Side Railroad.[51]

To the south, Pickett reached Five Forks—in time to find a disaster. While the Union infantrymen had broken the angle in the Confederate entrenchments, their cavalry comrades had pressed the right flank and front of the Confederate defenses.[52] In the center of the Confederate line at Five Forks, Pegram's three field guns remained in action. Contending against the Federals in his front and the growing pressure from those to the east, the young Southern artilleryman ordered his gunners to deliver their canister low into the advancing blue lines. Pegram directed the defense of the Five Forks crossroads from horseback until a bullet hit his left arm and side, fatally wounding him. The battlefield where he fell was a little less than eight miles west of the one where, about two months earlier, his brother, Brig. Gen. John A. Pegram, had been killed.[53]

By the time young Willie Pegram went down, the attackers had reached the mouths of his field pieces. The Federal cavalry soon overwhelmed the remaining defenses of Five Forks.[54] Pickett's survivors fled to the north, and it was "every man for himself," one of them candidly acknowledged. Among the Confederate prisoners was Joseph Abbitt, a former shopkeeper from a small village more than sixty miles to the west-northwest—Appomattox Court House.[55]

The casualties of Pickett's Division at Five Forks can only be estimated, but probably about 545 of its officers and men were either killed or wounded. The Federals captured on the order of another 2,000 to 2,400. Relative to the Confederate casualties, the total Union losses at Five Forks were light, about 830.[56]

In the aftermath of the calamity on April 1, Pickett's reputation collapsed. A few days after the battle, a Southern cavalryman informed his wife that the Five Forks defeat "would not have taken place if Gen. Picket had been in his proper place." Pickett almost certainly did not know, and surely did not care, about the opinion of this trooper who could not spell his name correctly. Losing his standing with his revered army leader was a far different matter. A week after the Five Forks debacle, Lee relieved Pickett from his assignment. The division commander evidently never received the order, however, as he remained with the remnants of his unit.[57]

While defeat raised ill will among the Confederates, victory did the same among the Federals. As noted, Grant had lost confidence in Warren long before Five Forks, when he faltered during the Battles of the Wilderness and Spotsylvania in 1864. More recently the general in chief had concluded that the V Corps's commander had mishandled the Battle of the White Oak Road. Grant and Sheridan faulted him for arriving late at Five Forks, and before the battle even began, they seemed to expect that he would fail there. On the eve of the engagement, Grant had given Sheridan carte blanche to fire Warren. While the Federals prepared their attack, Sheridan fumed that Warren was slow in moving his divisions into position. During combat, while the cavalry leader himself accompanied the infantrymen who broke through Pickett's defenses, the V Corps's commander was not at the front.

Just as the Union attack culminated in triumph, all of this past history came to a boil. After the Federals cut Ford's Road and corralled hundreds of prisoners, brevet Col. Frederick T. Locke, Warren's adjutant general, trotted up to Sheridan to report these accomplishments. The staff officer was shocked to have Sheridan explode at him: "Tell General Warren, by God! I say he was not at the front. That is all I have got to say to him." The stunned Colonel Locke managed to ask, "Must I tell General Warren that, sir?" "Tell him that, sir!" Sheridan stormed. Mortified, Locke rode away.[58]

Around 7:00 p.m. brevet Col. George A. Forsyth, one of Sheridan's aides, brought Warren a field order that abruptly ended his career with the Army of the Potomac: "Major-General Warren, commanding Fifth Army Corps, is relieved from duty, and will report at once for orders to Lieutenant-General Grant, commanding Armies of the United States."[59] The broken corps commander rode to Sheridan and asked him to reconsider the decision. The heat of combat was still on the fiery cavalryman, who dismissed Warren's request in the same temper that he had directed at Locke: "Reconsider? Hell! I don't reconsider my determination."[60]

Hoping to clear his reputation, Warren soon asked for a court of inquiry. Grant, first as commanding general of the army and then as president, delayed his repeated requests. Finally in December 1879 a court began an investigation and collected more than seventeen hundred pages of testimony from Southern and Northern veterans of Five Forks. The findings largely vindicated Warren but were not published until November 1882, about three months after the hero of Little Round Top had died.[61]

Warren had a stronger case than Sheridan's in the Five Forks controversy. His corps won an overwhelming victory in the battle, and he directed it ably from appropriate places on the battlefield. But Warren was not cashiered for his actions, or inaction, at Five Forks. Sheridan dismissed Warren because of shortcomings that the fiery cavalryman—and Grant—saw in his leadership well before that battle. Historian Stephen Sears has suggested that "had the same fate been visited upon one or two of the Army of the Potomac's less-than-stellar corps commanders back in 1862 or 1863, to serve as an indelible lesson to that army's high command, a kind of rough justice might have been the result. As it was, General Warren became a martyr to no cause at all."[62]

For the Southerners, as well for Warren, Five Forks was a disaster, but its consequences were not unexpected. On the morning of April 1, before the battle was fought but after the Federals reached Dinwiddie Court House, Gen. Robert E. Lee sent one of his last handwritten letters to President Davis from the field. He predicted that the Northerners would take advantage of their "superior" numbers of cavalrymen and cut the South Side and Danville Railroads. The general advised the chief executive to prepare "for the necessity of evacuating" Petersburg and Richmond "at once."[63]

For the Federals, Five Forks represented a splendid victory, but Grant, characteristically, did not pause to celebrate. He viewed the success as just one part of a larger operation. When the news of Sheridan's victory reached Grant's field headquarters at the site of Dabney's Mill, his staff officers staged a hand-shaking, hat-throwing, backslapping demonstration. The general, cigar in mouth, maintained his usual stoicism. He questioned the courier who brought the news, stepped into his tent, and began writing dispatches. Grant handed these messages to an orderly, emerged from the canvas shelter, and told his staff: "I have ordered an immediate assault along the lines."[64]

The hour, however, had grown too late for an attack that night. It was 8:30 p.m. when Grant informed General Meade of the outcome at Five Forks. The two exchanged several messages and determined that a general advance would begin at 4:00 a.m. on April 2. This large-scale operation eventually would be labeled the "Ninth Union Offensive" at Petersburg and would be the last of them.[65]

After nine and a half months at Petersburg, the Federals stood poised for a massive attack that would take the city. The blow would fall most heavily on a stretch of the far western Confederate siege lines, the sector between the Duncan and Church Roads. Three brigades of Lt. Gen. Ambrose P. Hill's Corps held this front and its neighboring area. General Hill spent the night of April 1–2, the last of his life, with his wife and two daughters in a cottage just west of Petersburg.[66]

The Federals prepared to advance along a broad front. On the Union right, east and southeast of Petersburg, Maj. Gen. John G.

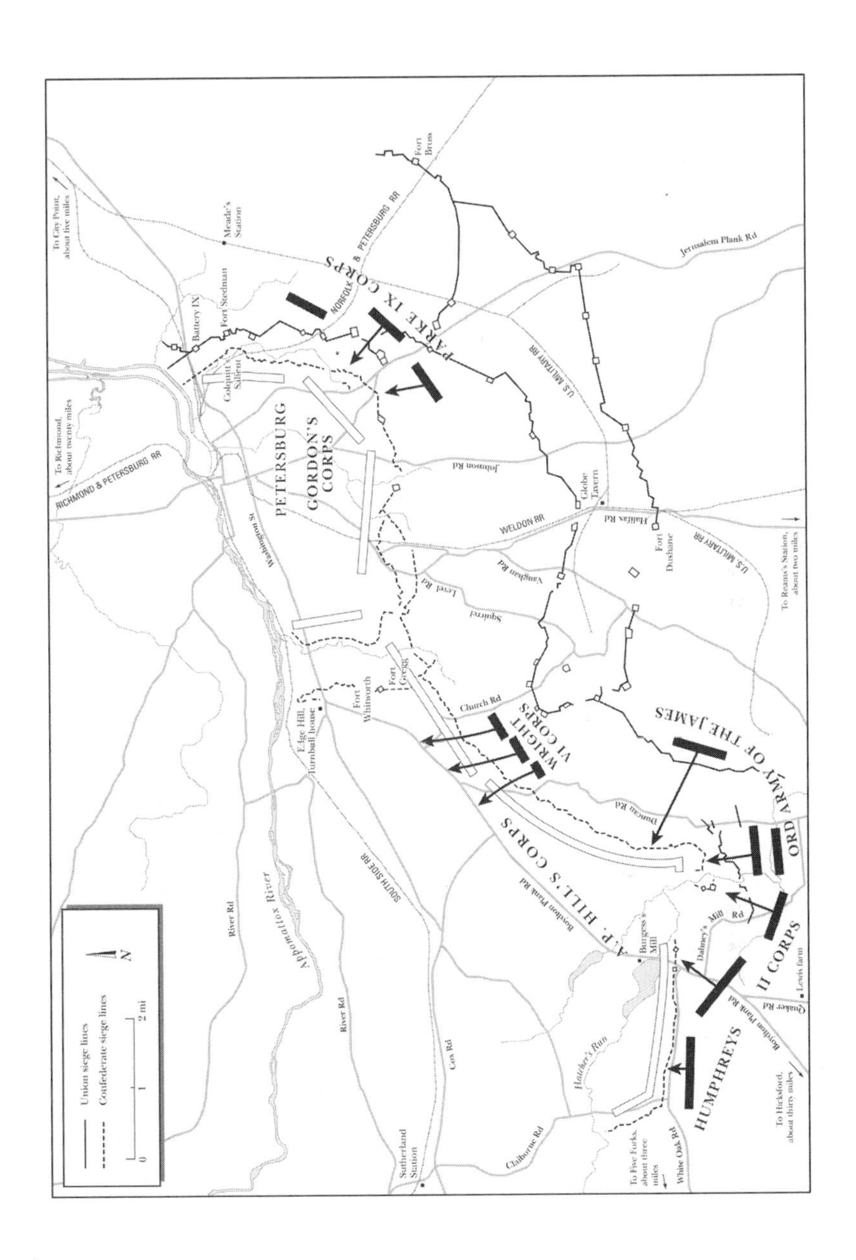

MAP 10. Final Assault at Petersburg, April 2, 1865

Parke's IX Corps would go forward. To its left, three divisions of Wright's VI Corps formed to assault the entrenchments held by Hill's veterans.[67]

Brig. Gen. Lewis A. Grant, known as the "other Grant," was the reliable leader of the VI Corps's Vermont Brigade and played an important role in preparing the April 2 assault. General Grant scouted the Confederate defenses and gave his small-unit commanders detailed plans for the attack. When Grant was wounded while on the picket line on April 1 and rendered unable to make the next day's advance, he already had contributed much to its success.[68]

Other Union forces also stood ready. On Wright's left was the XXIV Corps of the Army of the James. This unit was directed by Maj. Gen. John Gibbon, who had formerly commanded the famous Black Hat Brigade and later a division that had withstood Pickett's Charge at Gettysburg. Humphreys's II Corps also stood at hand.[69]

At 4:30 a.m. on Sunday, the second, the Federals launched what later would be recognized as the final assault on Petersburg. General Parke's IX Corps moved out of its works and advanced on both sides of the Jerusalem Plank Road. It encountered defenses that were held thinly but determinedly by Maj. Gen. John B. Gordon's Corps. Parke's advance was checked.[70]

Wright's VI Corps, west of the IX Corps, gained the distinction of breaking the line, a success that led to the fall of Petersburg and put Lee on the road to Appomattox. "At 4:15 there was a streak of gray in the heavens," Porter recounted, "which soon revealed another streak of gray formed by Confederate uniforms in the works opposite, and the charge was ordered. The thunder of hundreds of guns shook the ground like an earthquake, and soon troops were engaged all along the lines."[71]

The three divisions of the VI Corps crossed the damp ground between the lines and overran the rifle pits in front of the main Confederate defenses. A New Englander described the chevaux-de-frise that the attackers encountered as "made up of large round poles bored through with two inch holes and sticks drove through them and sharpened very sharp making one continuous bristling saw horse at least 4 ½ feet high." The Federals hacked their way through these and other obstacles.[72]

After a brief but vicious fight, the VI Corps broke the main defenses. A member of the Union Sixth Maryland related: "We had quite a lively time with the enemy when we entered [the Confederate works], although I do not think it lasted more than five minutes." "At a quarter past five," as Porter remembered it, a message from Wright arrived at Grant's field headquarters "that he had carried the enemy's line and was pushing in."[73]

Pride of success, swirled in the confusion of combat, led the Northern victors to lodge rival, irresolvable claims. Twenty of the forty-two VI Corps regiments that made the April 2 assault asserted in one way or another that they had been first to break the Southern defenses or plant their colors on them. At least four accounts identified Capt. Charles G. Gould of Company H, Fifth Vermont, as the first attacker to scale the Confederate works.[74] This young New Englander was severely wounded but lived to receive the Congressional Medal of Honor, as did Sgt. John E. Buffington of Company C, Sixth Maryland, another claimant of the honor of being the initial attacker to breach the Rebel defenses.[75] While the veterans argued during the postwar years about which individual or unit had been first into the Confederate lines, one observer made a realistic assessment of their disputes. "No man could then tell—no man can now tell—whose colors were first to have been planted on the works," he declared, "or whose men were first to have entered those works, except in his own immediate brigade front."[76]

Whoever had been first into the defenses, thousands of other soldiers followed and opened gaps that could not be repaired. Hill's men retreated north toward the Appomattox River and northeast to the inner fortifications of the city. A triumphant New Yorker related: "[We] fired into the running Rebs, and also into some wagons which were passing. We also twisted off the telegraph wires with our bayonets, continuing our firing at everything in sight."[77]

Chief engineer brevet Maj. Gen. John G. Barnard estimated the Union casualties in the breakthrough assault at eleven hundred killed and wounded. Southern losses remain unknown. In his commendably thorough study of the April 2 attack, historian A. Wilson Greene states that the number of Confederates captured doubtless exceeded those killed or wounded.[78]

Other attacks against the strong entrenchments around Petersburg—and elsewhere throughout the war—very often had made only limited gains or had ended in disastrous failures. But here the early morning assault of the VI Corps achieved what historian Earl Hess terms "the most decisive breakthrough of a heavily fortified line in the war."[79] The chief factor in this success probably was that as commanding as the Confederate fortifications were, the winter's attrition and Grant's continuous movements, probes, and attacks had thinned the ranks of the defenders. In the area of the breakthrough, Hill had only three brigades while four of his brigades defended six miles of fieldworks. Hill's entire front was held by fewer than fourteen hundred troops per mile, or a ratio of less than one soldier a yard.[80] Lee's overall defensive manning was even weaker, so he could not shift units to help Hill. The entire Southern front was held by eleven hundred men per mile, and as one meticulous historian of the April 2 attack has pointed out, that number is about one-tenth "as strong in manpower as [Lee's] line of battle at Fredericksburg had been in December 1862." On the night before the April 2 assault, Wright confidently had predicted that the VI Corps would "make the fur fly" and would break the Confederate line within fifteen minutes, because he knew it was held by reduced manpower.[81]

Other factors contributed to the achievement. The Federals had gained the Confederate picket line on March 25, allowing them to study the enemy's defenses and giving them staging room for their assault. Another element was the sound planning of Lewis A. Grant, whom historian Greene identifies as "the tactical architect of the offensive."[82] And the VI Corps infantrymen may have sensed that the defenders' morale had declined, a realization that raised their own spirits and contributed to the victory.[83]

Not long after soldiers of the VI Corps began swarming through the Southern lines, Hill learned of their success. It was probably after 5:00 a.m. when one of his staff officers brought the alarming news to the cottage where he had spent the night. Hill first went to Lee's headquarters at the nearby William Turnbull house and then set out with some aides for the right of his line. The general and his party soon observed the growing disaster: Federal infantrymen were moving through what had been the Confederate rear while Southern foot soldiers and wagons were retreating toward the inner works of Petersburg.[84]

While making his way along Cattail Run, Hill directed that some Confederate field guns should be deployed to hinder the Federals' approach to Lee's headquarters and to the city's inner defenses. The corps commander rode on with a lone aide, Sgt. George W. Tucker, into a stretch of woods north of the Boydton Plank Road. There, probably sometime after 6:30 a.m., they encountered Cpl. John W. Mauk and Pvt. Daniel Wolford of the 138th Pennsylvania, two among the hundreds of Federals drifting in the wake of the VI Corps's breakthough.[85]

Sergeant Tucker gamely tried to protect his commander by approaching the two Northerners and ordering them to surrender. Corporal Mauk sensed the bluff and said to his comrade, "I cannot see it. Let's shoot them." Both Federals fired. Private Wolford missed; Mauk shot Hill dead.[86] Tucker escaped and carried the sad news to Lee's headquarters.[87]

Hill was dead, his defensive line torn open, and the Federals were moving toward Petersburg's inner fortifications. Lee well understood the meaning of the morning's events, and shortly after 10:00 a.m. he advised Secretary of War John C. Breckinridge of the grave circumstances. "I see no prospect of doing more than holding our position here till night," the commander stated. "I am not certain that I can do that." Lee intended to abandon Petersburg, retreat to the north bank of the Appomattox River during the night, and eventually pull his forces together near the Richmond and Danville Railroad. He gave Secretary Breckinridge his honest counsel: "I advise that all preparations be made for leaving Richmond to-night."[88]

Davis received Lee's dispatch to Breckinridge while attending that Sunday morning's service in Saint Paul's Episcopal Church in Richmond. The church sextant walked down the aisle to the chief executive's pew, located about halfway between the narthex and chancel, and handed the president the fateful message.[89] Davis left the congregation and went on foot to his office in the Customs House, where he began gathering his cabinet and preparing to leave the capital. That evening he walked to the executive mansion and waited for a carriage to take him to the Richmond and Danville Railroad depot.[90]

Late that night, accompanied by five cabinet members—Postmaster General John H. Reagan, Attorney General George Davis, Secretary of State Judah P. Benjamin, Secretary of the Navy Stephen R. Mallory, and Secretary of the Treasury George A. Trenholm—Davis boarded a train for Danville. Secretary Breckinridge remained behind to oversee the evacuation of Richmond. Later he would ride to Petersburg to confer with Lee and eventually would join the presidential party.[91]

However disheartening Davis found it to flee from Richmond with his small retinue, Lee faced a far more difficult task in escaping from Petersburg with thousands of soldiers. The general could only hope that the city's inner works would delay the Federals long enough for his men to withdraw in cohesive units. Just south of his headquarters at the Turnbull house, and not far northeast of where the VI Corps had broken Hill's line, stood two of these now-crucial fortifications—Forts Whitworth and Gregg, named for the farms on which they were constructed.[92] Perhaps 350 of Hill's remaining veterans held Fort Gregg while more than 200 soldiers defended Fort Whitworth.[93]

General Gibbon's XXIV Corps exploited the opportunity won by the VI Corps and swung northeast toward these two forts. Wright, after his morning's success, had reformed a good part of his corps and had deployed it on the left of the men from the Army of the James. Gibbon, however, was not interested in help from the VI Corps; instead, he was determined to have his own soldiers win the honor of gaining Whitworth and Gregg, the last barriers west of Petersburg. In truth, Gibbon needed no assistance from the VI Corps or any other unit as his XXIV Corps deployed eight or nine attackers for each of the Confederate defenders.[94]

FIG. 1. This February 1865 photograph shows that the stress of a bloody Civil War took a toll on President Abraham Lincoln. Library of Congress.

FIG. 2. Lt. Gen. Ulysses S. Grant was an acquaintance of Confederate Lt. Gen. James Longstreet since their West Point days. General Longstreet warned Southerners that General Grant, "will fight us every day and every hour till the end of this war." Library of Congress.

FIG. 3. Maj. Gen. William T. Sherman waged "hard war" but then exceeded his authority in order to give lenient surrender terms. National Archives.

FIG. 4. Maj. Gen. George G. Meade was overruled by General Grant at one important juncture of the Appomattox campaign, but overall General Meade performed reliably throughout the pursuit of the Army of Northern Virginia. Library of Congress.

FIG. 5. Confederate president Jefferson Davis resisted surrender longer than nearly all of his senior generals and cabinet officers. National Archives.

FIG. 6. After the fall of Petersburg, Confederate general Robert E. Lee attempted to join forces with Gen. Joseph E. Johnston. This strategy failed. General Grant's skillful, relentless pursuit ran General Lee to ground at Appomattox Court House. Library of Congress.

FIG. 7. After Lee's capitulation at Appomattox Court House, Gen. Joseph E. Johnston intended to maintain his own Army of Tennessee in the field as a viable organization, to keep it well away from General Sherman's much larger force and to negotiate the best possible surrender terms for his men. Library of Congress.

FIG. 8. During the last weeks of the war, Confederate general Pierre Gustave Toutant Beauregard, like General Johnston, tried to get President Davis to accept the South's defeat. National Archives.

FIG. 9. The figure in the middle ground and the ones on the rampart in the background suggest the massive size of Fort Fisher, which defended the favorite approach of blockade runners into Wilmington, North Carolina, the Confederacy's last major port. Library of Congress.

FIG. 10. This image shows that trees stood inside and near Fort Stedman in Petersburg, Virginia. They were a rarity. During the long siege of Petersburg, soldiers used most of the trees, fences, and scrub growth in the area for defenses, firewood, or huts. Library of Congress.

FIG. 11. Alfred R. Waud drew infantrymen of the V Corps attacking Pickett's Division at Five Forks, a road junction south of the crucial South Side Railroad. Waud wrote on the back of this sketch: "The last charge at the Battle of Five Forks, April 1st, 1865." Library of Congress.

FIG. 12. The trenches and chevaux-de-frise (logs with sharpened stakes through them) seen here helped the Confederates hold Petersburg for more than nine months. Library of Congress.

FIG. 13. The camera position for this 1936 photograph was behind the right of Confederate Lt. Gen. Richard S. Ewell's line. The James Hillsman house stood on a commanding ridge; both the house and the ridge are seen in the background. Union artillery deployed on this high ground to the left and right of the home. These field guns supported the VI Corps's soldiers, who came down the slope to attack General Ewell's men. Sailor's Creek Battlefield Historical State Park.

FIG. 14. After two major battles were fought near Wilmer McLean's Manassas home, he fled the war and moved to Appomattox Court House. The conflict followed him, with Lee surrendering to Grant in McLean's parlor. Library of Congress.

FIG. 15. The modest home of James and Nancy Bennett, where Johnston agreed to terms with Sherman, contrasted with the stately McLean residence where Lee surrendered to Grant. Like many yeoman farmers, Bennett supplemented his income with other employments. Bennett Place State Historic Site.

Around 1:00 p.m. Gibbon's men stormed forward. They were met with what historian Hess calls "one of the classic, last-ditch defenses of the Civil War," particularly remarkable given that the larger situation was so hopeless for the Southerners. The defending fire was so heavy that the Federals had difficulty even reaching the ditch of Fort Gregg. Maj. Giles Buckner Cooke of Lee's staff described the action: "The enemy[,] gathering strength as he came by concentrating his forces[,] made an assault against our forts and was for some time repulsed with great slaughter."[95]

Gibbon's soldiers sustained their efforts, worked their way to the rear of Fort Gregg, and found the going there somewhat easier. The fighting was still intense, and the number of defenders declined by the minute. Major Cooke concluded that the attacking force was "too strong to be resisted and after a long continued and desperate effort [the enemy] carried Fort Gregg and the other forts in line with it."[96] "There were so many Federals coming over the parapet in the last charge," one Confederate explained, "we could not shoot them all."[97]

Gibbon acknowledged losing 714 total casualties that day, and doubtless most of them were incurred at Fort Gregg. The victors claimed that in taking the fortification they killed 56 Confederates and captured about another 250.[98] "The interior of the fort was a pool of blood," wrote one of the Federals, "a sight which can never be shut from memory. The rebels had recklessly fought to the last." The Southerners put up far less resistance at Fort Whitworth. There the Federals found 2 of their dead and 2 of their wounded inside the fort, and they captured about 70 defenders.[99]

West of Gibbon, the Union II Corps rolled forward with only one of Hill's divisions retreating in front of it. This isolated unit offered a fine target, but Meade diluted its pursuit by ordering Humphreys to send two of his divisions to support the VI Corps, which did not need their help. Only one division of the II Corps, led by Brig. Gen. Nelson A. Miles, a young leader who had a commendable record in the eastern theater, continued to track Hill's retreating men.[100]

By the late morning some of the Confederates began to overcome the shock of the VI Corps's breakthrough. A significant defensive stand occurred at Sutherland Station well to the west of Petersburg. Here the Southerners took up a line about half a mile long. Their front ran along the Cox Road, just south of the South Side Railroad and parallel to it. The Confederate left flank was thrown back to the north to cover the rail line.[101]

When General Miles's division reached Sutherland Station, it made two unsuccessful frontal assaults. It probably was approaching 4:00 p.m. when the unit tried a third time and knocked in the Confederate left flank. The Federals then gained the South Side Railroad, an objective that long had eluded them during the bitter months of the siege of Petersburg.[102]

At Sutherland Station, as at Fort Gregg, Lee gained time that he vitally needed to organize his men and wagons for an orderly retreat from Petersburg. Hill's Corps had been breached and its leader killed, but it had put up a creditable fight. Also Lt. Gen. James Longstreet's and General Gordon's Corps had held their lines until nightfall. Covered by darkness, the Confederates abandoned Petersburg and Richmond. "As we passed through Petersburg," one Southern infantryman recalled, "the sidewalks of the city were filled with weeping women and children, lamenting the fate which they knew daylight would bring upon them."[103]

The nine-and-a-half-month-long drama at Petersburg ended during the early morning hours of Monday, April 3. Around midnight Sgt. William T. Wixcey of the First Michigan Sharpshooters, a IX Corps unit, pulled himself out of his picket trench and, armed with an officer's revolver, crawled forward to scout the Confederate defenses. He discovered that everything "was quiet—absolutely quiet, in fact too much quiet—along the line." At 3:10 a.m. Sergeant Wixcey's regiment, with the Second Michigan on its left, advanced and confirmed that Petersburg had been abandoned. A few minutes after 4:00 a.m., soldiers of the First Michigan Sharpshooters raised their regimental flag over the city's courthouse.[104]

Soon after dawn Mayor William W. Townes and Councilman Charles Collier walked west from Petersburg while carrying a white flag. Hordes of triumphant Union soldiers rushed past them, far more interested in entering the city than in accepting its formal surrender. The two civilians returned to Petersburg satisfied that they had accomplished their mission although not quite as they had intended.[105]

The Confederates had lost Petersburg, but Lee had escaped. His soldiers remained in cohesive units and his supply wagons secure. Lee intended to move west, distance his forces from Grant's masses, and continue the war.

Grant understood his enemy's intention and knew that the Union's task was not finished. The Federals had taken Petersburg, but its capture was incidental to the destruction of Lee's field forces. Grant, too, would continue the war.

CHAPTER SEVEN

To Sailor's Creek

For years Union strategy in the eastern theater of the Civil War had aimed at capturing Richmond, but the fall of the Confederate capital proved an anticlimax. The Army of the Potomac did not enter the prized city but instead pursued the Army of Northern Virginia.[1] The troops of the Army of the James who did go into the capital went there because it stood directly in their path.

On Monday, April 3, 1865, Maj. Gen. Edward O. C. Ord happened to be at Petersburg. Maj. Gen. Godfrey Weitzel, who was less well known than many other Union generals who tried to capture Richmond, commanded the Army of the James on that historic day. It fell to General Weitzel to send the message that Northerners had waited long years to read: "We took Richmond at 8.15 this morning."[2]

The African American soldiers of brevet Maj. Gen. August V. Kautz's division of the XXV Corps extended themselves to enter the city ahead of a white division belonging to the XXIV Corps. In his official report, Weitzel declined to declare a winner of the race between the two units. He stated that it remained "a matter of dispute, both divisions claiming the credit."[3]

Weitzel's soldiers, white and black, gained a city in chaos. Lt. Gen. Richard S. "Old Baldy" Ewell, once a corps commander in the Army of Northern Virginia, commanded the Department of

Richmond and had ordered the capital's garrison to retreat during the night of April 2–3. General Ewell also directed that the tobacco and cotton in the city's warehouses be burned to deny these valuable crops to the Federals. At first his soldiers were able to limit the flames to these targeted buildings, but looters later set fires that jumped out of control. A trooper of the Twenty-fourth Virginia Cavalry jotted in his diary: "What [a] terrible morning—Richmond burning, gunboats burning and their magazines exploding."[4]

Gangs of looters took over the streets. "After night-fall Richmond was ruled by the mob," one resident asserted. "In the principal business section of the city they surged in one black mass from store to store, breaking them open, robbing them, and in some instances (it is said) applying the torch to them." Evelina "Lina" Brooke related that she pushed her "way down to the Commissary Department . . . only to find myself at two o'clock in the night in the midst of a riot, and to become an eyewitness to the conflagration of my beloved Richmond. The explosions at the Arsenals, Laboratory, and Armory suggested my return & home I went."[5]

The night's fires eventually destroyed more than twenty square blocks, enveloping the core of the city's commercial area. The section of Richmond from Capitol Square to the James River earned a grim nickname—the Burnt District. Expecting "to move the next day," Lina Brooke lamented, "we had stored our supplies in what is now the 'burnt district[,]' where they shared the fate of every thing else."[6]

One of Weitzel's aides related that parties of Union soldiers "were at once made to scour the city and press into service every able-bodied man, white or black, and make them assist in extinguishing the flames." This officer went on to contend that "the fire was extinguished and perfect order restored in an incredibly short time after we occupied the city." Weitzel himself went so far as to claim: "The people received us with enthusiastic expressions of joy."[7]

President Abraham Lincoln spent April 3 touring Petersburg, the other strategic prize that his soldiers had just won. Secretary of War Edwin M. Stanton was horrified by the prospect of this visit and urged his chief against it. "I will take care of myself," President Lincoln promised his dour cabinet officer. In the late afternoon of the third, the president returned to City Point and received Weitzel's message announcing the fall of Richmond. Lincoln declared he would go there next.[8]

While Lincoln prepared to visit the fallen capital of the Confederacy, Lt. Gen. Ulysses S. Grant concentrated on continuing operations against the field forces of Gen. Robert E. Lee. On the night of April 3, a young Union officer wrote a diary entry that General Grant would have endorsed: "We heard today that Richmond has been evacuated and is in flames. Well, let it burn, we do not want it. We are after Lee, and we are going to have him."[9]

But General Lee did not wait for the Federals to encircle his command. By the time the Northern officer had made his diary entry, the Confederate commander already had achieved his goals for the daylight hours of April 3: Lee had extricated his forces from the Richmond and Petersburg defenses in coherent units, and he had started moving them away from the Union masses that threatened to engulf them.

During that Monday, Ewell pulled his troops out of the works around the capital and marched them to the Tomahawk Baptist Church about fifteen miles to the southwest.[10] Properly referred to as "Ewell's Reserve Corps," this command included the Richmond garrison troops and two divisions. One of them formally belonged to Lt. Gen. James Longstreet's Corps, but because it had been serving near Ewell's men in the capital's defenses, it was attached to the Reserve Corps.[11]

South of Ewell's command, Maj. Gen. William Mahone's Division of Lt. Gen. Ambrose P. Hill's Third Corps held the Howlett Line along the Bermuda Hundred front. General Mahone had earned promotion to two-star rank with his successful counterattack during the Battle of the Crater. With Petersburg lost, he led his division back to Chester Station, withdrew through Chesterfield Court House, and headed for Goode's Bridge over the Appomattox River.[12] This span would carry the retreating Confederates across the Appomattox River about eight miles east

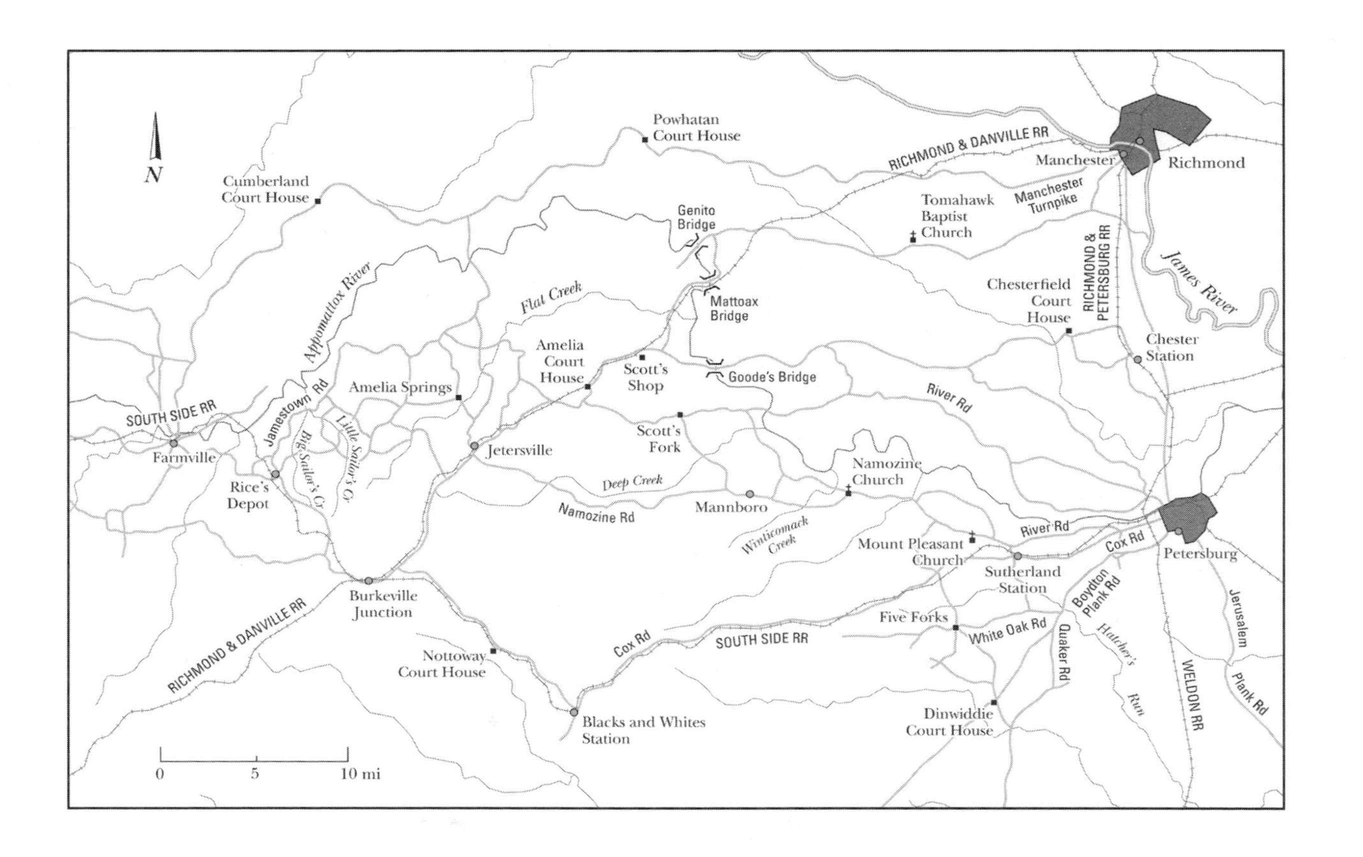

MAP 11. Petersburg to Sailor's Creek

of Amelia Court House, which was on the Richmond and Danville rail line about halfway between Petersburg and Danville.[13]

Below Mahone's column, Maj. Gen. John B. Gordon's Corps also was in motion. When the Federals began their final assault on Petersburg, two of General Gordon's divisions had held the siege lines east of the city; another, the works immediately south of it.[14] On the night of April 2–3, Gordon's Corps began withdrawing from these positions, a movement overseen by Maj. Giles Buckner Cooke of Lee's staff.[15] On the following day the command made a long march and that evening camped east of Goode's Bridge.[16]

Of the three divisions of General Longstreet's Corps, only one had been at the front when the Federals broke the Petersburg lines on April 2.[17] Another was operating with Ewell's Reserve Corps, and Maj. Gen. George E. Pickett's had been knocked apart at Five Forks.

To the right of Longstreet's lone division lay Petersburg's western defenses, which were the responsibility of General Hill's Corps. After Hill's death on April 2, one of his division commanders served a brief interim; then the corps was attached to Longstreet's Corps.[18] Two of its divisions had been driven back during the final Union assault on Petersburg. The third, Mahone's, was retreating independently of them and to the north.

In the far west was the nominal corps of Lt. Gen. Richard H. Anderson that in reality consisted of Maj. Gen. Bushrod R. Johnson's Division. General Johnson's brigades, along with General Pickett's remnants, now were fleeing northward. Maj. Gen. Fitzhugh Lee's cavalrymen covered this column while it looked for a place to cross the Appomattox River.[19]

Lee had been able to extract a considerable force, at least fifty-four thousand effectives, from the Richmond and Petersburg defenses.[20] He had set these soldiers moving westward, and a viable strategy remained open to them. They might elude their pursuers, follow the Richmond and Danville Railroad into North Carolina, join forces with Gen. Joseph E. Johnston, and strike in combination with him against either Grant or Maj. Gen. William T. Sherman.[21] On April 3 Lee's immediate goal was Amelia Court House, where he hoped to draw food and other supplies.[22]

In addition to this conventional strategy, another option lay open to the Confederates—guerrilla warfare. Bitter partisan fighting already had been waged during the Civil War in Missouri, Kentucky, Tennessee, Virginia, and elsewhere.[23] In the spring of 1865, the Federals faced the possibility that the Confederates might continue this style of warfare, employing it on a larger scale, as an alternative to the regular operations that Generals Lee and Johnston had been conducting. In an April 7 diary entry, Maj. Henry Hitchcock of General Sherman's staff considered this unhappy possibility: "But suppose that Lee's remnant and Johnston's force should also speedily fall or be broken to pieces, and the whole organization of the 'C.S.A.,' as such, be destroyed, east of the Mississippi, Texas still remains to be occupied, if not reconquered, and the 'guerrilla question' then comes up. It may be a good many months yet before all serious armed opposition to the Government shall cease."[24]

Major Hitchcock, and Federal leaders senior to him, rightly was concerned about the possibility that a dying Confederacy might turn in desperation to guerrilla warfare. Moving from a conventional to an irregular strategy might raise the morale of soldiers who had been fighting in the field for years and, by the spring of 1865, had begun to despair of victory. Partisan fighting appealed to some historical memories, if not the realities, of resistance to the British in the South during the Revolutionary War. Guerrilla bands would defend hearth and home; waging local defense, rather than serving in an army distant from a combatant's family, might strengthen morale.[25] If Lee, Johnston, and the commanders of the smaller field forces disbanded their armies, and if most of these soldiers became partisans, thousands of men would be under arms across the Confederacy. These guerrillas could prolong the war for months or even years, exhaust the Union's armies, and undermine—if not destroy—political support for the Northern war effort.[26]

On April 4, the second day of Lee's westward march from Petersburg, Confederate president Jefferson Davis issued a ringing proclamation, which was intended to rally morale after the fall of Richmond. The Southern cause was not lost, the commander in chief declared, but rather had entered "a new phase of a struggle, the memory of which is to endure for all ages, and to shed ever increasing lustre upon our country."[27]

Although some historians have interpreted the April 4 proclamation to be a call for guerrilla warfare, nowhere in the declaration did President Davis ask Southerners to fight specifically as partisans.[28] The April 4 proclamation is better read as a desperate attempt to raise the morale of an obviously dying Confederacy. Davis's experiences at West Point, during the Mexican-American War, and as secretary of war all encouraged him to value conventional military operations and to shun irregular warfare.[29] The Confederate commander in chief put his confidence in the field forces of Lee, Johnston, and other commanders, not in unreliable guerrillas.[30]

Davis's most successful army commander, Robert E. Lee, favored conventional rather than irregular warfare. When the Confederate Congress in 1864 had provided for organizing partisan units, Lee opposed the policy. He warned the president that it would encourage "many deserters & marauders" to "commit depredations on friend & foe alike."[31] The prominent Confederate artilleryman Brig. Gen. Edward Porter Alexander wrote that just before the Appomattox surrender Lee explained to him his reasons for not turning to guerrilla resistance.[32] Many other Southern officers opposed irregular warfare, and virtually every cabinet member advised Davis against it.[33]

These Confederate senior leaders had good reasons for rejecting partisan warfare. Sustained guerrilla operations required a popular base; by the spring of 1865, Confederate morale had fallen too low to support this option. Moreover, Southern leaders knew that the Confederate government would not be able to control the bands of bushwhackers that would roam the countryside, and they abhorred the social breakdown that irregular warfare would cause. William Preston Johnston, Davis's closest aide, reported the president as stating, "Guerrillas become brigands, and any government is better than that." General Alexander said that Lee opposed a partisan strategy for the same reason. Lawless bands would rob and plunder throughout the South, and it would take the country years to recover from the social disintegration that would follow.[34]

Having lost Petersburg and Richmond, Lee did not scatter his men to fight as guerrillas. He maintained them in conventional units and continued to pursue regular warfare. Lee directed his soldiers to Amelia Court House, taking his first step toward Johnston's forces and intending to draw supplies at this town on the Richmond and Danville Railroad.

Grant correctly assessed Lee's intention. The Union commander predicted to Maj. Gen. Philip H. Sheridan on the morning of April 3 that the Confederates would "make a stand at Amelia Court-House." Grant saw the significance of Burkeville Junction, a key transportation center where the Richmond and Danville and the South Side Railroads came together, about forty miles west of Petersburg and roughly eighteen miles southwest of Amelia Court House. If the Federals gained this point, they would frustrate the possibility of Lee's linking with Johnston in North Carolina.[35]

Grant made his priorities clear to General Sheridan: first, intercept Lee's army; second, "secure Burkeville." To achieve these objectives, Grant had a more than adequate force in Maj. Gen. George G. Meade's Army of the Potomac, which was supplemented by General Ord's Army of the James. The senior Union commander could keep his line of supply secure, occupy Richmond and Petersburg, and still send seventy-six thousand soldiers after Lee.[36]

Many years later a Union veteran wrote: "Now the memorable chase began." Sheridan's cavalry led the pursuit on April 3. Early that morning the Union troopers struck a rearguard force in the vicinity of Namozine Church, a Presbyterian meeting house about eighteen miles west of Petersburg. A few North Carolina cavalry regiments and part of Johnson's Division tried to resist the Federals and lost 350 men captured, among them Brig. Gen. Rufus Barringer, a cavalry brigade commander.[37] Throughout the day Sheridan rounded up hundreds of other prisoners. "Up to this hour," the cavalryman reported to Grant at 4:10 p.m. on the third, "we have taken about 1,200 prisoners." The woods were full of deserters and stragglers.[38]

The Union infantry joined the cavalry in the pursuit made on

April 3. Brevet Maj. Gen. Charles Griffin, an artilleryman turned infantry commander who was well respected by his men, had succeeded the unfortunate Maj. Gen. Gouverneur K. Warren at the head of the V Corps. He pushed his new command through the area where the Namozine Church fighting had taken place and went into camp on Deep Creek, about seven miles to the northwest.[39] Led by Maj. Gen. Andrew A. Humphreys, the II Corps followed the V Corps and bivouacked about four miles behind it near Winticomack Creek, a tributary of the Appomattox River.[40]

Behind these two corps Maj. Gen. Horatio G. Wright's VI Corps halted for the night around Mount Pleasant Church near Sutherland Station. Maj. Gen. John G. Parke left one division of his IX Corps to guard the South Side Railroad, the prized rail line that the Federals recently had won. General Parke's other two divisions followed General Wright's corps along the River Road and, like it, camped near Sutherland Station.[41]

While General Meade's Army of the Potomac made these marches, Ord's Army of the James also took up the pursuit. Two of Ord's divisions occupied Richmond, and two divisions from Maj. Gen. John Gibbon's XXIV Corps and one from the XXV Corps started after Lee. These three divisions acted as Grant's left wing, moving westward along a line to the south of the Army of the Potomac.[42] They headed for Burkeville Junction, the crucial junction of the South Side and the Richmond and Danville Railroads.[43] On April 3 Ord's soldiers tramped along the Cox Road, which roughly paralleled the tracks of the South Side Railroad. The "men marched well," their commander reported, and halted for the night about three miles west of Sutherland Station.[44]

The next day, April 4, Lee's forces moved toward Amelia Court House, their first objective since leaving Petersburg. The advance of Longstreet's column, accompanied by its commander and Lee, marched into the village that morning. Some of Hill's old units, now formally under Longstreet, began entering Amelia around 4:00 p.m., and General Anderson's Corps and Gen. Fitzhugh Lee's cavalrymen followed later.[45]

While things went well for these commands on the fourth, Ewell's Reserve Corps fared badly that day. In the morning it left its bivouac near the Tomahawk Baptist Church and headed west. In the afternoon Ewell reached the Genito Bridge over the Appomattox River. He had expected to find the old span in ruins, but he was dismayed to learn that a pontoon bridge had not been thrown at the site as planned. It was here—at the Genito Bridge crossing of the Appomattox and on the second afternoon out of Petersburg—that events began to turn against the Confederates.[46] Ewell spent irretrievable time searching for a crossing point. Late that night his exhausted men made their way over the Mattoax Bridge and camped on hilly ground south of the Appomattox, but they were nearly ten miles from Lee's main body.[47]

Ewell's misfortune influenced other units. Gordon's Corps moved from Goode's Bridge to Scott's Shop, about five miles east of Amelia Court House, and waited there for Ewell.[48] Mahone's Division, formerly of Hill's Corps and now assigned to Longstreet, headed west from Chesterfield Court House and camped not far from Goode's Bridge. In view of Ewell's unhappy discovery at the Genito span, Mahone remained near Goode's Bridge, holding it open for Old Baldy if he could find no better crossing.[49] As a result of Ewell's delay and its ripple effects, Lee decided to spend the night at Amelia Court House. The halt would prove fatal.[50]

While the Southerners gathered around Amelia Court House, the president of the United States visited the city that only a morning earlier had been the Confederate capital. Lincoln stepped ashore from a small barge on the James River and toured Richmond with a party of fewer than twenty people. He entered what had been the office of the Confederate president. One of Weitzel's staff officers recalled Lincoln sitting in what he assumed had been Davis's chair, looking "far off with a serious, dreamy expression."[51]

More than one member of the president's entourage feared an attempt on his life, and some alarming incidents did take place. A man in a Confederate uniform appeared to aim a shoulder arm at Lincoln, and that evening two suspicious persons tried to board his ship. Nothing came of these episodes, and Lincoln spent most of the afternoon of April 4 in the former Rebel bastion unharmed.[52] Ten days later, however, he would be assassinated in his own capital.

While the commander in chief toured Richmond, his military subordinates pursued Lee, although most of them spent the fourth moving at a modest pace. That day the II Corps found itself delayed by the Federal cavalry in front of it. General Humphreys's men completed only a short march from their campground near Winticomack Creek to Deep Creek. Wright's VI Corps did not go far on the fourth, either, advancing from Mount Pleasant Church to a point two miles beyond the Winticomack. The Union left wing, Ord's Army of the James, continued to move westward along the South Side Railroad and the Cox Road. General Gibbon's two divisions, followed by the one from the XXV Corps, stopped for the night at Wilson's Station on the South Side Railroad. From there Grant wired to Secretary Stanton: "All of the enemy that retain anything like organization have gone north of the Appomattox, and are apparently headed for Lynchburg. Their losses have been very heavy."[53]

Ten miles or more to the east of Grant and Ord at Wilson's Station, Parke's IX Corps halted for the night at Ford's Depot, which was also on the South Side Railroad. This command soon dropped out of the chase after Lee and took up other important work. The soldiers of the IX Corps guarded the rail line and realigned its tracks to the gauge used by Grant's military trains. Although left without a role in the pursuit, these men remained proud of their contributions to the Appomattox campaign. The day before Lee's surrender, an officer of the Fifty-sixth Massachusetts would write to his mother: "We are very foot sore but very much elated at our successes. I hope to see the war closed soon."[54]

The IX Corps stopped pursuing Lee after April 4, and on that day only two Federal commands, Sheridan's Cavalry Corps and General Griffin's V Corps, put any pressure on the Confederates. Brig. Gen. Ranald S. Mackenzie pushed his small mounted division from Deep Creek to a crossroads about a mile south of Amelia Court House, where he camped for the night.[55] Another Federal cavalry division reached Jetersville, some eight miles southwest of Amelia Court House, near the end of the fourth and severed the Richmond and Danville Railroad about eight miles above Burkeville Junction. There the Richmond and Danville line intersected the South Side Railroad; Grant correctly had identified the junction as crucial to the retreating Southerners. As the day came to an end, Sheridan's troopers began entrenching across the Richmond and Danville.[56]

Also on April 4 the V Corps's movements constricted the Confederates as well. Griffin drove his command a grueling twenty-five miles that day, from Deep Creek to Jetersville, and joined the cavalrymen near them in throwing up breastworks.[57] By nightfall of the fourth Griffin had more than twelve thousand Federal infantrymen within eight miles of the Confederates gathering around Amelia.[58] This force was so large that it was unlikely Lee would be able to open the Richmond and Danville line.

The Confederate commander would learn about this roadblock later, but on the morning of the fourth he faced a more immediate concern—a food shortage. Lee had directed his forces to Amelia Court House and, hindered by Ewell's delayed crossing of the Appomattox, halted them there to rest and draw food and other supplies in the village. Anticipating the loss of Petersburg and Richmond, commissary officers had gathered 350,000 rations in the capital that were to be shipped down the Richmond and Danville tracks to Amelia. Lee rode into the courthouse town on the morning of the fourth and learned that, for whatever reason, the food had not arrived. There were ample artillery supplies—caissons, ammunition, and harnesses—but no ration boxes.[59]

Confederate wagons trundled off into the countryside to collect whatever foodstuffs could be found. The foragers spent their time to little purpose. During the morning of April 5, the supply wagons began returning to Amelia with pathetically light loads. Early that afternoon the Confederate columns set out for the next station down the rail line, Jetersville, and beyond it, Danville.[60]

The Southerners trudged southwest from Amelia Court House, with their cavalry riding in their advance. Longstreet's Corps, moving without the remnants of Pickett's Division, led the infantry. Pickett's survivors accompanied Anderson's Corps, which fell in behind Old Pete's columns. Ewell's Corps broke its camp northeast of Amelia and began entering the village about the time Longstreet and Anderson left it. Gordon's Corps also had spent the night northeast of the court house and it took up the rearguard.[61]

As the lead columns approached Jetersville, skirmish fire crackled across the Confederate line of advance. Lee, Longstreet, and Maj. Gen. William H. F. "Rooney" Lee rode into a patch of woods to assess the situation. Gen. Rooney Lee, the senior commander's second son and a cavalry division leader, explained that dismounted horsemen barred the road into Jetersville. He also reported that Federal infantrymen soon would reinforce these troopers. The situation was in fact worse than what he described: Griffin's V Corps already was in their path and as strongly entrenched as its cavalry comrades were.[62]

The senior Lee concluded that he could not open the Richmond and Danville rail line and changed his operational plan. He had lost time at Amelia Court House; he wanted to avoid battle and keep moving. Lee abandoned his move on Jetersville and instead swung to his right toward Amelia Springs, which was about three miles to the north.[63] From there the Confederates would strike west for Farmville on the South Side Railroad. If Lee reached that town ahead of the Federals, he could continue west and outpace his pursuers; if not, he could veer south, toward Johnston.[64]

Hoping to distance themselves from their enemies at the Jetersville roadblock, the Confederates marched into the night of April 5. Splashing across Flat Creek, Longstreet's and Anderson's Corps pressed beyond Amelia Springs before halting in exhaustion. In the darkness, columns of weary soldiers stretched behind them for miles.[65]

While Lee lost time on Wednesday, April 5, the Union pursuit accelerated. Grant needed no encouragement but received some anyway in the contents of a heartening dispatch he received that day from Sheridan. The cavalryman provided some sharply accurate intelligence: Lee himself and his entire army were at or near Amelia Court House. Sheridan then suggested an aggressive operational plan: "We can capture the Army of Northern Virginia if force enough can be thrown to this point [Jetersville], and then advance upon it."[66]

Grant saw this opportunity as clearly as his cavalryman did.

During April 5 he continued to accompany Ord's command, the Federal left wing, while it made an impressive advance along the South Side Railroad. Gibbon's two divisions of the XXIV Corps covered an exhausting twenty-eight miles that Wednesday, moving from Wilson's Station to Burkeville Junction. The lone division of the XXV Corps halted well to the east at Blacks and Whites Station, where it would spend the rest of the campaign guarding the rail line.[67]

Like Gibbon's soldiers, the II and VI Corps pushed hard on the fifth. They had made little progress on the fourth, and likely as a result, Meade ordered them under way in the dead of night. Humphreys's corps was to move at 1:00 a.m. on Wednesday, April 5, with Wright's to follow. The two commands met their challenging departure times, but the II Corps soon found that it again would be delayed by some of Sheridan's troopers, who occupied the roadway. Complained Lt. Col. Theodore Lyman of Meade's staff, "That's the way with those cavalry bucks: they bother and howl about infantry not being up to support them, and they are precisely the people who are always blocking up the way; it was so at Todd's Tavern, and here again, a year after."[68] Humphreys's foot soldiers spent the early morning hours resting by the roadside and eating rations. Sometime after 7:00 or 8:00 a.m., their route opened, and they used this opportunity well. After marching fifteen miles or more, the II and VI Corps both closed on Jetersville.[69]

Grant's forces were significantly better placed at the end of April 5 than they had been the previous day. On the fourth only Griffin's corps and Sheridan's cavalry had pressured the Confederates. At darkness on the fifth, the II, V, VI, and Cavalry Corps all had concentrated at Jetersville, and the head of Ord's column had reached Burkeville Junction, fewer than ten miles to the southwest.[70]

The Army of the Potomac's soldiers marched well on April 5, but their commander was ill. Meade had not been healthy since March 31, Lieutenant Colonel Lyman reported, and then he suffered a chill and "violent fever" on April 4. That night the general had a "distressing cough." On the morning of the fifth, his staff officers put him in a wagon, and he spent the day traveling to Jetersville.[71]

Grant also headed for that same little community during the night of the fifth. In a dispatch that Sheridan had written to his chief that afternoon, the cavalryman had hinted: "I wish you were here yourself." Grant received this communication at 6:30 p.m. and acted on Sheridan's suggestion. Leaving Ord and his officers, the Federal commander rode Cincinnati, his large bay horse, through the darkness. Accompanied only by a small party, Grant made his way cross-country in the moonlight and reached Sheridan's picket line at about 10:30 p.m. The commander and his cavalry chief ate a late-night supper and then called on the ailing Meade at his nearby camp.[72]

Sheridan was largely responsible for convening this conference, which was held in the dead of night. The aggressive cavalryman had become impatient with Meade's pursuit plan and earlier that day had suggested that a visit by Grant would spur the effort to cut off Lee. Long after the war, Grant recalled that during this late-night meeting he explained to Meade that he did not want to follow Lee; indeed, he wanted to get ahead of him. Grant was concerned that Meade's orders "would allow the enemy to escape." Time was of the essence because, Grant surmised, "Lee was moving right then."[73]

As Grant's aide-de-camp Lt. Col. Horace Porter explained the matter, Meade had different ideas than Grant's about how the Army of the Potomac should operate during the next day. Meade believed that Lee would move by his right flank and to the north, and the Union commander had issued orders accordingly to his own army. Sheridan and Grant, however, concluded that Lee would march by his left flank, to the south. Grant, as Lieutenant Colonel Porter later summarized, "changed the dispositions that were being made so as to have [Meade's] army unite with Sheridan's troops in swinging round toward the south, and heading off Lee in that direction." As Grant recalled the meeting, once he explained what he wanted done, "Meade changed his orders at once."[74]

Grant may have seen in Meade's illness an opportunity to intervene in the affairs of his army without unduly offending the temperamental hero of Gettysburg. In the change of dispositions referred to by Porter, Wright's VI Corps was shifted from the right of the Army of the Potomac to the left. There it would operate with Sheridan's cavalry, a combination that had proved effective during the 1864 Shenandoah Valley campaign. Griffin's V Corps took station on the army's right.[75]

Grant had assessed correctly that Lee would continue to move through the night of the fifth and sixth. Leaving the Federals behind at Jetersville, he departed Amelia Springs and intended to go by way of Deatonville and Rice's Depot to Farmville. Maintaining the order in which they had left Amelia Court House, Longstreet's, Anderson's, Ewell's, and Gordon's Corps marched. Lee rode with Longstreet at the head of the column.[76] The vital supply wagons traveled between Ewell and Gordon.[77]

Since leaving Richmond and Petersburg, the Confederates had made long marches on little rest and few rations. Showers fell on their haggard columns during the morning of Thursday, April 6. The Federal cavalry was dangerously active, as it had been throughout the pursuit, and it probed at the Confederate wagon train.[78]

The Union infantry also moved vigorously that morning. Humphreys's men started north from Jetersville, but when an escort party from corps headquarters spotted the Confederate main body moving westward, the II Corps swung to the left in pursuit.[79] Wright's VI Corps came to its support while Griffin's V Corps continued north toward Painesville. Ord's exhausted soldiers rested until 11:00 a.m. and then set out for Farmville.[80]

For their part, the Federal troopers menaced the Southern wagons so greatly that by 11:00 a.m. Anderson and Ewell were forced to halt. They would have to allow at least some of the vehicles to pass, or else Gordon would be cut off while he tried to cover the lengthy supply train. This break in the march was anything but the restful one that the Southern infantrymen badly needed. Many of Ewell's men spent three hours deployed, as he explained, "to cover the passage of the trains." Even after this halt, most of the supply wagons remained between the Reserve Corps and Gordon's Corps, the army's rearguard. Gordon protected this crucial convoy by, in Ewell's words, "constantly fighting."[81]

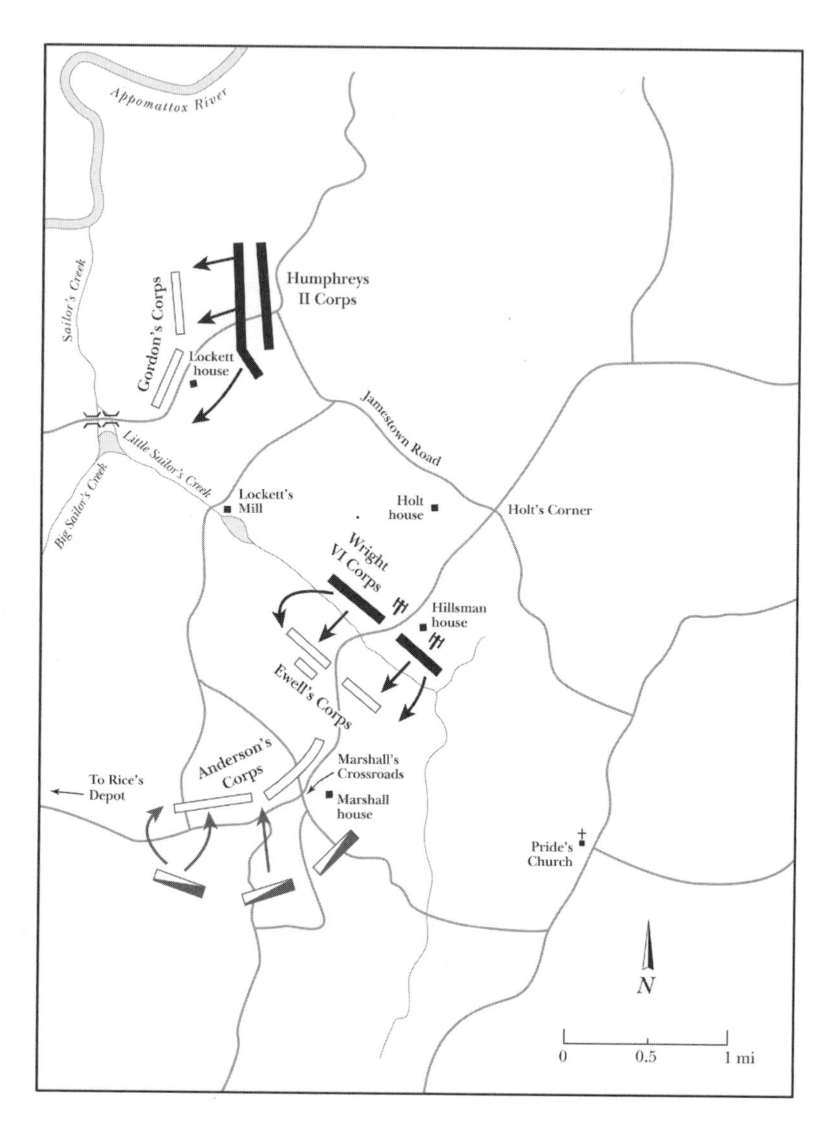

MAP 12. Battle of Sailor's Creek, April 6, 1865

Farther up in the Confederate column, the Union troopers created more trouble. At Holt's Corner, a country intersection near the modest home of overseer James Holt, Federal horsemen moved in front of Anderson and obliged him to spend much of the middle of the day clearing his roadway. While Anderson and Ewell were delayed, Longstreet continued his march to Rice's

Depot. A two-mile gap opened between his corps and the other Confederate units.[82]

Around 2:00 p.m. Ewell resumed his trek southwest toward Rice's Depot. He had crossed the small stream known as Little Sailor's Creek when he encountered Fitz Lee. The cavalryman gave him the unhappy news that the Federals had stalled Anderson not far down the road. Anderson had forced his way through Holt's Corner but was blocked again at the next junction—Marshall's Crossroads, evidently named for James N. "Swep" Marshall, whose farm was just east of it.[83] Here Anderson found that a "strongly posted" Union mounted contingent had cut the road in front of him.[84]

Acting quickly on Fitz Lee's disconcerting information, Ewell improvised a hasty plan. The infantry's route to Rice's Depot obviously had become dangerous for the slow-moving supply wagons. The main body of the train, rolling between Ewell and Gordon, was diverted onto the Jamestown Road, which ran northwest from Holt's Corner toward the Appomattox River. This roadway would carry the wagons away from the threatening enemy cavalry, and meanwhile Ewell would aid Anderson.[85] Gordon, receiving no word otherwise, assumed that the crucial supply vehicles were taking the main line of the infantry's march, as they had all day. At Holt's Corner he followed the wagon train onto the Jamestown Road.[86]

Ewell's Reserve Corps deployed across the road to Rice's Depot, forming his line parallel to Little Sailor's Creek and about three hundred yards south of it.[87] The position had little to recommend it. The narrow water course, less than four feet deep, offered no meaningful barrier to the enemy, and some brush pines provided the only cover.[88] Ewell was forced to hold this ground as best he could not only to help Anderson but also to defend himself. When Gordon's rearguard had moved off to follow the wagon train, it left open the road into the new Confederate rear. Masses of the Federal VI Corps now were bearing down on Ewell.[89]

Old Baldy improvised his stand as well as circumstances allowed. He had no artillery at hand; it had accompanied the army's reserve train. Ewell deployed his two divisions on one line, with the garrison troops in a second one. Many of these men, once department clerks and reservists in Richmond, were unused to marching. They had left the ranks by the hundreds during the long tramp from the capital to Little Sailor's Creek. The soldiers of the veteran divisions, too, had melted away. About six thousand of them had left the Richmond defenses on April 3; now fewer than half that number remained. All of the survivors—the veterans and the garrison troops—had marched the last two days without rations. "I saw men eating raw fresh meat as they marched in ranks," Ewell reported.[90]

Anderson had taken position just below Ewell on the road to Rice's Depot, but Union cavalry blocked his path. Anderson's left flank stood behind the right of the Reserve Corps. From there his line ran southwest for about a half mile and then curved westward for perhaps another three quarters of a mile. Anderson had only Johnson's Division and some of Pickett's survivors of Five Forks.[91]

Three Union cavalry divisions confronted Anderson.[92] At the same time, two divisions of the VI Corps, or about seven thousand men, descended on Ewell from the northeast.[93] The attackers closed on the Confederates like a vise.

Twenty field guns of the VI Corps were aligned along a ridge running through the James Hillsman farm; around 5:15 p.m. they opened on Ewell's tired and hungry soldiers.[94] Without artillery to reply, the defenders—only a few thousand of them, half of whom had never experienced a major engagement—endured the bombardment.[95] At 6:00 p.m. the VI Corps's veterans, who four days earlier had carried the Petersburg defenses, rolled forward.[96]

For a time Ewell's men staged a brave defense. They repulsed the first Federal advance and offered a counterattack. In this effort Col. Stapleton Crutchfield, an artilleryman who had served with then Maj. Gen. Thomas J. "Stonewall" Jackson during the glory days of the 1862 Shenandoah Valley campaign, was shot in the head and killed.[97]

The Union attackers reformed and advanced again. This time the dead weight of their numbers told, and they broke in both flanks of the defending line. Nearly thirty-four hundred Confederates surrendered. An Ohio soldier who saw a column of these prisoners the next day observed that "as a general thing they look'd pretty hard, drest in almost anything and everything."[98]

Ewell had gone to consult with Anderson and was away from his Reserve Corps when the fatal blow landed. He and his staff were captured when the Federals swarmed across the Marshall farm. Sgt. Angus Cameron, leading a squad on the Fifth Wisconsin's skirmish line, accepted the general's surrender. Sergeant Cameron's moment of fame passed quickly. His colonel complained that "a squad of cavalry" soon took the prisoners away from the infantrymen. Five other Confederate senior officers were caught up in the dissolution of the Reserve Corps and were captured: Maj. Gen. George Washington Custis Lee (the commander's eldest son), Maj. Gen. Joseph B. Kershaw, Brig. Gen. Seth Barton, Brig. Gen. Dudley DuBose, and Brig. Gen. James Simms.[99]

Anderson fared little better than Ewell had. Attacking at the same time as the VI Corps, the Union cavalrymen struck the right flank of Johnson's Division and drove it back into its own wagon train. Other Federal horsemen found the seam between Johnson's left and Pickett's right. As on Ewell's front, the exhausted Confederates soon were overwhelmed. Disaster ensued. While some of the defenders fled west through the woods, most surrendered. Ordnance Sgt. James W. Albright, one of Anderson's gunners, blamed the debacle on "too much straggling." Doubtless the wearying marches and dwindling rations had taken their toll. Sergeant Albright's own battalion entered the action with four guns and lost three of them.[100] In all, the Union cavalrymen garnered about twenty-six hundred prisoners, eight hundred mules, three hundred wagons, and fifteen field guns. Two more general officers, Brig. Gen. Eppa Hunton and Brig. Gen. Montgomery Corse, were captured.[101]

Reports of the calamity reached Lee, and Traveller, his horse, carried him back from Rice's Depot to a knoll overlooking Big Sailor's Creek. From here he could see Anderson's survivors fleeing across the valley east of him. "My God," Mahone heard Lee ask, "has this army dissolved?"[102]

The Army of Northern Virginia had not dissolved, but Sheridan's troopers and Wright's soldiers had destroyed Anderson's and Ewell's Corps. And the Confederate disaster did not end there. Gordon's Corps and the main baggage train also met a hard fate. Hoping to elude the Union cavalry, the wagon drivers had taken the Jamestown Road from Holt's Corner. Gordon had followed, but neither his men nor the supply train gained any respite from the harassing pursuit of the II Corps.[103]

Continuing to cover the wagons, Gordon struggled along the Jamestown Road for about two and a half miles. That brought him to the James S. Lockett house, which stood on a stretch of high ground that offered a defensive position. From this frame residence and its ridge, the road ran downhill for about three quarters of a mile.[104] The supply wagons lurched down this long slope into a bottomland where a pair of country bridges, just a few yards apart, would carry them across the confluence of Little and Big Sailor's Creeks.[105] Gordon ordered two of his divisions into a line along the high ground at Lockett's place. He hoped they would stand off their pursuers long enough for the wagons to make good their escape across the rickety double bridges.[106]

Sunset of April 6 was approaching when Humphreys's van closed in on Gordon's two rearguard divisions. The Southern teamsters tried to hasten across the double bridges, and a confused snarl of vehicles and stragglers clogged the low ground near the stream crossings. Major Cooke of Lee's staff, and doubtless other officers, attempted to sort out the tangle of supply and ambulance wagons.[107]

At 5:00 p.m. two divisions of the II Corps struck Gordon's thin line.[108] The Federals defeated Gordon much as they had Ewell, with a determined advance by a fresher, larger force that overlapped both flanks of the tired defenders. Once the Southern infantry gave way, the attackers descended on the beleaguered wagons at the double bridges. The scene at the water crossings, already confused, became chaotic. The Federals, Cooke related, "came rushing down upon our wagon train and ambulances at Sailor's Creek and such a scene as then ensued I never wish to behold again." The staff officer managed to clamber up the slope and out of the low ground, but he had to leave his exhausted horse in the creek.[109]

Capitalizing on its opportunity at Sailor's Creek, the II Corps on April 6, 1865, achieved one of the high points of its illustrious service in the Army of the Potomac. On that day the command bagged about seventeen hundred prisoners, more than three hundred wagons, seventy ambulances, and three field guns. Only the cover of darkness, which allowed a number of Gordon's men and vehicles to elude their pursuers, saved his corps from a calamity on the scale that befell Ewell's and Anderson's Corps.[110] The total Federal losses at Sailor's Creek came to 1,150; the Southern figure was more than six times that, or 7,700 men.[111]

For three days after April 6, 1865, the armies would endure more exhausting marches, harassing skirmishes, and running fights but no more major engagements. The Army of Northern Virginia—Lee's army, the pride of the South, and the bedrock of its hopes—had fought its last battle.

CHAPTER EIGHT

Spring Morning

Every day and night during the march from Petersburg, the Confederates became more famished and exhausted. Ordnance Sgt. James W. Albright, one of Lt. Gen. Richard H. Anderson's survivors of Sailor's Creek, characterized the artillerymen around him on April 6 as "poor, hungry tired men." A member of Company F of the Twenty-fourth Virginia Cavalry reported on April 5: "We fed our horses this morning[,] the first time since we left Richmond but get nothing for ourselves." The seemingly endless marching wore down the army's animals as well as its soldiers. Raleigh W. Downman of the Fourth Virginia Cavalry wrote to his wife on April 6 that since the fall of Petersburg his regiment had been "constantly in motion day & night, marching & fighting. Our horses are very fagged."[1]

By the time Downman wrote his letter, the soldiers of the Army of Northern Virginia were demoralized. At the beginning of the march westward, Gen. Robert E. Lee's veterans could believe they were undertaking a movement that freed them from the trenches of Petersburg. When day after day they passed abandoned wagons, dead animals, and scattered equipment, they could rationalize that this debris trimmed the army for its next battle. But by the time that darkness fell on the disaster at Sailor's Creek, only the most loyal Confederates could avoid despair. That night General Lee himself saw that many of his men had discarded their shoulder arms. Maj. Holmes Conrad, who directed a cavalry supply train, concluded on April 7 that the "Army seems spirit broken."[2]

Hunger, fatigue, and demoralization produced straggling and desertion. A trooper in the Twenty-fourth Virginia Cavalry reported that as early as the night of April 2–3, ten or twelve cavalrymen left his regiment. He estimated that eight or ten departed after dark on the fourth, and later another group followed them.[3] That same night of April 4, scores of deserters entered the picket lines of the V Corps. On the eighth, Lee's staff officer Maj. Giles Buckner Cooke acknowledged, "Our men straggled awfully."[4]

A firm accounting probably cannot be made of the numbers of Confederates who remained in the ranks and of those who left them between Petersburg and Appomattox Court House. A reasonable estimate can be suggested: at least 54,000 Southerners left Richmond and Petersburg. Lee lost about 980 men in the small actions between April 3 and 5 and another 7,700 at Sailor's Creek on the sixth. These losses left a potential strength on April 7 of 45,000, without taking into account deserters. During the minor engagements between Sailor's Creek and the Appomattox surrender—High Bridge, Farmville, Cumberland Church, Appomattox Station, and Appomattox Court House—Lee was to lose another 2,000 or more, reducing his potential strength on April 9 to less than 43,000.[5] On that day, a little more than 28,000 Confederates surrendered. Noting again that the numbers (other than paroles) can only be estimated, these figures suggest that about 15,000 men left the ranks during the march from Petersburg to Appomattox.[6]

Those who remained with their regiments faced a daunting situation. After the Battle of Sailor's Creek, the crossings of the Appomattox River west of that battlefield became crucial objectives for both forces. The combatants by then were deployed along a stretch of the Appomattox that cavalry could ford in places, but infantry could not.[7] If the Federals gained control of the bridges, they could deny Lee his best route toward North Carolina and Gen. Joseph E. Johnston.

Two crossing points were vital: High Bridge, about three miles north and slightly west of Rice's Depot, and the spans at Farmville

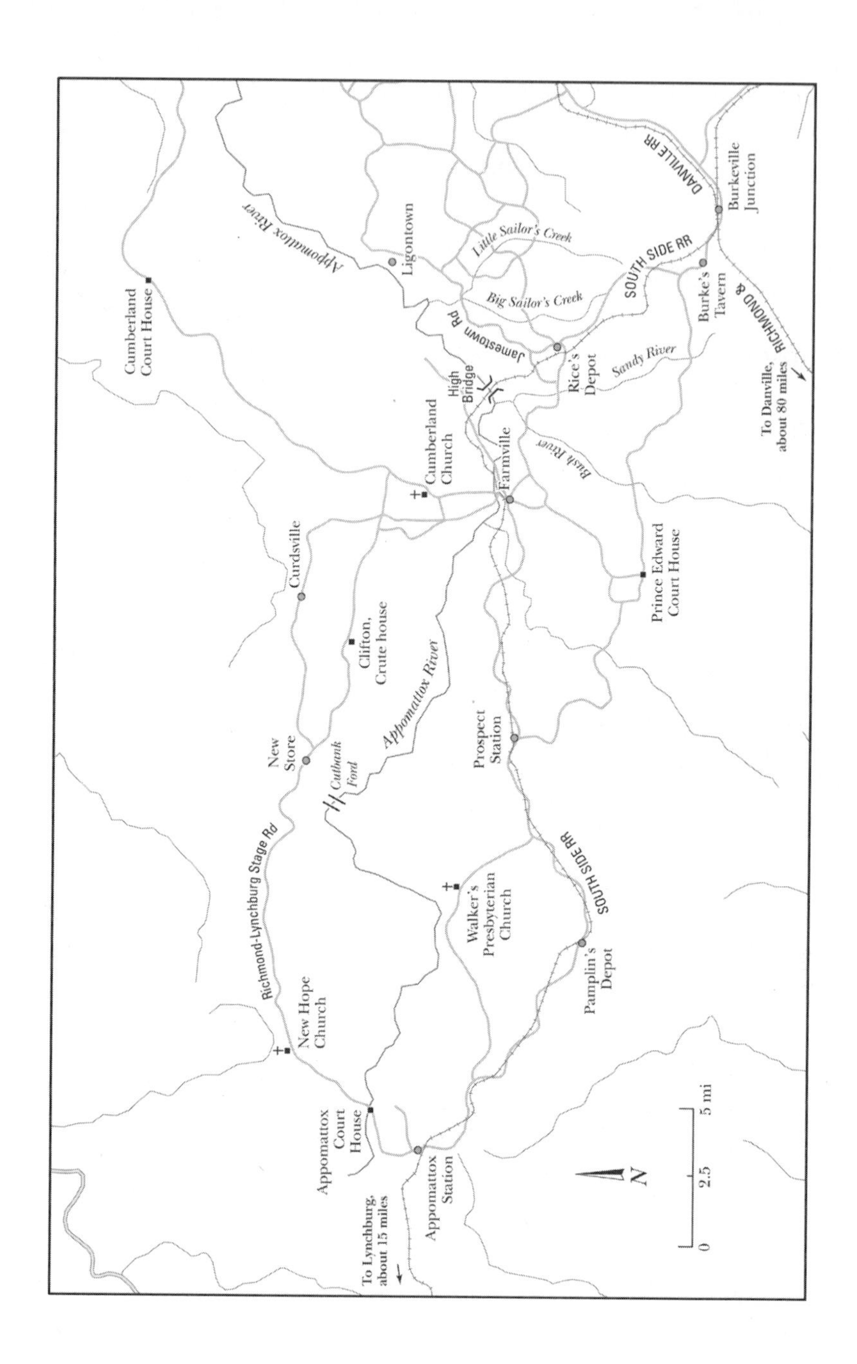

MAP 13. Sailor's Creek to Appomattox Court House

farther upstream. The South Side Railroad's High Bridge, begun in 1851 and completed on the last day of 1853, represented an impressive feat of construction as the first railway cantilever in North America. The span was well named: its 126 feet made it the world's highest railroad bridge of its length, so lofty that its first passengers became uneasy when their cars rolled out onto its elevated piers.[8] Lt. Col. Theodore Lyman marveled at the rural structure: "Nothing can more surprise one than a sudden view of this great viaduct, in a country like Virginia, where public works are almost unknown." The towering High Bridge was accompanied by a wagon bridge, which stood far below and parallel to it on its eastern, or downstream, side.[9] The other key point was the tobacco town of Farmville, four miles upstream, where the South Side Railroad again, if less dramatically, crossed the Appomattox. Here too a railway bridge was paired with a wagon one to the west of it.[10]

Maj. Gen. Edward O. C. Ord, who commanded the Army of the James and directed the left wing of the Union pursuit, was well aware of the importance of these crossings. Early on the morning of April 6, General Ord had dispatched a modest force representing three regiments to burn High Bridge. South of that imposing structure, these raiders encountered some of Maj. Gen. Fitzhugh Lee's cavalrymen. In a sharp action during the early afternoon of the sixth, the Confederates parried Ord's threat to the vital river crossing. They captured most of his strike force and, critically, kept High Bridge available for Lee's use.[11]

A sidebar story to this encounter south of High Bridge was the fatal wounding of Brig. Gen. James Dearing. Shot during the April 6 High Bridge fight, the Confederate general was taken to Lynchburg, where he lingered for seventeen days. He then became the last Confederate general officer to die of wounds received in combat.[12]

While the engagements took place on April 6 at High Bridge and Sailor's Creek, Lt. Gen. James Longstreet's Corps had remained near Rice's Depot. There it waited for the corps of Maj. Gen. John B. Gordon, General Anderson, and Lt. Gen. Richard S. Ewell. Of these groups, only General Gordon's command survived the Sailor's Creek disaster as a viable corps. While waiting for its comrades, General Longstreet's Corps also helped cover the vital High Bridge and Farmville crossings of the Appomattox.[13]

Federal infantry eventually approached Longstreet. Having sent a raiding party against High Bridge, Ord put in motion his main body—two divisions under Maj. Gen. John Gibbon—and it headed northwest from Burkeville Junction. During the late afternoon of the sixth, General Gibbon found the Confederate positions around Rice's Depot. Longstreet's veterans had used the day to entrench themselves well, and Gibbon had to prepare carefully before hazarding an attack. As historian Chris Calkins's reliable narrative *The Appomattox Campaign* points out, darkness fell before the Federals could mount an offensive.[14]

Through the night of April 6–7, Gordon's Corps retreated from Sailor's Creek to High Bridge and then crossed to the north bank of the Appomattox.[15] Lee directed Maj. Gen. William Mahone to take responsibility for the survivors of Anderson's Corps in addition to General Mahone's own division. General Ewell's Reserve Corps had been virtually destroyed at Sailor's Creek. The Army of Northern Virginia now was effectively reduced to two corps: Longstreet's and Gordon's. Mahone's Division remained nearer to Gordon's Corps than to its own, Longstreet's Corps, and continued to operate with it. Mahone's soldiers, as fatigued as Gordon's men, followed them across High Bridge and trudged onto the north bank of the Appomattox near the dawn of April 7.[16]

Moving without Mahone, Longstreet's Corps left Gibbon behind at Rice's Depot, walked through the night, and reached Farmville in the early hours of the seventh. The town of fifteen hundred residents stood on the south bank of the Appomattox. Here Longstreet's hungry marchers linked with their supply trains, quickly drew their rations, and pressed across the river to eat them.[17] Gordon's Corps and Mahone's Division planned to use High Bridge to cross the Appomattox. The Confederates then could destroy all the bridges in the area and hinder Lt. Gen. Ulysses S. Grant's pursuit.[18]

The Southerners failed to carry out this plan fully. Many years after the war, Col. Thomas M. R. Talcott, the commander of the army's engineer brigade, offered a credible explanation. As Colonel Talcott told the story, Lee instructed Gordon to destroy the bridges. The engineers were ordered to place the kindling that would start fires on High Bridge and its neighboring wagon crossing and then to await a command to apply the torch from Mahone or one of his staff officers. When no such order arrived, Lt. Col. William W. Blackford rode to find the division commander, who was about four miles away on the road to Farmville. Mahone gave his authorization to start the kindling, and Lieutenant Colonel Blackford galloped back to Talcott. The engineers started both bridges on fire, but by then the van of Maj. Gen. Andrew A. Humphreys's II Corps was approaching the valuable spans.[19]

General Humphreys's command had left the double bridges on the Sailor's Creek battlefield at about 5:30 a.m. on April 7. His lead division, which had not fought at Sailor's Creek, closed on High Bridge around 7:00 a.m. The unit had a chance, if it moved quickly, to capture both the lofty span and the wagon bridge, which would allow a vigorous Northern pursuit to continue.[20]

Flames were dancing up from the wagon bridge when the first pursuing Northerners reached the scene. Col. Isaac W. Starbird's Nineteenth Maine dashed out onto the lower span. Three companies of the Down Easters deployed in loose order and engaged Talcott's engineers, who were not used to being under fire and welcomed an infantry brigade dispatched by Mahone.[21] The remaining members of the Nineteenth Maine, covered by their skirmishing comrades, poured water from their canteens on the flames or beat on them with their tents and anything else at hand. The intrepid New Englanders saved the wagon bridge, and the rest of the Nineteenth Maine's brigade soon pressed across to the north bank. Colonel Starbird, however, was severely wounded.[22]

Towering above this action on the wagon bridge, another drama played out on High Bridge. Here too Talcott's engineers had set their fires a bit late. Union pioneers raced onto the bridge and attacked the flames. Ax-wielding members of the Nineteenth Maine, who had been lumbermen in civilian life, joined them from the wagon bridge. The Federals lost the battle for the northernmost three spans but chopped a gap that saved the remainder of the lofty structure. Repairing High Bridge would take months, but the wagon bridge far below it remained available for immediate use.[23]

Mahone deployed a loose-order line and tried to recover the wagon bridge. At first he enjoyed success, some of it at the expense of the Seventh Michigan and Fifty-ninth New York. One of the Wolverines long afterward recalled that his regiment "was put in advance on the skirmish line to feel the rebel position and we went a little too fast and lost connection with our left [and the] enemy got in the rear and gobbled up very near the entire regiment." This Seventh Michigan soldier remained a prisoner until the Confederate surrender two days later and made some revealing observations about Southern logistics during the Appomattox campaign. He and his fellow prisoners shared their own rations with their captors since the Confederates "had had nothing to eat for 24 hours." The Michigan prisoner himself received no more food until April 9: "They had nothing to give us[,] as they had nothing for themselves."[24]

The Confederates took some prisoners, but by about 9:00 a.m., another division from the II Corps reached the scene. Mahone recognized that he was outnumbered, called in his skirmish line, and retreated northwest. The Federals had gained undisputed control of the wagon bridge.[25]

Securing this river crossing allowed the Federals to continue their dogged pursuit of the Southerners. Two of Humphreys's divisions followed Mahone. The third went after Gordon's Corps, which took the line of the South Side Railroad toward Farmville.[26]

Brig. Gen. Thomas A. Smyth, an Irishman who had come to the United States in 1854, led the pursuit of Gordon. His brigade caught up with the Confederates outside of Farmville, where a Southern marksman shot him in the face and knocked him from his horse. A week later, an officer of the 108th New York described the scene: General Smyth "fell mortally wounded . . . when about to give the command forward,! [*sic*] to his brave boys who were about to make a charge on the enemy near Farmville. . . . The troops upon seeing their adored leader thus stricken down, stood motionless, neither advancing nor retreating, seeming for a time like a multitude struck dumb."[27] As historian William Marvel relates in his scholarly work *Lee's Last Retreat*, this hesitation by the Federals and a Confederate counterattack allowed Gordon to turn north and move away from his pursuers.[28]

Smyth had been completely paralyzed by his wound. The New York officer who saw him fall wrote: "The General was at once removed to comfortable quarters where he received the best of treatment but he could not be saved." Smyth died at about 4:00 a.m. on April 9, the day of Lee's surrender.[29] In Civil War memory, Thomas A. Smyth would be paired with James Dearing as the last Northern and Southern general officers to die in combat.

When the Federals gained the north bank of the Appomattox, the campaign entered its final phase. Lee turned his attention to Cumberland Church, which stood about five miles north of High Bridge.[30] A mid-eighteenth century building, Cumberland Church was an unpretentious Presbyterian meeting house that was painted but without a steeple. Lee recognized that this rural place of worship stood at a point where the Union units that had crossed the Appomattox near High Bridge might cut his line of march.[31]

Lee concentrated the Army of Northern Virginia accordingly. Longstreet's Corps, having crossed the Appomattox at Farmville, continued north to a position southeast of Cumberland Church. Gordon's Corps arrived on Longstreet's left and deployed facing east. Mahone's Division also outpaced its II Corps pursuers, reached Cumberland Church, and formed on Gordon's left along a line that looked north.[32] Mahone's position was the most vulnerable sector of the army's new position, and Gen. Fitzhugh Lee dispatched some of his cavalrymen to bolster it.[33]

The Northerners continued to move energetically. Recovered from the check it had received outside of Farmville, the II Corps turned north, and by 1:00 p.m. its lead units approached Cumberland Church.[34] While a drizzly afternoon passed, Humphreys learned that the entire Army of Northern Virginia was in his front, entrenched in a semicircle running from north of the country meeting house to southeast of it, with the Confederate flanks stretching well beyond his own. Humphreys believed that Maj.

Gen. Horatio Wright's VI Corps, like his own, was on the north side of the Appomattox. When the II Corps's commander heard firing from the direction of Farmville, he concluded that he could attack Lee's works in front and that General Wright's command would hit their rear. Humphreys sent the right of his corps forward around 4:15 p.m. No attack developed from the south, and his own effort was repulsed with, as he put it, "considerable loss."[35]

It was likely the gunfire Humphreys had heard came from an encounter that took place between Cumberland Church and Farmville. Some Union troopers spotted a Confederate supply train moving through that area and descended on it. The Southerners successfully defended their wagons, captured brevet Brig. Gen. J. Irvin Gregg, and chased off the Union cavalry.[36]

Meanwhile two of Maj. Gen. Philip H. Sheridan's divisions spent April 7 riding from the Sailor's Creek battlefield, through Rice's Depot, and on to Prince Edward Court House.[37] Their occupation of this county seat would make it harder for Lee to turn south and move toward North Carolina.[38] General Grant also had a sizable infantry force on his strategically important southern flank. On the seventh Maj. Gen. Charles Griffin's V Corps moved through Rice's Depot and reached Prince Edward Court House around 7:30 p.m.[39]

Large Union units also were concentrating at Farmville. Ord's command, two divisions of Gibbon's XXIV Corps, passed through the town and bivouacked west of it. Two African American brigades from the XXV Corps joined them.[40] The last of Grant's infantry, Wright's VI Corps, reached Farmville along with the rear of Ord's column. After dark this corps gained the north bank of the Appomattox and camped there.[41]

Grant himself had arrived at Farmville a little before noon on the seventh. One of his Ohio infantrymen described the village: "Tis a nice town containing 3 churches and several fine businesses [and] houses." The general made his headquarters on the expansive piazza of the Prince Edward Hotel, an imposing brick structure.[42]

Wearing a muddy uniform and smoking a cigar, Grant conferred with Ord, Gibbon, and Wright. The Union commander was heartened by a report received from a reliable civilian the previous night. It related that after his capture at Sailor's Creek, Ewell had expressed the hope Lee would surrender.[43] Grant also had heard from General Sheridan that eight trains with supplies for Lee were waiting for his famished army at Appomattox Station. This depot was fewer than twenty miles west along the rail line from Sheridan's present location at Prospect Station. Grant's cavalryman was confident that he could reach these stores, which were essential to the Confederates, before they could.[44]

Grant considered this and other favorable intelligence, then he remarked quietly to the officers around him on the Prince Edward Hotel porch, "I have a great mind to summon Lee to surrender." At 5:00 p.m. Grant wrote a two-sentence dispatch to his opponent, inviting him to capitulate.[45]

Lee received Grant's message sometime after 9:00 p.m. It arrived, as Longstreet long afterward recalled, while he and Lee were sitting together in a cottage near Cumberland Church. Lee read Grant's dispatch and handed it without comment to his senior corps commander. Longstreet considered the text, passed the paper back to his chief, and said tersely, "*Not yet.*"[46]

Lee answered Grant, asking what terms the Union commander would offer for his surrender. As soon as Lee sent this reply, he ordered his men to march yet again. The bone-weary Confederates would make their third consecutive night march.[47] Whatever the cost, the Army of Northern Virginia could not remain in its semicircle around Cumberland Church. The Federals inevitably would cut off the routes to the west and encircle it.

Brig. Gen. Reuben Lindsay Walker, who had been given responsibility for the army's reserve artillery, led the way from Cumberland Church. At 1:00 a.m. on April 8 General Walker set out with his field guns and wagon train, and throughout the day he headed the army's westward trek.[48]

After Walker's departure, Longstreet's command struggled on a muddy road toward Curdsville, more than five miles northwest of Cumberland Church.[49] Mahone's Division resumed operating with Longstreet's Corps, and Lee himself also accompanied the general he called his "Old War Horse."[50] Taking another road,

Gordon's Corps marched to New Store, which is more than five miles west of Curdsville.[51] Gordon's route was shorter than Longstreet's, but his road conditions were no better—and his straggling was worse. Fitz Lee provided a rearguard for both corps.[52]

These Confederate movements were well under way on the morning of April 8 when Grant received Lee's reply. The Federal commander wrote to his opponent for the second time, making it clear that Lee's men would be paroled but would not go to prison camps. Grant also tried to remove Lee's pride as an obstacle to the surrender of his army. The Federal general expressed his willingness to meet with Lee's subordinates rather than insisting that Lee himself must capitulate.[53]

Grant left Farmville, crossed the Appomattox, and caught up with Maj. Gen. George G. Meade and his staff. One of General Meade's officers noticed that Grant "was in high spirits" and addressed Meade as "Old Fellow."[54] Grant's mood was good that morning of the eighth, but he suffered a severe headache that afternoon. Lt. Col. Horace Porter believed the affliction was "the result of fatigue, anxiety, scant fare, and loss of sleep" and reported that "by night he grew much worse." Meade, too, was still ill.[55] Doubtless the pursuit created stresses that affected the health of both senior commanders.

Grant and Meade continued to travel with the II Corps, which spent the eighth making a creditable pursuit of Gordon's Corps.[56] Humphreys's soldiers began the day by advancing past the empty Confederate fieldworks at Cumberland Church and ended it bivouacking in the fields west of New Store. Along its route, the II Corps garnered four abandoned field guns. Wright's VI Corps closed on Humphreys's men and then marched on a road parallel to them. It covered about seventeen miles on the eighth and camped that night near New Store.[57]

South of the Appomattox, the Federals broke their camps early that Saturday morning, intending to move rapidly and block Lee's route to the west. Two of Sheridan's cavalry divisions spearheaded the pursuit. They left Prince Edward Court House, rode through Prospect Station at about 6:00 a.m., and headed for Walker's Church, roughly ten miles southeast of Appomattox Court House.[58]

On the seventh, Sheridan had told Grant that eight supply trains were waiting for Lee at Appomattox Station. They made a fine target for the Union cavalrymen, who had intended to ride in that direction in any case to cut off Lee's retreat. On the morning of April 8, a scout brought Sheridan word that four trainloads of provisions were standing at Appomattox Station. While this more recent intelligence reduced the size of the prize, it identified Lee's immediate destination. Sheridan quickly sent his troopers toward Appomattox Station.[59]

One Confederate force already had reached Appomattox Station—Walker's artillery reserve and accompanying wagon train. This contingent had led the Army of Northern Virginia's march throughout the eighth. About 3:00 p.m. Walker's hungry and exhausted men and horses went into park less than half a mile north of Appomattox Station.[60] Ignorant that any Federal cavalry roamed so far west, Walker did not deploy any pickets. His security depended largely on a cavalry escort, or a small brigade of roughly five hundred troopers. Writing two days later, Brig. Gen. William N. Pendleton, chief of the army's artillery, characterized Walker's camp as "defenseless."[61]

Late in the afternoon, the van of a Federal cavalry division reached Appomattox Station. It was led by brevet Maj. Gen. George A. Custer, a young officer who had made an undistinguished West Point record but then had a distinguished Civil War career. Before General Custer's horsemen reached the station, one of the four Confederate supply trains made its escape. A few troopers of Company K, Second New York Cavalry, demanded the engineers surrender the other three. The railroad men quickly complied. Without meeting any resistance, Custer's cavalrymen gained large quantities of food, clothing, and other supplies.[62]

Custer's lead brigade rode north from the depot, spotted Walker's artillery park, and around 4:00 p.m. struck it. Walker used dismounted cavalrymen to anchor his flanks, and he deployed some of his field pieces along a slight ridge.[63] Two of the Confederate batteries no longer had guns, but their crews carried shoulder arms. Dense trees and brush also helped Walker check the initial Union attack. The Southern defense was so stout that Custer credited Walker with two divisions of infantry.[64]

As more of Custer's cavalrymen joined their comrades, the Federal horsemen renewed their attacks and continued the fight into the darkness. Custer estimated that it was "nearly 9 o'clock at night" when his troopers made a general advance that finally carried Walker's position. The young general reported that his division captured "twenty-four pieces of artillery, all [of the enemy's] trains, several battle-flags, and a large number of prisoners. Our loss was slight."[65]

Custer's captures at Appomattox Station, and other events near the depot, underscored some harsh realities confronting the Confederates. First the surrender of the supply trains represented a heart-sickening loss to the destitute Army of Northern Virginia. Next the presence of Union cavalrymen at Appomattox Station meant that Lee's westward line of march had been cut. Finally it was likely that masses of Federal infantrymen soon would close up on the troopers.[66]

Ord had followed the cavalrymen and had driven his soldiers sternly. "I marched my men," he later reported to Grant, "from daylight on the 8th until 10:00 a.m. on the 9th of April, except three hours." Ord encouraged his tramping columns of white and African American troops with a series of rallying cries: "Legs will win this battle, men!" "It rests with us to head them off!" And "they can't escape, if you will keep up to it!" Sensing that victory might be near, Ord's infantrymen averaged nearly two miles an hour.[67] General Griffin's V Corps trailed Ord, making a march that its commander called "very slow and tedious."[68]

While Ord's and Griffin's deep ranks of infantry moved up behind Sheridan's cavalrymen, Humphreys and Wright relentlessly closed in from the east on the debilitated Army of Northern Virginia. By the night of April 8, the Southerners no longer had room to maneuver. The vigorous Federal pursuit had put the Confederates in a vise.

Lee well knew the situation was desperate when his headquarters tent was pitched for the night of April 8–9 about a mile northeast of Appomattox Court House.[69] In what was to be Lee's last council of war, that Saturday evening he conferred with Longstreet, Gordon, and Fitz Lee. The army's only alternative to surrendering was to open the road west of Appomattox Court House and then to move toward Lynchburg. The action at Appomattox Station had confirmed that the Union cavalry was west of the courthouse. Fitz Lee and Gordon were to push aside Sheridan's troopers and clear the army's route to the west. If they encountered Federal infantry as well as cavalry, they were to inform Lee immediately.[70]

Perhaps in an effort to buy time, Lee sent Grant a second message. He denied that in his first dispatch he had intended to propose surrendering his army, maintaining that he had only meant to ask about terms. He offered to meet Grant between the picket lines of the two forces and to discuss not the Army of Northern Virginia's capitulation but, instead, general peace terms. Lee made this offer despite his knowledge that Grant was not authorized to negotiate a settlement of the war. Grant's handling of the preliminaries to the February Hampton Roads conference and President Abraham Lincoln's response to the March Ord-Longstreet episode had established that Grant would meet with Lee for two purposes only: to discuss minor, purely military issues or to accept the surrender of the Army of Northern Virginia.[71]

About sixteen miles east of Lee's bivouac, Grant and Meade spent the night at Clifton, the spacious two-story home of Joseph Crute. The house had been deserted and most of its furnishings removed, but a bed was found for Grant in an upstairs room. His staff slept on the parlor floor, and Meade and his officers camped a few hundred yards from the house.[72]

Around midnight Lee's second message to Grant arrived at Clifton. The communication angered Brig. Gen. John A. Rawlins, Grant's chief of staff, who believed that the Confederate commander was trying to bargain when he had no option other than surrender.[73] Grant seemed more disappointed than angry. He was still suffering with his migraine headache and had not been able to sleep. The general told his staff officers, "It looks as if Lee still means to fight; I will reply in the morning."[74]

Grant's headache kept him from sleeping. Sometime after 4:00 a.m. on April 9, the general, Lieutenant Colonel Porter, and some other staff officers walked to Meade's camp for an early morning cup of coffee. Grant then wrote his third dispatch to Lee, stating flatly that he had no authority to negotiate a general peace and that nothing could come of the meeting Lee had suggested for later that morning. The Federal commander made it clear that the war could be ended only by a Confederate surrender.[75]

Sunrise on Sunday, April 9, 1865, brought a foggy morning that became warm with a blue, cloudless sky.[76] Before daybreak Fitz Lee and Gordon began preparing to carry out what would be the last offensive of the Army of Northern Virginia. They would attempt to move Sheridan's cavalry out of the way and open the Stage Road west from Appomattox Court House.[77] Gordon deployed his corps at the western edge of the Court House, along a line running from the southeast to northwest. Fitz Lee's cavalrymen extended his right flank.[78]

At daylight the Southerners advanced, at first encountering only a lone dismounted cavalry brigade and two three-inch rifles of Battery A, Second United States Artillery.[79] Much stronger cavalry—and infantry—forces were not far away.

The last attack of the Army of Northern Virginia met the same experience as many others during the Civil War: it won initial success before it ended in failure. In an early achievement, some North Carolina cavalrymen captured the pair of field guns. As one of the attackers remembered it, some of the Union artillerymen "went into the woods, some took shelter under the gun carriages, and all quit firing." When Maj. Erasmus Taylor of Longstreet's staff recalled this successful action many years later, the section of two guns became a full battery: "When the advance began on this morning of the 9th of April, 1865, our van-guard encountered a battery of the enemy at once, which they charged and captured, bringing into our lines guns, horses, officers and men."[80]

Fitz Lee's troopers hit their opponents in front and on their northern flank and drove the Federals back. To the left of the Southern cavalry, Gordon brought forward his corps. By about 8:30 a.m. the Confederates had opened the Stage Road.[81]

Lee made his command post on a knoll about a mile and a half northeast of Appomattox Court House, or about midway between his two corps, with Gordon ahead and Longstreet to the rear. The morning's fog prevented the Confederate commander from seeing Gordon's fight along the Stage Road. Lee nonetheless could hear the infantry and artillery fire coming from the west.[82]

Gordon well understood that having opened the Stage Road, he must keep it secure so the army could continue its westward march. He left one North Carolina brigade and little else to guard the road against threats from the west. Gordon swung nearly all of his men in a great wheel to the left to clear the way for the wagons and artillery and to protect the essential roadway against a counteraction from the south.[83]

Gordon and Fitz Lee had achieved all that they could, and now the rapid advance of Grant's southern wing—Sheridan, Ord, and Griffin—paid the North a decisive dividend. With aggressive cavalry rides and hard infantry marches, these commands had outpaced their opponents and had taken Appomattox Station. Then they had turned east. Now they would seal the fate of the Army of Northern Virginia at Appomattox Court House.

The first challenge to the Confederates came when the Union cavalry arrived from Appomattox Station. The Confederates then faced not just a lone dismounted brigade but masses of Sheridan's horsemen.[84] During the ensuing action, the Federals shot down the color bearer of the Fourteenth Virginia Cavalry. Sgt. John Donaldson of the Fourth Pennsylvania captured his flag, the last of the hundreds of such trophies seized in battle during the Civil War.[85]

The arrival of the Federal infantry proved fatal to Gordon. For two days Ord had driven hard his soldiers, telling them, among other things, that their legs would win the next battle. Two full divisions of the Army of James, under Gibbon's immediate command, now emerged from the woods in the rear of the Union troopers. They drove back the lone North Carolina brigade still facing west, and soon they threatened Gordon's right flank and rear. Ord galloped past his tired soldiers, swinging his hat and shouting in triumph: "Your legs have done it, my men! Your legs have done it!"[86]

Griffin's V Corps had followed Ord and came up on his right, pressuring Gordon from the southwest and south. The Confederates were forced to withdraw toward Appomattox Court House.[87]

The massed ranks of Ord's and Griffin's infantrymen had settled the matter. Lee could move no farther west.

The eastern half of the Federal vise also was closing. Humphreys's II Corps and Wright's VI Corps advanced west from New Store and approached Appomattox Court House from the east. While Longstreet's men staggered westward on the Stage Road, Humphreys's advanced guard nipped at their heels. Along Wright's marching column, the word arrived that Lee had been cut off at Appomattox Court House. This report, Lieutenant Colonel Lyman exulted, "gave us new wings!"[88]

Lee recognized that the end was near. The noise of the combat west of the village was growing louder, closer. This sound meant that Gordon had been unable to control the Stage Road. Lee sent for Longstreet and described the position to him. The commander's Old War Horse asked if sacrificing the Army of Northern Virginia could benefit the Confederacy elsewhere. After Lee gave a negative reply, Longstreet stated that the situation spoke for itself. Mahone joined the two senior generals; years later, Longstreet remembered that "Mahone thought it time to see General Grant."[89]

After conversing with Longstreet and Mahone, Lee summoned an orderly, Sgt. George W. Tucker, and assistant adjutant generals Lt. Col. Charles Marshall and Lt. Col. Walter Taylor. The Confederate commander had not yet received Grant's reply to his request for a meeting. At about 8:30 a.m. Lee and his three escorts began riding east, thinking it most likely that Grant would be accompanying the Federal troops approaching from that direction. Lee's small party rode along the Stage Road past Longstreet's rearguard position, and around 9:00 a.m. it encountered the II Corps's picket line.[90]

Lieutenant Colonel Marshall rode ahead to clarify matters with the Federals. He met Lt. Col. Charles A. Whittier, Humphreys's adjutant, and explained that Lee had approached the Federal lines to learn about the meeting proposed for 10:00 a.m. The situation was quickly resolved because Lieutenant Colonel Whittier had delivered Lee's second dispatch to Grant at Clifton and was carrying the reply that the Federal commander had written earlier that morning. Marshall conducted Whittier to Lee, who read Grant's dispatch. Grant declined a meeting and stated that peace would come when the Southerners lay down their arms.[91]

Lee recognized that Grant's message meant that the end had arrived. He directed Marshall to write a dispatch to the Union commander, requesting a meeting for the purpose of surrendering the Army of Northern Virginia. Whittier explained to Lee that Grant was no longer in the area; he had gone to join Sheridan, who was west of Appomattox Court House.[92] Lee no doubt concluded from this information that arranging the meeting would take some time, and he told Marshall to write another message, asking for a truce until the surrender terms were put in place.[93]

Whittier carried these dispatches to Meade, who had left Clifton that morning and traveled behind the II Corps. Although feeling better, the commander of the Army of the Potomac was still riding in an ambulance wagon. Meade wrote to Lee, assuring him that his correspondence would be forwarded to Grant, but Meade also suggested that Lee send the same communication to Grant elsewhere through the Federal lines. Meade granted a short truce and offered to extend it if he learned Lee had agreed to Grant's terms.[94] Acting on Meade's advice, Lee sent Grant a dispatch through Sheridan's front that repeated the request for a meeting to discuss the surrender of his army.[95]

Having learned that Grant was not east but west of him, Lee and his escorts turned back in that direction. Close to where the Stage Road crossed the Appomattox River, with the courthouse not far beyond, they turned off into an apple orchard that belonged to the Sweeneys, a family well known for its musical talent. Joel Walker Sweeney, a minstrel performer, was even said to have invented the five-string banjo.[96] Here at the Sweeney orchard, Lee waited for a third and last dispatch from Grant.[97]

West of the Sweeney property, Capt. Robert Sims of Longstreet's staff carried Lee's truce request from Appomattox Court House into Sheridan's lines. Captain Sims encountered Custer, who refused the cease-fire offer and brazenly followed the courier into the Confederate position. Custer found Gordon and demanded that the Army of Northern Virginia surrender to Sheridan. The brash young Federal was referred to Longstreet, who sharply upbraided him. As one of Longstreet's staff officers tersely summarized the episode, Custer's demand "was declined and he was escorted back."[98]

Longstreet put an end to Custer's one-man effort to settle matters, but Lee and Meade had agreed to a cease-fire. After 10:00 a.m. it began to go into effect. Casualties continued to be inflicted, though, until word of the truce reached every unit. An exploding artillery round brought down Pvt. William Montgomery of the 155th Pennsylvania on the V Corps's skirmish line near Appomattox Court House. He passed away nineteen days later and was believed to be the last Union enlisted man to die in the campaign. Lt. Hiram Clark, a tall young man in the 185th New York, the V Corps, also fell victim to artillery fire and became the final Northern officer killed at Appomattox. Sgt. Robert W. Parker of the Second Virginia Cavalry, killed in the action west of the village, is thought to have been the last casualty of the Army of Northern Virginia.[99] The total Union losses at Appomattox Court House came to about 225; the Confederate figure was estimated at 500.[100] The great majority of these casualties took place during the morning's fighting west of the courthouse.

While the truce was sporadically taking hold, Grant, as Whittier had told Lee, was putting in an active morning. Having written to his opponent from Clifton, he headed west on the Stage Road with his staff and followed the II and VI Corps. Meade's ambulance, with its accompanying officers, had taken the same route. Grant still suffered from his migraine headache, and the condition of the Stage Road—churned to mud by the feet of thousands of infantrymen—made the ride difficult. Not far west of New Store, Grant and his party turned left. Rather than continue following Humphreys's and Wright's men on the muddy Stage Road, they rode south toward the Appomattox River while Meade's cavalcade stayed on the main road running west to Appomattox Court House. Grant and his staff waded the Appomattox at Cutbank Ford, and fewer than eight miles from the Stage Road, they reached Walker's Church. Here they turned west toward Sheridan's lines.[101]

About four miles west of Walker's Church, Grant and his officers halted to rest themselves and their mounts. Just before noon, Lt. Charles E. Pease of Meade's staff, his horse foaming, caught up with them.[102] He handed the three-star general Lee's third dispatch, forwarded by Meade, and he informed Grant of the truce. The Federal commander now read the words that he and millions of others had long awaited: Lee requested an interview for the purpose of surrendering the Army of Northern Virginia. When Grant finished reading Lee's message, his migraine headache disappeared.[103]

Grant dismounted and, sitting along the roadside, wrote a reply to Lee. The Union commander explained that he had left the Stage Road for the Farmville and Lynchburg Road and gave his present location. He told Lee that he would "push forward to the front, for the purpose of meeting you."[104]

Lt. Col. Orville E. Babcock, accompanied by Lt. William Dunn, set out with this reply to Lee. Grant and the rest of his staff followed, riding the six miles to Appomattox Court House at a slower pace than that of the two couriers. Along the way, Grant received a now-superfluous duplicate message that Lee, at Meade's recommendation, had sent through Sheridan's lines.[105]

While Grant and his staff rode toward Sheridan's position, Lieutenant Colonel Babcock and Lieutenant Dunn found Lee waiting in the Sweeney orchard, and they delivered Grant's message. Lee called on Marshall to ride with him, along with Pvt. Joshua O. Johns, a cavalryman from Lynchburg who served as an orderly. Babcock and Dunn followed the three Confederates toward Appomattox Court.[106]

Riding ahead to find a worthy location for the meeting, Marshall and Private Johns entered a village that soon would take a prominent place in American history. In 1845 the little community of Clover Hill had become the seat of a new county and had been re-designated Appomattox Court House. The river, whose headwaters were nearby, and the county carried the same name, which early white Virginians believed was derived from a native tribe, the Apumetec. By 1865 Appomattox Court House had become a prosperous settlement, featuring the county courthouse, county jail, two stores, a law office, tavern, blacksmith shop, stable, and several residences.[107]

At first Marshall had trouble finding among these buildings a suitable one for the conference; then Wilmer McLean offered his home.[108] McLean's story was among the strangest of the Civil War. In 1861 he had owned Yorkshire, a large house northeast of Manassas, Virginia, and a ford across the Bull Run stream carried his name. After two major battles were fought near his home, McLean, in his late forties and with a pregnant wife, decided he had seen enough warfare. He determined to move to the haven of Appomattox Court House, where he bought two tavern buildings and a substantial brick residence.[109] McLean had fled the war, but it had followed him.

Having decided on McLean's fine brick house, Marshall sent Johns to inform Lee, Babcock, and Dunn of the location. When these three officers arrived, they climbed the seven steps of the front porch, entered the front hall, and went into the parlor to the left.[110] Johns stayed with Traveller and the other horses in the home's fenced front yard.[111] Babcock asked Dunn to wait outside, too, and alert the group to Grant's arrival.[112]

One of Sheridan's staff officers guided Grant and his party to the McLean house, apparently mistaking a turn along the way. Lee waited about half an hour for their arrival. En route to Appomattox Court House, Grant met Sheridan and Ord and invited them to join him.[113]

When the group arrived at McLean's yard, Grant dismounted and handed his reins to an orderly. Cincinnati and Traveller now grazed in the same front yard. Grant entered the house alone. Horace Porter later explained: "The members of [Grant's] staff, Generals Sheridan and Ord, and some other general officers who had gathered in the front yard, remained outside, feeling that General Grant would probably prefer his first interview with General Lee to be, in a measure, private." In a few minutes Babcock appeared at McLean's front door and extended Grant's invitation to enter. Porter recorded: "It was then about half-past one on Sunday, the 9th of April."[114]

The two senior commanders, direct opponents since Union

forces had entered the Wilderness about eleven months earlier, shook hands cordially. Lee wore a new uniform; Porter surmised that "in deference to General Grant," he "had dressed himself with special care for the purpose of the meeting."[115] Grant's boots and some of his clothes were stained with mud, collected during his morning ride from Clifton to Appomattox Court House by way of Walker's Church.[116]

Grant and Lee seated themselves and made small talk about their service during the Mexican-American War. It was the defeated Confederate, not the victorious Federal, who directed the conversation to the subject at hand. Lee asked about Grant's terms for the surrender. The Union commander replied that the Southern officers and men would lay down their arms, take paroles, and go to their homes. They would promise not to fight again unless they were properly exchanged for Northern prisoners. The Federals would treat all the weapons, ammunition, and supplies the Confederates surrendered as captured property. Lee readily agreed to these terms.[117]

With that acquiescence, the main business of the meeting had been achieved. All that remained were the details of the surrender. Perhaps because Lee's agreement to the essential point had been reached so easily, Grant, as Porter recalled it, "went on to talk at some length in a very pleasant vein about the prospects of peace."[118]

Again it was Lee who returned the discussion to the main issue by suggesting that Grant write out his terms. Col. Ely S. Parker, the son of a Seneca chief and Grant's military secretary, brought an order book and, from the back of the parlor, a small wooden table. Pulling on a cigar, Grant wrote out the surrender conditions.[119]

During the recent meeting on the *River Queen*, Grant had conducted himself as though he were familiar with President Lincoln's ideas about how the war should end. The conditions of surrender that the Union commander wrote at Appomattox were consistent with the president's desire for a lenient peace. Grant's terms required only that the Confederates take paroles and surrender their "arms, artillery, and public property." The officers could keep their side arms, horses, and baggage.[120]

In the final sentence of the terms, Grant included a fundamentally important provision that went beyond his authority over military affairs and entered the area of civil policy. Grant wrote that once the paroles were taken and arms surrendered, "each officer and man will be allowed to return to their homes, not to be disturbed by United States authority so long as they observe their paroles and the laws in force where they may reside."[121]

With that sentence, Grant made the remarkable pledge that Lee, his officers, and his men would not go to prison camps, would not be charged with treason, and would not face reprisals—so long as they honored their paroles and federal laws. This provision was a matter of civil policy, and Grant must have felt confident that it was consistent with the guidance of his commander in chief. The promise of no reprisals carried the spirit of Lincoln's direction to "let 'em up easy." At the same time, the insistence that the defeated Southerners must respect federal laws matched the president's views on national authority.[122]

Lee carefully read this sentence and the others before it. When he finished he remarked, "This will have a very happy effect upon my army." Before signing the final copy of the document, Lee asked if his enlisted men, as well as officers, would be allowed to keep their horses. Grant's first reaction was that the terms did not permit it. Two facts influenced him to modify his position: the Confederate cavalrymen and artillerymen had brought their own horses into their army, and these animals would be helpful during the spring planting. Grant stated that he would not revise the written terms, but he would instruct the officers accepting the paroles to let any man who claimed a horse or mule to keep it. In another act of generosity, after Lee signed the final version of the terms, Grant said he would send twenty-five thousand rations to the surrendered army.[123]

Delivering the rations, allowing the enlisted men and officers to take home their animals, and letting officers keep their side arms—all of these actions made steps toward the lenient peace that Lincoln, and Grant, wanted. But the truly significant point of the surrender document appeared in its last sentence. The other concessions, as historian Brooks Simpson has written, "however magnanimous, paled beside Grant's assurance that as long as the paroled Confederates obeyed the law, they would not be disturbed by United States authorities. . . . Grant was fully aware of the implications of the offer; he knew that he had taken an important step toward the establishment of a lasting peace settlement, holding out the promise of lenient treatment in exchange for absolute submission."[124]

The immediate result of Lee's signing the surrender document was that more than twenty-eight thousand Southerners and their arms were removed from the war. When all the abandoned and captured field guns were accounted, the Army of Northern Virginia surrendered about 180 pieces of artillery.[125] A large number of the infantrymen who took paroles no longer had shoulder arms, and Humphreys surmised that seeing the end approaching, many soldiers had thrown away their weapons.[126]

While many discarded their guns, it was more remarkable that so many Confederates remained with their regiments to the end of the campaign. Thousands stayed in the ranks and endured extreme hardships, but no amount of hard marching on low rations and little sleep could overcome the misfortunes at the Genito Bridge, Amelia Court House, Sailor's Creek, Appomattox Station, and elsewhere. Nor could Lee or his subordinates devise any clever plan to elude the relentless Federal pursuit.

For the Northerners, the victory began with Grant's unwavering determination to close out the Appomattox campaign. Sheridan and Ord directed aggressive pursuits that cut off Lee's westward march. Meade had been overruled by his chief at a key point during the campaign, but he performed reliably. Other Union senior commanders also contributed to the victory. The last spotlight fell on the men in the ranks: marching hard for a week and fighting well when necessary, they brought an end to the Army of Northern Virginia.

The dignified general who had surrendered that army left McLean's house and, accompanied by Marshall and Johns, rode back to deliver the news to his waiting men. Robert E. Lee and the Army of Northern Virginia, the man and the organization that had carried the Confederacy's best hopes, no longer served the

Southern cause. About 160 miles to the south, another Confederate field force remained at large. A week after the Appomattox surrender, an officer in the II Corps wrote home. Although he misspelled his enemy's name, he made an apt observation: "All minds are now anxiously turned towards Johnson and Sherman."[127]

CHAPTER NINE

A Scrap of Paper

At Goldsboro, North Carolina, on March 23, 1865, two days after the Battle of Bentonville, Maj. Gen. William T. Sherman finished combining his force with Maj. Gen. John M. Schofield's two corps. General Sherman then had eighty-one thousand effectives, giving him an overwhelming numerical advantage over his opponent, Gen. Joseph E. Johnston. Furthermore the strategic situation decisively favored the Federals. "They may unite Johnston & [Gen. Robert E.] Lee," Sherman explained to his wife, Ellen, on March 26, "when[,] if they make the further mistake of holding on to Richmond, I can easily take Raleigh and the Roanoke, when Richmond will be of little use to them. If Lee lets go of Richmond the People of Virginia will give up."[1]

After the Battle of Bentonville, General Johnston had retreated north to Smithfield, North Carolina. One of his motives for attacking Sherman on March 19 had been to raise the morale of his men, and in this effort, he succeeded. The day after the Battle of Bentonville, one of Johnston's soldiers summarized the engagement for his wife; his cheery version of events would have pleased the general himself. "We went down on Saturday," Duncan Campbell related, "and on Sunday afternoon attacked two corps of Sherman's Army. We killed some few[,] caught some few[,] and brought off as trophies two cannon. Night put an end to the Contest, and we retired to our lines[.]" On March 27 Johnston him-

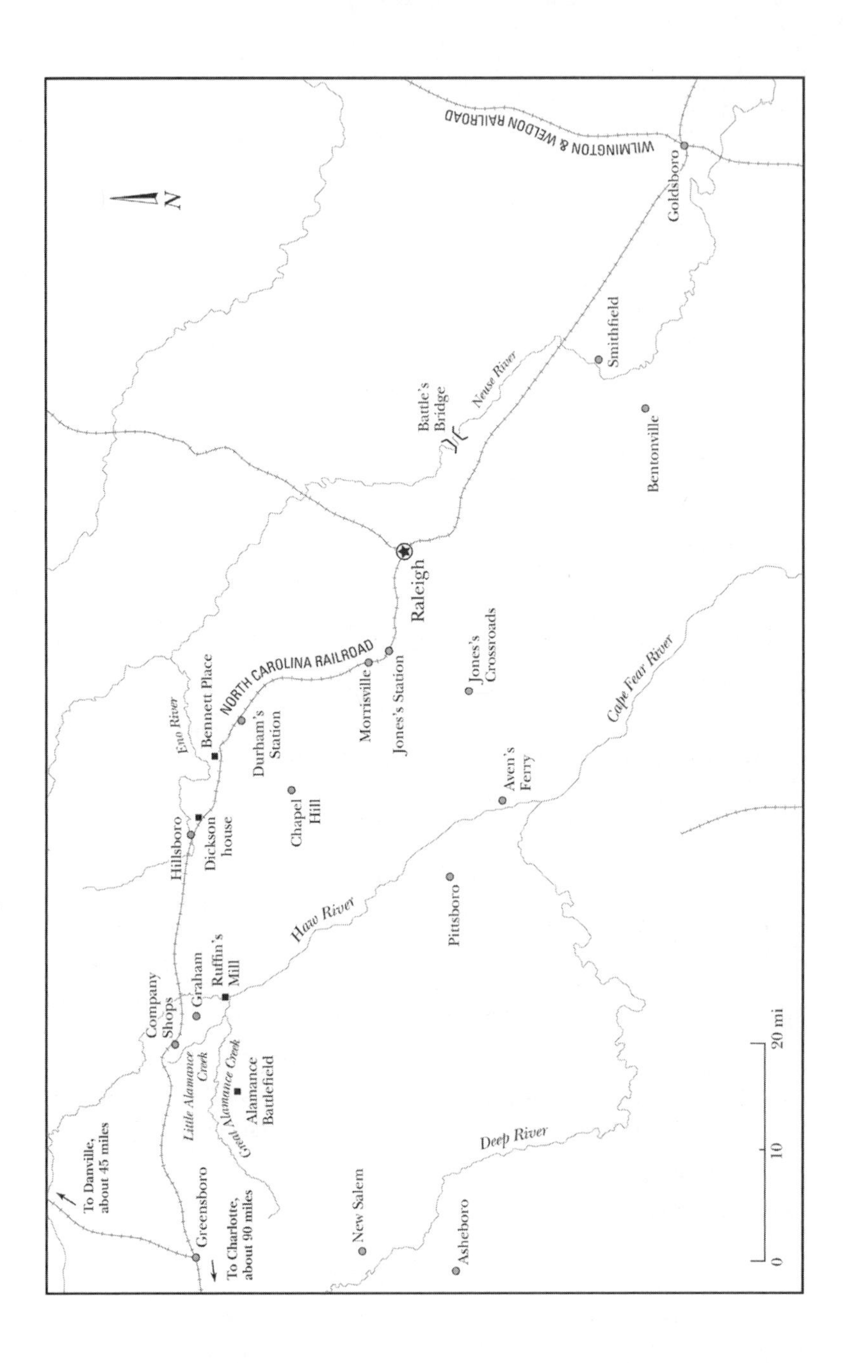

MAP 14. Bentonville to the Bennett Place

self reported to General Lee, the general in chief, "The spirit of the army is greatly improved and is now excellent."[2]

After Bentonville Confederate morale was healthy, and Johnston still had a viable strategy. If Lee could elude Lt. Gen. Ulysses S. Grant, Johnston could link his force with the Army of Northern Virginia. Johnston and Lee together might then confront Sherman.

This strategy would be very difficult to execute, but at least one event in early April heartened the Confederates. Some survivors of Gen. John B. Hood's disastrous Tennessee campaign joined Johnston. These additions gave Johnston an aggregate strength of about thirty thousand men, representing a significantly larger force than the Confederates had had at Bentonville.[3]

Bolstered by these reinforcements, on April 9 Johnston reorganized the main Confederate field force in the western theater for the final time. The name "Army of Tennessee," long the designation of the largest Southern command west of the Appalachians, returned, and the Army of the South ended its brief history.[4]

On the morning of April 10, the Army of Tennessee began moving from Smithfield toward Raleigh, the capital of North Carolina. Johnston camped for the night of April 10–11 between those two cities at Battle's Bridge over the Neuse River. There at 1:00 a.m. on the eleventh, he received crushing news from President Jefferson Davis, who had fled Richmond by taking a train to Danville. A dispatch from the chief executive informed Johnston of a scout's report that Lee had surrendered at Appomattox. President Davis had no "official intelligence," but he acknowledged there was "little room for doubt."[5]

Lee's surrender reinforced a view that Johnston probably had held since taking command—that is, the war no longer could be won in the field. Fighting another battle against Sherman's hosts was out of the question; the Confederates would be far too heavily outnumbered. Nor would Johnston scatter his men and urge them to fight as partisans.[6]

With a military victory no longer possible, as historian Mark Bradley points out in his superb work *This Astounding Close*, Johnston's first objective was to keep the Army of Tennessee in the field as a viable organization.[7] That goal probably explains why Johnston did not officially announce the surrender of the Army of Northern Virginia. The Confederate commander knew full well that his soldiers eventually would learn of the calamity, and he may have thought it better that the reality become gradually established by days of rumors rather than by the sudden shock of an official announcement.[8]

Johnston's second objective was to keep his small command beyond the reach of Sherman's enormous one. He had to prevent the Army of Tennessee from being encircled as the Army of Northern Virginia had been. Then there remained only one other goal for Johnston—to negotiate the best possible terms for his men and, perhaps, the rest of the Confederacy.[9]

Johnston realized that these objectives would be difficult to accomplish, and he knew that his commander in chief held a far more optimistic view of the South's prospects in the field. Davis's communications from Danville carried no indication that he agreed with Johnston that the time had arrived to negotiate terms with the Federals. Far from planning to surrender, Davis was preparing to leave Danville with what remained of his government, which amounted to the five cabinet officers who had fled Richmond with him. The commander in chief intended to continue eluding the Federals and directing the Confederate war effort.[10]

While serving a civilian superior who held an unrealistic understanding of the Confederacy's military plight, Johnston faced a determined opponent. On the Palm Sunday of the Appomattox surrender, Sherman wrote to Ellen: "Tomorrow we move straight against Joe Johnston wherever he may be." Good to these words, the next day Sherman marched directly at Johnston, leaving behind Goldsboro and the bleak area around it. Brig. Gen. John M. Oliver, once a pharmacist and a court recorder and now a brigade commander in the XV Corps, described the region in a letter to his wife: "The country is poor through which we have passed & the condition of the people is terrible. The Reb army took almost everything & we were forced to take the balance."[11]

While the Federals headed for Smithfield, the news that Petersburg and Richmond had been captured elevated their spirits.

Capt. Solon A. Carter, the assistant adjutant general of Brig. Gen. Charles J. Paine's African American division, wrote his wife, Emily, that when the troops learned about the triumphs in Virginia, "such shouting and huzzahing as there was throughout the army you never heard. The wildest enthusiasm prevailed." Some of the "more demonstrative" of General Paine's soldiers, Captain Carter told his spouse, "expressed their satisfaction by standing on their heads . . . and cutting up all sorts of antics." The first of Sherman's confident soldiers reached Smithfield about 10:00 a.m. on April 11.[12]

Johnston pursued his strategy of keeping the Army of Tennessee out of Sherman's reach. The day that the Federals reached Smithfield, the Confederates marched toward Raleigh. Stifling weather led many of them to fall out of the ranks.[13] When the Southerners reached the state capital, it soon became apparent that they had no intention of defending it and instead would continue to retreat from Sherman's hosts.

About eighty miles west and a little north of Raleigh, Davis's train arrived in Greensboro on the afternoon of April 11. No crowd of citizens turned out to greet the Confederate president. Reports that Lee had surrendered at Appomattox and fears that Union cavalry raiders led by Maj. Gen. George Stoneman of western New York were headed for Greensboro probably had crushed local morale. A journalist described the town: "The streets were swimming in mud, and the houses were in a deplorable condition."[14]

Davis asked Gen. Pierre Gustave Toutant Beauregard, Johnston's second in command, to join him at Greensboro for a conference. It was an awkward meeting between two leaders who long had been at odds. Davis had lost trust in General Beauregard, but now at Greensboro he had to turn to this vain subordinate for information about the Confederacy's military situation and strategic prospects.[15] Beauregard presented Davis with a grim picture of where matters stood: Sherman was closing on Raleigh, General Stoneman was leading a destructive cavalry raid in Virginia and central North Carolina, and the Federals had taken Selma, Alabama, and soon would gain Mobile.[16] Beauregard's dark briefing failed to persuade Davis that the war was lost. A presidential aide described Davis at Greensboro as still showing "a great deal of fight."[17]

Davis then directed Johnston, another general with whom he had a bitter relationship, to come to Greensboro. Johnston put Lt. Gen. William J. Hardee in temporary command and instructed him to continue moving the army away from Sherman. Johnston left for Greensboro at midnight of April 11–12.[18]

Early on the morning of the twelfth, two couriers arrived at Sherman's headquarters in Smithfield with the monumental news from General Grant of the Appomattox surrender. Sherman wrote at once to his military superior and strong friend: "I hardly Know how to express my feelings, but you can imagine them." In view of later events, Sherman's next two sentences were noteworthy: "The terms you have given Lee are magnanimous and liberal. Should Johnston follow Lee's example I shall of course grant the Same."[19]

Rumors of Lee's surrender were swirling in Greensboro when Johnston arrived there after 8:00 a.m. on the twelfth. Johnston went first to meet with Beauregard, then at noon Davis summoned them.[20] The two generals called on the president at the home of Col. John Taylor Wood, his nephew and aide. Three cabinet members were present: Secretary of State Judah P. Benjamin, Secretary of the Navy Stephen R. Mallory, and Postmaster General John H. Reagan.[21] Johnston later wrote that he and Beauregard assumed they had been called to give military advice about pursuing or ending the war. But the president asked neither general anything and instead presented his own unrealistic plans for raising more troops and continuing resistance. Johnston demurred with this scheme, and Davis abruptly adjourned the meeting.[22]

There were other important developments that evening of April 12. Secretary of War John C. Breckinridge made a hard ride from Danville, eluded Stoneman's raiders, and arrived with a detailed report that confirmed Lee's surrender.[23] Beauregard and Johnston, now firmly convinced that the Confederate cause had become hopeless, conferred with Secretary Breckinridge. Johnston told him that the only power left to Davis "was that of terminating the war." Breckinridge made a commitment: he would give Johnston the chance to say this directly to the commander in chief at the next cabinet meeting. Johnston and Beauregard also learned that evening that they had the support of Secretary Mallory.[24]

While the Confederacy's senior leaders were conferring in Greensboro on April 12, General Hardee carried out Johnston's directive that the Army of Tennessee should keep moving away from Sherman. That morning the last Southern units passed through Raleigh and continued to fall back along the line of the North Carolina Railroad.[25]

During the Confederate retreat through the state capital, cavalry Capt. William W. Gordon called at the home of Kenneth Rayner, one of Raleigh's prominent citizens. The residents told Captain Gordon "the dreadful news of Lee's surrender" that had begun widely circulating among Southern soldiers and civilians. In his diary, Gordon reported his reaction: "I couldnot credit it. My mind couldn't grasp or comprehend so vast a misfortune." The ladies of the Rayner household "were all in tears and almost in despair at the news from Va., the retreat of our Army, the prospect of the citys being pillaged by our cavalry during the night and the certain advent of the Yankees in the morning. I left them with many, many regrets."[26]

As the ladies at the Rayner home feared, the pursuing Federals entered Raleigh the next day, April 13, but North Carolina's state capital avoided the hard fate of Atlanta, Georgia, and Columbia, South Carolina. Rayner and other civic leaders helped calm the situation. Historian Bradley is correct, however, in giving "the lion's share of credit" for the quiet occupation of Raleigh to Sherman's officers and men.[27]

While the Federals were securing Raleigh on the morning of the thirteenth, Davis held another meeting with his advisers in the president's room at Colonel Wood's home. Davis had again called in Johnston and Beauregard, an invitation that doubtless was the result of Breckinridge's promise to Johnston. When the generals arrived, the chief executive already was meeting with his cabinet members. Breckinridge and Attorney General George Davis had joined the group; Secretary of the Treasury George A. Trenholm was seriously ill and unable to attend.[28]

Unlike Johnston, Beauregard, and most of his cabinet, Davis had not yet accepted the reality of the Confederates' defeat. As at the previous meeting, the president again spoke wildly optimistically about how the Southern war effort still might be pursued. Davis made it clear that he wanted to hear from Johnston and Beauregard not about a policy of making peace with the Federals but about a strategy for continuing the war.[29] After the chief executive finished his grandiose address, he turned to Johnston, who, with the rest of Davis's audience, sat in stunned silence. The commander in chief had to prod his general into giving his views.[30]

Johnston first tersely reviewed the Confederacy's military situation and prospects in much the same bleak terms as Beauregard had related to Davis two days earlier. But then Johnston moved from the subject of strategy to policy, the purview of civilians. He began introducing the case for a change from armed resistance to negotiated peace. Johnston told the president and his cabinet that the South had been overrun and its resources depleted; the Federals were much stronger than the Confederates were and could grow more so. Johnston bluntly reported that his own men were deserting in large numbers every day. With no chance of military victory remaining, Johnston concluded, "it would be the greatest of human crimes to continue the war."[31] As historian Mark Grimsley observed, "Johnston thus did what no American commander has ever done, before or since: he exercised the full weight of his military position to tell his government how to conclude a war."[32]

During Johnston's stark presentation, Davis avoided looking at the general. The president kept his head down and gave his attention to a scrap of paper, which he continually folded and unfolded. When Johnston finished, another awkward silence held the room, and Davis continued to focus on his piece of paper. Finally the commander in chief asked Beauregard for his views.[33] The general replied, "I concur in all General Johnston has said." Still looking down at his scrap of paper, Davis polled his civilian advisers. All except Secretary Benjamin advised negotiating a peace.[34]

With the cabinet's overwhelming vote, Davis edged toward accepting the reality of the Confederacy's situation. After yet another pause, the president finally looked up from his paper.

Davis skeptically asked Johnston to propose a course of action, pointing out that the Federal government "refuses to treat with us." Johnston asked his commander in chief for permission to begin corresponding with Sherman. Davis reluctantly agreed, expressing doubt about the "ultimate results."[35]

The president dictated a letter to be signed by Johnston and sent to Sherman. It proposed that Sherman agree to suspend "active operations" and ask Grant to do the same, "the object being to permit the civil authorities to enter into the needful arrangements to terminate the existing war."[36] The Confederate senior leaders sent this letter to Lt. Gen. Wade Hampton, Johnston's cavalry chief, to be carried to Sherman. For unknown reasons, it was delayed between Greensboro and General Hampton's headquarters, which were about six miles east of Hillsborough.[37]

Johnston had gained what he wanted—that is, Davis's permission to open the communications that would lead to the surrender of the Army of Tennessee. Johnston left Greensboro that evening, the thirteenth, to return to his army. Davis remained in the city until the fifteenth.[38]

While the last conference of the Confederate high command took place in Greensboro, the Army of Tennessee continued to retreat. Lt. Gen. Alexander P. Stewart and Lt. Gen. Stephen D. Lee, the Confederacy's youngest three-star general, took their corps toward Hillsborough, which one officer characterized as "certainly a pretty place," and camped there on the evening of the thirteenth.[39] Hardee's Corps marched through Chapel Hill and stopped for the night two miles west of it.[40] The Confederates had gained a day's march on Sherman, whose men remained in Raleigh during April 13.[41]

On the morning of Good Friday, April 14, Johnston rejoined his army at Hillsborough, and the Confederates struck out to the west. Generals Lee's and Stewart's Corps reached the North Carolina Railroad bridge crossing of the Haw River near Graham, and Hardee's Corps moved to Ruffin's Mill, located about four miles downstream on the Haw.[42]

Sherman assumed that Johnston's logistics would keep him tied to the North Carolina Railroad. He decided to direct his infantry west from Raleigh to Asheboro, which is due south of Greensboro. Sherman ordered brevet Maj. Gen. Judson Kilpatrick's cavalrymen to do nothing more than "keep up a show of pursuit." On the fourteenth General Kilpatrick's troopers rode to Durham's Station on the North Carolina Railroad about a dozen miles southeast of Hillsborough.[43]

More than 250 miles to the north and shortly after 8:00 p.m. that Good Friday, President Abraham Lincoln and Mary Todd Lincoln boarded a carriage at the front portico of the White House. After collecting their theater guests for the night—Maj. Henry Rathbone and his fiancée, Clara Harris—the Lincolns continued to Ford's Theatre, where Laura Keene starred in a popular 1850s British comedy *Our American Cousin*.[44]

That same night a Confederate courier brought the delayed Davis-Johnston letter to Kilpatrick's headquarters at Morrisville, a dozen or so miles west and a little north of Raleigh, up the North Carolina Railroad from the capital. Sherman received this communication at midnight of Good Friday, April 14–15.[45]

Sherman promptly replied to Johnston, agreeing to meet with him and arrange for a suspension of hostilities. The Union commander made the commitment that his infantry would move no farther than Morrisville and asked that Johnston hold his own men in place. Sherman proposed a settlement based on the Appomattox terms. Sherman offered to ask Grant not to direct any troops to North Carolina and also stated that he himself would suspend Stoneman's raid. Significantly Sherman's reply did not address what Davis doubtless regarded as the main point of the Confederate correspondence—a request for a cease-fire so that the "civil authorities" could negotiate an end to the war. Sherman directed his aide and a telegraph operator to go to Morrisville, where they would await Johnston's answer and send it by wire to Raleigh.[46]

On the morning of April 15, Johnston had not received Sherman's message with its request that he maintain his position, so he had no reason to constrain his movements. On that Saturday the Army of Tennessee again marched away from the grasp of Sherman's masses. Hardee's Corps crossed three dangerously flooded water barriers: the Haw River, Little Alamance Creek, and

Great Alamance Creek. It camped for the night at Alamance, the militia-Regulator battlefield of 1771.[47]

North of Hardee's Corps, Stewart's and Lee's infantrymen passed through Graham and Company Shops. (This latter community had originated in 1854, when the North Carolina Railroad established its maintenance and repair shops there. In 1886 the railroad's officials moved these operations to Manchester, Virginia, and the next year a committee of locals renamed the town Burlington.[48]) Stewart's and Lee's veterans trudged past the railroad shops and bivouacked about fifteen miles short of Greensboro.[49]

While the Army of Tennessee moved westward on that mid-April Saturday, it encountered dejected veterans of the former Army of Northern Virginia who were returning to their homes. Any of Johnston's men who had doubted the terrible news from Virginia now faced incontrovertible proof of the disaster. Col. Joseph F. Waring, commander of the Jeff Davis Legion, entered in his diary on April 15: "Paroled prisoners from Virginia say that Gen. Lee has surrendered his army. . . . God help the cause[.]"[50]

During that evening of April 15, Davis moved beyond the range of immediate communication with Johnston. At 6:00 p.m. the president and his cabinet left Greensboro. Stoneman's raiders had wrecked the tracks, and the presidential entourage was forced to travel by horseback and wagon. Secretary Trenholm was nearly immobilized and had to be lifted into an ambulance. The forlorn group headed southwest for Charlotte, near the South Carolina border.[51]

On the day Davis fled Greensboro, the fifteenth, Sherman continued to keep his cavalry active north and northwest of Raleigh and to shift his infantry westward. During that Saturday Kilpatrick's horsemen held Durham's Station and Chapel Hill. The advanced elements of Maj. Gen. Henry W. Slocum's wing threw a pontoon bridge across the Cape Fear River at Aven's Ferry. Maj. Gen. Oliver O. Howard's wing started for Pittsboro, which was more than thirty-five miles east of Asheboro.[52]

On the morning of Easter Sunday, April 16, Johnston received Sherman's message offering to meet with him. Johnston rode to Greensboro, intending to discuss Sherman's communication with Davis.[53] Reaching the city, the general found that his president had left without notifying him. Johnston saw an opportunity to pursue negotiations with Sherman on his own, unhindered by Davis's overly optimistic assessment of the situation in the field. Johnston, however, did take Beauregard's sound advice of inviting Breckinridge to the proceedings, for the secretary of war could run political interference with Davis.[54] The Confederate commander wrote to Breckinridge and then asked Hampton to arrange a meeting with Sherman.[55]

Johnston directed Stewart and Lee to stop their corps at Greensboro and instructed Hardee to halt his at New Salem, seventeen miles south of there. Johnston gave some guidance about the cavalry's dispositions to Hampton and to Maj. Gen. Joseph Wheeler, Hampton's young subordinate.[56] Carrying out these orders, the Army of Tennessee made its last effective marches.

Having seen to the movements of his forces, Johnston took a train from Greensboro to Hillsborough. From there he traveled southeast about a mile to Hampton's headquarters at the Alexander Dickson home. Locals would call this two-story white farmhouse "the last headquarters of the Confederacy." Here Johnston remained until his meeting with Sherman.[57]

Hampton's request for a conference reached Kilpatrick, who relayed it to Sherman at Raleigh. Hampton proposed that the two principals should meet at 10:00 a.m. the next day, halfway between the Confederate lines at Hillsborough and the Union ones at Durham's Station.[58] Sherman quickly instructed Kilpatrick to arrange the meeting and advised him to move the time to noon. Having sent this telegram, the general joked to a staff officer: "The war is over—[my] occupation's gone!"[59]

Confident that Johnston would respect the conditions for the negotiations and halt his units, Sherman restricted the movements of his own commands on that Easter Sunday. General Slocum's wing stopped at Aven's Ferry on the Cape Fear River. General Howard's wing advanced no farther than Morrisville, which sits far to the east of Howard's earlier objective at Pittsboro. Most of the command, Howard noted, was "brought back" to campsites "immediately west of the city of Raleigh."[60]

The weather proved fine on April 17; one of Sherman's corps commanders called it a "beautiful day." At 8:00 a.m. that Monday Sherman and some of his staff officers waited at the Raleigh depot for the North Carolina Railroad car that would take them to Durham's Station. From there they would travel by horseback on the Hillsborough Road to their meeting with Johnston and his officers. While Sherman's party was boarding, the telegraph operator ran from the depot and informed the general that a coded message was arriving from Morehead City. Acting on the operator's information, Sherman held his locomotive and car for about half an hour. The translated telegram tragically validated the telegraph employee's conduct: it was Secretary of War Edwin M. Stanton's report to Sherman of President Lincoln's assassination.[61]

This stunning news "fell on me with terrible force," Sherman later wrote. The general swore the telegraph operator to secrecy, and the general and his officers made the twenty-six-mile rail trip from Raleigh to Durham's Station. Kilpatrick met Sherman and provided him and his staff with mounts and an escort. A trooper with a white flag took the lead, and the Union party set out on the road to Hillsborough.[62]

At 10:00 a.m. Johnston and Hampton, accompanied by staff officers and an escort, left the Dickson house and traveled toward Durham's Station. Maj. Henry B. McClellan rode ahead, carrying a flag of truce. The members of Johnston's entourage passed on their left the modest home of James and Nancy Bennett.[63]

At noon the two flag bearers met one another about four miles west of Durham's Station. Sherman later wrote that "word was passed back to us that General Johnston was near at hand, when we rode forward and met General Johnston on horseback, riding side by side with General Wade Hampton. We shook hands and introduced our respective attendants."[64]

Colonel Waring of the Jeff Davis Legion, who commanded Johnston's escort, had an unflattering first impression of the Federal commander's appearance. "Sherman is hard-featured & ill-favoured," he entered in his diary that day. Sherman, on his part, emphasized in his memoirs that he and Johnston had not met before but that they quickly reached good terms with one another.[65]

Sherman asked where they could meet in private, and Johnston said he had passed a small farmhouse not far back. The generals and their escorts rode to the Bennett Place, settled in 1846 by James and Nancy Bennett, their sons Lorenzo and Alphonzo, and daughter Eliza Ann.[66] In 1860 Bennett owned 189 acres, valued at $800, on which his family raised hogs and grew corn, wheat, oats, and potatoes.[67] Like most yeoman farmers, James Bennett supplemented his income with other employments. He sold horse feed, tobacco plugs, whiskey, and meals and lodging to travelers; he was also a tailor and cobbler.[68]

The Bennett home stood just north of the Hillsborough Road. It was a simple wood frame structure, contrasting with Wilmer McLean's fine brick residence. Near the main house and north of the road, the Bennetts had a kitchen, a dairy, and a smokehouse and across the Hillsborough Road was their well and a barn or stable. Among these buildings, only the house was suitable for a meeting of senior officers. The Bennetts withdrew to their kitchen, and the staff officers and escorts lounged under the shade trees or leaned against the fencing.[69]

As soon as the two generals were alone, Sherman showed Johnston the message reporting the Lincoln assassination. Genuinely distressed by this news, Johnston denounced the act and said he hoped that Sherman did not charge it to the Confederate government. Sherman's main concern was that the assassination might lead to further violence, particularly in Raleigh.[70]

Turning to the immediate subject of the meeting, Sherman urged that further resistance was useless and that since Lee had surrendered, Johnston could honorably do the same. Johnston referred to his original, April 13, message to Sherman that called for the military leaders to suspend operations and for the "civil authorities" to arrange an end to the war. As Davis had predicted, Sherman dismissed this idea on the grounds that the national government did not recognize the Confederacy. The Federal commander offered his opponent the terms that Grant had given Lee at Appomattox.[71]

Doubtless Johnston expected Sherman to state, as he had, that the Federal government did not recognize the Confederacy's civil authorities. But Johnston intended that the April 13 letter would give him the opportunity to negotiate in person with Sherman. After granting that the Appomattox terms were "magnanimous," Johnston played his best card: the Army of Northern Virginia had been surrounded, but the Army of Tennessee remained in the field and at a considerable distance from Sherman's force. The Confederate general then offered to take a long step, suggesting that "instead of a partial suspension of hostilities, we might . . . arrange the terms of a permanent peace."[72]

Sherman questioned Johnston's authority to secure a wide-ranging peace agreement, one that would include not only his own field force but all other remaining Confederate commands. Could he control armies other than his own? In his memoirs the Union general wrote that Johnston "intimated that he could procure authority from Mr. Davis." Sherman decided that it would be wise to adjourn the present meeting. Johnston needed time to obtain his president's authority for a larger surrender. Sherman also wanted to return to Raleigh before the news of the assassination broke there.[73]

In his memoir, Johnston emphasized another reason for the adjournment. As Johnston recalled it, the only sticking point during their initial session was the question of amnesty for the Confederacy's senior civilian leaders. Johnston was pleased at Sherman's willingness to discuss a general peace settlement. Sherman agreed to a general amnesty for Southerners but refused to include Davis and his cabinet. According to Johnston, granting amnesty for the Confederacy's senior civilian leaders was the main unresolved issue that afternoon.[74]

The stalemate over this point, according to Johnston, led to their agreement to adjourn until noon the next day. Johnston also wrote that he wanted time to bring Breckinridge into the negotiations since the secretary's relationship with Davis might help resolve the amnesty issue.[75]

When Sherman returned to Raleigh, he found that his soldiers had heard and rapidly spread the report of Lincoln's murder. "Yesterday the news of the assassination of President Lincoln reached us," staff officer Carter informed his wife on April 18, "and cast a gloom over the whole army. What a dreadful thing it is[.]" A member of the Eighty-fifth Illinois, which was camped southwest of Raleigh, observed that the commander in chief's death filled "the army with sorrow for he had done the best in his power to quell the rebellion." To the north, the news of the assassination shocked Grant's veterans as well as Sherman's. Two weeks after the terrible event, an officer of the 108th New York wrote that although he knew the report of Lincoln's death was "but too true, still I do not realize it. It does not seem possible that the man who was with our Army at the opening of our late decisive campaign can now lie cold in death."[76]

To Sherman's alarm, the reaction of many of his soldiers shifted quickly from a stunned sorrow to a vengeful anger. The immediate concern of Federal senior officers was that their men's wrath would lead to the destruction of Raleigh. Sherman himself; Maj. Gen. John A. "Black Jack" Logan, commander of the XV Corps; Mayor William H. Harrison; and other prominent citizens took prompt action and maintained the peace.[77]

While Sherman returned to Raleigh and dealt with this crisis, Johnston went back to the Dickson house on the afternoon of the seventeenth. He made no effort to gain Davis's authority to negotiate for all of the Confederacy's remaining armies, but he did send immediately for Breckinridge.[78] Johnston evidently believed that the secretary of war's participation in the negotiations would give him all the standing he needed.

Breckinridge, accompanied by Postmaster General Reagan and North Carolina governor Zebulon B. Vance, arrived at the Dickson house in the dead of night of April 17–18. Johnston briefed them on his meeting with Sherman. Reagan offered to draft a surrender document based on the Johnston-Sherman discussions on the seventeenth and on a series of additional terms Johnston wanted included. During the morning of Tuesday, April 18, Reagan was still working on this document when Johnston left for the Bennett Place.[79]

While Johnston rode toward Sherman, his men were deserting in droves from their camps around Greensboro and New Salem. Once rumors about their commander's April 13 letter to Sherman began circulating, more Southerners began to leave their units. After Johnston opened communications with his opposite number, as the general's biographer puts it, "quietly but steadily the number of deserters increased."[80] An epidemic of so-called French leave moved through the entire army in mid-April. An officer in Hardee's Corps identified April 17 as the day "the army perished—a mob remained." "As of April 18, 1865," writes historian Bradley, "Johnston commanded an army in name only."[81]

The two commanders again met at the Bennetts' modest farmhouse on April 18. Johnston opened the discussion by stating he had the authority to surrender all of the Confederacy's armies, but he wanted some guarantees of political rights for the Southern veterans. Sherman explained that Lincoln's December 1863 amnesty proclamation had pardoned all Confederate soldiers below the rank of brigadier general and that Grant's Appomattox terms had extended this pardon to all officers, including Lee. Johnston remained dissatisfied. According to Sherman, Johnston stated that both his officers and his men "were unnecessarily alarmed about this matter, as a sort of bugbear."[82]

While the generals considered this issue, Johnston asked that Breckinridge participate in the meeting. Sherman objected on the grounds that Breckinridge was a cabinet member of a government that Sherman's civilian authorities did not recognize. Johnston believed Breckinridge's presence was essential to his authority for surrendering all of the Confederacy's armies. He then urged Sherman to permit the Kentuckian to enter the discussions in his role as a Confederate major general. In this capacity, Breckinridge was acceptable to Sherman, and Breckinridge soon joined the two generals in the Bennett house.[83]

Sometime after Breckinridge's arrival, a courier came from the Dickson house with a collection of papers, including the document Reagan had drafted. Intending to provide a "basis of pacification," it called for "a general suspension of hostilities" and for the Confederates to disband their armies and recognize the authority of the Constitution and the federal government. In return, Southerners would receive some guarantees: the existing state governments would continue to function, Southerners would have all of the political and personal rights given them by the Constitution or state laws, and no one would be prosecuted for participating in the war. Johnston read the document out loud and remarked that Sherman already had accepted all of its provisions, except a general amnesty that would include Davis and his cabinet.[84] Sherman dismissed Reagan's effort, saying its preamble was "long" and its surrender terms "general and verbose."[85]

Sherman rapidly wrote out his own draft of the surrender terms that he called a "Memorandum or basis of agreement." Sherman had been dismissively critical of Reagan's submission, but significantly, he kept it close at hand while he wrote his own document. And although Sherman had faulted the postmaster general's effort as wordy, his own proved to be twice as long.[86] While the Union commander worked, Johnston gazed out a window, and for a brief time, he drifted into the Bennetts' yard and studied a Union soldier's Spencer carbine. Sherman finished writing and then, he later recalled, declared that his terms were "the best I could do, and [Johnston and Breckinridge] readily assented."[87]

The two Confederate generals had every reason to assent, because Sherman's document must have exceeded their best hopes. His memorandum began by having the two armies enter a cease-fire; if either side chose to break it, the respective army was to give forty-eight hours' notice. The Confederates would disband their armies and turn in their weapons to the arsenals of the Southern states. The executive branch of the national government would recognize the state governments then existing in the South, and federal courts would be reestablished in the region. The executive branch also would guarantee "the political rights and franchises" of the citizens of the Southern states and not disturb them as long as they lived peaceably. Finally the federal government would declare "a general amnesty."[88]

Johnston was delighted to sign Sherman's document. Its terms said nothing about slavery, but by April 1865 the institution was, as a practical matter, dead. At one point in the discussions, Johnston and Breckinridge had acknowledged this reality. No doubt thousands of other white Southerners by then had arrived at the same conclusion. Johnston's surrender of all remaining Confederate armies would not end slavery, but it would confirm its demise. And other than slavery, as historian Grimsley notes, Sherman's memorandum essentially "restored the status quo antebellum."[89] Historian Bradley asserts, "The true victor at the Bennett farm on April 18 was Joe Johnston."[90]

Historians Brooks Simpson and Jean Berlin have aptly described Sherman's actions on April 18, 1865. "Sherman's self-confidence and belief that soldiers were better equipped than politicians to settle the conflict," they write, "got the better of him. The man who claimed he would not 'complicate any points of civil policy' proceeded to do just that; in so doing he usurped the authority of his military and civilian superiors in an effort to take his own turn as a politician making peace."[91]

Why did Sherman leave his own realm of military affairs and enter into national policy? Why did the Federal commander who stood second to none in making hard war against the South offer Johnston such liberal surrender terms?

First Sherman felt sure he knew what peace terms Lincoln had wanted, and now he presumed President Andrew Johnson wanted them, too. Sherman had left the City Point conference with an overall impression that Lincoln sought a quick end to the war and lenient treatment of the defeated South. Second Sherman was confident he knew Lincoln's views on continuing the operation of civil governments and on granting a general amnesty.[92] Third Sherman was concerned that in the wake of Lincoln's assassination, enraged Northerners might demand sweeping vengeance or that the South would turn to guerrilla resistance and years of chaotic lawlessness would follow. By quickly making a lenient peace that disbanded the Confederate armies, Sherman hoped to thwart these unhappy possibilities.[93] Finally Sherman wanted Johnston to surrender promptly in order to avoid further, extended field operations. In his memoirs Sherman stated that all of his senior officers "dreaded the long and harassing pursuit of a dissolving and fleeing army—a march that might carry us back again over the thousand miles that we had just accomplished." Years later General Schofield also contended that because Johnston's army was not surrounded, "its surrender could not have been compelled."[94]

For these reasons, Sherman moved from military affairs into civil ones. It was true that Grant had crossed the same line. He had agreed that the veterans of the Army of Northern Virginia would not go to prison camps, would not be charged with treason, and would not face reprisals as long as they honored their paroles and obeyed federal laws. Lincoln had sanctioned Grant's terms, but Sherman's went much further into the arena of civil policy. Grant, as historian Simpson writes, had a far better understanding than Sherman did "of what the president would allow his generals to do."[95]

Sherman at some level recognized that he had taken some long steps into the realm of civil authority. He acknowledged in the last sentence of his memorandum that he and Johnston would have to "obtain the necessary authority" so that they could "carry out the above programme."[96]

At 4:00 p.m. the three generals left the Bennett Place. Johnston returned to the Dickson house while Breckinridge, with Reagan, set out with a copy of the surrender terms for Davis.[97] Sherman and his officers returned to Raleigh, and that night the field commander sent the surrender documents to Washington DC.[98]

While Sherman waited for the endorsement of his terms, he kept his troops active with daily reviews. The April 20 performance by General Paine's African American division proved to be the highlight of these parades.[99] Slocum characterized the review as "one of the most impressive" scenes of the war. "They were well drilled," he wrote, "dressed in new and handsome uniforms, and with their bright bayonets gleaming in the sun they made a splendid appearance." The black troops marched so smartly down the main streets of Raleigh that a Confederate officer, who was in the capital under a flag of truce, acknowledged that they "made a very fine appearance."[100]

While parades contributed to a festive atmosphere in the Federal ranks, desertions continued to reduce the Southern camps even as some general officers tried to restore morale. On the eve of the first Johnston-Sherman meeting, Waring of the Jeff Davis

Legion reported: "Gen. Hampton visited the Brigade to-day & made us an address. The men cheered him heartily. No surrender in him." On April 20 during the truce, cavalry officer Gordon entered in his diary: "Most of the men went over to [General Wheeler's headquarters] to hear him. I was told he said the Army had not been surrendered: that he would never surrender himself: that if a surrender took place he would give his corps ample notice of it, to escape if they saw fit."[101]

On the same day that young Wheeler exhorted his troopers, Lee sent Davis a somber letter, advising him that the entire area east of the Mississippi was "morally and physically unable to maintain the contest unaided with any hope of ultimate success." Guerrilla resistance could be offered, but it would lead only to "individual suffering and the devastation of the country." Lee bluntly recommended that "measures be taken for suspension of hostilities and the restoration of peace."[102]

Two days after Lee offered this stark counsel, Breckinridge and Reagan caught up with Davis in Charlotte and gave him the Bennett Place agreement. Davis still remained reluctant to accept terms even as generous as these terms were. He instead asked his cabinet members for their views in writing.[103] When Davis had polled his advisers in Greensboro, all of them except Benjamin had favored peace negotiations. At Charlotte the vote was unanimous: the president should endorse the Bennett Place document. Confronted with this unified reply, Davis wired Johnston his approval of the April 18 terms. The chief executive made one observation, which proved astute: he doubted that President Johnson would approve a settlement so favorable to the South.[104]

Davis's prediction understated the events that followed in Washington. The arrival of Sherman's terms ignited a firestorm. Secretary Stanton quickly compiled a list of nine reasons that the Bennett Place document was unacceptable.[105] At a meeting on the evening of April 21, Johnson and his advisers unanimously agreed that they would not approve the memorandum.[106]

Stanton first told Grant to notify Sherman that his terms had been rejected and that he must resume operations against Johnston. Later that same night of the twenty-first, the secretary of war changed his directive and instructed Grant to go to Sherman's headquarters, where Grant himself was to "direct operations" against the Confederates. The new guidance was not entirely pointed against Sherman. The idea that the general in chief should travel to Raleigh originated with Grant himself, who intended to shield his friend and subordinate from the uproar in Washington and to oversee the negotiations with Johnston.[107]

Historians Simpson and Berlin hit the right note in their assessment of Sherman's terms and of his outraged critics. "If in the end one is hard-pressed to defend Sherman's action," they write, "however, it is equally difficult to justify how many Northerners, including Secretary of War Edwin M. Stanton, responded to them." Some of the criticism of Sherman was groundless, and much of it was needlessly public. Stanton sent his nine-point refutation of the general's terms to the *New York Times*, which published it on April 23. Maj. Gen. Henry W. Halleck, until recently the army chief of staff and now the commander of the Military Division of the James, put in print a wildly erroneous report that Davis's gold train was moving south from Goldsboro and implied that Sherman could not be relied on to intercept it.[108]

Sherman found it unforgivable that Stanton and General Halleck, a friend since their prewar days in California, could arrive at such views and publicize them. He took revenge against both men. When the Union armies of the eastern and western theaters held their Grand Review of the Armies in Washington DC on May 23 and 24, Sherman very publicly refused to shake hands with the secretary of war.[109] In his 1875 memoirs the general also dealt harshly with both Stanton and Halleck.[110]

Grant, Sherman's superior and friend, was determined to protect him from the extreme rhetoric in Washington when he arrived in Raleigh on the morning of April 24. Sherman had seen some of the Northern press accounts of Lincoln's murder, and given the inflamed climate of opinion in the North, he was not surprised to learn from Grant that Johnson had rejected the Bennett Place agreement. But Sherman did not know about the fiery reaction his terms had stirred at the April 21 cabinet meeting and elsewhere in Washington, and Grant did not tell him about it. Only after Grant left North Carolina did Sherman learn from the *New York Times* how virulently Stanton and others had assailed him.[111]

When the two generals were alone in Sherman's office, Grant subtly but clearly conveyed to Sherman that he had strayed into civil affairs and that he must get Johnston to surrender on the Appomattox terms. Understanding the course correction that Grant wanted, Sherman immediately sent two dispatches to Johnston. The first gave the forty-eight hour's notice, called for in the April 18 agreement, that Sherman would end the Bennett Place truce. The second explained why: Sherman had been ordered to avoid civil negotiations and to take the surrender only of Johnston's command and no other commands on the Appomattox terms.[112] These communications showed Grant that Sherman understood the situation, and the general in chief ignored Stanton's directive to supersede Sherman in conducting field operations.[113]

At 5:00 p.m. on April 24, the day Grant met with Sherman, Johnston received Davis's endorsement of the Bennett Place terms and, about an hour later, Sherman's two dispatches. Confronted with the new situation presented in Sherman's messages, Johnston wired Breckinridge for instructions. Davis would not agree to Johnston's surrendering on the Appomattox terms. The president directed Breckinridge to order the Army of Tennessee to continue to retreat, but the secretary of war knew that Johnston would reject this directive. Breckinridge instead suggested that the cavalry and some of the light field guns be sent to the Trans-Mississippi and that the infantry and most of the artillery be disbanded but with a plan to reassemble.[114]

The next day, April 25, Johnston held his last council of war. Beauregard and the Army of Tennessee's corps and division commanders joined him at the Dickson house. These senior leaders agreed that Breckinridge's plan could not be carried out.[115] Johnston intended to resume his negotiations with Sherman independent of any guidance from Davis.

Early in the evening of the twenty-fifth, Johnston issued his final marching orders to the Army of the Tennessee. The corps commanders were to ready their units for a move late the next morning. The army would head for Salisbury, about fifty miles down the North Carolina Railroad from Greensboro.[116]

On Tuesday, April 25, Johnston also answered Sherman's two dispatches. He replied to the first by asking for another truce and another meeting. Answering the second, Johnston argued for a settlement that went beyond the Appomattox terms. He contended that disbanding the Army of Northern Virginia had "afflicted this country with numerous bands having no means of subsistence but robbery," so Sherman should "agree to other conditions."[117]

On the same day, the Union soldiers completed their last marches of the Carolinas campaign, with the XVII Corps of Howard's wing moving to Jones's Station on the North Carolina Railroad ten miles west of Raleigh and the XX Corps of Slocum's wing going to Jones's Crossroads about fifteen miles southwest of the city.[118] Other commands stood ready to advance on the twenty-sixth, but as it turned out, the Federals had made their final bivouacs in the western theater.

That evening Sherman received Johnston's first dispatch, asking for another conference. Sherman replied that he would meet him at noon the next day at the Bennett Place. Johnston's second message, questioning the Appomattox terms, did not arrive until around 7:00 a.m. the following morning.[119] Sherman did not answer it. He had direct guidance from his superiors that Johnston was to surrender under the Appomattox terms, leaving no room for negotiation. In any case, Sherman would be meeting with Johnston in a matter of hours after receiving his second dispatch.

On Wednesday morning, April 26, believing a Confederate surrender was eminent, Sherman held his units in place. Johnston intended to begin the movement toward Salisbury that he had ordered on the previous day. At 11:00 a.m. the Southerners began a march—of sorts. Entire regiments remained in their camps, refusing to move again. Many soldiers deserted. Convinced that they would soon be surrendered, they saw no reason to wait to receive a parole.[120]

The dissolution of the Army of Tennessee did not matter because Johnston would sign a surrender document that same

Wednesday afternoon. On the morning of the twenty-sixth, Sherman left his Raleigh headquarters, expecting to meet Johnston at the Bennett Place at noon. "General Johnston was delayed by an accident to his train," Sherman related, "but at 2 p.m. [he] arrived." For the third time the two generals entered the modest North Carolina farmhouse.[121]

At the time of this conference, Grant was still in Raleigh, where he would remain until the next morning.[122] He saw no reason to oversee Sherman's conduct of the meeting with Johnston. Three other senior officers accompanied their commander to the Bennetts' house: Howard, Schofield, and Maj. Gen. Frank P. Blair, Jr.[123]

Sherman began the session by calling on Johnston to surrender under the terms Grant had given Lee. Johnston argued that the Appomattox settlement was inadequate, and he again sought further guarantees for his men. Sherman was limited by the direct instructions from his superiors, so the conversation stood at an impasse. Sherman called on Schofield, who suggested that the two commanders sign one document closely resembling the Appomattox surrender and then a second one that would list the terms Johnston wanted. As Schofield recalled long years afterward, Johnston made a remark to the effect of "I think General Schofield can fix it."[124] Johnston knew that after any agreements were signed, Sherman would take most of his command to Washington and that Schofield would remain with a smaller force to oversee the Confederate demobilization and maintain order. Johnston was confident that Schofield would carry out any terms included in the second document.[125]

Schofield drafted first what he titled "Terms of a military convention," consisting of five points and presenting terms nearly identical to the ones offered at Appomattox. Johnston and Sherman signed this agreement, and later that day in Raleigh, Grant endorsed it. After the Bennett Place signing, Johnston, Sherman, and Schofield discussed what additional terms might be included in the second document.[126]

The next day, April 27, Schofield and Johnston met to prepare the additional terms. The Confederate commander listed the points he wanted included. Johnston was particularly concerned that his men have food and transportation, which would be in the interests not only of his men but also of Southern civilians and the Federal troops charged with maintaining order in the postwar South.[127]

Schofield read this and Johnston's other entries, reduced them from eight to six, and wrote a document he titled "Military Convention of April 26, 1865.—Supplemental Terms." Points 1 and 4 addressed Johnston's concern about transportation, and point 3 stated that his soldiers could keep their horses and other private property. Schofield also provided the Southern veterans with 250,000 rations and wagons to haul them.[128]

The second point of Schofield's Supplemental Terms carried the greatest potential for controversy. As in Sherman's rejected April 18 document, it called for the Confederate soldiers to deposit their arms at their state capitals. Even more striking, this second provision allowed each brigade to keep one-seventh of its small arms. Johnston and Schofield signed the Supplemental Terms, and Sherman endorsed and sent them to Washington.[129]

The Johnson administration accepted the Supplemental Terms, including its remarkable second provision. Writing about it a generation later, Schofield remained taken aback that this entry survived the scrutiny of the nation's civilian leaders.[130]

Although Johnston's surrender, as he originally proposed, did not include all of the remaining Southern armies, it nonetheless was the largest of the Civil War. In February Lee had given Johnston authority over the Department of South Carolina, Georgia, and Florida; Johnston commanded the soldiers of those states and North Carolina. In total, the Bennett Place surrender covered nearly ninety thousand Confederates.[131]

Confederate defeat in the Carolinas was inevitable perhaps as early as January 1865, when Johnston became army commander, and certainly by April 9, when the Army of Northern Virginia surrendered. Davis still would not acknowledge this reality. Even after Johnston surrendered on April 26, the president refused to give up the cause, and he continued to flee his Federal pursuers.

Johnston played the lead role in ending the war in the Carolinas. After Lee's surrender, and perhaps earlier, Johnston decided that his best course was to maintain a coherent force, keep it well away from Sherman, and negotiate the best terms possible for his army and perhaps the entire Confederacy. Johnston was remarkably successful in reaching these goals. First the morale of his army remained resilient after the disastrous loss of Petersburg and Richmond and then the fatal surrender of Lee's army. Only when Johnston began negotiating the capitulation of the Army of Tennessee did it dissolve in desertion.

As for his second goal, Johnston fully succeeded in keeping his army beyond Sherman's grasp. While Sherman occupied Raleigh and the area around it, the Confederates continued to move, and by the time of the Bennett Place meetings, they were five march days away from their foes. Sherman could have run the Confederates to ground, but it would have taken considerable effort and would have increased the risk that the Army of Tennessee would break up into guerrilla bands.

Johnston met and exceeded his third goal. Supported by Beauregard and others during the Greensboro conference, Johnston secured Davis's permission to begin negotiations with Sherman. After Davis left Greensboro on April 15, he was unable to communicate directly with his field commander, and Johnston exploited this opportunity. With Breckinridge providing political cover, Johnston met with Sherman. Johnston's military position was more viable than Lee's had been, and he accordingly was able to do more negotiating. Johnston initially reached a wide-ranging peace agreement with his hard-war opponent that left the defeated South in a far better position than its leaders could have hoped. Even after the Johnson administration vetoed Sherman's original terms, Johnston still gained a settlement for his troops that was superior to the one Lee had accepted for his soldiers.[132]

Johnston's men, before their morale collapsed, made an essential contribution to their commander's achievement at the Bennett Place. The first element in Johnston's plan was that the Army of Tennessee must remain a viable field force. It did so until Johnston began his discussions with Sherman. The men in the ranks endured strenuous marches and other hardships and stayed with their colors long enough to get Johnston a bargaining position at the Bennett Place.

The Southern defeat was in part the result of Sherman's generalship. Sherman, like Grant, remained tightly focused on securing a victory in the field. He understood the value of his advantage in resources and managed his logistics wisely. Sherman's operational plans were superior to those of his opponents. For far too long, the Confederate forces lacked central direction and remained widely scattered. Sherman executed a strategy that took advantage of their weaknesses.

If Sherman made an operational error in the Carolinas, it was at Bentonville. There he stood content to ward off Johnston's blows of desperation and then resume a campaign of movement when a hammer blow on the second or third day of the battle might well have destroyed the Army of the South.

This lost opportunity hardly mattered. Sherman looked beyond the Bentonville battlefield to the objective of joining his forces with Schofield's two corps. This combination proved strategically decisive as Sherman closed out the Carolinas campaign without waging another major battle.

Like every successful general, Sherman owed his victory to the men who carried out his plans. The soldiers of the Army of the Tennessee compiled a praiseworthy record during the Carolinas campaign. They served their country well, and they appreciated the victory they won. Shortly after the war ended, an Indiana veteran wrote that the men around him "were a tired but happy lot of boys."[133] Sherman's soldiers completed long marches and fought hard battles, and if more effort had been needed, they stood ready to give it. While the Bennett Place truce was in effect, one staff officer promised his father that "if it should become necessary for this army to pursue the Rebels further, the lesson of war that the South has already learned will be as nothing to that which we would teach them."[134]

The western veterans were proud of their service in the field and of their performance in the Grand Review of the Armies. When the soldiers gathered in the nation's capital for two days of celebratory parades, many, including Sherman himself, expected that smart marching by the spit-and-polish army from the eastern theater would upstage his men. It did not happen. On the first day of that memorable event, the paper-collar Army of the Potomac made some basic marching mistakes, and too many of its men were distracted by the crowd along Pennsylvania Avenue. On the second day, the rough-hewn western Army of the Tennessee made an impressive showing.

Many years later, Sherman was still proud when he wrote about his men in the grand review: "Many good people, up to that time, had looked upon our Western army as a sort of mob; but the world then saw, and recognized the fact, that it was an army in the proper sense, well organized, well commanded and disciplined; and there was no wonder that it swept through the South like a tornado."[135]

CHAPTER TEN

Scattered Embers

With the surrender of Gen. Joseph E. Johnston, Federal forces extinguished the once-raging bonfire of Confederate military resistance. But some embers remained scattered across the South, and they continued to glow. Each was small but had to be stamped out against the possibility, however slight, that the fire would rekindle.

In March 1865 Selma, Alabama, remained a valuable city to the Southern war effort. It stood more than forty miles west of the former Confederate capital at Montgomery and represented the last significant logistical center in the Deep South.[1] A fifty-acre complex included a city arsenal, iron works, powder mill and magazine, niter works, machine shop and other factories, and warehouses. Selma was also an important transportation hub; it was located on the north bank of the Alabama River and at the intersection of the Alabama and Mississippi Rivers Railroad and the Tennessee and Alabama River Railroad.[2]

Selma became the target of young Maj. Gen. James H. Wilson, who had graduated sixth in the West Point Class of 1860 and then demonstrated both administrative and combat skills during a sterling Civil War career. General Wilson mobilized about thirteen thousand Union cavalrymen in the northwestern corner of Alabama for what would become one of the most memorable raids of the Civil War.[3] On March 22, the day after the Battle of Bentonville and three days before the attack on Fort Stedman, Wilson's troopers set out for Selma in three columns. By March 29, they had covered almost 150 miles.[4]

Lt. Gen. Nathan Bedford Forrest's Cavalry Corps of the Department of Alabama, Mississippi, and East Louisiana opposed Wilson's horsemen. General Forrest once had been the most feared among the South's cavalrymen. His biographer Brian Steel Wills relates that Forrest learned the value of inciting dread in his rivals during his youth, which was spent in antebellum Tennessee's rough backwoods. "Perhaps the most important trait that Forrest developed from his early years on the frontier," writes Wills, "was the art of intimidation." During most of the Civil War, Forrest's name struck alarm across the North, but in late March 1865 it no longer was the case because he commanded so few men. Forrest initially faced Wilson's raiders with only about fifteen hundred troopers.[5]

Wilson's commanding advantage in numbers was further strengthened by an intelligence coup. On the morning of April 1, a Federal patrol captured a courier carrying dispatches signed by Brig. Gen. William H. Jackson, who commanded one of Forrest's cavalry divisions, and Maj. Charles W. Anderson, Forrest's aide-de-camp. "I now knew exactly where every division and brigade of Forrest's corps was," Wilson claimed in his memoirs, "that they were widely scattered and that if I could force the marching and fighting with sufficient rapidity and vigor, I should have the game entirely in my hands."[6]

Wilson pressed his advantage, and Forrest, heavily outmanned, could raise only light opposition to the Union raiders. On the afternoon of April 2, the Federals reached Selma. Wilson found that the city's fortifications "consisted of a bastioned line on a radius of nearly three miles, extending from the Alabama River below to the same above the city." The fieldworks around Selma were strong, but their value was diluted because they lacked an adequate number of defenders. "The place was well fortified, but we didn't have men enough to man the trenches," a Mississippi cavalryman pointed out. "They were from five to ten steps apart in the ditches." Forrest assembled about seven thousand defenders, many of whom were hastily impressed militia.[7]

Late on the afternoon of April 2, the Federal cavalrymen attacked the Selma fortifications. Forrest's veteran horsemen put up a creditable defense; a member of the First Mississippi Cavalry claimed that his regiment was the last to give way. The militiamen, however, fled their posts. A Georgian wrote that they "threw away everything they could shed without checking [their] speed."[8]

The Federal cavalrymen gave an excellent account of themselves at Selma. Wilson wrote about them with considerable pride: "The troops dismounted, sprang forward with confident alacrity, and in less than fifteen minutes, without ever stopping, wavering or faltering, had swept over the works and driven the rebels in confusion toward the city. . . . The troops, inspired by the wildest enthusiasm, swept everything before them and penetrated the city in all directions."[9] The able brevet Maj. Gen. Emory Upton, one of Wilson's subordinates, helped plan this dramatically successful assault against the fortified city, and an episode at Selma influenced General Upton's postwar work on new tactics for the army. Upton took note when Brig. Gen. Eli Long's division, armed with Spencer repeating carbines, gained auspicious results by attacking dismounted and in a single-rank, loose-ordered formation.[10]

The Union horsemen had gained the Deep South's last major military depot. General Long's division paid for its success with more than 300 casualties. Long himself suffered a paralyzing head wound, and one of his brigade leaders and two regimental commanders also were wounded. "The immediate fruits of our victory [at Selma]," Wilson reported, "were 31 field guns and one 30-pounder Parrott which had been used against us, 2,700 prisoners, including 150 officers, a number of colors, and immense quantities of stores of every kind." For the entire raid, Wilson stated that his casualties were 99 killed, 598 wounded, and 28 missing and that he captured 288 artillery pieces and 6,820 prisoners.[11]

Pressing on after his victory at Selma, Wilson gained Montgomery on April 12. He then rode into Georgia and, after a rare Civil War nighttime engagement, captured Columbus during the dark hours of April 16.[12] Four days later Wilson took Macon, where the Confederates presented him with the news of General Johnston's armistice with Maj. Gen. William T. Sherman. Here Wilson ended his dramatic raid and established a headquarters. His cavalrymen then became available to search for the fleeing Confederate president Jefferson Davis.[13]

Forrest's troopers who survived the Battle of Selma soon would be surrendered along with the other soldiers in the Department of Alabama, Mississippi, and East Louisiana. After Johnston's capitulation, this department contained the only organized Confederate forces east of the Mississippi River. It was commanded by Lt. Gen. Richard Taylor, a Louisiana planter who was the son of the late president Zachary Taylor. Active in state politics before the war, he then served the Confederacy in both the eastern and western theaters.[14]

As early as September 1864, General Taylor had concluded that defeat in his theater was inevitable. He advised his far more optimistic commander in chief, President Davis, that "the best we could hope for was to protract the struggle until spring." By the time that season arrived, however, Taylor faced a hopeless situation. In March Maj. Gen. Edward R. S. Canby prepared for an operation against Mobile, Alabama, defended by energetic and popular Maj. Gen. Dabney H. Maury. General Canby had nearly fifty thousand Federals, far outnumbering the nine thousand men the Confederates had available early that month.[15] Supported by a naval operation, General Canby's troops occupied Mobile, the South's last major city, on April 12, 1865.[16]

Its conqueror, Canby, commanded the Military Division of West Mississippi, which included the states from Missouri south to the Gulf Coast and from Texas to Florida. Canby had the reputation of being a cautious field commander. On March 14 Lt. Gen. Ulysses S. Grant had complained about him to Secretary of War Edwin M. Stanton: "I am very much dissatisfied with General Canby. He has been slow beyond excuse."[17] After Canby took Mobile, General Grant's criticism was rendered irrelevant. Given the Union's enormous advantage in numbers, it remained only to negotiate Taylor's surrender, and Canby was certainly up to that task.

Taylor had believed for some time that the Confederates would not win their independence. The surrenders of Gen. Robert E. Lee and Johnston confirmed his view that the war was over. Like Johnston, he thought that his only course was to keep his men with their regiments and surrender them on the best terms possible. Just before capitulating, he advised one of his subordinates that "officers and soldiers must stand fast to their colors, present as bold a front as possible, and in the last extremity surrender en masse, upon such terms as are never granted to any but an organized national army."[18]

In mid-April Taylor and Canby wrote one another about the possibility of a prisoner exchange. Taylor concluded from the "tenor and tone" of Canby's correspondence that the time had come to begin negotiations. He proposed to meet with Canby, when and where the Federal general chose, so that the two of them could draft a document that would "become the basis of final action within the sphere of the authority confided to us."[19]

On April 29 Taylor and Canby met at Jacob and Mary Magee's farm on the Mobile and Ohio Railroad a dozen miles north of Mobile. An infantry brigade and a brass band grandly escorted Canby to the site. Taylor's entrance was less imposing: he arrived on a railroad handcar with only its operators and a lone staff officer.[20]

The two generals conferred alone in one of the Magees' rooms and agreed to a war-ending truce based on the same terms that General Sherman originally had offered Johnston. The officers then enjoyed what Taylor called a "bountiful luncheon," and champagne corks popped. The Union band serenaded the gathering with "Hail Columbia" and then played "Dixie." Taylor returned to his headquarters camp, no doubt as pleased as Johnston had been on the afternoon of April 19.[21]

Canby soon learned that President Andrew Johnson had disapproved the original Sherman-Johnston terms. The day after the Magee farm meeting, Canby sent Taylor a dispatch that explained this development and offered him essentially the same conditions that General Lee had accepted at Appomattox. "There was no room for hesitancy," Taylor later wrote. "Folly and madness combined would not have justified an attempt to prolong a hopeless contest." Like other Confederate leaders, Taylor emphatically rejected guerrilla resistance. The soldiers must "remain intact" and accept a general surrender, he explained to General Maury; otherwise, "they will be hunted down like beasts of prey, their families will be persecuted, and ruin thus entailed not only upon the soldiers themselves, but also upon thousands of defenseless Southern women and children."[22]

On the evening of May 2, Taylor accepted Canby's offer of the Appomattox terms. Two days later the generals met again, this time at Citronelle, on the rail line about forty miles north of Mobile. Taylor surrendered his command. On paper it numbered about twenty-five thousand soldiers, but as historian Sean Michael O'Brien notes, far fewer were "actually present."[23]

On May 8 Canby's men began issuing paroles to the surrendered Confederates of the Department of Alabama, Mississippi, and East Louisiana. The victorious Federals gave the former Confederates rations and transportation home. These considerations encouraged the defeated Southerners to appear in person and take the paper that documented their capitulation. Thousands of Confederate deserters presented themselves at Meridian, Mississippi, and flooded the parole process. Taylor himself finally asked the Federals to stop issuing the documents.[24]

Two days after the victors began paroling Taylor's veterans, Union cavalrymen captured the Confederate president. Davis had left Charlotte, North Carolina, on April 26, intending to elude Federal pursuers, cross the lower Southern states, and reach the Trans-Mississippi. From this far western theater, Davis believed that no matter how bleak Confederate military affairs appeared to others, he could continue the fight.[25] Rather than join the flight from Charlotte, Attorney General George Davis had resigned, explaining to the president that he was responsible for orphaned children. Nor did Adjutant and Inspector General Samuel Cooper, well into his sixties and ill, leave Charlotte with the president. Five cabinet members did: Secretary of the Treasury George A. Trenholm, Secretary of War John C. Breckinridge, Secretary of State Judah P. Benjamin, Secretary of the Navy Stephen R. Mallory, and Postmaster General John H. Reagan.[26]

During the next week Davis and his remaining followers traveled about 180 miles from Charlotte to Abbeville in western South Carolina. Ailing Secretary Trenholm resigned on April 27, and Davis gave his duties to Postmaster General Reagan. Gen. Braxton Bragg, the most star crossed of the president's field commanders, joined the group on May 1.[27]

On the afternoon of May 2, Davis conferred with the military members of his entourage: Secretary (and Major General) Breckinridge, General Bragg, and the officers of the president's cavalry escort. Once again, the commander in chief spoke unrealistically about continuing resistance. The situation, he contended, was no worse than at the nadir of the American Revolutionary War. His military leaders made it clear that they remained with him to protect him, but in no way did they share his wildly optimistic view of the Confederacy's future.[28]

Davis and his party left Abbeville in the dead of night of May 2–3. The president's band of loyalists soon dissolved further. On the third Secretary Benjamin, probably for Davis's benefit, said that he was leaving for a diplomatic mission to Cuba and the Bahamas and would join the commander in chief in Texas. Benjamin fled to Florida and eventually took a passage to England. He died in Paris in 1884.[29] Secretary Mallory resigned on the third and went his own way.[30] During the night of May 5, Breckinridge, who was supervising the rear of the escort column, decided to ride south toward Florida, whether the president took that route or not. The two men never saw each other again.[31]

Varina Davis, the president's wife, had left Richmond before it was evacuated. She went to Charlotte, departed before her husband's arrival there, and with their four children, traveled independently of him. Acting on information from his scouts, Davis rode ahead of his group and, near midnight on May 6–7, found Varina and her escorts camped near Dublin, Georgia. Although the president knew it would slow the pace, he decided to combine the two parties, and they began traveling together on May 7.[32]

By early May the rate of Davis's flight hardly mattered. Union forces inevitably would run him to ground. With the end of Wilson's raid and the surrender of Taylor's men, large numbers of

Federals had been freed to search for the fleeing Confederate president and his entourage. From his Macon headquarters, Wilson directed an aggressive patrolling of Georgia. In the superheated climate of Northern opinion after President Abraham Lincoln's assassination, Davis was accused of complicity in that heinous crime. At the urging of Secretary Stanton and other advisers, President Johnson signed a May 2 proclamation declaring Davis a conspirator in the assassination and offering for his arrest a reward of $100,000, or double the one for John Wilkes Booth.[33]

On the night of May 9–10, Jefferson and Varina Davis and their remaining escorts camped in a clearing a mile north of Irwinville, Georgia. Just before dawn on the tenth, the Fourth Michigan Cavalry and a detachment of the First Wisconsin Cavalry struck their encampment and captured the Confederate president.[34] Davis, who had insisted on continuing the Southern war effort longer than the circumstances warranted, now was forced to accept the reality of his own situation. "God's will be done," he quietly told his captors.[35]

Federal authorities held Davis in a casement of Fort Monroe, Virginia, for two years. Northern emotions, which boiled in the immediate aftermath of President Lincoln's assassination, soon cooled. "With striking speed," writes historian William C. Davis, "the vindictiveness over the war and Lincoln's assassination collapsed under the weight of relief that the long ordeal was done. Though feelings remained high against the Southern leaders, sheer exhaustion seemingly sapped Northerners of the energy to prosecute them." No charges of conspiracy or treason were brought against Davis, and he was released in May 1867.[36]

Three days after Davis's capture and more than a month after the Appomattox surrender, the last battle of the Civil War was fought. Col. Theodore H. Barrett, commander of the Federal garrison on Brazos Santiago, Texas, took a force of about eight hundred Federals from that island and led it up the north bank of the Rio Grande. He evidently believed he could reach Brownsville without resistance. On May 13 Colonel Barrett was attacked by about thirteen hundred Confederates under Col. John S. "Rip" Ford at Palmito Ranch, a small dwelling about fifteen miles east of Barrett's objective.[37] Colonel Ford hit the Union soldiers hard and drove them back to the Texas coast.[38]

Palmito Ranch, the final land engagement of the conflict, produced several "lasts" of the Civil War. "The last volley of the war," Barrett stated in his official report, "it is believed, was fired by the Sixty-second U.S. Colored Infantry about sunset of the 13th of May, 1865, between White's Ranch and the Boca Chica, Tex." Pvt. Ferdinand Gerring, of German descent, was believed to be the last Confederate fatality. Veterans of the Thirty-fourth Indiana presented the family of Pvt. John Jefferson Williams with a medallion that recognized him as the last soldier killed in the Civil War.[39] The Battle of Palmito Ranch was notable for these "lasts" and for the ethnic mix of its participants: Anglos, Mexicans, African Americans, and others.[40]

Ford's success created the irony that the Confederacy lost the Civil War but won the conflict's last battle. It quickly became apparent that his victory was meaningless. Ford's men learned from their Union prisoners that Richmond had been captured and Lee had surrendered more than a month earlier. This information destroyed morale. The victors of Palmito Ranch rapidly headed for Brownsville, where they began leaving Confederate service without waiting for formal discharges.[41]

Ford's triumph on May 13 was also rendered irrelevant by a larger event. The battle was fought in the Trans-Mississippi Department, and a little less than two weeks after it took place, Gen. Edmund Kirby Smith surrendered all the troops within that jurisdiction. General Kirby Smith's Civil War career, which began as a brigade commander at First Manassas, was marked by feuds with brother officers and disagreements with Richmond authorities. His Trans-Mississippi region had been cut off from the rest of the Confederacy since the loss of Vicksburg and Port Hudson, Mississippi, in July 1863. By the spring of 1865, his command was far too weak to contend against the Union forces that began concentrating against it.[42]

During the second week of May 1865, Kirby Smith met at Marshall, in eastern Texas, with political leaders from the Trans-Mississippi's four slave states. The governors of Missouri, Arkansas, and Louisiana and a representative of the ailing Texas governor attended the conference. In an apparent attempt to rally what little morale remained on the far western home front, these politicians grandly declared the conditions under which they would accept surrender. They presumptuously stated terms that were more similar to the ones that Sherman had originally offered Johnston at the Bennett Place than to those Grant had given Lee at Appomattox. This posturing by the governors was futile. Freed by Taylor's capitulation, Union forces already were massing on the borders of the Trans-Mississippi, the last existing military department of the Confederacy. Federal authorities would not have to accept anything less from their opponents than the Appomattox terms.[43]

The politicians and Kirby Smith were not ready to acknowledge defeat, but many soldiers were. Without waiting to be surrendered, they began acting as if they had been. In the middle of May, Brig. Gen. Samuel B. Maxey acknowledged that he could not depend on the service of his division. Maj. Gen. John G. Walker predicted that the men of his cavalry division would "lay down their arms at the first appearance of the enemy."[44] On May 16 Maj. Gen. John B. Magruder bluntly advised Kirby Smith: "Nothing more can be done except to satisfy the soldiers, to induce them to preserve their organization, and to send them in regiments, &c., to their homes, with as little damage to the community as possible." Then General Magruder made a direct appeal: "For God's sake act or let me act."[45]

But Kirby Smith had no intention of surrendering. On May 18 he loftily announced that he was moving his headquarters from Shreveport, Louisiana, to Galveston, Texas, where he apparently believed he could rally enough reliable troops to continue the war. He soon was proven wrong. While he traveled from Louisiana to Texas, the remaining units of his army of the Trans-Mississippi dissolved. On May 21 the Confederate soldiers holding Galveston rioted, and two days later the Houston garrison went on a rampage. The pattern continued along a line running from below the Red River to east of San Antonio, with disturbances occurring at Clarksville, Henderson, Crockett, La Grange, and Gonzales.[46]

If Kirby Smith failed to accept the reality behind these events, some of his senior officers did grasp it. Lt. Gen. Simon B. Buckner and two other subordinates whom the commander had left in Shreveport rode a steamboat to New Orleans and met at length with Canby, who had taken Taylor's surrender earlier that month. On May 26 they agreed to accept the Appomattox terms, pending the approval of Kirby Smith.[47]

The men in the ranks and their senior officers had forced Kirby Smith's hand. They had taken what remained of his command—fewer than 17,700 soldiers took paroles—into the last major surrender of the war. Kirby Smith grudgingly endorsed the May 26 terms and issued an ungracious farewell to his veterans: "I am left a Commander without an army—a General without troops. You have made yr. choice. It was unwise & unpatriotic, But it is final. I pray you may not live to regret it." On June 26 Kirby Smith entered Mexico with a band of former Confederate military and political leaders.[48] He eventually settled in Tennessee, where he died in 1893, the last of the full Confederate generals to pass away.[49]

Kirby Smith's surrender did not include the Native Americans in his department who had fought for the Confederacy.[50] The last of their leaders to capitulate was Brig. Gen. Stand Watie. In 1835 he had accepted the national policy of removing the Cherokees from Georgia and resettling them in the Indian Territory, and he became the leader of the minority Treaty Party of his people. When the Civil War began, the Cherokees tried to remain neutral, but eventually the majority party declared for the Union while the minority party supported the South. Watie became a Confederate brigadier general and led his men into battle at Wilson's Creek, Missouri; Pea Ridge, Arkansas; and elsewhere. On June 23 he rode into Doaksville in the Indian Territory and surrendered his Cherokees and the Creeks, the Seminoles, and the Osages who had served with them. Nearly sixty years old, Watie was the last Confederate general to surrender.[51]

With Watie's capitulation, the last of the scattered embers was extinguished. The Union had been preserved, the Constitution upheld, and slavery ended. These goals had been achieved at an unimaginable human cost. The estimate usually given for the Civil War's total casualties is 620,000, a figure that exceeds the 1860 population of Connecticut or Arkansas and doubles that of Vermont.[52]

No doubt the actual statistic is higher than this approximation. The often-cited number of 620,000 is misleading. First it represents no more than a crude estimate of the war's total military casualties. The number usually given for the total Federal losses is about 360,000. It is hard to have much confidence in this figure. Historian Drew Gilpin Faust shows that it is the result of a series of upward revisions that the War Department made over a period of about twenty years following the conflict. Southern casualty statistics are even less reliable. Given the weaknesses in Confederate record keeping, Faust rightly regards the number usually stated for Southern military deaths "as an educated guess." Another problem with the 620,000 figure is that it excludes civilian deaths, which historian James McPherson has estimated at 50,000.[53] The precise statistics will never be known, and it hardly matters. The numbers are so large that they numb the mind. They cannot convey the human suffering caused by the war or the consequences of so many lives lost, so many lives broken.

Southerners endured horrifying losses, only to be left with stark defeat. In North Carolina, Col. Joseph F. Waring saw Johnston's surrender approaching, and he grimly acknowledged that "the South is [to] go back to the 'Union.' It is a bitter pill." On the day the fighting ended in Virginia, Ordnance Sgt. James W. Albright wrote in his diary that he "felt like an old horse, who had been faithful until age unfit him for work—turned out to die. Many shed tears as we bade one another goodbye and started south." A Louisiana cavalryman despaired: "Everything we had fought for and believed in had come down to nothing."[54]

For four years thousands of Southerners performed hard, dangerous duties, and no one appreciated their loyal service more than their general in chief. Lee's final orders to his men ended eloquently: "With an increasing admiration of your constancy and devotion to your country, and a grateful remembrance of your kind and generous considerations for myself, I bid you all an affectionate farewell."[55]

Unlike their opponents, the Federals enjoyed a sense of victory. They also, like many veterans of all wars, felt enormous relief. After John A. Boon completed his service in the western theater, he wrote to his wife on April 20, 1865: "I have no news to write but you may believe I am glad the war is over." "No words could tell our gladness at the final accomplishment of this great work," declared an Ohio soldier, "nor our deep sense of relief when we fully realized that we had fought our last battle." For many, the deliverance from the ordeal was accompanied by a remorse for those comrades who had not been so fortunate. A veteran of the Fifty-seventh New York proudly marched in the Grand Review of the Army of the Potomac, but after the majestic parade, his thoughts turned to those who had not lived to see the celebration. "They sleep their soldiers rest," he wrote, "under the green mounds of the blood-dyed Wilderness, amidst the sighing pines and hemlocks of the Carolinas and Georgia, or their bones are bleaching yet on the fatal field of Chickamauga."[56]

Thousands of Union veterans would take pride for decades in the victory that had been won, the hardships that had been endured, and the camaraderie that had been gained. Long years after the Civil War ended, J. H. Baylis, a veteran of the Fifty-ninth Illinois, wrote a heartfelt piece of correspondence to William McAdams, an officer of his former regiment. After reminiscing about their victorious service together in the "Old 59th," Baylis closed his letter with two poignant sentences: "I brought home with me eleven gun shots and two other wounds received by a battery wagon running over me. My good wishes to all the comrades."[57]

NOTES

1. Terrible Times of Shipwreck

1. Diary of Joseph F. Waring, entry for Saturday, January 14, 1865, Joseph Frederick Waring Papers, Southern Historical Collection, University of North Carolina at Chapel Hill.

2. Mary Boykin Miller Chesnut, *Mary Chesnut's Civil War*, ed. C. Vann Woodward (New Haven CT: Yale University Press, 1981), 706–7, quotation 707; and Craig L. Symonds, *Joseph E. Johnston: A Civil War Biography* (New York: Norton, 1992), 341.

3. Joseph T. Glatthaar, *General Lee's Army: From Victory to Collapse* (New York: Free Press, 2008), 446.

4. A. Wilson Greene, *The Final Battles of the Petersburg Campaign: Breaking the Backbone of the Rebellion* (Knoxville: University of Tennessee Press, 2008), 77; and Earl J. Hess, *In the Trenches at Petersburg: Field Fortifications & Confederate Defeat* (Chapel Hill: University of North Carolina Press, 2009), 287.

5. Hess, *Trenches at Petersburg*, 218.

6. U.S. War Department, *The War of the Rebellion: A Compilation of the Official Records of the Union and Confederate Armies* (Washington DC: Government Printing Office, 1880–1901), series 1, vol. 46, pt. 2:1258. Hereafter cited as OR, and unless otherwise stated, all references are to series 1.

7. Douglas Southall Freeman, *Lee's Lieutenants: A Study in Command* (New York: Charles Scribner's Sons, 1942–44), 3:624; OR, 46, 2:1265; and J. Tracy Power, *Lee's Miserables: Life in the Army of Northern Virginia from the Wilderness to Appomattox* (Chapel Hill: University of North Carolina Press, 1998), 260.

8. Power, *Lee's Miserables*, 261.

9. Power, *Lee's Miserables*, 308.

10. Power, *Lee's Miserables*, 308.

11. Greene, *Final Battles*, 89. See also Hess, *Trenches at Petersburg*, 224–25.

12. Joseph T. Glatthaar, *Soldiering in the Army of Northern Virginia: A Statistical Portrait of the Troops Who Served under Robert E. Lee* (Chapel Hill: University of North Carolina Press, 2001), 174.

13. Power, *Lee's Miserables*, 261, 306–7; and OR, 46, 2:1254.

14. Richard M. McMurry, *Two Great Rebel Armies: An Essay in Confederate Military History* (Chapel Hill: University of North Carolina Press, 1989), 14.

15. These themes are developed in works such as Thomas Lawrence Connelly's *Army of the Heartland: The Army of Tennessee, 1861–1862* (Baton Rouge: Louisiana State University Press, 1967) and *Autumn of Glory: The Army of Tennessee, 1862–1865* (Baton Rouge: Louisiana State University Press, 1971); Grady McWhiney, *Braxton Bragg and Confederate Defeat*, vol. 1, *Field Command* (New York: Columbia University Press, 1969); and Thomas Lawrence Connelly and Archer Jones, *The Politics of Command: Factions and Ideas in Confederate Strategy* (Baton Rouge: Louisiana State University Press, 1973).

16. Richard M. McMurry, *John Bell Hood and the War for Southern Independence* (Lexington: University Press of Kentucky, 1982), 182; and Chris E. Fonvielle, Jr., *The Wilmington Campaign: Last Rays of Departing Hope* (Campbell CA: Savas, 1997), 325–26.

17. Robert L. Kerby, *Kirby Smith's Confederacy: The Trans-Mississippi South, 1863–1865* (New York: Columbia University Press, 1972), 381–82, 383.

18. Kerby, *Kirby Smith's Confederacy*, 382–83.

19. Kerby, *Kirby Smith's Confederacy*, 399.

20. OR, ser. 4, 3:989, 1182, cited in Judith Lee Hallock, *Braxton Bragg and Confederate Defeat vol. 2*(Tuscaloosa: University of Alabama Press, 1991), 256; and W. W. Goldsborough, "Grant's Change of Base," in R. A. Brock, ed., *Southern Historical Society Papers* (Richmond VA: Southern Historical Society, 1876–1959), 29(1901):290.

21. Herman Hattaway and Richard E. Beringer, *Jefferson Davis, Confederate President* (Lawrence: University Press of Kansas, 2002), 387; Steven E. Woodworth, *Davis and Lee at War* (Lawrence: University Press of Kansas, 1995), 332; and William C. Davis, *Jefferson Davis: The Man and His Hour* (New York: HarperCollins, 1991), 592.

22. Gary W. Gallagher, *The Confederate War* (Cambridge: Harvard University Press, 1997), 58.

23. Diary of Joseph F. Waring, entry for Saturday, January 14, 1865, Joseph Frederick Waring Papers.

24. Woodworth, *Davis and Lee at War*, 309–11. The congressional resolution also called on Davis to reinstate Gen. Joseph E. Johnston in command of the Army of Tennessee.

25. William J. Cooper, *Jefferson Davis, American* (New York: Alfred A. Knopf, 2000), 509.

26. Two important sources on Lincoln as commander in chief are T. Harry Williams, *Lincoln and His Generals* (New York: Alfred A. Knopf, 1952); and

Herman Hattaway and Archer Jones, *How the North Won: A Military History of the Civil War* (Urbana: University of Illinois Press, 1983), especially 695–96.

27. Joseph T. Glatthaar, *Partners in Command: The Relationships between Leaders in the Civil War* (New York: Free Press, 1994), 230.

28. Bruce Catton, *Grant Moves South, 1861–1863* (Boston: Little, Brown, 1960), 3; and Grady McWhiney, *Southerners and Other Americans* (New York: Basic Books, 1973), 69.

29. Brooks D. Simpson, *Ulysses S. Grant: Triumph over Adversity, 1822–1865* (Boston: Houghton Mifflin, 2000), 14; and Horace Porter, *Campaigning with Grant: General Horace Porter*, ed. Wayne C. Temple (New York: Bonanza Books, 1961), 47.

30. Simpson, *Ulysses S. Grant*, 463; and Adam Badeau, *Grant in Peace: From Appomattox to Mount McGregor; A Personal Memoir* (Freeport NY: Books for Libraries Press, 1971; reprint of Hartford CT: S. S. Scranton, 1887), 459–60.

31. John F. Marszalek, *Sherman: A Soldier's Passion for Order* (New York: Free Press, 1993), 499. Mark Grimsley, Brooks D. Simpson, Lee Kennett, and other historians have made a strong case that white Southerners blamed Sherman for more destruction in Georgia than his forces committed. Mark Grimsley, *The Hard Hand of War: Union Military Policy toward Southern Civilians, 1861–1865* (Cambridge: Cambridge University Press, 1995), 196–200; Brooks D. Simpson, introduction, in Henry Hitchcock, *Marching with Sherman*, ed. M. A. DeWolfe (Lincoln: University of Nebraska Press, 1995; reprint of New Haven CT: Yale University Press 1927), vii, viii; Lee Kennett, *Marching through Georgia: The Story of Soldiers and Civilians during Sherman's Campaign* (New York: HarperCollins, 1995), especially 308–24; and Brooks D. Simpson and Jean V. Berlin, eds., *Sherman's Civil War: Selected Correspondence of William T. Sherman, 1860–1865* (Chapel Hill: University of North Carolina Press, 1999), 759–60. See also Marszalek, *Sherman*, 297, 316.

32. "The Opposing Forces at Petersburg and Richmond, December 31st, 1864," in Robert U. Johnson and Clarence C. Buel, eds., *Battles and Leaders of the Civil War* (reissue, New York: Thomas Yoseloff, 1956), 4:594; *OR*, 46, 1:61; and *OR*, 47, 1:42.

33. Ulysses S. Grant to William T. Sherman, December 27, 1864, in Ulysses S. Grant, *The Papers of Ulysses S. Grant*, ed. John Y. Simon (Carbondale: Southern Illinois University Press, 1967–91), 13:168 and 169. See also Mark L. Bradley, *Last Stand in the Carolinas: The Battle of Bentonville* (Campbell CA: Savas Woodbury, 1996), 2, 4; and Nathaniel Cheairs Hughes, Jr., *Bentonville: The Final Battle of Sherman and Johnston* (Chapel Hill: University of North Carolina Press, 1996), 2.

34. Edward Hagerman, *The American Civil War and the Origins of Modern Warfare: Ideas, Organization, and Field Command* (Bloomington: Indiana University Press, 1988), 279, 283–84, 287.

35. Hagerman, *American Civil War*, 288.

36. James M. McPherson, *Battle Cry of Freedom: The Civil War Era* (New York: Oxford University Press, 1988), 827–28; and Joseph T. Glatthaar, *The March to the Sea and Beyond: Sherman's Troops in the Savannah and Carolinas Campaigns* (New York: New York University Press, 1985), 110. For a scholarly biography of Orlando M. Poe, see Paul Taylor, *Orlando M. Poe: Civil War General and Great Lakes Engineer* (Kent OH: Kent State University Press, 2009). General Poe's direct descendant then-Lt. Bryce Poe II flew an RF-80A in the Korean War's first reconnaissance sortie, which was also the first combat jet reconnaissance sortie flown by the United States Air Force. Poe served a distinguished air force career, retired in 1981 as a full general, and died in 2000. Robert Frank Futrell, *The United States Air Force in Korea, 1950–1953* (Washington DC: U.S. Air Force, 1983), 27; and "4-Star Air Force General Bryce Poe II Dies," *Washington Post*, December 8, 2000, B-6.

37. Bruce Catton, *A Stillness at Appomattox* (Garden City NY: Doubleday, 1953), 321.

38. Cooper, *Jefferson Davis*, 509–10; Charles W. Sanders, Jr., "Jefferson Davis and the Hampton Roads Peace Conference: 'To Secure Peace to the Two Countries,'" *Journal of Southern History* 63, no. 4 (November 1997): 808–9; Thomas E. Schott, *Alexander H. Stephens of Georgia: A Biography* (Baton Rouge: Louisiana State University Press, 1988), 439; Davis, *Jefferson Davis*, 589; and Jefferson Davis to F. P. Blair, January 12, 1865, in Abraham Lincoln, *The Collected Works of Abraham Lincoln*, ed. Roy P. Basler (New Brunswick NJ: Rutgers University Press, 1953–55), 8:275. Cooper believes Davis agreed to the Blair mission partly because the president saw a chance "to silence his critics who faulted him for not pursuing peace more vigorously" (Cooper, *Jefferson Davis*, 510). Sanders argues that Davis did not pursue negotiations with Lincoln solely to discredit the Southern peace movement but that he sincerely believed they offered a chance to avoid military defeat and secure an independent Confederacy. Sanders, "Jefferson Davis," 803–26.

39. Davis, *Jefferson Davis*, 590; Schott, *Alexander H. Stephens*, 439; and Abraham Lincoln to F. P. Blair, January 18, 1865, in Lincoln, *Collected Works*, 8:276.

40. Davis, *Jefferson Davis*, 590. Sanders points out that while it may appear that Lincoln had reneged on the idea of negotiations by the generals, the facts of this part of the Hampton Roads story remain "a bit of a mystery." Sanders, "Jefferson Davis," 814–15.

41. James Z. Rabun, "Alexander H. Stephens and Jefferson Davis," *American Historical Review* 58, no. 2 (January 1953): 310, 317; and Ezra J. Warner and W. Buck Yearns, *Biographical Register of the Confederate Congress* (Baton Rouge: Louisiana State University Press, 1975), 155–56.

42. McPherson, *Battle Cry of Freedom*, 650, 693–94.

43. McPherson, *Battle Cry of Freedom*, 650, 664.

44. Schott, *Alexander H. Stephens*, 440; and Davis, *Jefferson Davis*, 590.

45. Davis, *Jefferson Davis*, 590–93; and Schott, *Alexander H. Stephens*, 441–43.

46. Schott, *Alexander H. Stephens*, 443; and Brooks D. Simpson, *Let Us Have Peace: Ulysses S. Grant and the Politics of War and Reconstruction, 1861–1868* (Chapel Hill: University of North Carolina Press, 1991), 73.

47. Simpson, *Let Us Have Peace*, 73–74.

48. McPherson, *Battle Cry of Freedom*, 822; and Abraham Lincoln to William H. Seward, January 31, 1865, in Lincoln, *Collected Works*, 8:279.

49. Diary of Joseph F. Waring, entry for Tuesday, February 7, 1865, Joseph Frederick Waring Papers; Schott, *Alexander H. Stephens*, 443; and McPherson, *Battle Cry of Freedom*, 822, 824.

50. Davis, *Jefferson Davis*, 590; and Simpson, *Let Us Have Peace*, 72–73.

51. Fonvielle, *Wilmington Campaign*, 329.

52. Sherman to Dearest Ellen, December 31, 1864, in Simpson and Berlin, *Sherman's Civil War*, 785; and Thomas Ward Osborn, *The Fiery Trail: A Union Officer's Account of Sherman's Last Campaigns*, ed. Richard Harwell and Philip N. Racine (Knoxville: University of Tennessee Press, 1986), 75.

2. Fort Fisher and Wilmington

1. Bradley, *Last Stand*, 1; and Fonvielle, *Wilmington Campaign*, 193.

2. Fonvielle, *Wilmington Campaign*, between 26 and 27 (map), 35 (map), 36; Charles M. Robinson III, *Hurricane of Fire: The Union Assault on Fort Fisher* (Annapolis: Naval Institute Press, 1998), 30; and Ethan S. Rafuse, *A Single Grand Victory: The First Campaign and Battle of Manassas* (Wilmington DE: S. R. Books, 2002), 171.

3. Fonvielle, *Wilmington Campaign*, 72.

4. Fonvielle, *Wilmington Campaign*, 41–42; and William Lamb, "The Defense of Fort Fisher," in Johnson and Buel, *Battles and Leaders*, 4:642.

5. Fonvielle, *Wilmington Campaign*, 109; and Russell F. Weigley, *A Great Civil War: A Military and Political History, 1861–1865* (Bloomington: Indiana University Press, 2000), 417. See also Thomas O. Selfridge, Jr., "The Navy at Fort Fisher," in Johnson and Buel, *Battles and Leaders*, 4:655.

6. Fonvielle, *Wilmington Campaign*, 129–30.

7. Fonvielle, *Wilmington Campaign*, 114; Ezra J. Warner, *Generals in Gray: Lives of the Confederate Commanders* (Baton Rouge: Louisiana State University Press, 1995), 140; and Fonvielle, *Wilmington Campaign*, 232.

8. Fonvielle, *Wilmington Campaign*, 38, 119.

9. Fonvielle, *Wilmington Campaign*, 109–11, 112–13, 119.

10. Fonvielle, *Wilmington Campaign*, 102, 121, 122, 124–25; Selfridge, "Navy at Fort Fisher," in Johnson and Buel, *Battles and Leaders*, 4:655; Weigley, *Great Civil War*, 417; and OR, 47, 2:3.

11. Fonvielle, *Wilmington Campaign*, 132–34, 151–53, 178.

12. Fonvielle, *Wilmington Campaign*, 145, 146 (map), 161, 172; and Selfridge, "Navy at Fort Fisher," in Johnson and Buel, *Battles and Leaders*, 4:657.

13. Fonvielle, *Wilmington Campaign*, 192–93.

14. Fonvielle, *Wilmington Campaign*, 106; Ezra J. Warner, *Generals in Blue: Lives of the Union Commanders* (Baton Rouge: Louisiana State University Press, 1964), 497; and [Solon A. Carter] to My own precious wifey, January 22, 1865, Solon A. Carter Papers, United States Army Heritage and Education Center, Carlisle PA.

15. Fonvielle, *Wilmington Campaign*, 198; and OR, 47, 1:168, 680–81.

16. Fonvielle, *Wilmington Campaign*, 204, 436.

17. Fonvielle, *Wilmington Campaign*, 181.

18. Fonvielle, *Wilmington Campaign*, 88–89, 182; and R. E. L. Krick, "The Men Who Carried This Position Were Soldiers Indeed: The Decisive Charge of Whiting's Division at Gaines's Mill," in Gary Gallagher, ed., *The Richmond Campaign of 1862: The Peninsula and the Seven Days* (Chapel Hill: University of North Carolina Press, 2000), 181–216.

19. Fonvielle, *Wilmington Campaign*, 182; and OR, 42, 3:1360.

20. Fonvielle, *Wilmington Campaign*, 88–89; and Hallock, *Braxton Bragg*, 221–22.

21. OR, 42, 1:999; and Hallock, *Braxton Bragg*, 231, 232.

22. OR, 46, 2:1015; and Fonvielle, *Wilmington Campaign*, 182–83.

23. Fonvielle, *Wilmington Campaign*, 34, 183.

24. Fonvielle, *Wilmington Campaign*, 24 (map), 182–83.

25. Fonvielle, *Wilmington Campaign*, 199, 203, 204; and OR, 46, 1:396.

26. Fonvielle, *Wilmington Campaign*, 207, 208.

27. OR, 46, 1:396; and Fonvielle, *Wilmington Campaign*, 209, 210, 211 (map), 212, 218–19.

28. Fonvielle, *Wilmington Campaign*, 219; and Warner, *Generals in Blue*, 354–55.

29. Warner, *Generals in Blue*, 5.

30. Fonvielle, *Wilmington Campaign*, 220 (map), 221, 222–24; and OR, 46, 2:1053.

31. Fonvielle, *Wilmington Campaign*, 226–27, 235 (map).

32. Fonvielle, *Wilmington Campaign*, 228.

33. Fonvielle, *Wilmington Campaign*, 155, 228–29, 232; and OR, 46, 1:398.

34. Fonvielle, *Wilmington Campaign*, 233–34, 237, 242.

35. Fonvielle, *Wilmington Campaign*, 240–41.

36. Fonvielle, *Wilmington Campaign*, 245, 247; and Lamb, "Defense of Fort Fisher," in Johnson and Buel, *Battles and Leaders*, 4:650.

37. Fonvielle, *Wilmington Campaign*, 249–50; and Lamb, "Defense of Fort Fisher," in Johnson and Buel, *Battles and Leaders*, 4:650.

38. Fonvielle, *Wilmington Campaign*, 245, 250, 252, 254, 255, 257; and Selfridge, "The Navy at Fort Fisher," in Johnson and Buel, *Battles and Leaders*, 4:660.

39. Selfridge, "The Navy at Fort Fisher," in Johnson and Buel, *Battles and Leaders*, 4:661; and Fonvielle, *Wilmington Campaign*, 260.

40. Fonvielle, *Wilmington Campaign*, 261, 263, 265, 266, 268, 269, 273.

41. Fonvielle, *Wilmington Campaign*, 269–73.

42. Fonvielle, *Wilmington Campaign*, 274–75; and OR, 46, 1:416.

43. OR, 46, 2:1064, 1065.

44. OR, 46, 2:1061.

45. Fonvielle, *Wilmington Campaign*, 281, 284–85, 289.

46. Fonvielle, *Wilmington Campaign*, 292–93; Lamb, "Defense of Fort Fisher," in Johnson and Buel, *Battles and Leaders*, 4:653; and Fonvielle, *Wilmington Campaign*, 291 (map).

47. Fonvielle, *Wilmington Campaign*, 293–94; and Lamb, "Defense of Fort Fisher," in Johnson and Buel, *Battles and Leaders*, 4:653.

48. Fonvielle, *Wilmington Campaign*, 295–96; and OR, 46, 1:410.

49. Fonvielle, *Wilmington Campaign*, 273; and Warner, *Generals in Blue*, 366.

50. Fonvielle, *Wilmington Campaign*, 289; and Warner, *Generals in Blue*, 107.

51. Fonvielle, *Wilmington Campaign*, 306.

52. Fonvielle, *Wilmington Campaign*, 303, 307. The cause of the explosion remained uncertain. There is a judicious discussion in Fonvielle, *Wilmington Campaign*, 305–6.

53. Fonvielle, *Wilmington Campaign*, 307, 320, 462.

54. Fonvielle, *Wilmington Campaign*, 461; and Warner, *Generals in Gray*, 335.

55. Fonvielle, *Wilmington Campaign*, 461; and Hallock, *Braxton Bragg*, 239–40.

56. Fonvielle, *Wilmington Campaign*, 461.

57. Hallock, *Braxton Bragg*, 242.

58. Hallock, *Braxton Bragg*, 245; and Katherine M. Jones, *Heroines of Dixie: Confederate Women Tell Their Story of the War* (Indianapolis: Bobbs-Merrill, 1955), 356.

59. Hallock, *Braxton Bragg*, 245; Fonvielle, *Wilmington Campaign*, 320, 327, 328; and Solon [A. Carter] to My own precious Emily, February 7, 1865, Solon A. Carter Papers.

60. Fonvielle, *Wilmington Campaign*, 331–32.

61. Fonvielle, *Wilmington Campaign*, 332.

62. Fonvielle, *Wilmington Campaign*, 333–34.

63. OR, 47, 1:50–55; Warner, *Generals in Blue*, 451–53; Edwin B. Coddington, *The Gettysburg Campaign: A Study in Command* (reprint, New York: Morningside Bookshop, 1979), 310–15; A. Wilson Greene, "'A Step All-Important and Essential to Victory': Henry W. Slocum and the Twelfth Corps on July 1–2, 1863," in Gary W. Gallagher, ed., *The Second Day at Gettysburg: Essays on Confederate and Union Leadership* (Kent OH: Kent State University Press, 1993), 94–101; and David G. Martin, *Gettysburg, July 1* (Conshohocken PA: Combined Books, 1995), 523–35.

64. OR, 47, 1:46–50; Warner, *Generals in Blue*, 237; Marion V. Armstrong, *Unfurl Those Colors! McClellan, Sumner, and the Second Army Corps in the Antietam Campaign* (Tuscaloosa: University of Alabama Press, 2008), 182, 187,

189; Stephen W. Sears, *Chancellorsville* (Boston: Houghton Mifflin, 1996), 260–81; and Harry W. Pfanz, *Gettysburg—the First Day* (Chapel Hill: University of North Carolina Press, 2001), 227–57.

65. OR, 47, 1:191–93.

66. OR, 47, 1:17; and U.S. War Department, *Atlas to Accompany the Official Records of the Union and Confederate Armies* (Washington DC: Government Printing Office, 1891–95), plate 144 (hereafter cited as OR *Atlas*). Slocum detailed his troubles in OR, 47, 1:419–20.

67. OR, 47, 1:168, 680–81.

68. Henry W. Slocum, "Sherman's March from Savannah to Bentonville," in Johnson and Buel, *Battles and Leaders*, 4:684.

69. Fonvielle, *Wilmington Campaign*, 335, 357–58, 479–80; and Warner, *Generals in Blue*, 97.

70. Solon [A. Carter] to My own darling Emily, February 12, 1865, Solon A. Carter Papers; and Solon [A. Carter] to My own darling wife, February 15, 1865, Solon A. Carter Papers.

71. Hallock, *Braxton Bragg*, 245–47.

72. Hallock, *Braxton Bragg*, 246–47.

73. Fonvielle, *Wilmington Campaign*, 332, 366, 379–80; and photocopy of [Solon A. Carter] to My own Precious Em & darling "Dedie," February 21, 1865, Solon A. Carter Papers.

74. Fonvielle, *Wilmington Campaign*, 385, 386; and OR, 47, 2:1228.

75. Fonvielle, *Wilmington Campaign*, 386.

76. OR, 47, 1:964. Cox's much neglected operation is well detailed in Fonvielle, *Wilmington Campaign*, 391, 393, 400–404, 406, 408–15.

77. Fonvielle, *Wilmington Campaign*, 394, 413–14.

78. Fonvielle, *Wilmington Campaign*, 396, 398, 413–14.

79. Hallock, *Braxton Bragg*, 247; and Fonvielle, *Wilmington Campaign*, 421–22, 424.

80. Fonvielle, *Wilmington Campaign*, 427–29; Hallock, *Braxton Bragg*, 247; and OR, 47, 2:1155.

81. Catton, *Stillness at Appomattox*, 329.

82. Solon [A. Carter] to My own darling Emily, February 12, 1865, Solon A. Carter Papers.

3. In the Carolinas

1. OR, 47, 1:911, 912, 973.

2. OR, 47, 1:973.

3. OR, 47, 1:43.

4. Bradley, *Last Stand*, 21; Warner, *Generals in Gray*, 22–23; and Connelly and Jones, *Politics of Command*, 82–84.

5. Joseph E. Johnston, *Narrative of Military Operations, Directed, during the Late War between the States, by Joseph E. Johnston* (New York: Appleton, 1874),

371–72; and R. E. Lee to John C. Breckinridge, February 21, 1865, in Robert E. Lee, *The Wartime Papers of Robert E. Lee*, ed. Clifford Dowdey and Louis H. Manarin (Boston: Little, Brown, 1961), 906.

6. McWhiney, *Southerners and Other Americans*, 98–99.

7. Connelly, *Autumn of Glory*, 518–20; and Diary of Colonel Joseph F. Waring, entry for February 20, 1865, Joseph Frederick Waring Papers, Southern Historical Collection, University of North Carolina at Chapel Hill.

8. Bradley, *Last Stand*, 22; and OR, 47, 2:1084. Sherman's numbers at this time are given in OR, 47, 1:42.

9. Bradley, *Last Stand*, 21–22; and OR *Atlas*, plate 143.

10. Bradley, *Last Stand*, 21; Warner, *Generals in Gray*, 124–25; and Perry Jamieson, "William Joseph Hardee," in Roger J. Spiller, Joseph M. Dawson III, and T. Harry Williams, eds., *Dictionary of American Military Biography* (Westport CT: Greenwood Press, 1984), 2:444.

11. Bradley, *Last Stand*, 21; and Warner, *Generals in Gray*, 137.

12. Bradley, *Last Stand*, 21–22; Freeman, *Lee's Lieutenants*, 1:262–63; Leonne M. Hudson, *The Odyssey of a Southerner: The Life and Times of Gustavus Woodson Smith* (Macon GA: Mercer University Press, 1998), 219; and Warner, *Generals in Gray*, 281.

13. Bradley, *Last Stand*, 22; and OR *Atlas*, plates 76 and 143.

14. Bradley, *Last Stand*, 22.

15. Bradley, *Last Stand*, 22; and Connelly, *Autumn of Glory*, 521.

16. Connelly, *Autumn of Glory*, 520, 521. Wheeler is sometimes referred to as a lieutenant general. After a thorough examination of the question, historian Eric J. Wittenberg concludes that he was not promoted beyond major general. See Eric J. Wittenberg, *The Battle of Monroe's Crossroads and the Civil War's Final Campaign* (New York: Savas Beatie, 2006), 255–58. At the end of the war, Wheeler was signing himself as a major general. OR, 47, 1:1129.

17. [William T. Sherman] to Dear Brother, January 22, 1865, in Simpson and Berlin, *Sherman's Civil War*, 808; and Slocum, "Sherman's March," in Johnson and Buel, *Battles and Leaders*, 4:687.

18. John G. Barrett, *Sherman's March through the Carolinas* (Chapel Hill: University of North Carolina Press, 1956), 50–51; and Hughes, *Bentonville*, 3.

19. F. Y. Hedley, *Marching through Georgia: Pen-Pictures of Every-Day Life in General Sherman's Army, from the Beginning of the Atlanta Campaign until the Close of the War* (Chicago: Donohue, Henneberry, 1885), 356; typescript of the Diary of Capt. George F. Glossbrenner, entry for Friday, [February] 3, [1865], George F. Glossbrenner Papers, United States Army Heritage and Education Center, Carlisle PA; and Edwin Williams to My Dear Father and Mother and All, March 22, 1865, Edwin Williams Papers, United States Army Heritage and Education Center, Carlisle PA.

20. Typescript of the Diary of Capt. George F. Glossbrenner, entry for Friday, [February] 10, [1865], George F. Glossbrenner Papers.

21. Barrett, *Sherman's March*, 51; and Slocum, "Sherman's March," in Johnson and Buel, *Battles and Leaders*, 4:685–86n, quotation 686n.

22. Warner, *Generals in Gray*, 123; and Barrett, *Sherman's March*, 69.

23. Bradley, *Last Stand*, 23 and 468n51.

24. Slocum, "Sherman's March," in Johnson and Buel, *Battles and Leaders*, 4:686; and Connelly, *Autumn of Glory*, 521.

25. Marion Brunson Lucas, *Sherman and the Burning of Columbia* (College Station: Texas A&M University Press, 1976), 70.

26. Lucas, *Sherman and the Burning*, 53, 65–66, 68; and Barrett, *Sherman's March*, 72–74, 78.

27. Lucas, *Sherman and the Burning*, 98, 128. Lucas offered a well-balanced assessment of responsibility for the fire (163–67), which concluded: "There was no one fire which burned Columbia, but a series of fires over the space of forty-eight hours, none of which can be identified positively as the act of a single individual or group of individuals. . . . The best analysis, with Columbia a virtual firetrap on February 17, 1865, is that the fire was an accident of war." Lucas, *Sherman and the Burning*, 165. See also Grimsley, *Hard Hand of War*, 202.

28. Typescript of the Diary of Johann Heinrich Sudkamp, translated from the German by M. Philibertha, Johann Heinrich Sudkamp Papers, entries undated, United States Army Heritage and Education Center, Carlisle PA; and typescript of the Diary of Capt. George F. Glossbrenner, entry for Friday, [February] 3, [1865], George F. Glossbrenner Papers.

29. Typescript of the Diary of Capt. George F. Glossbrenner, entry for Saturday, [February] 18, [1865], George F. Glossbrenner Papers.

30. R. E. Lee to Jefferson Davis, February 19, 1865, in Lee, *Wartime Papers*, 906; *OR*, 47, 2:1238; and R. E. Lee to Jefferson Davis, February 23, 1865, in Lee, *Wartime Papers*, 909.

31. Woodworth, *Davis and Lee at War*, 310; and R. E. Lee to John C. Breckinridge, February 19, 1865, in Lee, *Wartime Papers*, 904.

32. R. E. Lee to John C. Breckinridge, February 19, 1865, in Lee, *Wartime Papers*, 904; Symonds, *Joseph E. Johnston*, 127–28; and Chesnut, *Mary Chesnut's Civil War*, 482–83.

33. R. E. Lee to John C. Breckinridge, February 19, 1865, in Lee, *Wartime Papers*, 904; and R. E. Lee to John C. Breckinridge, February 21, 1865, in Lee, *Wartime Papers*, 906.

34. *OR*, 47, 2:1247.

35. Woodworth, *Lee and Davis at War*, 314.

36. Johnston, *Narrative of Military Operations*, 371–72.

37. Bradley, *Last Stand*, 27; Johnston, *Narrative of Military Operations*, 371–72; and *OR*, 47, 1:43. This number for Sherman's strength is as of February 28, within a week of Johnston's reinstatement. See also *OR*, 47, 3:74, which credits Schofield with 34,003 men as of March 31.

38. *OR*, 47, 2:1408.

39. *OR*, 47, 2:1408; and Symonds, *Joseph E. Johnston*, 344.

40. *OR*, 47, 2:1408.

41. *OR*, 47, 2:1257; and Hallock, *Braxton Bragg*, 247–48.

42. *OR Atlas*, plate 142; and Bradley, *Last Stand*, 75.

43. *OR*, 47, 2:1247.

44. Bradley, *Last Stand*, 47 and 470n44; and Barrett, *Sherman's March*, 93.

45. Barrett, *Sherman's March*, 96, 97.

46. Barrett, *Sherman's March*, 96.

47. *OR*, 44:743, 799.

48. Bruce Catton, *This Hallowed Ground: The Story of the Union Side of the Civil War* (Garden City NY: Doubleday, 1956), 374.

49. Typescript of the Diary of Capt. George F. Glossbrenner, entry for Monday, [February] 6, [1865], George F. Glossbrenner Papers.

50. Glatthaar, *March to the Sea*, 122; and Daniel Oakey, "Marching through Georgia and the Carolinas," in Johnson and Buel, *Battles and Leaders*, 4:678.

51. Glatthaar, *March to the Sea*, 122; and Oakey, "Marching through Georgia," in Johnson and Buel, *Battles and Leaders*, 4:672.

52. Slocum, "Sherman's March," in Johnson and Buel, *Battles and Leaders*, 4:688; and *OR*, 47, 2:803, 817.

53. Glatthaar, *March to the Sea*, 60, 63, 65.

54. Barrett, *Sherman's March*, 98, 99.

55. Bradley, *Last Stand*, 58, 59, 71.

56. Oakey, "Marching through Georgia," in Johnson and Buel, *Battles and Leaders*, 4:675; typescript of the Diary of Capt. George F. Glossbrenner, entry for March 4, [1865], George F. Glossbrenner Papers; and Slocum, "Sherman's March," in Johnson and Buel, *Battles and Leaders*, 4:687.

57. Symonds, *Joseph E. Johnston*, 347; and *OR*, 47, 2:1321.

58. Symonds, *Joseph E. Johnston*, 347; and Oliver Otis Howard, *Autobiography of Oliver Otis Howard* (New York: Baker & Taylor, 1907), 2:136.

59. *OR*, 47, 1:1053, 1054; and *OR*, 47, 2:1333, 1339.

60. Catton, *This Hallowed Ground*, 377; and Oakey, "Marching through Georgia," in Johnson and Buel, *Battles and Leaders*, 4:677–78, quotation 677.

61. *OR*, 47, 2:721; Catton, *This Hallowed Ground*, 377; Grimsley, *Hard Hand of War*, 202; and Simpson and Berlin, *Sherman's Civil War*, 821.

62. Catton, *This Hallowed Ground*, 377; Grimsley, *Hard Hand of War*, 202; and John A. Boon to Dear Family, April 3, 1865, typescript of John A. Boon Letters, John A. Boon Papers, Civil War Miscellaneous Collection, United States Army Heritage and Education Center, Carlisle PA.

63. *OR*, 47, 1:974, 973.

64. *OR*, 47, 1:974, 973.

65. Hallock, *Braxton Bragg*, 248; Bradley, *Last Stand*, 74–75; and *OR*, 47, 2:1338.

66. Bradley, *Last Stand*, 74–75; Hallock, *Braxton Bragg*, 251; OR, 47, 1:1078; and OR, 47, 2:1350. There are various spellings of this battlefield's name, including "Wise Fork" or "Wise Forks" and "Wise's Fork" or "Wise's Forks." The Historical Preservation Group, the local organization that has worked to preserve and interpret the battlefield, uses "Wyse Fork." http//www.historical preservationgroup.org/projects_wf_battlefield.html, accessed March 7, 2013. As the text notes, the engagement is also known as the Second Battle of Kinston.

67. Hallock, *Braxton Bragg*, 251; OR, 1:522, 1068; and Edwin Williams to My Dear Father and Mother and All, March 7, 1865, Edwin Williams Papers.

68. Hallock, *Braxton Bragg*, 251; and OR, 47, 1:994, 997, 1078.

69. OR, 47, 1:994.

70. Hallock, *Braxton Bragg*, 251; OR, 47, 2:1350; and OR, 47, 1:1087.

71. OR, 47, 1:994.

72. Hallock, *Braxton Bragg*, 251; Bradley, *Last Stand*, 75; OR, 47, 1:994; and OR, 47, 2:1360.

73. Hallock, *Braxton Bragg*, 251; OR, 47, 2:1363; and OR, 47, 1:1088.

74. Bradley, *Last Stand*, 86–104. Bradley gives an order of battle for Monroe's Crossroads in *Last Stand*, 417–19. The battle is well detailed in Wittenberg, *Battle of Monroe's Crossroads*.

75. Barrett, *Sherman's March*, 135; and [Solon A.] Carter to My own darling Emily, March 12, 1865, Solon A. Carter Papers, United States Army Heritage and Education Center, Carlisle PA.

76. Slocum, "Sherman's March," in Johnson and Buel, *Battles and Leaders*, 4:688; and Edwin Williams to My Dear Father and Mother and All, March 22, 1865, Edwin Williams Papers.

77. Slocum, "Sherman's March," in Johnson and Buel, *Battles and Leaders*, 4:690; and Bradley, *Last Stand*, 76.

78. Bradley, *Last Stand*, 114; Dave Roth, "The General's Tour: The Battle of Averasboro North Carolina, March 15–16, 1865," *Blue & Gray Magazine* 16, no. 1 (Fall 1998): 63; and Hallock, *Braxton Bragg*, 252. Smithville, a plantation, should not be confused with the town of Smithfield.

79. OR, 47, 2:1373.

80. OR, 47, 2:1372.

81. OR, 47, 2:1373.

82. OR, 47, 2:1372.

83. R. E. Lee to Jefferson Davis, March 14, 1865, in Lee, *Wartime Papers*, 915; and OR, 47, 2:1395.

84. OR, 47, 2:1395.

85. Bradley, *Last Stand*, 112, 119.

86. OR, 47, 1:234; and Bradley, *Last Stand*, 70 (map).

87. OR, 47, 1:382–83; and Bradley, *Last Stand*, 70 (map).

88. OR, 47, 2:802 and 822.

89. Typescript of the Diary of Capt. George F. Glossbrenner, entry for March 9, [1865], George F. Glossbrenner Papers; and OR, 47, 2:867.

90. Bradley, *Last Stand*, 120, 124 (map).

91. OR, 47, 2:867.

92. OR, 47, 2:835; and Bradley, *Last Stand*, 119, 120.

93. Bradley, *Last Stand*, 120, 121–22; and James S. Pula, "Battle in the Swamp: Cogwell's Federal Brigade at the Battle of Averasboro," *Civil War Regiments* 6, no. 1 (1998): 66.

94. Bradley, *Last Stand*, 122, 124 (map); and Warner, *Generals in Blue*, 560.

95. Bradley, *Last Stand*, 122–23.

96. Bradley, *Last Stand*, 124 (map), quotation 125–26.

97. Bradley, *Last Stand*, 125–26, quotation 126.

98. Bradley, *Last Stand*, 127–28; and OR, 47, 1:1126, 1074.

99. Bradley, *Last Stand*, 128, 129.

100. OR, 47, 1:484; Warner, *Generals in Blue*, 115–16; and Nathaniel Cheairs Hughes, Jr., and Gordon D. Whitney, *Jefferson Davis in Blue: The Life of Sherman's Relentless Warrior* (Baton Rouge: Louisiana State University Press, 2007), 100–126.

101. Hughes and Whitney, *Jefferson Davis in Blue*, xi, xii.

102. OR, 47, 1:484; and Bradley, *Last Stand*, 130 (map).

103. Bradley, *Last Stand*, 129, 131; and OR, 47, 1:484.

104. OR, 47, 1:448; and Bradley, *Last Stand*, 131.

105. Bradley, *Last Stand*, 132; Wade Hampton, "The Battle of Bentonville," in Johnson and Buel, *Battles and Leaders*, 4:701; and Bradley, *Last Stand*, 140.

4. Bentonville

1. Bradley, *Last Stand*, 137; and Sam Davis Elliott, *Soldier of Tennessee: General Alexander P. Stewart and the Civil War in the West* (Baton Rouge: Louisiana State University Press, 1999), 80. For the order of battle of the Army of the South during the Battle of Bentonville, see Bradley, *Last Stand*, 437–47.

2. OR, 47, 2:1399.

3. Bradley, *Last Stand*, 140; and OR *Atlas*, plate 135-A.

4. Bradley, *Last Stand*, 136; and OR, 47, 1:205.

5. OR, 47, 1:913.

6. Bradley, *Last Stand*, 309; and OR, 47, 1:1057. Bradley states that the Confederates brought sixteen thousand men to the battlefield. This number is a little higher than what Johnston gave in his official report (OR, 47, 1:1057) and higher than the total of the field return that Johnston submitted to Lee (OR, 47, 1:1057), but that return does not include all of the Army of the South's artillery or its cavalry or some troops who reached the army after the return was prepared. Bradley explains how he arrived at his figure in *Last Stand*, 505n31.

7. OR, 47, 1:43; and OR, 47, 2:1411.

8. Mark Grimsley, "Learning to Say 'Enough': Southern Generals and the Final Weeks of the Confederacy," in Mark Grimsley and Brooks D. Simpson, eds., *The Collapse of the Confederacy* (Lincoln: University of Nebraska Press, 2001), 57; and OR, 47, 2:1395.

9. Grimsley, "Learning to Say 'Enough,'" in Grimsley and Simpson, *Collapse of the Confederacy*, 57–58; and Johnston, *Narrative of Military Operations*, 372.

10. Grimsley, "Learning to Say 'Enough,'" in Grimsley and Simpson, *Collapse of the Confederacy*, 58; Johnston, *Narrative of Military Operations*, 389; and OR, 47, 1:1057.

11. OR, 47, 2:1411.

12. OR, 47, 2:1415.

13. Bradley, *Last Stand*, 142, 483–84n26. Bradley points out that long after the war Hampton claimed he had identified for Johnston the location of each of Sherman's four marching corps, but in a dispatch written on the afternoon of March 18, 1865, the cavalryman admitted he did not know which one was in his immediate front. Hampton, "Battle of Bentonville," in Johnston and Buel, *Battles and Leaders*, 4:701; and OR, 47, 2:1430.

14. Johnston, *Narrative of Military Operations*, 384.

15. Hampton, "Battle of Bentonville," in Johnston and Buel, *Battles and Leaders*, 4:701. This postwar account remains the best source on Hampton's reply to Johnston. As Bradley points out, "If Hampton's reply to Johnston was a written message, it has not come down to us." Bradley, *Last Stand*, 483n26. Again, Hampton's dispatch to Johnston on the afternoon of March 18 makes it extremely doubtful that he was able to identify the four Union corps for Johnston that morning. OR, 47, 2:1430. See also OR, 47, 2:1429.

16. Johnston, *Narrative of Military Operations*, 384; and Bradley, *Last Stand*, 483n26.

17. OR, 47, 2:1429; and Bradley, *Last Stand*, 142. Bradley states that "Johnston himself concedes that the Bentonville plan was Hampton's." Bradley, *Last Stand*, 485n46. Johnston's memoir acknowledges Hampton's major contributions to the plan, but neither Johnston's memoir nor his official dispatches credit the plan entirely to Hampton. Perhaps it is fair to say that Johnston conceived a concept of operations and Hampton suggested the details of the plan, which Johnston endorsed and for which he took responsibility. Johnston proposed the plan's fundamental element: striking south from Smithfield to attack Sherman while he was on the march to Goldsboro. OR, 47, 2:1415. Hampton selected the battlefield, as Johnston acknowledged. His memoir refers to "the ground selected by General Hampton, and adopted from his description." Johnston, *Narrative of Military Operations*, 386. Hampton also suggested the initial troop deployments. Hampton, "Battle of Bentonville," in Johnston and Buel, *Battles and Leaders*, 4:702–3. As commander of the Army of the South, Johnston ultimately assumed responsibility for the plan.

18. Johnston, *Narrative of Military Operations*, 384, 384–85. In his memoir, Johnston called this cartography "the map of North Carolina." In his report to Lee, he called it "the State map." OR, 47, 1:1056.

19. Hughes, *Bentonville*, 47.

20. OR, 47, 1:1057; and OR, 47, 2:1428, 1435.

21. Bradley, *Last Stand*, 148–49.

22. Bradley, *Last Stand*, 149; and OR, 47, 1:1057.

23. Bradley, *Last Stand*, 309; and see note 6 of this chapter.

24. Bradley, *Last Stand*, 148–49; Johnston, *Narrative of Military Operations*, 386; and Elbert L. Little, *National Audubon Society Field Guide to North American Trees* (New York: Alfred A. Knopf, 1996), 397. Johnston's official report suggests that contrary to the advantage that Hampton expected, the thickets of blackjack oak trees delayed the Confederate deployment. OR, 47, 1:1056.

25. Mark A. Moore, *Moore's Historical Guide to the Battle of Bentonville* (Campbell CA: Savas, 1997), 18 (map); and Bradley, *Last Stand*, 161.

26. Moore, *Moore's Historical Guide*, 19n5; and Bradley, *Last Stand*, 357.

27. Bradley, *Last Stand*, 148, 149; and Hughes, *Bentonville*, 48–49.

28. OR, 47, 2:1427–28.

29. OR, 47, 2:1429.

30. OR, 47, 2:803, 822.

31. Bradley, *Last Stand*, 146.

32. Hampton, "Battle of Bentonville," in Johnson and Buel, *Battles and Leaders*, 4:702; and Bradley, *Last Stand*, 146–48, 150–52, 154–59.

33. Bradley, *Last Stand*, 154; and Hughes, *Bentonville*, 64.

34. John C. Hood, family number 966, Bentonville Township, Johnston County Census Records, Johnston County Heritage Center, Smithfield NC; and Bradley, *Last Stand*, appendix E, 449 (map). After the battle the Federals burned Hood's carriage shop, storehouse, and turpentine distillery and the Methodist church. Historian Mark Bradley surmises that this destruction was in retaliation for the murder of Federal prisoners. Bradley, *Last Stand*, 402–3. See also Moore, *Moore's Historical Guide*, 90.

35. Bradley, *Last Stand*, 342; and Mark L. Bradley, "The Battle of Bentonville, March 19–21, 1865: Last Stand in the Carolinas," *Blue & Gray Magazine* 13, no. 2 (Holiday 1995): 15 (map). Gen. Joseph E. Johnston made his headquarters on the John Benton farm. The exact site remains unknown. It may have been in Benton's log house or a nearby field. Historian Nathaniel Cheairs Hughes, Jr., concludes the "exact location of Johnston's headquarters is unknown. It is likely that he used either Benton's log house or a tent or tents pitched nearby" (Hughes, *Bentonville*, 287n22). Hughes's text indicates that Johnston used Benton's house as his headquarters at some point during the battle. See Hughes, *Bentonville*, 199. Historian Mark Bradley discusses the problem of locating Johnston's headquarters in *Last Stand*, 509n71. In Bradley's text, he refers to the Benton "farm" as Johnston's headquarters,

leaving open the question whether Johnston used the house, tents, or both. See Bradley, *Last Stand*, 380. The state highway historical marker identifies the area but not the specific location of the headquarters. North Carolina Division of Archives and History marker, State Road 1197 (Bentonville Road).

36. "Bentonville History Trail," wayside marker on the Bentonville Battlefield State Historic Site; and Hughes, *Bentonville*, 49.

37. Bradley, *Last Stand*, 146, 319 (map), 484n37.

38. Hughes, *Bentonville*, 56; Symonds, *Joseph E. Johnston*, 350; and Bradley, *Last Stand*, 165–66.

39. Johnston, *Narrative of Military Operations*, 385; and OR, 47, 1:1056. See also Bradley, *Last Stand*, 144.

40. Hughes, *Bentonville*, 44. Hughes also identifies another error in Hardee's map. See Hughes, *Bentonville*, 36.

41. Hughes, *Bentonville*, 44–45.

42. Hughes, *Bentonville*, 45; and Bradley, *Last Stand*, 148. Robert Snead owned an estate of about two thousand acres five miles northwest of Bentonville. He died in 1857, and it is likely, but not certain, that his son George Poindexter Snead hosted Hardee. Four other sons served in the Confederate army; George, a Unionist, remained home and probably was in the house on the night of March 18–19, 1865. Interview with Candice Snead Atwood, great-great granddaughter of Robert Snead, resident of Four Oaks, North Carolina, September 2, 2010. Hardee and his division commander Maj. Gen. Lafayette McLaws both believed this man's name was "Sneed." OR, 47, 2:1428; and Hughes, *Bentonville*, 44. It is highly probable that the generals heard the name pronounced but did not see it in writing. The family spelling is Snead. Interview with Candice Snead Atwood; interview with Talmadge Snead, great-great grandson of Robert Snead, resident of Four Oaks NC, August 27, 2010; and interview with Robert H. Snead, great-great grandson of Robert Snead, resident of Fort Meade FL, August 30, 2010.

43. On December 20, 1860, South Carolina adopted its cataclysmic ordinance; two days later a meeting of friends of the Union convened in Smithfield, the seat of Johnston County, and passed an anti-secession resolution. Heritage of Johnston County Book Committee, *The Heritage of Johnston County, North Carolina, 1985* (Winston-Salem NC: Hunter, 1985), 23. In the 1864 gubernatorial election, Johnston and Randolph were the only counties to vote for peace candidate William W. Holden over Zebulon Vance. Hugh Talmage Lefler and Albert Ray Newsome, *North Carolina: The History of a Southern State* (Chapel Hill: University of North Carolina Press, 1973), 476; and Hughes, *Bentonville*, 45.

44. Hughes, *Bentonville*, 45, 52.

45. Bradley, *Last Stand*, 166.

46. Bradley, *Last Stand*, 185 (map); Warner, *Generals in Gray*, 255, 256; and Bradley, *Last Stand*, 167.

47. Bradley, *Last Stand*, 185 (map); and Hughes, *Bentonville*, 59, 60.

48. Warner, *Generals in Gray*, 204, 297; and Hughes, *Bentonville*, 60.

49. Bradley, *Last Stand*, 204–5, 222; and Hughes, *Bentonville*, 143, 145–48.

50. Hughes, *Bentonville*, 60–61; and Johnston, *Narrative of Military Operations*, 386. Historian Mark Bradley aptly points out that Johnston distanced himself from the decision by writing about it in his memoir in the passive voice: Hardee "was directed" to send McLaws to General Hoke's support. Bradley, *Last Stand*, 179.

51. Bradley, *Last Stand*, 154; OR, 47, 1:25; and William T. Sherman, *Memoirs of Gen. W. T. Sherman* (New York: C. L. Webster, 1892), 2:303.

52. OR, 47, 2:903–4; and typescript of the Diary of Capt. George F. Glossbrenner, entry for Sunday, March 19, [1865], George F. Glossbrenner Papers, United States Army Heritage and Education Center, Carlisle PA.

53. Slocum, "Sherman's March," in Johnson and Buel, *Battles and Leaders*, 4:692.

54. Bradley, *Last Stand*, 226, 259.

55. Hughes, *Bentonville*, 64–89, quotation 93, 96; and OR, 47, 1:72, 71.

56. Bradley, *Last Stand*, 309. These numbers admittedly are estimates. Bradley explains how he arrived at them in *Last Stand*, 505n31.

57. Hughes, *Bentonville*, 161, 173 (map); and Bradley, *Last Stand*, 374.

58. OR, 47, 1:1056; and Johnston, *Narrative of Military Operations*, 389. Johnston also mentioned the need to remove the wounded in communications to Lee on March 21 and 23, 1865. See OR, 47, 1:1055.

59. Symonds, *Joseph E. Johnston*, 351; and Grimsley, "Learning to Say 'Enough,'" in Grimsley and Simpson, *Collapse of the Confederacy*, 58.

60. Bradley, *Last Stand*, 340; and Hughes, *Bentonville*, 165.

61. Moore, *Moore's Historical Guide*, 54 (map), 55.

62. Bradley, *Last Stand*, 347. Bradley's fifty-five thousand for Sherman's strength on March 20 matches well with Sherman's muster roll strength on March 1 (fifty-seven thousand) and Slocum's total casualties on March 19 (eleven hundred). His figure for Johnston's strength on March 20 seems to add four thousand cavalry reinforcements to Johnston's numbers on March 19 (sixteen thousand), without taking into account Johnston's losses on March 19.

63. OR, 47, 1:1059.

64. Bradley, *Last Stand*, 330–31, 333; and OR, 47, 1:72. The official report of Federal casualties for the Battle of Bentonville combines the figures for March 19–21; doubtless the Fourteenth Michigan and Sixteenth Illinois suffered nearly all, if not all, of their losses on March 20.

65. OR, 47, 1:1056, 1057; Johnston, *Narrative of Military Operations*, 389; and Grimsley, "Learning to Say 'Enough,'" in Grimsley and Simpson, *Collapse of the Confederacy*, 58. Nathaniel Cheairs Hughes questions the idea that Johnston remained at Bentonville on March 21 because Sherman might make a costly attack and points to the lack of ambulances as the explanation. Hughes, *Bentonville*, 177–78, 209. In his official report Johnston gave the

possibility of an unsound Federal attack as one reason for staying on the field on March 20. Johnston, in his report and his memoir, did not mention this likelihood as a consideration for offering battle on March 21. His official report can be read, however, to imply that the reasons given for staying on the twentieth still applied on the twenty-first. In any case, Hughes is on solid ground when he contends that removing the wounded was a more compelling factor than hoping for Sherman to make a mistake.

66. Bradley, *Last Stand*, 377 (map).

67. Bradley, *Last Stand*, 60; Hitchcock, *Marching with Sherman*, 110; and Sherman, *Memoirs*, 2:304.

68. Bradley, *Last Stand*, 371–73, 393–94.

69. Hughes, *Bentonville*, 199–204, 206–7.

70. Bradley, *Last Stand*, 393; and OR, 47, 1:1059.

71. Bradley, *Last Stand*, 404.

72. Sherman, *Memoirs*, 2:304.

73. Hughes, *Bentonville*, 230.

74. Bradley, *Last Stand*, 400.

75. Moore, *Moore's Historical Guide*, 91. Census records show that in 1860 the Harpers had only three children living with them. John Harper, family number 974, Bentonville Township, Johnston County Census Records, Johnston County Heritage Center, Smithfield NC.

76. Moore, *Moore's Historical Guide*, 91.

77. OR, 47, 1:913.

78. OR, 47, 1:28; and Sherman, *Memoirs*, 2:306.

79. OR, 47, 1:43.

80. OR, 47, 2:1454.

5. Late Winter at Petersburg

1. "Opposing Forces at Petersburg and Richmond," in Johnson and Buel, *Battles and Leaders*, 4:594; and R. E. Lee to James A. Seddon, December 26, 1864, in Lee, *Wartime Papers*, 879.

2. OR, 46, 1:61.

3. Brooks D. Simpson, "Great Expectations: Ulysses S. Grant, the Northern Press, and the Opening of the Wilderness Campaign," in Gary Gallagher, ed., *The Wilderness Campaign* (Chapel Hill: University of North Carolina Press, 1997), 5.

4. Edward G. Longacre, *The Cavalry at Appomattox: A Tactical Study of Mounted Operations during the Civil War's Climactic Campaign, March 27–April 9, 1865* (Mechanicsburg PA: Stackpole Books, 2003), 43; Greene, *Final Battles*, 29; and Warner, *Generals in Blue*, 350. See also Edward G. Longacre, *Army of Amateurs: General Benjamin F. Butler and the Army of the James, 1863–1865* (Mechanicsburg PA: Stackpole Books, 1997), 187.

5. Greene, *Final Battles*, 29.

6. Chris M. Calkins, *The Appomattox Campaign: March 29–April 9, 1865* (Conshohocken PA: Combined Books, 1997), 80.

7. Hess, *Trenches at Petersburg*, xv.

8. Hess, *Trenches at Petersburg*, 141. The distance from Petersburg to Globe Tavern was three and a half miles. Andrew A. Humphreys, *The Virginia Campaign of '64 and '65* (New York: Charles Scribner's Sons, 1883), map in the back matter of volume 2; and Noah Andre Trudeau, *The Last Citadel: Petersburg, Virginia, June 1864–April 1865* (Boston: Little, Brown, 1991), 145 (map). The Battle of Globe Tavern is also known as the Second Battle of the Weldon Railroad.

9. Warner, *Generals in Blue*, 241; Catton, *Stillness at Appomattox*, 51; and Gordon C. Rhea, "The Testing of a Corps Commander: Gouverneur Kemble Warren at the Wilderness and Spotsylvania," in Gary W. Gallagher, ed., *The Spotsylvania Campaign* (Chapel Hill: University of North Carolina Press, 1998), 61–77. See also William D. Matter, "The Federal High Command at Spotsylvania," in Gallagher, *Spotsylvania Campaign*, 57.

10. Hess, *Trenches at Petersburg*, 141. Hess surveys the Battle of Globe Tavern earlier in this book, 129–35.

11. Hess, *Trenches at Petersburg*, 141.

12. William C. Wyrick, "The Coming of Spring, 1865," *Blue & Gray Magazine* 25, no. 1 (Campaign 2008): 12.

13. Simpson, *Ulysses S. Grant*, 380.

14. Humphreys, *Virginia Campaign*, map in the back matter of volume 2.

15. Humphreys, *Virginia Campaign*, 2:310, 312; Arthur W. Bergeron, Jr., "The Battle of Hatcher's Run, February 5–7, 1865," *Civil War Magazine* 67 (April 1998): 44; and Hess, *Trenches at Petersburg*, xix–xx. When Hess introduces the structure of Union offensives, Confederate offensives, and raids that he imposes on the Petersburg Campaign, he acknowledges his debt to historian Richard J. Sommers (Hess, *Trenches at Petersburg*, xvii). In Sommers's monumental study of Chaffin's Bluff and Poplar Spring Church, he introduced the idea of dividing the siege of Petersburg into a series of separate operations, a construct that furthered the detailed examination of each of these segments and improved a student's understanding of the campaign as a whole. See Richard J. Sommers, *Richmond Redeemed: The Siege at Petersburg* (Garden City NY: Doubleday, 1981), xii. The structure Hess applies to the campaign varies somewhat from the one Sommers introduced in his superbly detailed *Richmond Redeemed*. Hess, *Trenches at Petersburg*, xx–xxi.

16. Humphreys, *Virginia Campaign*, 2:312; OR, 46, 1:365–66; and Douglas Southall Freeman, *R. E. Lee: A Biography* (New York: Charles Scribner's Sons, 1934–35), 3:535.

17. Greene, *Final Battles*, 27.

18. Greene, *Final Battles*, 100; and OR, 46, 1:191, 253.

19. OR, 46, 1:366; and Humphreys, *Virginia Campaign*, 2:314.

20. *OR*, 46, 1:192.

21. Freeman, *R. E. Lee*, 3:535–36n46.

22. *OR*, 46, 1:381; Humphreys, *Virginia Campaign*, 2:310; and Warner, *Generals in Gray*, 111. Like Joseph Wheeler, John B. Gordon sometimes is referred to as a lieutenant general, but there is no conclusive evidence that he attained that rank. Warner, *Generals in Gray*, xvii, xviii.

23. Bergeron, "Battle of Hatcher's Run," 46; and Humphreys, *Virginia Campaign*, 2:313.

24. *OR*, 46, 1:254, 366.

25. *OR*, 46, 1:254–55; and Noah Andre Trudeau, *Out of the Storm: The End of the Civil War, April–June 1865* (Boston: Little, Brown, 1994), 16n.

26. *OR*, 46, 1:254, 293.

27. *OR*, 46, 1:390; and Warner, *Generals in Gray*, 232.

28. *OR*, 46, 1:368, 390.

29. *OR*, 46, 1:255; and Robert Tilney, *My Life in the Army: Three Years and a Half with the Fifth Army Corps, Army of the Potomac, 1862–1865* (Philadelphia: Ferris & Leach, 1912), 182.

30. *OR*, 46, 1:255; Greene, *Final Battles*, 105; Theodore Gerrish, *Army Life: A Private's Reminiscences of the Civil War* (Portland ME: Hoyt, Fogg & Donham, 1882), 223; and Avery Harris, "Personal Reminiscences of the Author from August 1862 to June 1865, War of the Rebellion," 268, Avery Harris Papers, United States Army Heritage and Education Center, Carlisle PA. Writing long after the event, Harris misdated this episode by a day.

31. Greene, *Final Battles*, 105; Henry Kyd Douglas, *I Rode with Stonewall* (Chapel Hill: University of North Carolina Press, 1940), 327; and Warner, *Generals in Gray*, 232.

32. J. C. Goolsby, "Crenshaw Battery, Pegram's Battalion, Confederate States Artillery," *Southern Historical Society Papers* 28 (1900): 369.

33. *OR*, 46, 1:370; photocopy of the Journal of Charles Barnet (Barnt?), entry for February 7, [1865], Charles Barnet (Barnt?) Papers, Ronn Palm Collection, United States Army Heritage and Education Center, Carlisle PA; and *OR*, 46, 1:256.

34. *OR*, 46, 1:381; and Thomas L. Livermore, *Numbers and Losses in the Civil War in America* (Boston: Houghton Mifflin, 1900), 134. Among the historians offering the thousand-man figure are Bergeron, "Battle of Hatcher's Run," 49; Trudeau, *Last Citadel*, 322; Greene, *Final Battles*, 105; and Hess, *Trenches at Petersburg*, 232.

35. *OR*, 46, 1:257.

36. *OR*, 46, 1:194.

37. Power, *Lee's Miserables*, 243–44; and Greene, *Final Battles*, 97. Pointing out that the Confederates energetically improved their defenses through the winter, Greene emphasizes that many Southern soldiers held remarkably positive attitudes. See Greene, *Final Battles*, 64–66. He and historian

Earl Hess note that the Federals had a desertion problem of their own that season. Greene, *Final Battles*, 59–60; and Hess, *Trenches at Petersburg*, 228.

38. Hess, *Trenches at Petersburg*, 233; and Humphreys, *Virginia Campaign*, 2:315.

39. Hess, *Trenches at Petersburg*, 233.

40. Greene, *Final Battles*, 105; Wyrick, "Coming of Spring, 1865," 12; and John B. Gordon, *Reminiscences of the Civil War* (New York: Charles Scribner's Sons, 1904), 420. Offering a rough estimate long after the fact, Gordon made the entire Petersburg front three miles longer than historian Wyrick does.

41. Davis, *Jefferson Davis*, 590; Freeman, *Lee's Lieutenants*, 3:643; and James Longstreet, *From Manassas to Appomattox: Memoirs of the Civil War in America* (Bloomington: Indiana University Press, 1960), 583.

42. Jeffry D. Wert, *General James Longstreet: The Confederacy's Most Controversial Soldier: A Biography* (New York: Simon & Schuster, 1993), 397; and Longstreet, *From Manassas to Appomattox*, 584.

43. Davis, *Jefferson Davis*, 592; Freeman, *Lee's Lieutenants*, 3:643; and Longstreet, *From Manassas to Appomattox*, 584.

44. Longstreet, *From Manassas to Appomattox*, 585–86. The second Longstreet-Ord meeting took place on February 28, not February 23, as Longstreet's memoir seems to indicate. See also Wert, *General James Longstreet*, 397; and Longstreet, *From Manassas to Appomattox*, 583–85. Robert E. Lee to Ulysses S. Grant, March 2, 1865, quoted in Longstreet, *From Manassas to Appomattox*, 585.

45. Wesley Merritt, "Sheridan in the Shenandoah Valley," in Johnson and Buel, *Battles and Leaders*, 4:521; and Gordon, *Reminiscences*, 388.

46. OR, 46, 2:802.

47. Long after the event, Gordon said Lee summoned him at about 2:00 a.m. one night during "the first week of March, 1865." Gordon, *Reminiscences*, 385. Freeman dated this summons as the "night of March 3," based on Lee's visit with Davis on the fourth. See Freeman, *R. E. Lee*, 4:7.

48. R. E. Lee to Jefferson Davis, March 2, 1865, in Lee, *Wartime Papers*, 911.

49. Freeman, *R. E. Lee*, 4:7; Gordon, *Reminiscences*, 385–86; and Greene, *Final Battles*, 23.

50. Gordon, *Reminiscences*, 386–89. In recounting this meeting decades later, Gordon directly quoted Lee and himself at lengths far greater than it is likely he could have remembered. See, for example, Gordon, *Reminiscences*, 401–2. Despite its weaknesses, Gordon's account, as historian Mark Grimsley points out, may provide "one of the best windows into Lee's thought during this critical period" (Grimsley, "Learning to Say 'Enough,'" in Grimsley and Simpson, *Collapse of the Confederacy*, 49).

51. Freeman, *R. E. Lee*, 4:8–9; and Gordon, *Reminiscences*, 390–93.

52. Ulysses S. Grant to Robert E. Lee, March 4, 1865, quoted in Longstreet, *From Manassas to Appomattox*, 587; and Freeman, *R. E. Lee*, 4:9. See

also Michael B. Ballard, *A Long Shadow: Jefferson Davis and the Final Days of the Confederacy* (Jackson: University Press of Mississippi, 1986), 21.

53. Gordon, *Reminiscences*, 393–94; and Freeman, *R. E. Lee*, 4:9, 10.

54. Freeman, *R. E. Lee*, 4:11.

55. Freeman, *R. E. Lee*, 4:11–12; Gordon, *Reminiscences*, 397; and Hess, *Trenches at Petersburg*, xx.

56. Gordon, *Reminiscences*, 398–99, 401; and Trudeau, *Last Citadel*, 289.

57. Robert E. L. Krick, "The Assault on Fort Stedman March 25, 1865," *Civil War Magazine* 67 (April 1998): 51; and Greene, *Final Battles*, 157. In July 2014, Grant Gates of Petersburg National Battlefield provided information about the Otway P. Hare house. See also James A. Walker, "Gordon's Assault on Fort Stedman, March 25th, 1865—a Brilliant Achievement," *Southern Historical Society Papers* 31 (1903): 19.

58. Mark Mayo Boatner III, *The Civil War Dictionary* (New York: McKay, 1959; reprint, New York: Vintage Civil War Library, 1961), 793; and OR, 42, 1:793.

59. William C. Wyrick, "Lee's Last Offensive: The Attack on Fort Stedman March 25, 1865," *Blue & Gray Magazine* 25, no. 1 (Campaign 2008): 11 and photo, 12; John F. Hartranft, "The Recapture of Fort Stedman," in Johnson and Buel, *Battles and Leaders*, 4:584; Dave Roth et al., "Lee's Assault on Fort Stedman," *Blue & Gray Magazine* 25, no. 1 (Campaign 2008): 52; and Hess, *Trenches at Petersburg*, 65.

60. Trudeau, *Last Citadel*, 335, gives the Colquitt's Salient–Fort Stedman distance as 282 yards. In November 2010 the author measured the distance from the outer line of the main works at Colquitt's Salient to the outer line of Fort Stedman's main works at about 260 yards, a figure roughly comparable to Trudeau's. Historians often have given 200 yards as the distance between the "lines," a distance that would have been less than that between the fortifications themselves. Greene, *Final Battles*, 112; Krick, "Assault on Fort Stedman," 51; and the Petersburg National Battlefield's Battle of Fort Stedman Trail Guide (brochure), n.p.

61. Trudeau, *Last Citadel*, 335; and Warner, *Generals in Gray*, 58.

62. Trudeau, *Last Citadel*, 335.

63. Humphreys, *Virginia Campaign*, 2:317; Wyrick, "Lee's Last Offensive," 11; and Hess, *Trenches at Petersburg*, 249.

64. Gordon, *Reminiscences*, 408; Wyrick, "Lee's Last Offensive," 11; and Hess, *Trenches at Petersburg*, 249.

65. Krick, "Assault on Fort Stedman," 51; and Gordon, *Reminiscences*, 399–400, 406.

66. Krick, "Assault on Fort Stedman," 52; and OR, 46, 1:62.

67. OR, 46, 1:355, 361.

68. George L. Kilmer, "Gordon's Attack at Fort Stedman," in Johnson and Buel, *Battles and Leaders*, 4:579n; OR, 46, 1:341; and Catton, *A Stillness at Appomattox*, 47–48.

69. Kilmer, "Gordon's Attack at Fort Stedman," 4:579n.

70. OR *Atlas*, plate 62, number 9; and Johnson and Buel, *Battles and Leaders*, 4:538 (map). Some primary sources identify these Union batteries with roman numerals, others with arabic numerals. In February 2002, historian Chris Calkins, then at Petersburg National Battlefield, provided information about Rushmore's plantation.

71. OR, 46, 1:70; Warner, *Generals in Blue*, 359–60; and Greene, *Final Battles*, 28.

72. Freeman, *R. E. Lee*, 4:12.

73. Freeman, *R. E. Lee*, 4:12.

74. OR, 47, 2:1454.

75. Gordon, *Reminiscences*, 405; and Freeman, *R. E. Lee*, 4:13.

76. Trudeau, *Last Citadel*, 337.

77. Trudeau, *Last Citadel*, 337; Freeman, *R. E. Lee*, 4:16; and Wyrick, "Lee's Last Offensive," 21. Hess gives a larger number for the reserve force. Hess, *Trenches at Petersburg*, 250. The Confederate order of battle and formation for the Fort Stedman assault are stated variously. Freeman had two brigades of Maj. Gen. Henry Heth's Division also in support of the attack. Trudeau, who discusses this subject carefully in *Last Citadel*, 438, drops them out. Wyrick mentions them in the text of his article "Lee's Last Offensive," 22, but excludes them from an order of battle that accompanies it.

78. Trudeau, *Last Citadel*, 335.

79. According to Gordon, Lee questioned him about a "strong line of infantry in the ravine behind the fort [Stedman] and the three other forts in the rear which command Fort Stedman." Gordon, *Reminiscences*, 403. Lee presumably learned about these forts from Gordon's own reporting. They became a point of controversy.

80. Trudeau, *Last Citadel*, 335; and Greene, *Final Battles*, 112.

81. Trudeau, *Last Citadel*, 336, 438.

82. Gordon, *Reminiscences*, 407–10. Writing in *Reminiscences* long after Reconstruction, Gordon liked stories that illustrated the combatants' respect for one another and played to the theme of reunion—for example, the Gordon and Barlow episode at Gettysburg (151–53) and Chamberlain's men giving the surrendering Southerners a "soldierly salute" at Appomattox (444).

83. Gordon, *Reminiscences*, 407; Hartranft, "Recapture of Fort Stedman," in Johnson and Buel, *Battles and Leaders*, 4:585; and Trudeau, *Last Citadel*, 338–39.

84. Trudeau, *Last Citadel*, 339; and Kilmer, "Gordon's Attack at Fort Stedman," 4:580.

85. Trudeau, *Last Citadel*, 341.

86. Trudeau, *Last Citadel*, 339, 342.

87. Trudeau, *Last Citadel*, 343.

88. Humphreys, *Virginia Campaign*, quotation 2:317, 319–20; and Wyrick, "Lee's Last Offensive," 49–50. "Through the failure of the three guides, we

had failed to occupy the three forts in the rear, and they were now filled with Federals." See Gordon, *Reminiscences*, 411.

89. Greene, *Final Battles*, 112; Freeman, *R. E. Lee*, 4:16; and Trudeau, *Last Citadel*, 438.

90. Hartranft, "Recapture of Fort Stedman," in Johnson and Buel, *Battles and Leaders*, 4:584; and Stephen Sears, *Landscape Turned Red: The Battle of Antietam* (New Haven CT: Ticknor & Fields, 1983), 266.

91. Hartranft, "Recapture of Fort Stedman," in Johnson and Buel, *Battles and Leaders*, 4:584, 588.

92. OR, 46, 1:345; and Hartranft, "Recapture of Fort Stedman," in Johnson and Buel, *Battles and Leaders*, 4:585, 585–86.

93. Hartranft, "Recapture of Fort Stedman," in Johnson and Buel, *Battles and Leaders*, 4:586–87; Trudeau, *Last Citadel*, 348; and Humphreys, *Virginia Campaign*, 2:319.

94. Simpson, *Ulysses S. Grant*, 413, 415–17; Humphreys, *Virginia Campaign*, 2:320; and OR, 46, 1:318.

95. OR, 46, 1:347; and Hartranft, "Recapture of Fort Stedman," in Johnson and Buel, *Battles and Leaders*, quotation 4:588, 588–89. Historian William C. Wyrick argues that Hartranft gave himself "the lion's share of credit for the recapture of Fort Stedman." Wyrick points to the large numbers of Confederates captured by the Third Maryland, 100th Pennsylvania, and other units. See Wyrick, "Lee's Last Offensive," 45–46. The Federals had won a total victory, and there was glory enough to share.

96. Greene, *Final Battles*, 114.

97. Humphreys, *Virginia Campaign*, 2:319; photocopy of the Diary of Ordnance Sgt. James W. Albright, entry for March 25, [1865], Virginia Historical Society, Richmond; Freeman, *R. E. Lee*, 4:18; and Humphreys, *Virginia Campaign*, 2:319.

98. Simpson, *Ulysses S. Grant*, 416; and Trudeau, *Last Citadel*, 352.

99. OR, 46, 1:71; and Trudeau, *Last Citadel*, 353.

6. The Fall of Petersburg

1. Simpson, *Ulysses S. Grant*, 418; Simpson, *Let Us Have Peace*, 78; and Sherman, *Memoirs*, 2:325.

2. Simpson, *Ulysses S. Grant*, 418; Simpson, *Let Us Have Peace*, 78; and Sherman, *Memoirs*, 2:326.

3. Sherman, *Memoirs*, 2:326.

4. Sherman, *Memoirs*, 2:326–27; David Herbert Donald, *Lincoln* (New York: Simon & Schuster, 1995), 574; and Donald C. Pfanz, *The Petersburg Campaign: Abraham Lincoln at City Point, March 20–April 9, 1865* (Lynchburg VA: H. E. Howard, 1989), 28.

5. Simpson, *Ulysses S. Grant*, 418–19.

6. Simpson, *Ulysses S. Grant*, 419; and Sherman, *Memoirs*, 2:327.

7. Peter S. Carmichael, "The Battles of Lewis Farm and White Oak Road, March 29–30, 1865," *Civil War Magazine* 67 (April 1998): 53.

8. OR, 46, 1:50.

9. Carmichael, "Battles of Lewis Farm," 53–54.

10. OR, 46, 1:1101.

11. Greene, *Final Battles*, 155; OR, 46, 1:1101; and Hess, *Trenches at Petersburg*, xx.

12. Calkins, *Appomattox Campaign*, 14; and Warner, *Generals in Gray*, 157.

13. Greene, *Final Battles*, 158, 159 (map); Carmichael, "Battles of Lewis Farm," 55–56; and Calkins, *Appomattox Campaign*, 201. In February 2002 historian Chris Calkins, then at Petersburg National Battlefield, provided information about the Lewis farm.

14. Carmichael, "Battles of Lewis Farm," 54.

15. "Lee's concentration at Five Forks resulted from a sound analysis of likely Federal intentions rather than any evaluation of actual Union troop movements." See Greene, *Final Battles*, 448n20.

16. Greene, *Final Battles*, 165.

17. Johnson and Buel, *Battles and Leaders*, 4:538–39 (maps).

18. Greene, *Final Battles*, 165. For a splendid history of the lore surrounding Pickett's Charge, see Carol Reardon, *Pickett's Charge in History and Memory* (Chapel Hill: University of North Carolina Press, 1997).

19. OR, 46, 1:1102; and Greene, *Final Battles*, 165.

20. OR, 46, 1:1102, 1299; Greene, *Final Battles*, 175–78; and Calkins, *Appomattox Campaign*, 201.

21. Greene, *Final Battles*, 170–74; and Calkins, *Appomattox Campaign*, 201. See also Carmichael, "Battles of Lewis Farm," 56.

22. Horace Porter, "Five Forks and the Pursuit of Lee," in Johnson and Buel, *Battles and Leaders*, 4:711; and OR, 46, 1:817, 1244.

23. Greene, *Final Battles*, 30–31; and Simpson, *Ulysses S. Grant*, 422.

24. Philip H. Sheridan, *Personal Memoirs of P. H. Sheridan* (New York: C. L. Webster, 1888), 2:161; and Ulysses S. Grant, *Personal Memoirs of U. S. Grant* (New York: C. L. Webster, 1886), 2:214–15.

25. OR, 46, 3:381; and Greene, *Final Battles*, 181–82.

26. OR, 46, 1:1299.

27. OR, 46, 1:1263–64.

28. Freeman, *R. E. Lee*, 4:36.

29. Greene, *Final Battles*, 183.

30. OR, 46, 1:1144, 1155, 1157.

31. OR, 46, 1:1130, 1123–24.

32. OR, 46, 1:1103; Porter, "Five Forks," in Johnson and Buel, *Battles and Leaders*, 4:711; OR, 46, 1:1244; and Ed Bearss and Chris Calkins, *Battle of Five Forks* (Lynchburg VA: H. E. Howard, 1985), 117.

33. Chris Calkins, "The Battle of Five Forks: Final Push for the South Side," *Blue & Gray Magazine* 9, no. 4 (April 1992): 19, 22. These numbers take into account the V Corps's losses at the Lewis farm and the White Oak Road, the cavalry's casualties at Dinwiddie Court House, and the cavalry units held in reserve.

34. Calkins, "Battle of Five Forks," 18. Pickett's casualties at Dinwiddie Court House would be one consideration in the difference between the two numbers.

35. OR, 46, 1:829; and Porter, "Five Forks," 4:711.

36. OR, 46, 1:829; Bearss and Calkins, *Five Forks*, 74; and OR, 46, 1:831, 1105. On Gravelly Run Methodist Episcopal Church, see Bearss and Calkins, *Five Forks*, 117–19.

37. Bearss and Calkins, *Five Forks*, 81; and Dave Roth, "So—What Are Shad? And How Did They Affect Confederate Fortunes at Five Forks?," *Blue & Gray Magazine* 9, no.4 (April 1992): 48.

38. Bearss and Calkins, *Five Forks*, 92; and OR, 46, 1:1105.

39. Calkins, "Battle of Five Forks," 41.

40. Porter, "Five Forks," 4:713.

41. Porter, "Five Forks," 4:713.

42. Porter, "Five Forks," 4:713.

43. Porter, "Five Forks," 4:713.

44. Calkins, "Battle of Five Forks," 41; and OR, 46, 1:869.

45. OR, 46, 1:832–33.

46. OR, 46, 1:833, 1105.

47. Porter, "Five Forks," 4:713.

48. Bearss and Calkins, *Five Forks*, 96–98, 101.

49. Bearss and Calkins, *Five Forks*, 82; and Calkins, "Battle of Five Forks," 48.

50. Bearss and Calkins, *Five Forks*, 82, 102.

51. Bearss and Calkins, *Five Forks*, 102.

52. Freeman, *Lee's Lieutenants*, 3:669–70.

53. Bearss and Calkins, *Five Forks*, 106; and Calkins, "Battle of Five Forks," 50.

54. Calkins, "Battle of Five Forks," 50; and Porter, "Five Forks," 4:714.

55. William A. Marvel, *A Place Called Appomattox* (Chapel Hill: University of North Carolina Press, 2000), 200.

56. Calkins, "Battle of Five Forks," 51; and Trudeau, *Out of the Storm*, 45.

57. Transcript of R. W. Downman to My dear wife, April 6, [1865], Downman Family Papers, 1699–1909, Virginia Historical Society, Richmond; Freeman, *R. E. Lee*, 4:112; and William Marvel, *Lee's Last Retreat: The Flight to Appomattox* (Chapel Hill: University of North Carolina Press, 2002), 159–60, 214–17.

58. Trudeau, *Out of the Storm*, 44. Warren referred to Locke as a colonel and his adjutant general; see OR, 46, 1:836. Colonel was his brevet rank; see Francis B. Heitman, *Historical Register and Dictionary of the United States Army, from Its Organization, September 29, 1789, to March 2, 1903* (Washington

DC: Government Printing Office, 1903; reprint, Urbana: University of Illinois Press, 1965), 1:637.

59. Bearss and Calkins, *Five Forks*, 109; and OR, 46, 3:420.

60. Bearss and Calkins, *Five Forks*, 110.

61. "General Warren at Five Forks, and the Court of Inquiry," in Johnson and Buel, *Battles and Leaders*, 4:723; David M. Jordan, *"Happiness Is Not My Companion": The Life of General G. K. Warren* (Indianapolis: Indiana University Press, 2001), 239–40, 246–47, 260; and Stephen W. Sears, *Controversies and Commanders: Dispatches from the Army of the Potomac* (Boston: Houghton Mifflin, 1999), 282, 284.

62. Sears, *Controversies and Commanders*, 284. Bruce Catton made a similar suggestion in *A Stillness at Appomattox*, 358.

63. R. E. Lee to Jefferson Davis, April 1, 1865, in Lee, *Wartime Papers*, 922; and Freeman, *R. E. Lee*, 4:35–36.

64. Porter, "Five Forks," 4:715.

65. Greene, *Final Battles*, 194; and Hess, *Trenches at Petersburg*, xx.

66. Greene, *Final Battles*, 202 (map), 257. See also map on 68.

67. Calkins, *Appomattox Campaign*, 44 (map).

68. Greene, *Final Battles*, 191–93, 196–97, 205. Historian Carol Reardon called Lewis A. Grant the "other Grant" in the title of her fine essay "The Other Grant: Lewis A. Grant and the Vermont Brigade in the Battle of the Wilderness," in Gallagher, *Wilderness Campaign*, 201–35.

69. Jeffry D. Wert, *Gettysburg Day Three* (New York: Simon & Schuster, 2001), 148; and Humphreys, *Virginia Campaign*, 2:366–67.

70. Greene, *Final Battles*, 332–40.

71. Porter, "Five Forks," 4:716.

72. Greene, *Final Battles*, 235. Devoting a chapter to this attack, Greene describes it in splendid detail in *Final Battles*, 215–51.

73. Greene, *Final Battles*, 239; and Porter, "Five Forks," 4:716.

74. Greene, *Final Battles*, 248, 249.

75. OR, 46, 1:1259; and Greene, *Final Battles*, 220–23, 249–50.

76. Greene, *Final Battles*, 251.

77. Trudeau, *Last Citadel*, 373.

78. Greene, *Final Battles*, 248.

79. Hess, *Trenches at Petersburg*, 273.

80. Hess, *Trenches at Petersburg*, 271; and Greene, *Final Battles*, 189.

81. Greene, *Final Battles*, 449–50n31; OR, 46, 3:423; and Hess, *Trenches at Petersburg*, 271.

82. Hess, *Trenches at Petersburg*, 271; and Greene, *Final Battles*, 205.

83. Greene, *Final Battles*, 62–63.

84. Greene, *Final Battles*, 257–59, 261; and James I. Robertson, Jr., *General A. P. Hill: The Story of a Confederate Warrior* (New York: Random House, 1987), 314–16.

85. Greene, *Final Battles*, 259–61.

86. Robertson, *General A. P. Hill*, 317–18; and Greene, *Final Battles*, 260–61.

87. Greene, *Final Battles*, 261, 263.

88. Freeman, *R. E. Lee*, 4:49; and OR, 46, 3:1378.

89. Cooper, *Jefferson Davis*, 523; and "A Walking Tour of St. Paul's" (brochure), Richmond VA, n.d.

90. Cooper, *Jefferson Davis*, 523.

91. William C. Davis, *An Honorable Defeat: The Last Days of the Confederate Government* (New York: Harcourt, 2001), 58, 60, 62–63, 65, 73.

92. Trudeau, *Last Citadel*, 381. Trudeau points out that contemporaries sometimes called Gregg and Whitworth "batteries" rather than forts; also, he and Greene both mention that the latter was occasionally referred to by other names. Trudeau, *Last Citadel*, 381n; and Greene, *Final Battles*, 489n12.

93. Greene, *Final Battles*, 287; and Hess, *Trenches at Petersburg*, 274.

94. Trudeau, *Last Citadel*, 383; and Greene, *Final Battles*, 294.

95. Hess, *Trenches at Petersburg*, 274; Greene, *Final Battles*, 297; and Giles Buckner Cooke Diary, entry for Sunday, April 2, [1865], Virginia Historical Society, Richmond.

96. Hess, *Trenches at Petersburg*, 275; Greene, *Final Battles*, 302; and Giles Buckner Cooke Diary, entry for Sunday, April 2, [1865].

97. Greene, *Final Battles*, 303.

98. OR, 46, 1:1174; and Greene, *Final Battles*, 307.

99. Trudeau, *Last Citadel*, 388; and Greene, *Final Battles*, 306, 307.

100. Greene, *Final Battles*, 322–23; and Warner, *Generals in Blue*, 322–23.

101. Greene, *Final Battles*, 323–24, 328 (map). There also are maps of Sutherland Station in Trudeau, *Last Citadel*, 358; and Calkins, *Appomattox Campaign*, 47.

102. Trudeau, *Last Citadel*, 396–97; and Greene, *Final Battles*, 324–30. Trudeau, 396, says it was "approaching 4 p.m." when the third attack began, and Greene states that "Miles logged the commencement of his third attack at 2:45 p.m., although the actual time may have been as much as an hour later" (327).

103. Trudeau, *Last Citadel*, 401.

104. Raymond J. Herek, *These Men Have Seen Hard Service: The First Michigan Sharpshooters in the Civil War* (Detroit: Wayne State University Press, 1998), 322, 325. Herek gives Wixcey's middle initial on page 428.

The brigade commander of the First Michigan Sharpshooters, brevet Col. Ralph Ely, who was not present at the flag raising, offered a slightly later time for this event. Herek, *These Men Have Seen Hard Service*, 501n103. For Colonel Ely's account, see OR, 46, 1:1047–48.

Wixcey was later promoted to color sergeant. See Herek, *These Men Have Seen Hard Service*, 341.

See also Herek's article about this episode: "First in Petersburg," *Michigan History* 82, no. 4 (July–August 1998): 49–51.

105. Greene, *Final Battles*, 353. On page 354 Greene evaluates three accounts of this episode and concludes that Collier's is the most reliable.

7. To Sailor's Creek

1. Catton, *Stillness at Appomattox*, 364.

2. Trudeau, *Out of the Storm*, 79; Warner, *Generals in Blue*, 548; and OR, 46, 3:509.

3. Trudeau, *Out of the Storm*, 80–81; and OR, 46, 1:1228.

4. Trudeau, *Out of the Storm*, 67, 68, 75; and typescript of the Diary of Cornelius Hart Carlton, entry for M[onday], [April] 3, [1865], Virginia Historical Society, Richmond.

5. Trudeau, *Out of the Storm*, 75; and Lina [Evelina] T. Brooke to My Dear Friend, July 27, 1865, Fredericka Holmes Trapnell Papers, Virginia Historical Society, Richmond.

6. Trudeau, *Out of the Storm*, 84; and Lina [Evelina] T. Brooke to My Dear Friend, July 27, 1865, Fredericka Holmes Trapnell Papers.

7. Thomas Thatcher Graves, "The Fall of Richmond: The Occupation," in Johnson and Buel, *Battles and Leaders*, 4:727; and OR, 46, 3:509.

8. Donald, *Lincoln*, 576; and Trudeau, *Out of the Storm*, 84–85.

9. Greene, *Final Battles*, 360.

10. Calkins, *Appomattox Campaign*, 68–69 and 56 (map).

11. OR, 46, 1:1269n*.

12. Greene, *Final Battles*, 18; and Calkins, *Appomattox Campaign*, 18, 58.

13. Calkins, *Appomattox Campaign*, 56 (map).

14. Calkins, *Appomattox Campaign*, 44 (map).

15. Calkins, *Appomattox Campaign*, 63; and Giles Buckner Cooke Diary, entry for Sunday, April 2, [1865].

16. Calkins, *Appomattox Campaign*, 68–69.

17. Calkins, *Appomattox Campaign*, 44 (map).

18. OR, 46, 1:1272n*.

19. OR, 46, 1:1274; and Calkins, *Appomattox Campaign*, 53–54.

20. Brooks D. Simpson, "Facilitating Defeat: The Union High Command and the Collapse of the Confederacy," in Grimsley and Simpson, *Collapse of the Confederacy*, 91. "The Opposing Forces in the Appomattox Campaign," in Johnson and Buel, *Battles and Leaders*, 4:753, estimates Lee's numbers at the beginning of the campaign at fifty-four thousand, acknowledging that this number excludes local troops and naval forces. Calkins, *Appomattox Campaign*, 63 and 200, gives a somewhat larger figure.

21. Simpson, "Facilitating Defeat," in Grimsley and Simpson, *Collapse of the Confederacy*, 91; Calkins, *Appomattox Campaign*, 63; and Grimsley, "Learning to Say 'Enough,'" in Grimsley and Simpson, *Collapse of the Confederacy*, 60–61.

22. OR, 46, 1:1265; Calkins, *Appomattox Campaign*, 63; and Grimsley, "Learning to Say 'Enough,'" in Grimsley and Simpson, *Collapse of the Confederacy*, 61.

23. Daniel E. Sutherland, "Guerrilla Warfare, Democracy, and the Fate of the Confederacy," *The Journal of Southern History* 68, no. 2 (May 2002): 263–64.

24. Henry Hitchcock to [Mrs. Hitchcock], April 7, 1865, in Hitchcock, *Marching with Sherman*, 292.

25. Sutherland, "Guerrilla Warfare," 266–69, 270–71.

26. William B. Feis, "Jefferson Davis and the 'Guerrilla Option': A Reexamination," in Grimsley and Simpson, *Collapse of the Confederacy*, 104–5.

27. Cooper, *Jefferson Davis*, 524.

28. Davis, *Jefferson Davis*, 608; Emory M. Thomas, *The Confederate Nation, 1861–1865* (New York: Harper & Row, 1979), 301; and Emory M. Thomas, *Robert E. Lee* (New York: W. W. Norton, 1995), 362. In *A Long Shadow*, historian Michael Ballard believes the April 4 proclamation proposed "a war of persistent guerrilla-type harassment," but at the same time "was an obvious attempt to rekindle public confidence" (57). Ballard also states: "Despite what some historians have written, Davis's words do not indicate an advocacy of guerrilla warfare per se" (71n14). See also Feis, "Jefferson Davis," in Grimsley and Simpson, *Collapse of the Confederacy*, 107. Sutherland is skeptical that the April 4 proclamation represented a call for guerrilla warfare. Sutherland, "Guerrilla Warfare," 291.

29. Feis, "Jefferson Davis," in Grimsley and Simpson, *Collapse of the Confederacy*, 113; and Sutherland, "Guerrilla Warfare," 274–76. Although the Mexican-American War was largely a conventional conflict, the invaders encountered guerrilla opposition. Historian Timothy Johnson persuasively argues that this activity might have been much greater had it not been for Maj. Gen. Winfield Scott's wise policies. Timothy D. Johnson, *Winfield Scott: The Quest for Military Glory* (Lawrence: University Press of Kansas, 1998), 186, 188, 194, 208, 209, 235.

30. Feis, "Jefferson Davis," in Grimsley and Simpson, *Collapse of the Confederacy*, 107.

31. Feis, "Jefferson Davis," in Grimsley and Simpson, *Collapse of the Confederacy*, 110.

32. Edward Porter Alexander, *Fighting for the Confederacy: The Personal Recollections of General Edward Porter Alexander*, ed. Gary W. Gallagher (Chapel Hill: University of North Carolina Press, 1989), 530–33. Alexander claimed to remember this conversation of guerrilla warfare in great detail long after the war. Historian William Marvel raises this caveat about Alexander's account in *Lee's Last Retreat*, 277n22. Alexander's details aside, there seems no reason to doubt his representation of Lee's position.

33. Feis, "Jefferson Davis," in Grimsley and Simpson, *Collapse of the Confederacy*, 110; and Sutherland, "Guerrilla Warfare," 291.

34. Sutherland, "Guerrilla Warfare," 291; Cooper, *Jefferson Davis*, 527; and Gallagher, *Fighting for the Confederacy*, 532. See also the Thirty-fifth Annual Fortenbaugh Memorial Lecture: George M. Frederickson, *Why the Confeder-*

acy Did Not Fight a Guerrilla War after the Fall of Richmond: A Comparative View (Gettysburg PA: Gettysburg College, 1996), 27–29.

35. OR, 46, 3:528; Simpson, "Facilitating Defeat," in Grimsley and Simpson, *Collapse of the Confederacy*, 95; and Calkins, *Appomattox Campaign*, 56 (map).

36. OR, 46, 3:528. A IX Corps division occupied Petersburg; see OR, 46, 1:1019. "Opposing Forces in the Appomattox Campaign," in Johnson and Buel, *Battles and Leaders*, 4:751, credits the Federals at the opening of the campaign with a total strength of 120,000. The number of Federal effectives who made the pursuit was significantly lower; see Calkins, *Appomattox Campaign*, 74, 201.

37. Frederick W. Oesterle, "Incidents Connected with the Civil War," 14, Frederick W. Oesterle Papers, United States Army Heritage and Education Center, Carlisle PA; and Calkins, *Appomattox Campaign*, 69–73. For the Namozine Church–Petersburg distance, see Calkins, *Appomattox Campaign*, 56 (map).

38. OR, 46, 3:529.

39. Warner, *Generals in Blue*, 190–91; OR, 46, 1:839; and Calkins, *Appomattox Campaign*, 56 (map), 74.

40. OR, 46, 1:680; and Calkins, *Appomattox Campaign*, 74, 57 (map), 72 (map).

41. OR, 46, 1:101, 107, 1019.

42. OR, 46, 1:1160, 1161.

43. OR, 46, 1: 55, 1161; and Calkins, *Appomattox Campaign*, 74.

44. Calkins, *Appomattox Campaign*, 74; OR, 46, 1:1161; and again Calkins, *Appomattox Campaign*, 74.

45. Freeman, *R. E. Lee*, 4:66; and Calkins, *Appomattox Campaign*, 76.

46. Christopher M. Calkins, "From Petersburg to Appomattox: A Tour Guide to the Routes of Lee's Withdrawal and Grant's Pursuit" (Philadelphia: Eastern National Park and Monument Association, 1983; reprint, Farmville VA: Farmville Herald, 1990), 14; and Marvel, *Lee's Last Retreat*, 44, 49–50.

47. OR, 46, 1:1296; Marvel, *Lee's Last Retreat*, 49; and William Marvel, "Retreat to Appomattox," *Blue & Gray* 18, no. 4 (Spring 2001): 9.

48. Calkins, "From Petersburg to Appomattox," 15; and Calkins, *Appomattox Campaign*, 77.

49. Calkins, *Appomattox Campaign*, 69; and Marvel, *Lee's Last Retreat*, 49.

50. See Marvel, *Lee's Last Retreat*, 49–50. And in the appendix (207–13), Marvel further assesses the Genito Bridge delay.

51. Trudeau, *Out of the Storm*, 190; and Thomas Thatcher Graves, "The Occupation," in Johnson and Buel, *Battles and Leaders*, 4:728.

52. Donald, *Lincoln*, 577.

53. OR, 46, 1:75, 101; Calkins, *Appomattox Campaign*, 78; and OR, 46, 3:545.

54. Calkins, *Appomattox Campaign*, 56 (map), 78–79; OR, 46, 1:1019; and J. [James W. Cartwright] to Dear Mother, April 8, 1865, James W. Cartwright

Correspondence, Cartwright Family Papers, United States Army Heritage and Education Center, Carlisle PA.

55. Calkins, *Appomattox Campaign*, 77.

56. Calkins, *Appomattox Campaign*, 56 (map); and OR, 46, 1:1149, 1157–58.

57. OR, 46, 1:86.

58. Calkins, *Appomattox Campaign*, 56 (map). On page 201, Calkins gives the strength of the V Corps on April 9 as 12,323. The unit fought no major battles between the fourth and the ninth.

59. Freeman, *R. E. Lee*, 4:66; Calkins, *Appomattox Campaign*, 75; and Marvel, *Place Called Appomattox*, 202.

60. Freeman, *R. E. Lee*, 4:71; and Calkins, *Appomattox Campaign*, 85.

61. Calkins, *Appomattox Campaign*, 90; and Marvel, *Place Called Appomattox*, 204.

62. Calkins, *Appomattox Campaign*, 91.

63. Calkins, *Appomattox Campaign*, 91; and Marvel, *Place Called Appomattox*, 204.

64. Calkins, *Appomattox Campaign*, 56 (map), 91; and Marvel, *Place Called Appomattox*, 204–5.

65. Calkins, *Appomattox Campaign*, 95; and Marvel, *Place Called Appomattox*, 205.

66. OR, 46, 3:573.

67. Calkins, *Appomattox Campaign*, 89; and OR, 46, 1:1161.

68. OR, 46, 1:75, 101, 681; and Theodore Lyman, *With Grant and Meade from the Wilderness to Appomattox*, comp. and ed. George R. Agassiz (Lincoln: University of Nebraska Press, 1994), 346.

69. OR, 46, 1:681, 905; Lyman, *With Grant and Meade*, 346; and Calkins, *Appomattox Campaign*, 56 (map).

70. Calkins, *Appomattox Campaign*, 57 (map).

71. Lyman, *With Grant and Meade*, 345, 345–46; and Calkins, "From Petersburg to Appomattox," 10.

72. OR, 46, 3:582; and Porter, "Five Forks," 4:720.

73. OR, 46, 3:582; Sheridan, *Personal Memoirs*, 2:177; and Grant, *Personal Memoirs*, 2:469.

74. Porter, "Five Forks," 4:720; and Grant, *Personal Memoirs*, 2:469.

75. Simpson, "Facilitating Defeat," in Grimsley and Simpson, *Collapse of the Confederacy*, 95.

76. Calkins, *Appomattox Campaign*, 97; OR, 46, 1:1265; and Freeman, *R. E. Lee*, 4:81–82.

77. Calkins, *Appomattox Campaign*, 99.

78. Calkins, *Appomattox Campaign*, 97; and OR, 46, 1:1107.

79. OR, 46, 1:681, 906.

80. OR, 46, 1:840, 1174.

81. Freeman, *R. E. Lee*, 4:88–90; and OR, 46, 1:1294.

82. Calkins, *Appomattox Campaign*, 105. Holt is identified in Marvel, *Lee's Last Retreat*, 67.

83. OR, 46, 1:1294; and Marvel, *Lee's Last Retreat*, 68. Marvel deduced "Swep" Marshall's identity from census records (255n01).

Calkins, *Appomattox Campaign*, 118, explains that "Sailor's" Creek—rather than "Sayler's," "Saylor's," or "Sailer's"—was the Civil War spelling.

84. OR, 46, 1:1294.

85. OR, 46, 1:1294; Calkins, *Appomattox Campaign*, 105; and Marvel, "Retreat to Appomattox," 14 (map).

86. Freeman, *R. E. Lee*, 4:90.

87. Calkins, *Appomattox Campaign*, 111 (map); and OR, 46, 1:1295.

88. Calkins, *Appomattox Campaign*, 110; and OR, 46, 1:1295.

89. Freeman, *Lee's Lieutenants*, 3:702–3; and Freeman, *R. E. Lee*, 4:90.

90. OR, 46, 1:1295.

91. Calkins, *Appomattox Campaign*, 111 and 111 (map).

92. Calkins, *Appomattox Campaign*, 111 (map).

93. Calkins, *Appomattox Campaign*, 108 and 111 (map).

94. Calkins, *Appomattox Campaign*, 108; and Marvel, *Lee's Last Retreat*, 67.

95. Calkins, *Appomattox Campaign*, 108; and Marvel, "Retreat to Appomattox," 16.

96. Calkins, *Appomattox Campaign*, 108.

97. OR, 46, 1:1297; Calkins, *Appomattox Campaign*, 109; and Freeman, *Lee's Lieutenants*, 3:705.

98. Calkins, *Appomattox Campaign*, 109, 111; and typescript of the Diary of Thomas Campbell, entry for Friday, April 7, [1865], Civil War Miscellaneous Collection, United States Army Heritage and Education Center, Carlisle PA.

99. OR, 46, 1:953; and Calkins, *Appomattox Campaign*, 111.

100. Calkins, *Appomattox Campaign*, 112; Marvel, "Retreat to Appomattox," 19; and photocopy of the Diary of Ordnance Sgt. James W. Albright, entry for April 6, [1865], Virginia Historical Society, Richmond.

101. Calkins, *Appomattox Campaign*, 112. Historian William Marvel suggests that a ninth Confederate general, Theodore W. Brevard, may have been captured at Sailor's Creek. See Marvel, *Lee's Last Retreat*, 92.

102. Marvel, *Lee's Last Retreat*, 91.

103. Calkins, *Appomattox Campaign*, 113.

104. Marvel, *Lee's Last Retreat*, 88–89; and Calkins, "From Petersburg to Appomattox," 31.

105. Marvel, *Lee's Last Retreat*, 89; and Christopher M. Calkins, "Thirty-Six Hours before Appomattox, April 6 and 7, 1865" (reprint, Farmville VA: Farmville Herald, 1998), 30 and 30 (map).

106. Marvel, *Lee's Last Retreat*, 89.

107. Calkins, *Appomattox Campaign*, 114; Marvel, *Lee's Last Retreat*, 89; Giles Buckner Cooke Diary, entry for Thursday, April 6, [1865].

108. Calkins, *Appomattox Campaign*, 114. On the dispositions of the two divisions of the II Corps, see also Calkins, "Thirty-Six Hours before Appomattox," 30 (map).

109. Marvel, *Lee's Last Retreat*, 89–90; and Giles Buckner Cooke Diary, entry for Thursday, April 6, [1865].

110. Calkins, *Appomattox Campaign*, 114; and Marvel, *Lee's Last Retreat*, 90.

111. Calkins, *Appomattox Campaign*, 202. In "Thirty-Six Hours before Appomattox," 2, Calkins offers a corrective to exaggerations of Confederate losses at Sailor's Creek. Freeman, for example, overstated the percentage they represented of Lee's total numbers. See Freeman, *Lee's Lieutenants*, 3:711.

8. Spring Morning

1. Photocopy of the Diary of Ordnance Sgt. James W. Albright, entry for April 6, [1865], Virginia Historical Society, Richmond; typescript of the Diary of Cornelius Hart Carlton, entry for Wednesday, [April] 5, [1865], Virginia Historical Society, Richmond VA; and transcript of R. W. Downman to My dear wife, April 6, [1865], Downman Family Papers, 1699–1909, Virginia Historical Society, Richmond.

2. Marvel, *Place Called Appomattox*, 215; and Marvel, *Lee's Last Retreat*, 127.

3. Typescript of the Diary of Cornelius Hart Carlton, entries for Tu[esday], [April] 4, and Wednesday, [April] 5, [1865]. Carlton became so ill that he barely could sit on his horse, and he himself dropped out of the ranks on April 7.

4. Marvel, *Lee's Last Retreat*, 52; and Giles Buckner Cooke Diary, entry for Saturday, April 8, [1865], Virginia Historical Society, Richmond.

5. "Opposing Forces in the Appomattox Campaign," in Johnson and Buel, *Battles and Leaders*, 4:753; and Calkins, *Appomattox Campaign*, 202.

6. "Opposing Forces in the Appomattox Campaign," in Johnson and Buel, *Battles and Leaders*, 4:753. This number of 15,000 falls at the low end of Marvel's estimated range of "at least 14,400, and perhaps as many as 20,400" deserters, but he begins his accounting period on March 10. See Marvel, *Lee's Last Retreat*, 205. Marvel (201–6) makes a strong case that desertion ran high during the retreat and that, logically enough, the farther away from the scene of operations a soldier lived, the less likely he was to desert.

7. Freeman, *R. E. Lee*, 4:97.

8. Calkins, "Thirty-Six Hours," 44 (map); Marvel, *Place Called Appomattox*, 31, 41; and Trudeau, *Out of the Storm*, 102.

9. Marvel, *Place Called Appomattox*, 31, 41; Lyman, *With Grant and Meade*, 352; and Marvel, "Retreat to Appomattox," 11 (photograph).

10. Calkins, *Appomattox Campaign*, 123–24; and Calkins, "Thirty-Six Hours," 48 (map).

11. Calkins, *Appomattox Campaign*, 101–5; and Trudeau, *Out of the Storm*, 102, 104–6.

12. Warner, *Generals in Gray*, 70.

13. Freeman, *Lee's Lieutenants*, 3:710; Humphreys, *Virginia Campaign*, 2:385; and Marvel, "Retreat to Appomattox," 12.

14. Calkins, *Appomattox Campaign*, 115.

15. Marvel, *Place Called Appomattox*, 214–15.

16. Calkins, *Appomattox Campaign*, 116; and Marvel, *Place Called Appomattox*, 215–16.

17. Calkins, *Appomattox Campaign*, 116, 123, 124.

18. Calkins, *Appomattox Campaign*, 116.

19. Marvel, *Lee's Last Retreat*, 121; and T. M. R. Talcott, "From Petersburg to Appomattox," *Southern Historical Society Papers* 32 (1904): 71. Mahone offered a different version of the story, in which he got Lee to modify a direct order; he presumptuously advised Lee as to how an order should best be given; and he shifted responsibility for firing the bridges to Gordon, a superior officer outside of his own chain of command. William Mahone, "On the Road to Appomattox," ed. William C. Davis, *Civil War Times Illustrated* 9, no. 9 (January 1971): 10–11, 42; and Marvel, *Lee's Last Retreat*, 121.

20. OR, 46, 1:674; and Calkins, *Appomattox Campaign*, 125.

21. OR, 46, 1:758, 763; and Marvel, *Lee's Last Retreat*, 121–22.

22. Calkins, *Appomattox Campaign*, 126; and OR, 46, 1:764.

23. OR, 46, 1:758; and Marvel, *Lee's Last Retreat*, 122.

24. OR, 46, 1:763–64; Calkins, *Appomattox Campaign*, 127; and Oesterle, "Incidents Connected with the Civil War," 14, Frederick W. Oesterle Papers.

25. Calkins, *Appomattox Campaign*, 127; Marvel, *Lee's Last Retreat*, 122; and OR, 46, 1:758.

26. Calkins, *Appomattox Campaign*, 128; and Marvel, *Lee's Last Retreat*, 124.

27. Warner, *Generals in Blue*, 465; OR, 46, 1:567; Marvel, *Lee's Last Retreat*, 126; and Charley [Charles E. Field] to Dear Hattie, April 16, 1865, Hattie Burleigh Papers, United States Army Heritage and Education Center, Carlisle PA.

28. Marvel, *Lee's Last Retreat*, 126.

29. Marvel, *Lee's Last Retreat*, 126; Charley [Charles E. Field] to Dear Hattie, April 16, 1865, Hattie Burleigh Papers; and Calkins, *Appomattox Campaign*, 141.

30. Marvel, *Lee's Last Retreat*, 124; Calkins, "Thirty-Six Hours," 53; and Calkins, *Appomattox Campaign*, 57 (map).

31. Calkins, "From Petersburg to Appomattox," 33; and Marvel, *Lee's Last Retreat*, 124.

32. Calkins, *Appomattox Campaign*, 132 (map).

33. Calkins, *Appomattox Campaign*, 131.

34. Calkins, *Appomattox Campaign*, 131.

35. Marvel, *Place Called Appomattox*, 217; Calkins, *Appomattox Campaign*, 133; and OR, 46, 1:674.

36. Calkins, *Appomattox Campaign*, 133–34; and Longacre, *Cavalry at Appomattox*, 163–65. Longacre offers a sensible analysis of Maj. Gen. Thomas L. Rosser's claim that he trapped Gregg.

37. OR, 46, 1:1120; and Calkins, *Appomattox Campaign*, 137. Prince Edward Court House is today's Worsham, Virginia. Calkins, *Appomattox Campaign*, 136.

38. Longacre, *Cavalry at Appomattox*, 167.

39. Calkins, *Appomattox Campaign*, 125, 137.

40. Calkins, *Appomattox Campaign*, 130, 136.

41. OR, 46, 1:907, 908.

42. Horace Porter, "The Surrender at Appomattox Court House," in Johnson and Buel, *Battles and Leaders*, 4:729; typescript of the Diary of Thomas Campbell, entry for Saturday, April 8 [1865], Civil War Miscellaneous Collection, United States Army Heritage and Education Center, Carlisle PA; Simpson, *Ulysses S. Grant*, 429; and Calkins, "Thirty-Six Hours," 56, 57 (photograph).

43. Simpson, *Ulysses S. Grant*, 429; and Porter, *Campaigning with Grant*, 459. Lt. Col. Theodore Lyman offered an account that ascribed similar remarks to some of Ewell's staff officers, as well as to the general himself, and cited them as speculating that if called on to surrender, Lee might do so. Lyman, *With Grant and Meade*, 354. They are reports of rumors; the specifics vary slightly, but the fundamental import is the same.

44. OR, 46, 3:633; Calkins, *Appomattox Campaign*, 57 (map); and Porter, *Campaigning with Grant*, 459. Sheridan referred to Appomattox Station as Appomattox Depot. Known then by either name, the town today is Appomattox, Virginia.

45. Simpson, *Ulysses S. Grant*, 429; and OR, 46, 3:619.

46. Calkins, *Appomattox Campaign*, 135; Marvel, *Lee's Last Retreat*, 132–33; and Longstreet, *From Manassas to Appomattox*, 619.

47. OR, 46, 3:619; Marvel, *Lee's Last Retreat*, 133; and Calkins, *Appomattox Campaign*, 138.

48. Marvel, *Lee's Last Retreat*, 57, 63, 146; and Calkins, *Appomattox Campaign*, 154.

49. Marvel, *Lee's Last Retreat*, 137; and Calkins, *Appomattox Campaign*, 138.

50. Calkins, *Appomattox Campaign*, 57 (map); and Marvel, *Lee's Last Retreat*, 135.

51. Calkins, *Appomattox Campaign*, 138.

52. Calkins, *Appomattox Campaign*, 57 (map), 147; and Marvel, *Lee's Last Retreat*, 137, 139.

53. OR, 46, 3:641; Simpson, *Ulysses S. Grant*, 430; and Marvel, *Lee's Last Retreat*, 140.

54. Lyman, *With Grant and Meade*, 354.

55. Simpson, *Ulysses S. Grant*, 430; Porter, *Campaigning with Grant*, 462; and Lyman, *With Grant and Meade*, 345, 355.

56. Calkins, *Appomattox Campaign*, 156.

57. Calkins, *Appomattox Campaign*, 147; Calkins, "From Petersburg to Appomattox," 10; and OR, 46, 1:675, 908.

58. OR, 46, 1:1120; and Marvel, *Lee's Last Retreat*, 142.

59. Marvel, *Lee's Last Retreat*, 142; Calkins, *Appomattox Campaign*, 150; and OR, 46, 1109.

60. Marvel, *Lee's Last Retreat*, 146; and Calkins, *Appomattox Campaign*, 152 (map).

61. Calkins, *Appomattox Campaign*, 154; and OR, 46, 1:1282.

62. Warner, *Generals in Blue*, 108–9; Marvel, *Lee's Last Retreat*, 147; Calkins, *Appomattox Campaign*, 152–53; and OR, 46, 1:1132.

63. Marvel, *Lee's Last Retreat*, 147; and Calkins, *Appomattox Campaign*, 154.

64. Marvel, *Lee's Last Retreat*, 147; Calkins, *Appomattox Campaign*, 154; and OR, 46, 1:1132.

65. Marvel, *Lee's Last Retreat*, 148, 149; and OR, 46, 1:1132.

66. Calkins, *Appomattox Campaign*, 155–56.

67. OR, 46, 1:1162; Calkins, *Appomattox Campaign*, 151–52; and Marvel, *Lee's Last Retreat*, 143.

68. OR, 46, 1:841.

69. Calkins, *Appomattox Campaign*, 155; and Calkins, "From Petersburg to Appomattox," 36 (map), 37.

70. Marvel, *Lee's Last Retreat*, 152–53; and Calkins, *Appomattox Campaign*, 155–56.

71. OR, 46, 3:641; Simpson, *Ulysses S. Grant*, 431; and Marvel, *Lee's Last Retreat*, 156–57.

72. Marvel, *Lee's Last Retreat*, 156; Calkins, *Appomattox Campaign*, 157; and Calkins, "From Petersburg to Appomattox," 35.

73. Porter, *Campaigning with Grant*, 462–63; and Simpson, *Ulysses S. Grant*, 431–32.

74. Porter, *Campaigning with Grant*, 463.

75. Porter, *Campaigning with Grant*, 463–64; and OR, 46, 3:664.

76. Longacre, *Cavalry at Appomattox*, 185; and Catton, *Stillness at Appomattox*, 375.

77. Calkins, *Appomattox Campaign*, 160; and Marvel, *Lee's Last Retreat*, 162–63.

78. Calkins, *Appomattox Campaign*, 160 (map).

79. Calkins, *Appomattox Campaign*, 156; Marvel, *Lee's Last Retreat*, 159; and OR, 46, 1:576.

80. Calkins, *Appomattox Campaign*, 161; Trudeau, *Out of the Storm*, 134; and transcript of the Reminiscences of Erasmus Taylor, 10, Virginia Historical Society, Richmond.

81. Marvel, *Lee's Last Retreat*, 163; and Trudeau, *Out of the Storm*, 135.

82. Trudeau, *Out of the Storm*, 134; and Freeman, *R. E. Lee*, 4:119.

83. Marvel, *Lee's Last Retreat*, 166; and Marvel, "Retreat to Appomattox," 52.

84. Calkins, *Appomattox Campaign*, 161, 162.

85. Calkins, *Appomattox Campaign*, 161; and Longacre, *Cavalry at Appomattox*, 188.

86. Calkins, *Appomattox Campaign*, 162; Marvel, "Retreat to Appomattox," 52; and Longacre, *Cavalry at Appomattox*, 193.

87. Marvel, *Lee's Last Retreat*, 170; and Calkins, *Appomattox Campaign*, 164.

88. Lyman, *With Grant and Meade*, 355, 356.

89. Marvel, *Lee's Last Retreat*, 171; and Longstreet, *From Manassas to Appomattox*, 625.

90. Marvel, *Lee's Last Retreat*, 171, 173.

91. Marvel, *Lee's Last Retreat*, 173; Humphreys, *Virginia Campaign*, 2: 392; and OR, 46, 3:664. There are small differences between the accounts of Humphreys and Marvel, who cites Marshall's memoirs, but the fundamental direction and outcome of their narratives are the same.

Humphreys referred to his staff officer as a colonel, the rank he received by brevet at the end of the war. Heitman, *Historical Register*, 1:1032.

92. OR, 46, 3:664; and Marvel, *Lee's Last Retreat*, 173.

93. OR, 46, 3:664.

94. Calkins, *Appomattox Campaign*, 168; Lyman, *With Grant and Meade*, 355; and OR, 46, 3:666. See also Lee's message to Grant on April 9 (the time when it was sent is not given), OR, 46, 3:665.

95. Calkins, *Appomattox Campaign*, 168; and OR, 46, 3:665. Marvel, *Lee's Last Retreat*, 173, indicates that Marshall sent two duplicate dispatches, based on information from Whittier to Marshall. See OR, 46, 3:664. Lee's dispatch, which appears on OR, 46, 3:665, directly mentions Meade's suggestion.

96. Marvel, *Lee's Last Retreat*, 177; and Marvel, *Place Called Appomattox*, 9–10, 76–77.

97. Marvel, *A Place Called Appomattox*, 9, 239.

98. Marvel, *Lee's Last Retreat*, 174–75; and transcript of the Reminiscences of Erasmus Taylor, 10.

99. Calkins, *Appomattox Campaign*, 165; Marvel, *Lee's Last Retreat*, 176; and Robert W. Parker, *Lee's Last Casualty: The Life and Letters of Sgt. Robert W. Parker, Second Virginia Cavalry*, ed. Catherine M. Wright (Knoxville: University of Tennessee Press, 2008), xxvi.

100. Calkins, *Appomattox Campaign*, 202.

101. Calkins, *Appomattox Campaign*, 169; and Simpson, *Ulysses S. Grant*, 432. The distance from the Stage Road to Walker's Church is calculated from Calkins, "From Petersburg to Appomattox," 28 (map).

102. Simpson, *Ulysses S. Grant*, 432; Marvel, *Lee's Last Retreat*, 179; and Calkins, *Appomattox Campaign*, 169.

103. Calkins, *Appomattox Campaign*, 169; OR, 46, 3:664; and Marvel, *Lee's Last Retreat*, 179.

104. Simpson, *Ulysses S. Grant*, 433; Calkins, *Appomattox Campaign*, 169; and OR, 46, 3:665.

105. Calkins, "From Petersburg to Appomattox," 37; Marvel, *A Place Called Appomattox*, 239; and Calkins, *Appomattox Campaign*, 169.

106. Calkins, *Appomattox Campaign*, 170; and Marvel, *Lee's Last Retreat*, 179.

107. Calkins, *Appomattox Campaign*, 170; and Marvel, *Place Called Appomattox*, 3–4, 222 (map).

108. Marvel, *Place Called Appomattox*, 239.

109. Marvel, *Place Called Appomattox*, 88, 114.

110. Marvel, *Place Called Appomattox*, 239–40; and Porter, *Campaigning with Grant*, 471.

111. Marvel, *Place Called Appomattox*, 240; and Porter, *Campaigning with Grant*, 472.

112. Marvel, *Place Called Appomattox*, 240.

113. Marvel, *Place Called Appomattox*, 240.

114. Simpson, *Ulysses S. Grant*, 433; and Porter, *Campaigning with Grant*, 472.

115. Porter, *Campaigning with Grant*, 472, 475.

116. Porter, *Campaigning with Grant*, 473.

117. Porter, *Campaigning with Grant*, 472–73, 475; and Simpson, *Ulysses S. Grant*, 434.

118. Simpson, *Ulysses S. Grant*, 434; and Porter, *Campaigning with Grant*, 476.

119. Porter, *Campaigning with Grant*, 476; and Simpson, *Ulysses S. Grant*, 74, 434.

120. Simpson, *Ulysses S. Grant*, 434; and OR, 46, 3:665.

121. Simpson, *Ulysses S. Grant*, 435; and OR, 46, 3:665. See also Simpson, "Facilitating Defeat," in Grimsley and Simpson, *Collapse of the Confederacy*, 96.

122. Simpson, *Ulysses S. Grant*, 434–35. Historian Jay Winik finds it "almost miraculous" that bloody civil warfare did not continue after the Confederate armies surrendered in April 1865. Instead, he contends, two nations became one, making "the story of April 1865 not just the tale of the war's denouement but, in countless ways, the story of the making of our nation." Jay Winik, *April 1865: The Month That Saved America* (New York: HarperCollins, 2001), xii, xiv. The last sentence of Grant's surrender terms took a long step toward reconciliation.

123. Porter, *Campaigning with Grant*, 477–78, 478–79, 483.

124. Simpson, "Facilitating Defeat," in Grimsley and Simpson, *Collapse of the Confederacy*, 96.

125. "Opposing Forces in the Appomattox Campaign," in Johnson and Buel, *Battles and Leaders*, 4:753; and Calkins, *Appomattox Campaign*, 188.

126. "Opposing Forces in the Appomattox Campaign," in Johnson and Buel, *Battles and Leaders*, 4:753.

127. Calkins, *Appomattox Campaign*, 175; and Charley [Charles E. Field] to Dear Hattie, April 16, 1865, Hattie Burleigh Papers.

9. A Scrap of Paper

1. OR, 47, 1:43; and W. T. Sherman to Dearest Ellen, March 26, 1865, in Simpson and Berlin, *Sherman's Civil War*, 836–37.

2. Grimsley, "Learning to Say 'Enough,'" in Grimsley and Simpson, *Collapse of the Confederacy*, 58; Duncan [Campbell] to My dear Wife, March 22, 1865, Campbell Family Papers, Southern Historical Collection, University of North Carolina at Chapel Hill; and OR, 47, 1:1057.

3. Johnston, *Narrative of Military Operations*, 373–74, 394. Johnston's muster rolls give him more than twenty-nine thousand men on April 7. OR, 47, 3:764, 766. Historian Mark Bradley, citing a manuscript source, credits him with more than thirty thousand. See Mark L. Bradley, *This Astounding Close: The Road to Bennett Place* (Chapel Hill: University of North Carolina Press, 2000), 79, 318–19n65.

4. Bradley, *This Astounding Close*, 80; OR, 47, 1:1061–66; and OR, 47, 3:733–34.

5. Johnston, *Narrative of Military Operations*, 396; and OR, 47, 3:777.

6. Bradley, *This Astounding Close*, 130.

7. Bradley, *This Astounding Close*, 131.

8. Bradley, *This Astounding Close*, 91.

9. Bradley, *This Astounding Close*, 130–31; and Johnston, *Narrative of Military Operations*, 372.

10. Cooper, *Jefferson Davis*, 525.

11. [William T. Sherman] to Dearest Ellen, April 9, 1865, in Simpson and Berlin, *Sherman's Civil War*, 853; Warner, *Generals in Blue*, 348; and John [Oliver] to My Dear wife, March 27, 1865, Box 39, Papers of Brig. Gen. John M. Oliver, Lewis Leigh Collection, United States Army Heritage and Education Center, Carlisle PA.

12. [Solon A. Carter] to My own precious Emily, April 9, 1865, Solon A. Carter Papers, United States Army Heritage and Education Center, Carlisle PA; and OR, 47, 1:30.

13. Johnston, *Narrative of Military Operations*, 396; and Bradley, *This Astounding Close*, 91.

14. Cooper, *Jefferson Davis*, 525; Warner *Generals in Blue*, 481; and Bradley, *This Astounding Close*, 136.

15. Bradley, *This Astounding* Close, 137; and McWhiney, *Southerners and Other Americans*, 98.

16. Bradley, *This Astounding Close*, 137.

17. Bradley, *This Astounding Close*, 63–64, 137–38, 138, 139; and Cooper, *Jefferson Davis*, 525.

18. McWhiney, *Southerners and Other Americans*, 97–98; OR, 47, 3:788; and Bradley, *This Astounding Close*, 95.

19. Bradley, *This Astounding Close*, 103; and W. T. Sherman to Lt. Gen. U. S. Grant, April 12, 1865, in Simpson and Berlin, *Sherman's Civil War*, 859.

20. Symonds, *Joseph E. Johnston*, 354; and Bradley, *This Astounding Close*, 140.

21. Bradley, *This Astounding Close*, 136–37, 140.

22. Johnston, *Narrative of Military Operations*, 396–97; and Symonds, *Joseph E. Johnston*, 354.

23. Bradley, *This Astounding Close*, 140; and Davis, *Honorable Defeat*, 130.

24. Johnston, *Narrative of Military Operations*, 397, 398; and Grimsley, "Leaning to Say 'Enough,'" in Grimsley and Simpson, *Collapse of the Confederacy*, 63–64.

25. Bradley, *This Astounding Close*, 95–96.

26. Diary of W. W. Gordon, entry for [April] 12th, [1865], Gordon Family Papers, Southern Historical Collection, University of North Carolina at Chapel Hill.

27. Bradley, *This Astounding Close*, 127.

28. Bradley, *This Astounding Close*, 141; and Davis, *An Honorable Defeat*, 73.

29. Bradley, *This Astounding Close*, 141–42; and Cooper, *Jefferson Davis*, 525.

30. Bradley, *This Astounding Close*, 142; and Symonds, *Joseph E. Johnston*, 354.

31. Grimsley, "Learning to Say 'Enough,'" in Grimsley and Simpson, *Collapse of the Confederacy*, 64; and Johnston, *Narrative of Military Operations*, 398, 398–99.

32. Grimsley, "Learning to Say 'Enough,'" in Grimsley and Simpson, *Collapse of the Confederacy*, 64.

33. Symonds, *Joseph E. Johnston*, 355.

34. Symonds, *Joseph E. Johnston*, 355; and Johnston, *Narrative of Military Operations*, 399.

35. Bradley, *This Astounding Close*, 142–43; and Symonds, *Joseph E. Johnston*, 355.

36. Bradley, *This Astounding Close*, 143; and OR, 47, 3:206, 207.

37. Bradley, *This Astounding Close*, 143, 148, 146.

38. Bradley, *This Astounding Close*, 145, 154.

39. Warner, *Generals in Gray*, 183; Bradley, *This Astounding Close*, 116; and Diary of Joseph F. Waring, entry for April 16, 1865, Joseph Frederick Waring Papers, Southern Historical Collection, University of North Carolina at Chapel Hill. See also Bradley, *This Astounding Close*, 130.

40. Bradley, *This Astounding Close*, 116, 130; and OR, 47, 1:1083.

41. OR, 47, 1:31.

42. Bradley, *This Astounding Close*, 146; and OR *Atlas*, plate 138.

43. OR, 47, 1:31; and OR *Atlas*, plate 138. See also W. T. Sherman to Maj. Gen. Kilpatrick, April 14, 1865, in Simpson and Berlin, *Sherman's Civil War*, 860.

44. Edward J. Steers, Jr., *Blood on the Moon: The Assassination of Abraham Lincoln* (Lexington: University Press of Kentucky, 2001), 104; and Michael W. Kauffman, *American Brutus: John Wilkes Booth and the Lincoln Conspiracies* (New York: Random House, 2004), 4.

45. Bradley, *This Astounding Close*, 148. The dating of events here follows Bradley, who presents strong evidence that Sherman was mistaken in his

memoirs as to when he received this important letter. Bradley, *This Astounding Close*, 333n45; and see OR, 47, 3:206–7.

46. OR, 47, 3:207; Sherman, *Memoirs*, 2:347; and Bradley, *This Astounding Close*, 148.

47. OR, 47, 1:1083; and Bradley, *This Astounding Close*, 151–52.

48. Bradley, *This Astounding Close*, 152; Durward T. Stokes, *Company Shops: The Town Built by a Railroad* (Winston-Salem NC: J. F. Blair, 1981), 125; and Don Bolden, *Alamance in the Past* (Burlington NC: P. N. Thompson Printing, 1979), 150–51.

49. Bradley, *This Astounding Close*, 152.

50. Bradley, *This Astounding Close*, 152; and Diary of Joseph F. Waring, entry for April 15, 1865, Joseph Frederick Waring Papers.

51. Bradley, *This Astounding Close*, 154; Davis, *An Honorable Defeat*, 146; and Cooper, *Jefferson Davis*, 527.

52. OR, 47, 1:31; and OR *Atlas*, plate 138.

53. Bradley, *This Astounding Close*, 154; and Symonds, *Joseph E. Johnston*, 355.

54. Bradley, *This Astounding Close*, 154; and Cooper, *Jefferson Davis*, 528.

55. Bradley, *This Astounding Close*, 154; and Symonds, *Joseph E. Johnston*, 355.

56. Bradley, *This Astounding Close*, 154–55; OR, 47, 3:865; and OR *Atlas*, plate 138.

57. Bradley, *This Astounding Close*, 156; and Dave Roth with Mark L. Bradley, "The General's Tour: The Road to Bennett Place," *Blue & Gray Magazine* 17, no. 1 (Fall 1999): 65.

58. Bradley, *This Astounding Close*, 155–56, 336n75; and Sherman, *Memoirs*, 2:347.

59. Bradley, *This Astounding Close*, 156, 336n75; and Marszalek, *Sherman*, 341.

60. Bradley, *This Astounding Close*, 156; and OR, 47, 1:210.

61. OR, 47, 1:937; Sherman, *Memoirs*, 2:347–48; and OR, 47, 3:220–21.

62. Marszalek, *Sherman*, 342; and Sherman, *Memoirs*, 2:348.

63. Bradley, *This Astounding Close*, 158.

64. Bradley, *This Astounding Close*, 158; and Sherman, *Memoirs*, 2:348.

65. Diary of Joseph F. Waring, entry for Monday, [April] 17, 1865, Joseph Frederick Waring Papers; and Sherman, *Memoirs*, 2:348–49.

66. Sherman, *Memoirs*, 2:348; Roth with Bradley, "The General's Tour," 64; and "A Brief History of the Bennett Family," Bennett Place State Historic Site, Durham NC, http://www.bennettplacehistoricsite.com/history/bennett-family/, accessed March 30, 2012.

67. Exhibits in the Visitor Center, Bennett Place State Historic Site, Durham NC, March 27, 2012.

68. Roth with Bradley, "The General's Tour," 64; and exhibits in the Visitor Center, Bennett Place State Historic Site.

69. Diorama at the Visitor Center, Bennett Place State Historic Site; Sherman, *Memoirs*, 2:349; and Symonds, *Joseph E. Johnston*, 356.

70. Sherman, *Memoirs*, 2:349.

71. Sherman, *Memoirs*, 2:349; and Johnston, *Narrative of Military Operations*, 402.

72. OR, 47, 1:32; and Johnston, *Narrative of Military Operations*, 403.

73. Sherman, *Memoirs*, 2:349, 350.

74. Johnston, *Narrative of Military Operations*, 403–4.

75. Johnston, *Narrative of Military Operations*, 404; and Sherman, *Memoirs*, 2:350. When the generals discussed the adjournment in their memoirs, each emphasized the factors he thought most important. Their accounts are not identical, but they are compatible. Sherman stated in his memoirs that with the exception of one minor point that Sherman said he could not remember Johnston making, Johnston's account was "quite accurate and correct." Sherman, *Memoirs*, 2:350.

76. [Solon A. Carter] to My own precious wifey, April 18, 1865, Solon A. Carter Papers; John A. Boon to My Dear Family, April 20, 1865, John A. Boon Papers, Civil War Miscellaneous Collection, United States Army Heritage and Education Center, Carlisle PA; and Charlie to My dear friend Hattie, April 28, 1865, Hattie Burleigh Papers, United States Army Heritage and Education Center, Carlisle PA.

77. Marszalek, *Sherman*, 344, 343–44; and Bradley, *This Astounding Close*, 165.

78. Johnston, *Narrative of Military Operations*, 404.

79. Bradley, *This Astounding Close*, 165, 167; and Johnston, *Narrative of Military Operations*, 404.

80. Bradley, *This Astounding Close*, 168–69; and Symonds, *Joseph E. Johnston*, 355.

81. Bradley, *This Astounding Close*, 169.

82. Sherman, *Memoirs*, 2:352. See also "Proclamation of Amnesty and Reconstruction," December 8, 1863, in Lincoln, *Collected Works*, 7:53–56.

83. Sherman, *Memoirs*, 2:352; and Bradley, *This Astounding Close*, 170.

84. Sherman, *Memoirs*, 2:353; OR, 47, 3:244–45, 806–7; and Johnston, *Narrative of Military Operations*, 405.

85. Sherman, *Memoirs*, 2:353.

86. Sherman, *Memoirs*, 2: 356–57; OR, 47, 3:243–44; Johnston, *Narrative of Military Operations*, 405; and Bradley, *This Astounding Close*, 172.

87. Bradley, *This Astounding Close*, 171; and Sherman, *Memoirs*, 2:353.

88. OR, 47, 3:243–44.

89. William T. Sherman to Lt. Gen. U. S. Grant, or Maj. Gen. Halleck, April 18, 1865, in Simpson and Berlin, *Sherman's Civil War*, 864; and Grimsley, "Learning to Say 'Enough,'" in Grimsley and Simpson, *Collapse of the Confederacy*, 66.

90. Bradley, *This Astounding Close*, 176.

91. Simpson and Berlin, *Sherman's Civil War*, 856.

92. Simpson and Berlin, *Sherman's Civil War*, 857; and OR, 47, 1:32–33.

93. Simpson and Berlin, *Sherman's Civil War*, 857; and William T. Sherman to Lt. Gen. U.S. Grant, or Maj. Gen. Halleck, April 18, 1865, in Simpson and Berlin, *Sherman's Civil War*, 864.

94. Bradley, *This Astounding Close*, 266; Sherman, *Memoirs*, 2:351; and John M. Schofield, *Forty-six Years in the Army* (New York: Century, 1897), 350.

95. Simpson and Berlin, *Sherman's Civil War*, 857; and Simpson, "Facilitating Defeat," in Grimsley and Simpson, *Collapse of the Confederacy*, 99.

96. OR, 47, 3:244.

97. Bradley, *This Astounding Close*, 177, 180, 203.

98. Bradley, *This Astounding Close*, 178, 206.

99. Marszalek, *Sherman*, 345; and Bradley, *This Astounding Close*, 199, 200.

100. H. W. Slocum, "Final Operations of Sherman's Army," in Johnson and Buel, *Battles and Leaders*, 4:757; and Diary of Joseph F. Waring, entry for Saturday, [April] 22, [1865], Joseph Frederick Waring Papers.

101. Diary of Joseph F. Waring, entry for Sunday, [April] 16, [1865], Joseph Frederick Waring Papers; and Diary of W. W. Gordon, entry for [April] 20, [1865], Gordon Family Papers.

102. R. E. Lee to Mr. President, April 20, 1865, in Lee, *Wartime Papers*, 939.

103. Bradley, *This Astounding Close*, 203; and Cooper, *Jefferson Davis*, 528.

104. Bradley, *This Astounding Close*, 203–4; and Cooper, *Jefferson Davis*, 528.

105. Bradley, *This Astounding Close*, 207–8.

106. Bradley, *This Astounding Close*, 207; and Simpson, *Ulysses S. Grant*, 445.

107. Bradley, *This Astounding Close*, 209; Simpson, *Ulysses S. Grant*, 445–46; and Simpson and Berlin, *Sherman's Civil War*, 857.

108. Simpson and Berlin, *Sherman's Civil War*, 857; Bradley, *This Astounding Close*, 208; Warner, *Generals in Blue*, 196; Sherman, *Memoirs*, 2:371; Bradley, *This Astounding Close*, 232; and again Sherman, *Memoirs*, 2:372–73.

109. Sherman, *Memoirs*, 2:373; and Marszalek, *Sherman*, 356–57.

110. Sherman, *Memoirs*, 2:372–73, 375–76, 377.

111. Simpson, *Ulysses S. Grant*, 446; Bradley, *This Astounding Close*, 211, 227–28; and Marszalek, *Sherman*, 349.

112. Bradley, *This Astounding Close*, 210–11; OR, 47, 1:34; and OR, 47, 3:293, 294.

113. Bradley, *This Astounding Close*, 211; and OR, 47, 1:34.

114. Bradley, *This Astounding Close*, 213; and OR, 47, 3:835.

115. Bradley, *This Astounding Close*, 213; and OR, 47, 3:836.

116. OR, 47, 3:837, 838; and OR *Atlas*, plate 135-A. The orders to Stewart and Hardee are marked 5:00 p.m. Lee's orders have no time given, but since his corps was to leave an hour earlier, it is likely that they too were issued early that evening.

117. OR, 47, 3:303, 304.

118. For the movement of the XVII Corps, see OR, 47, 1:99, 104; and OR *Atlas*, plate 138. The itinerary for the corps refers to "Jones' Cross-Roads"; the one for the Second Brigade, Third Division, states, "Encamped on Jones' plantation." OR, 47, 1:90, 101. And for the XX Corps's march, see OR, 47, 1:596; and OR *Atlas*, plate 138.

119. OR, 47, 1:34; and OR, 47, 3:303, 304. Sherman also received a third dispatch from Johnston, very soon after the second, seeking confirmation that the truce would continue through the third Bennett Place meeting. OR, 47, 3:312.

120. Bradley, *This Astounding Close*, 219.

121. Bradley, *This Astounding Close*, 214–15; and OR, 47, 1:34.

122. Bradley, *This Astounding Close*, 227.

123. Bradley, *This Astounding Close*, 214.

124. Bradley, *This Astounding Close*, 215–16; and Schofield, *Forty-six Years*, 351–52, quotation 351.

125. James L. McDonough, *Schofield: Union General in the Civil War and Reconstruction* (Tallahassee: Florida State University Press, 1972), 158–59. See also Donald B. Connelly, *John M. Schofield and the Politics of Generalship* (Chapel Hill: University of North Carolina Press, 2006), 165–66.

126. OR, 47, 3:313; and Bradley, *This Astounding Close*, 216.

127. McDonough, *John M. Schofield*, 158.

128. OR, 47, 3:321, 482; and Connelly, *John M. Schofield*, 165.

129. OR, 47, 3:482.

130. Schofield, *Forty-six Years*, 352. Historian Mark Bradley shared Schofield's reaction. See Bradley, *This Astounding Close*, 217.

131. Bradley, *This Astounding Close*, 217.

132. This appreciation of Johnston's achievement is based on details that are presented in Bradley's fine campaign study *This Astounding Close* and ideas that are developed in Grimsley's insightful essay "Learning to Say 'Enough,'" in Grimsley and Simpson, *Collapse of the Confederacy*.

133. Steven E. Woodworth, *Nothing but Victory: The Army of the Tennessee, 1861–1865* (New York: Alfred A. Knopf, 2005), 640.

134. Woodworth, *Nothing but Victory*, 636.

135. Marszalek, *Sherman*, 355–56; Catton, *This Hallowed Ground*, 399; and Sherman, *Memoirs*, 2:378.

10. Scattered Embers

1. OR *Atlas*, plate 148. Modern maps show the highway distance is longer than forty miles.

2. Edward G. Longacre, *Mounted Raids of the Civil War* (South Brunswick NJ: A. S. Barnes, 1975), 319; and OR *Atlas*, plate 148.

3. Warner, *Generals in Blue*, 566–67; and "Opposing Forces in Wilson's Raid, March 22d–April 20, 1865," in Johnson and Buel, *Battles and Leaders*, 4:759.

4. OR, 49, 1:350; "Wilson's Raid through Alabama and Georgia," in Johnson and Buel, *Battles and Leaders*, 4:759; and Longacre, *Mounted Raids*, 313.

5. Brian Steel Wills, *The Confederacy's Greatest Cavalryman: Nathan Bedford Forrest* (reprint, Lawrence: University of Kansas Press, 1992), 10, quotation 16; and Longacre, *Mounted Raids*, 314.

6. OR, 49, 1:358; OR, 49, 2:173, 174; and James Harrison Wilson, *Under the Old Flag: Recollections of Military Operations in the War for the Union, the Spanish War, the Boxer Rebellion, Etc.* (New York: D. Appleton, 1912), 2:211.

7. OR, 49, 1:359, 360; Trudeau, *Out of the Storm*, 160; and Longacre, *Mounted Raids*, 317. Wilson estimated the defenders at seven thousand. OR, 49, 1:361. And again see Trudeau, *Out of the Storm*, 160.

8. Trudeau, *Out of the Storm*, 165.

9. OR, 49, 1:360.

10. Wilson, *Under the Old Flag*, 2:222, 226; Perry D. Jamieson, *Crossing the Deadly Ground: United States Army Tactics, 1865–1899* (Tuscaloosa: University of Alabama Press, 1994), 6; and OR, 49, 1:438.

11. OR, 49, 1:361, 369.

12. OR, 49, 1:352, 363–64.

13. OR, 49, 1:352, 371–72; and Wilson, *Under the Old Flag*, 2:281–82.

14. Sean Michael O'Brien, *Mobile, 1865: Last Stand of the Confederacy* (Westport CT: Praeger, 2001), 217; and Warner, *Generals in Gray*, 299–300.

15. O'Brien, *Mobile, 1865*, 13–14, 217; and OR, 49, 1:92, 1045. For a fine study of wartime Mobile and its defense, see Arthur W. Bergeron, Jr., *Confederate Mobile* (Jackson: University Press of Mississippi, 1991).

16. O'Brien, *Mobile, 1865*, 211.

17. Warner, *Generals in Blue*, 68; O'Brien, *Mobile, 1865*, 17, 32; and OR, 48, 1:1164. Canby's biographer called him "prudent" in the title of his study of the general's life: Max L. Heyman, Jr., *Prudent Soldier: A Biography of Major General E. R. S. Canby, 1817–1873* (Glendale CA: A. H. Clark, 1959).

18. Richard Taylor, "The Last Confederate Surrender," in *The Annals of the War Written by Leading Participants North and South; Originally Published in the "Philadelphia Weekly Times"* (reprint, Dayton OH: Morningside, 1988), 68–69; and OR, 49, 2:1275.

19. OR, 49, 2:440.

20. Heyman, *Prudent Soldier*, 232; "Magee Farm—Kushla, Alabama," Alabama Tourism, http://www.alabamabeautiful.com/gulf-coast/magee-farm-kushla-alabama.html, accessed March 13, 2012; and O'Brien, *Mobile, 1865*, 217.

21. O'Brien, *Mobile, 1865*, 218; Richard Taylor, *Destruction and Reconstruction: Personal Experiences of the Late War* (New York: Appleton, 1879), 224–25; and Taylor, "Last Confederate Surrender," 69.

22. OR, 49, 2:531–32; Taylor, "Last Confederate Surrender," 70; and OR, 49, 2:1275.

23. O'Brien, *Mobile, 1865*, 218.

24. O'Brien, *Mobile, 1865*, 220–21. O'Brien states that Taylor reported some eight thousand men to be surrendered, but twenty thousand presented themselves for paroles. O'Brien, *Mobile, 1865*, 220–21.

25. Davis, *Jefferson Davis*, 626; and Cooper, *Jefferson Davis*, 526–27, 532.

26. Davis, *Jefferson Davis*, 626; Warner, *Generals in Gray*, 62; and Cooper, *Jefferson Davis*, 530.

27. Cooper, *Jefferson Davis*, 530.

28. Cooper, *Jefferson Davis*, 531.

29. Cooper, *Jefferson Davis*, 531; Davis, *Jefferson Davis*, 632; Trudeau, *Out of the Storm*, 384; and Eli N. Evans, *Judah P. Benjamin: The Jewish Confederate* (New York: Free Press, 1988), 399.

30. Davis, *Jefferson Davis*, 633; and Cooper, *Jefferson Davis*, 531.

31. Davis, *Jefferson Davis*, 632; and Davis, *An Honorable Defeat*, 320.

32. Trudeau, *Out of the Storm*, 284; and Cooper, *Jefferson Davis*, 532–33.

33. Cooper, *Jefferson Davis*, 533; William Hanchett, *The Lincoln Murder Conspiracies* (Urbana: University of Illinois Press, 1983), 64–65; and James L. Swanson, *Bloody Crimes: The Chase for Jefferson Davis and the Death Pageant for Lincoln's Corpse* (New York: William Morrow/HarperCollins, 2010), 268–69.

34. Cooper, *Jefferson Davis*, 534; and Trudeau, *Out of the Storm*, 291–94.

35. Trudeau, *Out of the Storm*, 294. Davis, *Jefferson Davis*, 637, directly quotes this same remark but puts it in a slightly different context.

36. Cooper, *Jefferson Davis*, 536; and Davis, *An Honorable Defeat*, quotation 384, 384–86.

37. Kerby, *Kirby Smith's Confederacy*, 419; and Jeffrey Wm Hunt, *The Last Battle of the Civil War: Palmetto Ranch* (Austin: University of Texas Press, 2002), 2, 23. Kerby gives an excellent synopsis of the Battle of Palmito Ranch. A longer account can be found in Trudeau, *Out of the Storm*, 299–310. For book-length treatments, see Hunt, *Last Battle of the Civil War*; and Phillip Thomas Tucker, *The Final Fury: Palmito Ranch, The Last Battle of the Civil War* (Mechanicsburg PA: Stackpole Books, 2001).

38. Kerby, *Kirby Smith's Confederacy*, 419.

39. OR, 48, 1:267; Tucker, *Final Fury*, 136, 152–53; and Trudeau, *Out of the Storm*, 310. Hunt assigns the last shot to a seventeen-year-old member of Capt. W. H. D. Carrington's Confederate command. Hunt, *Last Battle of the Civil War*, 122, 171.

40. Tucker, *Final Fury*, 166.

41. Kerby, *Kirby Smith's Confederacy*, 419.

42. Warner, *Generals in Gray*, 280; and Trudeau, *Out of the Storm*, 335.

43. Trudeau, *Out of the Storm*, 339–40; and Kerby, *Kirby Smith's Confederacy*, 416–17.

44. OR, 48, 2:1308, 1308–9. Kirby Smith assigned Maxey to duty as a major general, but President Jefferson Davis never appointed him to that rank. OR, 48, 2:1286; and Warner, *Generals in Gray*, 216.

45. *OR*, 48, 2:1308.

46. OR, 48, 2:1312; Kerby, *Kirby Smith's Confederacy*, 422–23; and Trudeau, *Out of the Storm*, 340.

47. Kerby, *Kirby Smith's Confederacy*, 425; and OR, 48, 2:600–601.

48. "Notes on the Union and Confederate Armies," in Johnson and Buel, *Battles and Leaders*, 4:768; OR, 48, 2:601; and Kerby, *Kirby Smith's Confederacy*, 426, 428.

49. Warner, *Generals in Gray*, 280.

50. Trudeau, *Out of the Storm*, 360.

51. Warner, *Generals in Gray*, 327–28; and Trudeau, *Out of the Storm*, 360.

52. Drew Gilpin Faust, *This Republic of Suffering: Death and the American Civil War* (New York: Alfred A. Knopf, 2008), xi, 266.

53. Faust, *This Republic of Suffering*, 255, 257; and McPherson, *Battle Cry of Freedom*, 619n53.

54. Diary of Joseph F. Waring, entry for Friday, April 21, 1865, Joseph Frederick Waring Papers, Southern Historical Collection, University of North Carolina at Chapel Hill; photocopy of the Diary of Ordnance Sgt. James W. Albright, entry for April 9, [1865], Virginia Historical Society, Richmond; and Trudeau, *Out of the Storm*, 243.

55. General Order, No. 9, April 10, 1865, in Lee, *Wartime Papers*, 935. Lt. Col. Charles Marshall wrote General Lee's farewell order, but Lee reviewed, revised, and signed it. Freeman, *R. E. Lee*, 4:149–50, 154.

56. John A. Boon to Dear Hannah, April 20, 1865, John A. Boon Papers, Civil War Miscellaneous Collection, United States Army Heritage and Education Center, Carlisle PA; Trudeau, *Out of the Storm*, 243; and Marti [Martin R. Connally] to My dear Hattie, May 29, 1865, Hattie Burleigh Papers, United States Army Heritage and Education Center, Carlisle PA.

57. J. H. Baylis to Mr. William McAdams, September 24, 1902, Lt. William McAdams Papers, Civil War Miscellaneous Collection, United States Army Heritage and Education Center, Carlisle PA.

BIBLIOGRAPHIC ESSAY

Many works treat the last campaigns of the American Civil War or particular aspects of them. This essay identifies some of the sources that supported this book's accounts of the conflict's final operations, and it points readers to materials for further study of them. It is not a comprehensive list of every title on the subject.

The armies that conducted the war's last campaigns have received considerable attention from historians. Douglas Southall Freeman's classic achievement *Lee's Lieutenants: A Study in Command*, 3 vols. (New York: Charles Scribner's Sons, 1942–44), examines the senior leaders of the Army of Northern Virginia and provides a narrative history of that famous field force. J. Tracy Power's *Lee's Miserables: Life in the Army of Northern Virginia from the Wilderness to Appomattox* (Chapel Hill: University of North Carolina Press, 1998), a much more recent work, is an insightful treatment of the command's last months. Equally helpful are two splendid works by Joseph T. Glatthaar: *Soldiering in the Army of Northern Virginia: A Statistical Portrait of the Troops Who Served under Robert E. Lee* (Chapel Hill: University of North Carolina Press, 2001) and *General Lee's Army: From Victory to Collapse* (New York: Free Press, 2008). The Army of Northern Virginia's cavalry is surveyed in Edward G. Longacre's *Lee's Cavalrymen: A History of the Mounted Forces of the Army of Northern Virginia, 1861–1865* (Mechanicsburg PA: Stackpole Books, 2002).

Of Thomas Connelly's two groundbreaking volumes on the Army of Tennessee, *Autumn of Glory: The Army of Tennessee, 1862–1865* (Baton Rouge: Louisiana State University Press, 1971) covers the final operations. On the Confederate cavalry in the western theater, see Edward G. Longacre, *Cavalry of the Heartland: The Mounted Forces of the Army of Tennessee* (Yardley PA: Westholme, 2009). On the artillery, consult Larry J. Daniel, *Cannoneers in Gray: The Field Artillery of the Army of Tennessee, 1861–1865* (University: University of Alabama Press, 1984).

Among the Federal armies, the Army of the Potomac has received the greatest attention from historians. In the 1950s that field force was the subject of a beautifully written trilogy by Bruce Catton. He related the last campaigns in *A Stillness at Appomattox* (Garden City NY: Doubleday, 1953). During the decades after Catton's eloquent work, more volumes appeared about the main Union army in the eastern theater: Stephen W. Sears, *Controversies and Commanders: Dispatches from the Army of the Potomac* (Boston: Houghton Mifflin, 1999); Jeffry D. Wert, *The Sword of Lincoln: The Army of the Potomac* (New York: Simon & Schuster, 2005); and Stephen R. Taaffe, *Commanding the Army of the Potomac* (Lawrence: University Press of Kansas, 2006). In 2002 Da Capo Press published the first title in a multivolume study *Army of the Potomac* by Russel H. Beatie. The series has not yet reached the late-war period. Readers interested in the cavalry in the eastern theater will enjoy Edward G. Longacre's *Lincoln's Cavalrymen: A History of the Mounted Forces of the Army of the Potomac, 1861–1865* (Mechanicsburg PA: Stackpole Books, 2000).

The Army of the Potomac has attracted far more interest than its counterpart in the western theater, the Army of the Tennessee. The high quality of a few works goes far to make up for this lack of quantity. Strongly recommended are Steven E. Woodworth, *Nothing but Victory: The Army of the Tennessee, 1861–1865* (New York: Alfred A. Knopf, 2005), and Joseph T. Glatthaar, *The March to the Sea and Beyond: Sherman's Troops in the Savannah and Carolinas Campaigns* (New York: New York University Press, 1985).

Before and while these armies conducted the final campaigns, political leaders made efforts to negotiate an end to the war.

Some useful sources on these peace initiatives include: James Z. Rabun, "Alexander H. Stephens and Jefferson Davis," *American Historical Review* 58, no. 2 (January 1953): 290–321; Charles W. Sanders, Jr., "Jefferson Davis and the Hampton Roads Peace Conference: 'To Secure Peace to the Two Countries,'" *Journal of Southern History* 63, no. 4 (November 1997): 803–26; and Thomas E. Schott, *Alexander H. Stephens of Georgia: A Biography* (Baton Rouge: Louisiana State University Press, 1988).

The last campaigns of the Civil War are surveyed in Noah Andre Trudeau's *Out of the Storm: The End of the Civil War, April–June 1865* (Boston: Little, Brown, 1994); it thoroughly covers every theater of the conflict. Another wide-ranging and helpful work is William C. Davis's *An Honorable Defeat: The Last Days of the Confederate Government* (New York: Harcourt, 2001). Every serious student must read Mark Grimsley and Brooks D. Simpson, eds., *The Collapse of the Confederacy* (Lincoln: University of Nebraska Press, 2001), a collection of essays that is full of insights into the final operations of the war. Jay Winik related what he found remarkable about the conclusion of the Civil War in *April 1865: The Month That Saved America* (New York: HarperCollins, 2001).

Many strong volumes that focus on individual campaigns were greatly helpful in writing this book. There is no better example than Chris E. Fonvielle Jr.'s meticulous *The Wilmington Campaign: Last Rays of Departing Hope* (Campbell CA: Savas, 1997). It will be decades, if ever, before this operation again will be covered so thoroughly. Readers also will enjoy Charles M. Robinson III's shorter and clearly written *Hurricane of Fire: The Union Assault on Fort Fisher* (Annapolis: Naval Institute Press, 1998). Rod Gragg deserves credit for initially giving Fort Fisher the attention it merits with his *Confederate Goliath: The Battle of Fort Fisher* (New York: HarperCollins, 1991).

A good place to begin exploring the Carolinas campaign is an old standby, John G. Barrett's *Sherman's March through the Carolinas* (Chapel Hill: University of North Carolina Press, 1956). Marion Brunson Lucas, in *Sherman and the Burning of Columbia* (College Station: Texas A&M University Press, 1976), offers a balanced assessment of a tragic episode of the operations in South Carolina. Mark L. Bradley's remarkably thorough *This Astounding Close: The Road to Bennett Place* (Chapel Hill: University of North Carolina Press, 2000) greatly furthered the writing of this book.

A. Wilson Greene's *The Final Battles of the Petersburg Campaign: Breaking the Backbone of the Rebellion* (Knoxville: University of Tennessee Press, 2008), which has appeared in two editions, offers a compelling and exhaustive treatment of its subject. Noah Andre Trudeau's pioneering survey of the entire Petersburg campaign, *The Last Citadel: Petersburg, Virginia, June 1864–April 1865* (Boston: Little, Brown, 1991), also deserves attention. Earl J. Hess's *In the Trenches at Petersburg: Field Fortifications & Confederate Defeat* (Chapel Hill: University of North Carolina Press, 2009) is essential to understanding the operations around the Cockade City. Although Richard J. Sommers's *Richmond Redeemed: The Siege at Petersburg* (Garden City NY: Doubleday, 1981) covers an earlier period than that treated in this book, it is mentioned here because of the high standard it sets for future work on Petersburg and other Civil War campaigns. Also noted here is Andrew A. Humphreys's classic publication *The Virginia Campaign of '64 and '65: The Army of the Potomac and the Army of the James*, 2 vols. (New York: Charles Scribner's Sons, 1883). Beginners may find these two volumes tedious reading, but advanced students will appreciate them as the work of an experienced and intelligent Union senior officer. Humphreys covered not only Petersburg but all the operations in the eastern theater from the Wilderness to the end of the war.

The straightforward narrative in Chris M. Calkins's *The Appomattox Campaign: March 29–April 9, 1865* (Conshohocken PA: Combined Books, 1997) provides an excellent introduction to the Appomattox campaign. Students then should turn to two scholarly and provocative works by William A. Marvel: *Lee's Last Retreat: The Flight to Appomattox* (Chapel Hill: University of North Carolina Press, 2002), a survey history of the last major operations in the eastern theater; and *A Place Called Appomattox* (Chapel Hill: University of North Carolina Press, 2000), a study of their setting. The contending cavalries played important roles during the Appomattox campaign, and their activities are well recounted in Edward G. Longacre's lively *The Cavalry at Appomattox: A Tactical Study of*

Mounted Operations during the Civil War's Climactic Campaign, March 27–April 9, 1865 (Mechanicsburg PA: Stackpole Books, 2003).

The last campaigns produced no battles on the scale of Gettysburg or Chickamauga, but Bentonville, Five Forks, Sailor's Creek, and a few other late-war engagements were sizable combat actions. As with the campaign books mentioned earlier, some fine battle studies enormously helped in writing this volume. Mark L. Bradley's extraordinarily detailed *Last Stand in the Carolinas: The Battle of Bentonville* (Campbell CA: Savas Woodbury, 1996) proved particularly valuable. Nathaniel Cheairs Hughes, Jr., *Bentonville: The Final Battle of Sherman and Johnston* (Chapel Hill: University of North Carolina Press, 1996), a shorter volume than Bradley's, was equally useful. Its thoughtful analysis of the battle will help both beginning and advanced students of Bentonville develop their thinking about that engagement. Robert P. Broadwater's *Battle of Despair: Bentonville and the North Carolina Campaign* (Macon GA: Mercer University Press, 2004) should not be overlooked; it is a fine introduction to the subject. Broadwater offers a brief account that does a good job of putting the battle into its larger context. None of the late-war engagements in the eastern theater have attracted the attention Bentonville has, but Five Forks received book-length treatment by Ed Bearss and Chris Calkins in *Battle of Five Forks* (Lynchburg VA: H. E. Howard, 1985).

Secondary works that cover other battles of the last campaigns include: Arthur W. Bergeron, Jr., "The Battle of Hatcher's Run, February 5–7, 1865," *Civil War Magazine* 67 (April 1998): 44–49; Peter S. Carmichael, "The Battles of Lewis Farm and White Oak Road, March 29–30, 1865," *Civil War Magazine* 67 (April 1998): 53–57; Robert E. L. Krick, "The Assault on Fort Stedman, March 25, 1865," *Civil War Magazine* 67 (April 1998): 50–53; and Eric J. Wittenberg, *The Battle of Monroe's Crossroads and the Civil War's Final Campaign* (New York: Savas Beatie, 2006). Detailed information about some of the battles of the last campaigns also can be found in the issues of *Blue & Gray Magazine* that are listed in the last paragraph of this essay.

Robert L. Kerby's study of the Trans-Mississippi theater, *Kirby Smith's Confederacy: The Trans-Mississippi South, 1863–1865* (New York:

Columbia University Press, 1972), has held up well over time. On some of the specific episodes of the war's last weeks, see: Arthur W. Bergeron, Jr., *Confederate Mobile* (Jackson: University Press of Mississippi, 1991); Chris J. Hartley, *Stoneman's Raid, 1865* (Winston-Salem NC: John F. Blair, 2010); Chris J. Hartley, "Stoneman's 1865 Raid in Central North Carolina 'Driving Dixie Down,'" *Blue & Gray Magazine* 26, no. 6 (2010); Jeffrey Wm. Hunt, *The Last Battle of the Civil War: Palmetto Ranch* (Austin: University of Texas Press, 2002); Edward G. Longacre, *Mounted Raids of the Civil War* (South Brunswick NJ: A. S. Barnes, 1975), for its chapter on Wilson's raid; Sean Michael O'Brien, *Mobile, 1865: Last Stand of the Confederacy* (Westport CT: Praeger, 2001); James L. Swanson, *Bloody Crimes: The Chase for Jefferson Davis and the Death Pageant for Lincoln's Corpse* (New York: William Morrow/HarperCollins, 2010); Richard Taylor, "The Last Confederate Surrender," in *The Annals of the War Written by Leading Participants North and South; Originally Published in the "Philadelphia Weekly Times"* (reprint, Dayton OH: Morningside, 1988), 67–71; and Phillip Thomas Tucker, *The Final Fury: Palmito Ranch, the Last Battle of the Civil War* (Mechanicsburg PA: Stackpole Books, 2001).

The two presidents who served as commanders in chief during these campaigns have received enormous attention. Among the numerous biographies of Abraham Lincoln, an excellent starting point is David Herbert Donald's *Lincoln* (New York: Simon & Schuster, 1995). Much can be learned about the president during the last days of the war from Donald C. Pfanz, *The Petersburg Campaign: Abraham Lincoln at City Point, March 20–April 9, 1865* (Lynchburg VA: H. E. Howard, 1989). Lincoln's papers are available in Abraham Lincoln, *The Collected Works of Abraham Lincoln*, ed. Roy P. Basler, 9 vols. (New Brunswick NJ: Rutgers University Press, 1953–55).

Lincoln's opposite number also has attracted many biographers. This work benefited from William J. Cooper, *Jefferson Davis, American* (New York: Alfred A. Knopf, 2000); William C. Davis, *Jefferson Davis: The Man and His Hour* (New York: HarperCollins, 1991); and Herman Hattaway and Richard E. Beringer, *Jefferson Davis, Confederate President* (Lawrence: University Press of Kansas, 2002). James M. McPherson's *Embattled Rebel: Jefferson Davis as Comander in Chief*

(New York: Penguin, 2014) appeared too late to be used in this book, but it is recommended here. On the Confederate president and the close of the war, see Michael B. Ballard, *A Long Shadow: Jefferson Davis and the Final Days of the Confederacy* (Jackson: University Press of Mississippi, 1986); and *The Papers of Jefferson Davis* (Baton Rouge: Louisiana State University Press, 1971–) now runs through 1879, in thirteen volumes.

Like Jefferson Davis, Ulysses S. Grant has been the subject of many biographies. This work profited from two particularly fine efforts by Brooks D. Simpson: *Ulysses S. Grant: Triumph over Adversity, 1822–1865* (Boston: Houghton Mifflin, 2000) and *Let Us Have Peace: Ulysses S. Grant and the Politics of War and Reconstruction, 1861–1868* (Chapel Hill: University of North Carolina Press, 1991). Serious students of the war must become familiar with that landmark of American literature, Ulysses S. Grant's *Personal Memoirs of U.S. Grant*, 2 vols. (New York: C. L. Webster, 1886), and with *The Papers of Ulysses S. Grant*, 18 vols., edited by John Y. Simon (Carbondale: Southern Illinois University Press, 1967–91).

There are several biographies of Grant's friend and comrade William T. Sherman. Readers can begin with John F. Marszalek, *Sherman: A Soldier's Passion for Order* (New York: Free Press, 1993); then move to William T. Sherman, *Memoirs of Gen. W. T. Sherman*, 2 vols. (New York: C. L. Webster, 1892); and Brooks D. Simpson and Jean V. Berlin, eds., *Sherman's Civil War: Selected Correspondence of William T. Sherman, 1860–1865* (Chapel Hill: University of North Carolina Press, 1999). Edward G. Longacre's *Worthy Opponents: William T. Sherman and Joseph E. Johnston: Antagonists in War—Friends in Peace* (Nashville: Rutledge Hill Press, 2006) succinctly relates the wartime careers of these two generals and suggests that their friendship after the war reflected the larger reconciliation between the two sections of the nation during the late nineteenth century.

There are many helpful works either by, or about, other important Federal commanders in the last campaigns. They include Donald B. Connelly, *John M. Schofield and the Politics of Generalship* (Chapel Hill: University of North Carolina Press, 2006); Max L. Heyman, Jr., *Prudent Soldier: A Biography of Major General E. R. S. Canby,*

1817–1873 (Glendale CA: A. H. Clark, 1959); Oliver Otis Howard, *Autobiography of Oliver Otis Howard*, 2 vols. (New York: Baker & Taylor, 1907); Nathaniel Cheairs Hughes, Jr., and Gordon D. Whitney, *Jefferson Davis in Blue: The Life of Sherman's Relentless Warrior* (Baton Rouge: Louisiana State University Press, 2007); James L. McDonough, *Schofield: Union General in the Civil War and Reconstruction* (Tallahassee: Florida State University Press, 1972); Eugene D. Schmiel, *Citizen-General: Jacob Dolson Cox and the Civil War Era* (Athens: Ohio University Press, 2014); John M. Schofield, *Forty-six Years in the Army* (New York: Century, 1897); Philip H. Sheridan, *Personal Memoirs of P. H. Sheridan*, 2 vols. (New York: C. L. Webster, 1888); Paul Taylor, *Orlando M. Poe: Civil War General and Great Lakes Engineer* (Kent OH: Kent State University Press, 2009); and James Harrison Wilson, *Under the Old Flag: Recollections of Military Operations in the War for the Union, the Spanish War, the Boxer Rebellion, Etc.*, 2 vols. (New York: D. Appleton, 1912).

Gen. Robert E. Lee was a central figure in the American Civil War and accordingly has attracted much attention. It is still well to begin with Douglas Southall Freeman's magisterial *R. E. Lee: A Biography*, 4 vols. (New York: Charles Scribner's Sons, 1934–35). By focusing on Lee's personality rather than his generalship, Emory Thomas made a significant contribution to the literature with his *Robert E. Lee: A Biography* (New York: W. W. Norton, 1995). Two valuable collections of Lee materials are *The Wartime Papers of Robert E. Lee*, edited by Clifford Dowdey and Louis H. Manarin (Boston: Little, Brown, 1961), and Douglas Southall Freeman and Grady McWhiney, eds., *Lee's Dispatches: Unpublished Letters of General Robert E. Lee, C.S.A. to Jefferson Davis and the War Department of the Confederate States of America, 1862–1865* (Baton Rouge: Louisiana State University Press, 1994).

The Confederate commander in the western theater during the late-war period is the subject of Craig L. Symonds's well-crafted biography *Joseph E. Johnston: A Civil War Biography* (New York: Norton, 1992). The general told his own story in Joseph E. Johnston, *Narrative of Military Operations, Directed during the Late War between the States* (New York: Appleton, 1874). Students also can pursue their interest with Longacre's previously mentioned Johnston-Sherman study, *Worthy Opponents*.

Works about or by other key Confederate leaders include: Edward Porter Alexander, *Fighting for the Confederacy: The Personal Recollections of General Edward Porter Alexander*, edited by Gary W. Gallagher (Chapel Hill: University of North Carolina Press, 1989); Sam Davis Elliott, *Soldier of Tennessee: General Alexander P. Stewart and the Civil War in the West* (Baton Rouge: Louisiana State University Press, 1999); Gary W. Gallagher and Joseph T. Glatthaar, *Leaders of the Lost Cause: New Perspectives on the Confederate High Command* (Mechanicsburg PA: Stackpole Books, 2004); John B. Gordon, *Reminiscences of the Civil War* (New York: Charles Scribner's Sons, 1904); Leonne M. Hudson, *The Odyssey of a Southerner: The Life and Times of Gustavus Woodson Smith* (Macon GA: Mercer University Press, 1998); James Longstreet, *From Manassas to Appomattox: Memoirs of the Civil War in America* (Bloomington: Indiana University Press, 1960); Richard M. McMurry, *John Bell Hood and the War for Southern Independence* (Lexington: University Press of Kentucky, 1982); Grady McWhiney, *Braxton Bragg and Confederate Defeat*, vol. 1, *Field Command* (New York: Columbia University Press, 1969); Judith Lee Hallock, *Braxton Bragg and Confederate Defeat*, vol. 2 (Tuscaloosa: University of Alabama Press, 1991); T. Michael Parrish, *Richard Taylor: Soldier Prince of Dixie* (Chapel Hill: University of North Carolina Press, 1992); James I. Robertson, Jr., *General A. P. Hill: The Story of a Confederate Warrior* (New York: Random House, 1987); Alfred Roman, *The Military Operations of General Beauregard in the War between the States, 1861 to 1865; Including a Brief Personal Sketch and a Narrative of His Services in the War with Mexico, 1846–48*, 2 vols. (New York: Harper & Brothers, 1884); Richard Taylor, *Destruction and Reconstruction: Personal Experiences of the Late War* (New York: Appleton, 1879); Jeffry D. Wert, *General James Longstreet: The Confederacy's Most Controversial Soldier: A Biography* (New York: Simon & Schuster, 1993); T. Harry Williams, *P.G.T. Beauregard: Napoleon in Gray* (Baton Rouge: Louisiana State University Press, 1955); and Brian Steel Wills, *The Confederacy's Greatest Cavalryman: Nathan Bedford Forrest* (reprint, Lawrence: University of Kansas Press, 1992).

While studying the final and other campaigns of the Civil War, some reference works may be helpful. Readers may want to have at hand: Mark Mayo Boatner III, *The Civil War Dictionary* (New York: McKay, 1959; reprint, New York: Vintage Civil War Library, 1961); Francis B. Heitman, *Historical Register and Dictionary of the United States Army, from Its Organization, September 29, 1789, to March 2, 1903*, 2 vols. (Washington DC: Government Printing Office, 1903; reprint, Urbana: University of Illinois Press, 1965); Thomas L. Livermore, *Numbers and Losses in the Civil War in America* (Boston: Houghton Mifflin, 1900), while recognizing the enormous difficulty of stating precisely any Civil War numbers and losses; Roger J. Spiller, Joseph G. Dawson III, and T. Harry Williams, eds., *Dictionary of American Military Biography*, 3 vols. (Westport CT: Greenwood Press, 1984); Ezra J. Warner's *Generals in Blue: Lives of the Union Commanders* (Baton Rouge: Louisiana State University Press, 1964) and *Generals in Gray: Lives of the Confederate Commanders* (Baton Rouge: Louisiana State University Press, 1995); and Ezra J. Warner and W. Buck Yearns, *Biographical Register of the Confederate Congress* (Baton Rouge: Louisiana State University Press, 1975).

Scholarly studies of the great American conflict of the 1860s are based on a strong foundation of primary sources. Students are particularly fortunate to have the U.S. War Department, *The War of the Rebellion: A Compilation of the Official Records of the Union and Confederate Armies*, 128 vols. (Washington DC: Government Printing Office, 1880–1901). These volumes hold a magnificent collection of correspondence and after-action reports that serve as the building blocks of every serious Civil War campaign or battle history.

While the *Official Records* present the formal documents of senior officers, archival collections hold letters and diaries that add the unvarnished perspective of enlisted soldiers and junior officers. In this regard, the Southern Historical Collection at the University of North Carolina–Chapel Hill; the United States Army Heritage and Education Center at Carlisle Barracks, Pennsylvania; and the Virginia Historical Society in Richmond, Virginia, preserve manuscripts that were valuable in writing this book. This work also drew on materials at the Johnston County Heritage Center in Smithfield, North Carolina, and in the Local History Collection of the May Memorial Library in Burlington, North Carolina.

More readily available than manuscript collections are the published accounts of officers, soldiers, and civilians. Among this enormous group of primary sources are: Theodore Lyman, *With Grant and Meade from the Wilderness to Appomattox*, compiled and edited by George R. Agassiz (Lincoln: University of Nebraska Press, 1994); Adam Badeau, *Grant in Peace: From Appomattox to Mount McGregor; a Personal Memoir* (Freeport NY: Books for Libraries Press, 1961; reprint, Hartford CT: S. S. Scranton, 1887); Henry Kyd Douglas, *I Rode with Stonewall* (Chapel Hill: University of North Carolina Press, 1940); Theodore Gerrish, *Army Life: A Private's Reminiscences of the Civil War* (Portland ME: Hoyt, Fogg & Donham, 1882); Thomas Ward Osborn, *The Fiery Trail: A Union Officer's Account of Sherman's Last Campaigns*, edited by Richard Harwell and Philip N. Racine (Knoxville: University of Tennessee Press, 1986); F. Y. Hedley, *Marching through Georgia; Pen-Pictures of Every-Day Life in General Sherman's Army, from the Beginning of the Atlanta Campaign until the Close of the War* (Chicago: Donohue, Henneberry, 1885); Henry Hitchcock, *Marching with Sherman*, edited by M. A. DeWolfe Howe (New Haven CT: Yale University Press, 1927; reprint Lincoln: University of Nebraska Press, 1995); Katharine M. Jones, *Heroines of Dixie: Confederate Women Tell Their Story of the War* (Indianapolis: Bobbs-Merrill, 1955); Horace Porter, *Campaigning with Grant: General Horace Porter*, edited by Wayne C. Temple (New York: Bonanza Books, 1961); Robert Tilney, *My Life in the Army: Three Years and a Half with the Fifth Army Corps, Army of the Potomac, 1862–1865* (Philadelphia: Ferris & Leach, 1912); Mary Boykin Miller Chesnut, *Mary Chesnut's Civil War*, edited by C. Vann Woodward (New Haven CT: Yale University Press, 1981); and Robert W. Parker, *Lee's Last Casualty: The Life and Letters of Sgt. Robert W. Parker, Second Virginia Cavalry*, edited by Catherine M. Wright (Knoxville: University of Tennessee Press, 2008).

Two well-known collections of primary sources are R. A. Brock, ed., *Southern Historical Society Papers*, 52 vols. (Richmond VA: Southern Historical Society, 1876–1959); and Robert U. Johnson and Clarence C. Buel, eds., *Battles and Leaders of the Civil War*, 4 vols. (reissue, New York: Thomas L. Yoseloff, 1956). The accounts found in these volumes are worthwhile but, given that they were written a considerable time after the war, should be approached with caution.

It is rewarding to visit places associated with the war's last operations. Many sites of the Petersburg and Appomattox campaigns are federally protected and professionally interpreted by the National Park Service. North Carolina's Division of State Historic Sites ably manages Fort Fisher, Bentonville, and the Bennett Place. Two nonprofit organizations, the Historical Preservation Group and the Averasboro Battlefield Commission, Inc., deserve credit for their efforts to preserve the Wyse Fork and Averasboro battlefields.

Visitors to these sites may want to carry along some maps, articles, and photographs. Several issues of *Blue & Gray Magazine* provide helpful guides to the last campaigns: 9, no. 4 (April 1992), on the Battle of Five Forks; 13, no. 2 (Holiday 1995), on the Battle of Bentonville; 16, no. 1 (Fall 1998), on the Battle of Averasboro; 17, no. 1 (Fall 1999), on the Bennett Place surrender; 18, no. 4 (Spring 2001), on the Appomattox Campaign; 25, no. 1 (Campaign 2008), on the Battle of Fort Stedman; and 26, no. 6 (2010), on Stoneman's Raid. While exploring the area of the Appomattox campaign or the Bentonville battlefield, travelers will benefit from: Chris M. Calkins's "From Petersburg to Appomattox: A Tour Guide to the Routes of Lee's Withdrawal and Grant's Pursuit" (Philadelphia: Eastern National Park and Monument Association, 1983; reprint, Farmville VA: Farmville Herald, 1990) and "Thirty-Six Hours before Appomattox, April 6 and 7, 1865" (reprint, Farmville VA: Farmville Herald, 1998); and Mark A. Moore, *Moore's Historical Guide to the Battle of Bentonville* (Campbell CA: Savas, 1997).

INDEX

Page numbers in italic indicate maps

In the Great Campaigns of the Civil War series

Six Armies in Tennessee: The Chickamauga and Chattanooga Campaigns
By Steven E. Woodworth

Fredericksburg and Chancellorsville: The Dare Mark Campaign
By Daniel E. Sutherland

Banners to the Breeze: The Kentucky Campaign, Corinth, and Stones River
By Earl J. Hess

The Chessboard of War: Sherman and Hood in the Autumn Campaigns of 1864
By Anne J. Bailey

Atlanta 1864: Last Chance for the Confederacy
By Richard M. McMurry

Struggle for the Heartland: The Campaigns from Fort Henry to Corinth
By Stephen D. Engle

And Keep Moving On: The Virginia Campaign, May–June 1864
By Mark Grimsley

Vicksburg Is the Key: The Struggle for the Mississippi River
By William L. Shea and Terrence J. Winschel

Now for the Contest: Coastal and Oceanic Naval Operations in the Civil War
By William H. Roberts

Counter-Thrust: From the Peninsula to the Antietam
By Benjamin Franklin Cooling

Spring 1865: The Closing Campaigns of the Civil War
Perry D. Jamieson